The publisher gratefully acknowledges the generous support of the Ahmanson Foundation Humanities Endowment Fund of the University of California Press Foundation.

Heroes of Empire

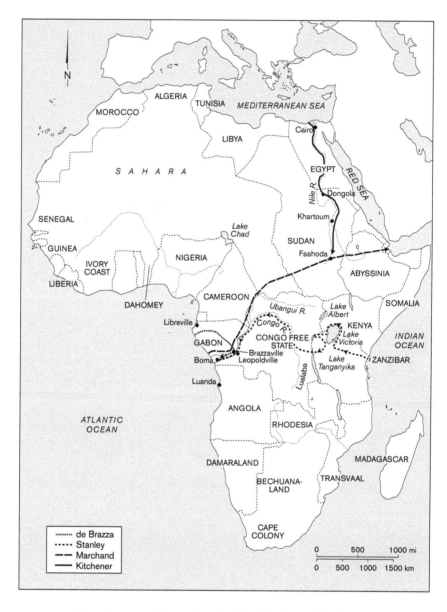

Four journeys: Brazza, Stanley, Marchand, and Kitchener.

Heroes of Empire

FIVE CHARISMATIC MEN AND THE
CONQUEST OF AFRICA

Edward Berenson

UNIVERSITY OF CALIFORNIA PRESS

BERKELEY   LOS ANGELES   LONDON

University of California Press, one of the most distinguished university presses in the United States, enriches lives around the world by advancing scholarship in the humanities, social sciences, and natural sciences. Its activities are supported by the UC Press Foundation and by philanthropic contributions from individuals and institutions. For more information, visit www.ucpress.edu.

University of California Press
Berkeley and Los Angeles, California

University of California Press, Ltd.
London, England

Library of Congress Cataloging-in-Publication Data

Berenson, Edward, 1949–.
    Heroes of empire : five charismatic men and the conquest of Africa / Edward Berenson.
        p.   cm.
    Includes bibliographical references and index.
    ISBN 978-0-520-23427-7 (cloth : alk. paper)
    1. Africa—Discovery and exploration—European.
2. Stanley, Henry M. (Henry Morton), 1841–1904.
3. Brazza, Pierre Savorgnan de, 1852–1905.   4. Gordon,
Charles George, 1833–1885.   5. Marchand, Jean-Baptiste,
1863–1934.   6. Lyautey, Louis Hubert Gonzalve, 1854–
1934.   7. Mass media—France—History—19th century.
8. Mass media—Great Britain—History—19th century.
9. Explorers—Europe—Biography.   10. Explorers—
Africa—Biography.   I. Title.
    DT3.B467   2011
    916.04'2309224—dc22   2010016819

19   18   17   16   15   14   13   12   11
10   9   8   7   6   5   4   3   2   1

FOR JIMMY, ANDREW, AND CHRIS

CONTENTS

ILLUSTRATIONS

FIGURES

MAPS

ACKNOWLEDGMENTS

IT IS A PLEASURE TO thank the many friends and colleagues who have given me vital help with this book. Four "official" readers—Alice Conklin, Stephen Howe, Mary Lewis, and Miles Taylor—offered invaluable, expert advice. So did J. P. Daughton and Ruth Harris, who took time away from their own work to comment on mine. Both read the manuscript from start to finish, and Ruth read parts of it more than once. I asked them to look at my work because I admire theirs so much. Other friends and colleagues read various chapters and, I think, made them better. For this, I thank Herrick Chapman, Julia Clancy-Smith, Annegret Fauser, Arno Mayer, Emmanuelle Saada, Jerrold Seigel, and Debora Silverman. I owe a special intellectual debt to Eva Giloi, who has taught me a great deal about Weber and charisma. The conference we organized together inspired parts of this book.

I have had the good fortune to present different chapters to very smart people in a variety of settings: the Bay Area French History Seminar at Stanford; the Annenberg Seminar in History at the University of Pennsylvania; the Center for Social Theory and Comparative History at UCLA; the Remarque Institute, Maison Française, and European History Workshop at NYU; the CUNY History Department Colloquium; the New York Intellectual and Cultural History Seminar; a Royal Holloway University seminar and Keele University colloquium; the Institut d'histoire moderne et contemporaine at the Ecole normale supérieure; and the seminars of colleagues in several other Parisian locales. It would take far too much space to offer the specific acknowledgment that each member of these groups deserves.

A great many archivists and librarians have helped at crucial points, and I wanted to salute one person in particular, Mathilde Leduc of the Stanley Archive in Tervuren, Belgium. She organized a research visit for me on very short notice and even arranged for me to work there when it normally would have been closed. Speaking of generous acts of friendship, I want to thank Annegret Fauser and Tim Carter for their hospitality in London and Nancy Green, Pierre Bouvier, Laura Downs, and Marie Laurence and Jean Netter for their hospitality in Paris.

I'm especially grateful to the wonderful people involved on the publishing side. Sandy Dijkstra's astute readings of the original book proposal gave me a crucial, initial boost, and she and her colleagues have backed me all along the way. At the University of California Press, Sheila Levine took time away from her extensive administrative duties to oversee this project. As always, I have benefitted enormously from her sage editorial advice. I'm grateful as well to the editors I've worked with at each stage of the process: Kate Marshall, Kalicia Pivirotto, Suzanne Knott, and Steven Baker. It's hard to imagine a better, more talented group.

At New York University I'm fortunate to enjoy the unique collegiality of the Institute of French Studies, where Laure Bereni, Herrick Chapman, Yasmin Desouki, Stephane Gerson, Françoise Gramet, Romain Lecler, Jackie Simon, and Frederic Viguier—plus dozens of visiting French colleagues—make the IFS a realm of personal and intellectual pleasure.

At home, my wife Catherine Johnson, a master of nonfiction prose, is a constant source of inspiration and loving support. Our three sons, Jimmy, Andrew, and Chris, have grown up in ways that amaze me all the time. They make me immensely proud; I dedicate this book to them.

Introduction

IN MARCH 1896, while France and Britain dickered over who would control Western and Central Africa, the government in Paris took a bold, if reckless, step. It sent a young army captain, Jean-Baptiste Marchand, up the Congo River and across the forbidding, malarial landscape of Central Africa, tugging a dismantled steamboat all the way. The goal was a tiny, abandoned Egyptian fort on the Upper Nile—a place called Fashoda that took him two years to reach. From there, Marchand and his band of 150 men were to claim a vast central African empire for France. They kept to this plan even when the British general Horatio Herbert Kitchener arrived on the scene with 25,000 soldiers, advanced weaponry, and an armada of gunships among the most destructive in the world. Marchand refused to back down, and his face-off with Kitchener in September 1898 brought their countries to the brink of war.

The two governments put their navies on alert, and influential British voices clamored for a fight. It mattered little that Lord Salisbury, Britain's prime minister, had privately deemed the African territory in question worthless, "wretched stuff." Had the French failed to withdraw, the nineteenth century could have ended with Europe's leading democracies at war. Fortunately for both sides, the government in Paris found itself paralyzed over the fate of Alfred Dreyfus, a Jewish army officer falsely accused of treason. France's foreign minister ordered Marchand home.

Although the African traveler ended with nothing concrete to show for his three-year ordeal, his extraordinary courage, dauntless optimism, and willingness to defend French interests against overwhelming odds made him a celebrated hero, martyr, and saint. The captain was said to embody the best of what it meant to be French. Amid the divisive Dreyfus Affair, Marchand brought the right, left, and center together in endorsing an imperial mission for France.

With Marchand, four other men rank among those who figured most prominently in France and Britain's unprecedented race for Africa between 1870 and 1914. These "heroes of empire" included Charles (Chinese) Gordon, one of four "Eminent Victorians" that the Bloomsbury writer Lytton Strachey saw as archetypes of the age; Henry Morton Stanley, famous for uttering "Dr. Livingstone, I presume" and infamous for his ruthless Congolese exploits; Pierre Savorgnan de Brazza, the "pacific conqueror" who has admirers in Africa to this day; and Hubert Lyautey, the dashing soldier-scholar who conquered Morocco for France. Although all five men hoped to improve African lives—and Brazza arguably did—they all contributed, wittingly or not, to a colonial enterprise that expressed and reinforced Europe's racial stereotypes about Africa and Africans and inflicted considerable suffering in what Stanley labeled the "Dark Continent."

Today we are justly skeptical of the heroism of such men, but in the late nineteenth century, most Europeans played down, denied, or ignored the violence that colonialism wrought, preferring to see our five exemplars of empire as extraordinary men. All five earned many of their countries' highest honors and created huge public enthusiasm. They stood out among the most important and best-known figures of their times. And they achieved such distinction, often as not, despite governments lukewarm to their imperial projects and accomplishments of uncertain, often dubious value. Given these fin-de-siècle realities, so different from the ones dominant nowadays, our purpose is not to judge the racial attitudes or humanitarian sensibilities of these individuals; it is historical: to examine how their contemporaries viewed them and understood the meaning of what they did.

From 1870 to 1914, what attracted ordinary citizens in Britain and France to empire were stories by and about the charismatic individuals who gave imperialism a recognizable, human face. These heroes allowed the mass of citizens to understand overseas expansion as a series of extraordinary, personal quests. It is true, as imperial historians have traditionally argued, that the majority of people in both countries took little interest in the details of overseas expansion—the geographical boundaries in question, the supposed economic advantages, the putative political gains, the strategic objectives involved.[1] But it does not follow, as historians once thought—although much less so nowadays—that the lion's share of British and French men and women remained indifferent to empire. The broad public in both countries may have been disinterested in the politics and economics of imperialism, even scorning them at times. But that disinterest did not extend to those who braved the scarcely imaginable dangers of unknown places and "savage" people, who revealed traits of character and personality widely admired in each society. If the political leaders and administrators who constituted what Ronald Robinson and John Gallagher called the "official mind" of imperialism focused on policy, ordinary citizens concentrated on heroes.[2]

In viewing imperialism this way, I am inspired not only by recent work on the culture of empire, which shows that images of empire figured prominently in British and French public life, but also by older accounts that criticized Robinson and Gallagher's magisterial study for ignoring "public opinion."[3] This term referred to the newspaper editorials and commentaries that promoted or resisted a government's foreign policies and sought to shape what elected officials and bureaucrats could do. Robinson and Gallagher maintained that policy makers operated largely independent of such external influences and made decisions based on their own values, traditions, and memories.[4] Although the historians who challenged the two British scholars tended to mistake the views of editorialists for those of the public at large, the critics were right to question the ability of policy makers to ignore the opinions of journalists and their readers. Thanks to the late nineteenth century's explosion of newsprint and its huge new audience, the power of journalism had reached unprecedented heights; so much so, that during the Fashoda crisis of 1898, Salisbury held regular meetings with Alfred Harmsworth, owner of the mass-circulation *Daily Mail*. There was no independent, largely self-contained "official mind" capable of deciding, without undo pressure or constraint, where, when, and how to intervene overseas.[5]

Such seems equally true of the "gentlemen capitalists," the bankers and financiers who, according to P. J. Cain and A. G. Hopkins, played the paramount role in shaping imperial policy, especially in key places like Egypt and South Africa.[6] Cain and Hopkins rightly linked "gentleman capitalists" to the gentlemen landowners who had long governed British society, arguing that the interests of overseas commerce dominated both groups' official mind. But the two economic historians doubtless overestimated the ability of this genteel alliance to achieve its imperial goals. During the period 1870–1914, a cacophony of voices and multiple centers of power competed to determine what directions the British Empire would take. Although bankers and elected leaders sometimes led the way, they often had to follow, or respond to, countless others—everyone from indigenous elites in overseas territories to British explorers, officials, soldiers, missionaries, and merchants on the spot.[7] At key moments during the late nineteenth century, no one enjoyed more imperial influence than the heroes who came to exercise an independent power of their own.

Among historians of the French Empire, the rough equivalent of the "official mind" has long been the notion that a tiny "colonial lobby," a compact group of legislators, high civil servants, businessmen, and journalists, single-handedly directed French imperial policy. They did so, the argument goes, by skillfully steering their country into overseas interventions and land seizures, often against the wishes of political leaders and behind the back of a public largely indifferent to the imperial game.[8] This view remained virtually impregnable until the 1990s, when it suddenly collapsed amid a welter of contemporary concerns: a xenophobic reaction against the suddenly visible presence of dark-skinned immigrants on French soil; the counterclaims of these immigrants and their descendents, now citizens of France; the controversy over Islamic headscarves in the schools; new revelations of French atrocities during the Algerian War (1954–62); and the return of repressed memories of slavery in former French colonies.[9] At century's end, France seemed to simmer in the afterlife of empire, in the uncomfortable evidence that colonialism had strongly affected the Hexagon itself. And if empire was everywhere in *this* fin-de-siècle, the same, many now argued, must have been true a century earlier. One result of this new sensibility was a fresh attention, even a preoccupation, with the history of French colonialism and especially with the large role historians now deemed it to have played in public life.

In this sense, the new French historiography mirrored the British. The old orthodoxy emphasizing "official mind," "colonial lobby," and public indifference to empire gave way to a new orthodoxy that presented late Victorian Britain and fin-de-siècle France as saturated with the imagery of empire. According to the newer work, the broad public in both countries found itself bombarded with pro-colonial propaganda, egged on by a chauvinistic press, and surrounded by advertising, popular entertainment, and consumer goods all brimming with explicit and implicit colonial themes.

As a whole, this work casts doubt on the notion that British and French citizens remained indifferent to empire during the late-nineteenth-century scramble for Africa. But it generally fails to gauge to what extent and in what ways individuals received or assimilated what historians have labeled the "popular culture of imperialism."[10]

One way to do just that is to examine the process of anointing heroes of empire and consider how ordinary people reacted to charismatic figures lauded in the press. What we find is an enthusiastic public response: masses of people crowding train stations and docks when their heroes returned from long African stays; equally large numbers flocking to ceremonies honoring or memorializing these heroes, especially when they were martyred to the imperial cause; stacks of adulatory letters—fan mail of sorts—written by people unknown to the men in question. Hero worship was hardly new to the late nineteenth century; its modern roots lay in the Napoleonic period, when the emperor himself seemed to become a world historical figure and when Admiral Lord Nelson died a martyr's death in defeating the French navy at Trafalgar in 1805.[11] But as popular as Napoleon and Nelson became, heroism was not yet a mass phenomenon; their era's relatively primitive state of literacy and communications limited the extent to which hagiographic material could percolate throughout society as a whole. Not until the late century did stories of heroism reach into the furthest recesses of British and French society, as millions of newspapers, illustrated magazines, children's books, song sheets, posters, and advertisements rolled off printing presses each and every day.[12]

These media stood out as key ingredients of the new democratic practices that emerged from the British Reform Bills of 1867 and 1884 and the restoration of French republican government in the 1870s. Not only did most British and French men now enjoy the right to vote; their political participation could be informed by an explosion of printed matter itself the result of new press freedoms and public education laws that gave nearly everyone the ability to read.[13] In this new cultural landscape, old hierarchies held less sway, and unprivileged individuals could achieve forms of status and recognition long the near-exclusive province of the wellborn. Heroes could now erupt from the middling and lower ranks of society and appear to exemplify their nations, precisely because they had come from the common stock. In a democratic age, exceptional individuals paradoxically owed a measure of their standing to being like everyone else.[14] This paradox allowed them to loom above their compatriots, the better to bring them together as a unified—or, at least, more unified—whole.

The era's new democratic culture and practice put a premium on unity. Those who appeared to embody the nation as a whole, who succeeded in uniting people across the boundaries of class, region, gender, and religion, could wield considerable power, whether or not they held public office. But since politicians in democratic societies necessarily identified themselves with a particular ideology or political group, they could never achieve universal public backing. The most popular heroes faced fewer limits of this kind. Such was especially true of imperial heroes, who appeared to represent their countries in conflicts with rival European powers or prospective colonial subjects and, in doing so, helped define what it meant to be British or French.[15] Magnifying the exceptional prominence of these figures was their apparent resemblance to heroes of ancient Rome, especially Caractacus and Vercingetorix, whose epic stories were well known and hugely popular in Victorian Britain and Third Republic France. Nineteenth-century writers and schoolbook authors cast Caractacus as at once a national and imperial hero, as defender of the British Isles and paragon of imperial Rome. Vercingetorix enjoyed a similar reputation except that he played a more indirect role in what were deemed the necessary successes of imperial Rome.[16]

The great status of the late nineteenth century's heroes of empire turned the imperialist steeplechase of these years into a powerful "heroic moment," a time when putatively great men transformed key episodes of British and French intervention overseas into high human drama and gave those episodes an emotional resonance central to their public appeal.[17] By attracting a large and avid following, these heroes gained enough political power not just to represent their countries' empires but to shape the nature and objectives of imperialism itself.

Beyond these imperial interventions, several other aspects of late-nineteenth-century British and French society and politics helped make the era a heroic moment. In these years, prominent leaders and commentators in both countries found their homelands wanting in virility, energy, spirit, and above all, public commitment to national strength. For many, the antidote to these ills would come from extraordinary individuals, heroes whose exemplary lives would inspire their fellow citizens to join them in reversing their nation's putative decline. Heroes from outside established structures of authority seemed especially important during the years after 1870, partly because elected political leaders did not, with certain notable exceptions (Disraeli, Gladstone), inspire their citizens or offer much beyond relatively orderly conservatism in government. British leaders sought to float "lazily downstream" and to guarantee, in Lord Salisbury's words, that "as little should happen as possible."[18] Meanwhile in France, a moderate conservatism and mostly dull political leaders held sway after the twin traumas of the Franco-Prussian War and Paris Commune (1870–71).

France's humiliating military defeat at the hands of Prussia made large numbers of people long for men who promised to restore French glory or who displayed traits and qualities deemed by tradition to have given the country its greatness and strength.[19] But the leaders of the new republic installed in the late 1870s viscerally opposed the idea of having any concrete individual embody their political system or represent its ideals. They had experienced too many Bourbons and too many Napoleons to allow any particular man to incarnate the new regime. They had become so hostile to executive authority that they invented a presidency empty of power and reserved that position for nondescript politicians, for unthreatening party men. Republicans were loath even to have a prime minister, preferring instead to create a Council of Ministers chaired by a *président du conseil*—a cabinet member who was first among equals rather than a true head of government.[20] Even under a strong président du conseil, governing majorities proved so unstable that it was impossible for any individual to represent the regime. Léon Gambetta (1838–82) came closest to playing this role, but his tenure as council president lasted but three short months.

Because the new republic inaugurated in 1870 dispersed power and weakened executive authority, its very institutions worked to exclude extraordinary men and prevent leaders from adding a charismatic aura to the purely bureaucratic authority they enjoyed. French citizens had to look elsewhere for heroes who could offer solace, protection, and revitalization to members of a nation whose faith in themselves and their country had been undermined. In this context, extraordinary individuals like Brazza and Marchand, who persevered through impossible circumstances and prevailed against the odds, emerged as saviors in whom many French men and women wanted to believe.

Britain lost no European wars during this period, but its army's performance during the Crimean War (1854–56) had been weak, and the powerful Indian rebellion of 1857, though ultimately unsuccessful, revealed the empire's apparently fragile state. So did Jamaica's racially charged Morant Bay disorders in 1865.[21] When the United States and Germany threatened Britain's economic dominance after 1870, and France appeared to challenge its imperial hegemony, a great many British commentators found the nation vulnerable to other powers and facing a relative, even absolute, decline.[22] Observers worried in particular about Prussia's crushing military victories over Austria (1866) and France (1870); Britain's small army seemed incapable of measuring up to Bismarck's fighting machine. Even the Royal Navy, which had long ruled the seas, now appeared to languish, as Admiral Sir Richard Hugh Spencer Bacon put it in 1888, at "the lowest level of efficiency . . . since the middle of the eighteenth century."[23] Fears of military weakness vis-à-vis Germany and even France produced a new genre of war-scare literature that reached its alarmist peak with H. G. Wells's *The War of the Worlds* (1898). This doomsday book built on William le Queux's *The Great War in England in 1897* (1894), which had gone through fourteen editions before Wells's novella appeared.[24]

Adding to this sense of post-1870s foreboding was the accelerating financial slide of Britain's landed elite, the country's traditional ruling group. In the 1880s, cheap North and South American farm products flooded the British market, hastening a collapse in agricultural prices already pressured by the worldwide economic downturn of that time. The result was a precipitous drop in British landed incomes and a threat to the status and power of the aristocracy.[25] Their economic fortunes suffered far more quickly than their political and cultural clout, which allowed members of the traditional elite and those who sympathized with them to present their own decline as the nation's decline.[26]

Motivated in part by these developments, Salisbury's 1883 essay, "Disintegration," published in the influential *Quarterly Review*, pointed in particular to a growing menace from below. For the future prime minister, Britain's electoral reforms announced a new age of mass politics in which the rabble would rule. "Things that have been secure for centuries," Salisbury wrote, "are secure no longer."[27] Such views echoed throughout the British Isles in this period, and not just among the landed elite. Like France, Great Britain threatened to become unmoored from long-standing forms of social organization and political authority. Radicals embraced these developments, but a great many others looked for salvation in heroes who appeared to possess tried and tested English virtues: "pluck," perseverance, energy, resolve, and a moral fortitude in tune with the evangelical Christianity that had swept the country in the first half of the nineteenth century.[28]

In both Britain and France, most heroes had traditionally been military men who risked their lives to achieve lofty goals. Because Western Europe knew no wars after the Franco-Prussian conflagration of 1870 and only one other since 1815, the search for military heroes had to focus on individuals acting abroad. Heroic virtues would be rediscovered among those who explored, conquered, and "civilized" in the arduous environments of Africa or "oriental" lands. Heroes of empire thus seemed ideally suited to provide models of character and behavior for the young and images of reassuring manliness for people yearning for certainty and unity in times when political, economic, or social developments otherwise pulled compatriots apart. Perhaps most important, these figures offered themselves as objects of veneration, though for different reasons and under different circumstances in Britain and France.

In Britain, where religious faith remained relatively strong throughout the nineteenth century, colonial heroes often appeared as Christian soldiers, as exemplars of a "muscular Christianity" who evoked worshipful responses. Charles Gordon was a paradigmatic case; he developed a charisma that retained much of the original religious meaning of the term.[29] In France, where a growing secularization reduced the influence, power, and legitimacy of Catholicism and the Church, emotions once directed toward religious figures now infused colonial heroes with an aura, even a spirituality, that could make them into secular saints.[30] As a result, our five heroes of empire all evoked strong public interest in exploring and claiming uncharted territories abroad, territories understood as arenas in which extraordinary, exemplary individuals could prove their—and the country's—worth. Such interest not infrequently came in moments when government officials in one country or the other shied away from new imperial commitments. For this reason, the colonial heroes' untraditional authority often pushed British and French governments further than they wanted to go, sometimes leading them into dead ends or foreign-policy disasters inexplicable but for the sway these individuals enjoyed. There was nothing rational about sending Gordon to Khartoum in 1884 or Stanley to rescue Emin Pasha three years later, or Marchand to Fashoda or even Lyautey to Morocco. The explanation for these ventures turns on the irrational enthusiasm they wrought.

Since these five men registered their feats of bravery and endurance far away from the European stage, they achieved their renown thanks to the penny papers that flew every day into millions of hands. Until midcentury, news and information, especially of distant places, had been largely reserved for a narrow elite of relatively affluent people. But in the 1860s and '70s, advances in publishing and news-gathering technology—high-speed rotary presses, automatic paper folders, linotype machines, news photography, railroads, and telephones—made cheap newspapers and low-priced books available to a rapidly expanding readership. Much of that readership was newly literate and drawn to accessible, "sensational" narratives of individuals and events. The penny press excelled at this mode of writing, and its editors hungered for gripping stories to tell, the kind of stories already popular in the French fiction of Jules Verne and in British adventure novels by George Henty and Henry Rider Haggard.[31]

These writers located many of their stories in Africa, and so would editors of the penny press.[32] As late as 1850, the continent's sub-Saharan interior remained largely unknown to Europeans, who had restricted their trading stations and settlements largely to the coasts.[33] To many, Africa seemed the most mysterious place on the globe, a "dark continent" with vast jungles and savage peoples, a land legendary for its wild animals, deadly diseases, hostile climate, and arduous terrain.[34] Tales persisted of headless monsters, cannibals, and hybrid, semihuman creatures more animal than man.[35] No other part of the planet seemed so unknown, and during the nineteenth century, an era par excellence of new knowledge and scientific discovery, Europeans felt ashamed of their ignorance. As a Scottish geographer wrote, Africa "is still humbling to that pride of knowledge which Europe very justly indulges with regard to the other quarters of the globe."[36] Europeans believed they knew something of Asia, Arabia, and the Americas and deemed those places to possess a modicum of civilized life. Africa alone appeared foreign to all civilization; in the nineteenth century a succession of European explorers and missionaries turned their attention to this last apparent challenge to the enlightened age.

Those who successfully met this challenge, who braved Africa's dangers and lifted its veil of mystery, provided precisely the kind of stories on which the new mass press thrived. If the prominence and ubiquity of these stories rightly turns our focus on them, it is crucial to consider their reception as well. Particularly illuminating are the letters written by ordinary people to four of our five colonial heroes. These letters reveal, among other things, the extent to which Stanley, Brazza, Gordon, and Lyautey embodied the era's ideal of manliness, defined as the ability to persist against all odds, to confront physical danger and the perils of the unknown, and to combine strength and fortitude with kindness toward women, "natives," and others needing gentle guidance backed by a firm, steady hand. The more crucial manliness seemed, the more commentators in fin-de-siècle Britain and France lamented its apparent decline.[37] Urbanization, an expanding consumer culture, the decline of physical labor, and the emancipation of women all conspired, or so it seemed, to create a weakened male, a man stripped of his virility and his distinctiveness from the "second" sex. Like many cultural phenomena, this "crisis of masculinity" lived in the *imaginary,* in a discourse-world neither true nor false but fully belonging to the reality it partially described.[38]

To combat the widely perceived masculine decline, middle- and upper-class men of the fin-de-siècle turned in growing numbers to sport and physical fitness as a way to restore virility. In Britain, these developments built on a previous "revival of chivalry" characteristic of the early and mid-Victorian periods (1837–86). The chivalric man, as Thomas Carlyle's influential writings described him, revealed a "muscular Christianity," a "Christian commitment to health and manliness" that manifested itself through "self-discipline and fearlessness."[39] Carlyle's version of Christianity rejected the supposedly feminized religiosity he associated with Catholicism and the High Church. He also distanced himself from a strain of evangelical Protestantism that remained influential up to midcentury, a strain that emphasized gentleness, self-sacrifice, and commitment to family life. Chivalric men worked hard and presented a tough exterior. Religion was important to them, but their Christianity had to "cultivate individual manliness," wrote Carlyle's disciple Thomas Hughes. Hughes's *The Manliness of Christ* (1880), printed in cheap editions intended for young and working-class readers, declared, "The conscience of every man recognizes courage as the foundation of manliness, and manliness as the perfection of human character, and if Christianity runs counter to conscience in this matter . . . Christianity will go to the wall."[40]

Britain's elite public schools adopted this muscular form of Christianity and the militant form of chivalry that accompanied it, applying its values to the competitive games and athletic contests increasingly central to the young man's life. The Boys' Brigade and other organizations aimed at working-class youth attempted to do the same. French schools paid less attention to sports and physical education, but towns and municipalities promoted athletic contests, and associations like Paul Déroulède's League of Patriots added gymnastics and shooting as well. Meanwhile, adult men took up fencing in surprisingly large numbers, as aristocratic and bourgeois elites revived the duel in an effort to resolve disputes while preserving honor and showing strength.[41] But since duelists rarely got hurt and most men did not excel at sport, observers in both countries wondered whether these pastimes did any good.[42] For this reason, the press focused all the more on the heroes said to embody the strength, power, and virility to which all men could aspire.

If explorers and conquerors stood out as sources of national strength, as fearless figures who engaged their compatriots emotionally and drew large numbers to them, they could not achieve their conquests in just any way. To qualify as genuine national heroes in the second half of the nineteenth century, they had to be peaceful conquerors—or appear as such—capturing territory in a "civilized," humane way or defending civilization against barbarism with their heroic acts. After 1850, the British and French sense of their own superiority turned in part on being more "civilized" than others, on their ability to resolve conflicts through negotiation and the example of a better life. The general absence of war after the revolutionary and Napoleonic periods, the decline of violent protest after midcentury, and the relative success of newly established police forces in taming and repressing violent crime all accustomed the British and French to a degree of everyday peacefulness largely unknown in Europe's past.[43] That peacefulness supposedly confirmed the advanced level of their societies, capping the long "civilizing process" that in Norbert Elias's telling had begun in the seventeenth century.[44]

When colonial violence occurred, as it often did, British and French commentators rarely saw it as initiated by their heroic emissaries. Instead, such men found themselves eulogized as martyrs to the civilizing process of colonialism. These Europeans, so it was said, preferred self-sacrifice to the dishonor of stooping to the violent methods of barbarous tribes. Sacrifice signaled superiority, the demonstration of which became one of the main goals of colonialism. The problem was that self-sacrifice and martyrdom often did not result in the acquisition of colonial territories. When Gordon died a martyr's death in Khartoum in 1885, it meant that Britain had lost its claims to the Sudan, a territory many considered crucial to Britain's hold on Egypt. Like the French after 1870, the British would learn after Khartoum to rebaptize defeats as victories by emphasizing the moral superiority of martyrdom.[45] But eventually, opinion leaders in both countries decided that martyrdom did not pay.

By the final decade of the nineteenth century, writers and political leaders openly approved violence in colonial conquest. Whereas the death and destruction of Stanley's African expeditions made him a great many enemies earlier in his career, when he returned home from his final voyage in 1890, British men and women seemed far more willing than before to accept, even endorse, his methods. The explorer's legendary toughness now seemed necessary to stem Britain's apparent decline and defend the empire against France's increasingly aggressive designs. In the religious realm, the new robust manliness found expression in a new understanding of the chivalric Christian man. Earlier in the century, chivalry required self-sacrifice in the form of forgiving those believed to have wronged British men. This attitude followed Christ's desire to forgive his oppressors. But after Gordon's martyrdom, Christian writers began to urge retribution rather than acceptance, a robust, militant response to setbacks and reverses rather than an effort to turn the other cheek.[46]

In France, Brazza's mild-mannered approach to colonization, his image as a "pacific conqueror," gave way in the late 1880s and 1890s to fiercer, more martial methods of conquest, as people in Indochina, Madagascar, and West Africa resisted French colonial penetration with considerable success. Increasingly, French colonialists maintained that pacific conquest was a contradiction in terms and that without sturdier, more effective efforts, the British would monopolize the colonial domain.[47]

Despite this apparent late-century consensus on the value of martial means, the heightened toughness offered no resolution to what historians would later identify as the "crisis of masculinity." The appalling death toll of Stanley's final expedition did not go unremarked, despite the perhaps unprecedented adulation the explorer received. And when Kitchener's Anglo-Egyptian forces slaughtered some 15,000 Islamic soldiers at Omdurman in 1898, even ardent colonialists like Winston Churchill found such a victory uncivilized and ungentlemanly.[48] The newly energized male of the fin-de-siècle could not be a brute. An excessively violent man would resemble savages abroad and appear to confirm the feminist view of men as unworthy of their superior position in society. But if, on the other hand, men were to become overly soft, pure figures of suffering and martyrdom, they risked appearing too feminine to undo the masculinity crisis apparently at hand.

The colonial figure who came closest to solving the twin problem of winning colonies while behaving in a civilized, relatively peaceful way was the French general Lyautey. This gentlemanly, cultivated military officer won Morocco for France and appeared to do so without excessive violence— even if his status as peaceful conqueror existed more in the French imaginary than in the Moroccan reality on the ground. And though journalists made him seem extraordinarily appealing, endlessly describing his elegant, svelte body, aristocratic bearing, intellectual refinement, and delicate taste, the whiff of homosexuality that surrounded him, even if largely absent from the press, made it difficult to see him as the answer to a widely perceived manly decline.

In a general sense, the era's fear of homosexuality partially subverted any focus on "intrepid" explorers and colonial fighters as models of a new, enhanced masculinity. There were, of course, several notable women explorers (Mary Kingley, Isabelle Eberhardt, Alexandra David-Neel), but the overwhelming majority of those who charted unknown territories in Africa, Asia, South America, and the North and South Poles were male.[49] On the one hand, these individuals appeared to be super-men, exhibiting extraordinary physical courage, exerting themselves far beyond the capacity of their fellows, and persevering in the face of the most daunting obstacles. On the other, their world seemed perhaps a little too male: explorers and other colonial pioneers operated in an environment populated almost exclusively by men. They lived together in close quarters, formed tight attachments, and often relied on young African or Asian men to cook for them and serve as interpreters and guides. David Livingstone was exceptional in having his wife accompany him on an important African journey.[50] Most explorers and the colonial military men who succeeded them remained unmarried until late in life—if they married at all. During their lengthy sojourns in Africa or Asia, they regularly became closely identified with one indigenous man or "boy"—Brazza with Malamine; Stanley with Kalulu.[51]

Many of the European men who traveled to the far reaches of the planet felt a dual motivation—attraction to the unknown and discomfort with European society. Future explorers often reported a difficulty fitting in and an unwillingness to adopt the conventions of bourgeois life, as well as problems relating to women and a lack of interest in them.[52] Lyautey fled to Indochina in part to escape a woman intent on marrying him. Stanley likewise avoided several would-be wives, and when he finally married late in life, he fathered no children. The colonial heroes' search for adventure abroad rather than the company of women at home does not, of course, constitute evidence of homosexuality. But by remaining unmarried, these men violated one of the era's central elements of masculine identity—being a father and head of a family. If the patriarchy of earlier times no longer existed, its vestiges remained important; men who had nothing to do with it did not seem fully masculine. Even those colonial figures who showed clear signs of heterosexuality by taking indigenous women as "temporary wives" and siring children with them still violated the norms of European family life. Brave and manly as they appeared, their example provided no resolution to the widely perceived deficit of manliness, a phenomenon heightened—or so it seemed at century's end—by the rise of feminism and the New Woman, believed to threaten manliness all the more.[53]

These ambiguities and dilemmas made the quest for an exemplary manliness, if anything, all the more pressing and encouraged journalists and colonial advocates to present their champions in the best possible light. When colonial heroes married—and Brazza, Stanley, and Lyautey eventually did—the press paid great attention to their weddings, to the selfless femininity of their wives, and to the children they sired—or, in Stanley's case, adopted. Gordon seemed so otherworldly, so much the ascetic disembodied saint, that his failure to marry could be explained away. As for Marchand, journalists focused on his paternal relationship to the African troops who had followed him across Africa and shared its rigors with him. When he returned to France in 1899, he brought several of his *tirailleurs sénégalais* along. By emphasizing the loyalty and devotion of Marchand's African charges, the reporters who covered his "triumphal" homecoming made him into a father figure so revered as to compensate for the lack of biological sons. Like our four other colonial heroes, Marchand's manliness remained largely intact.

By the early twentieth century, journalists, biographers, illustrators, and the public at large had devoted so much attention to these and other heroes of empire that to fully understand their surprising and, in some cases, enduring stature, it is helpful to turn to Max Weber's concept of charisma. In taking up this phenomenon, a religious notion Weber borrowed from the Protestant legal scholar Rudolf Sohm, the great German sociologist had much more in mind than the personal magnetism and star power we associate with certain movie idols, politicians, and business tycoons.[54]

For Weber, charisma was first and foremost a way of understanding authority, command, power, or influence (*Herrschaft* in German) that came neither from tradition nor from law. Throughout history, he wrote, most authority derived from one of two sources: political elders who traced their power back into the deep mists of time, or bureaucracies designed to administer and enforce laws developed through rational deliberation and debate. Both forms of authority rested on a structure of rules, whether in the form of "precedents handed down from the past" or, as in the case of bureaucracy, of "intellectually analyzable" statutes and procedures. But there was a third form of authority, opposed to the others in being "foreign to all rules."[55] This third, or residual, form harked back to the "gifts of grace" (charismata) that God originally gave to Christ and that later came to inhere in certain extraordinary individuals. "The term 'charisma,'" Weber wrote, refers "to a certain quality of an individual personality by virtue of which he is considered extraordinary and treated as endowed with super-natural, superhuman, or at least specifically exceptional powers or quali-ties. These are . . . not accessible to the ordinary person, but are regarded as of divine origin or as exemplary, and on the basis of them the individ-ual concerned is treated as a leader."[56] The authority of the charismatic person thus comes from his exceptional gifts and not from everyday ways and means.

Because charisma resides in certain extraordinary individuals, Weber's commentators have often thought it to be mainly a psychological phenom-enon, a secularized version of its original Christian meaning. But for We-ber, charisma required a relationship between the leader and his flock, and the best analysts have rightly understood Weberian charisma as at once psychological and sociological, as both a personal quality and a social phe-nomenon. Crucial as charismatic leaders are, their followers have a defin-ing role to play.[57] Weber insisted that an individual's charismatic qualities had to be validated by a group or community and that validation would come only if the individual in question regularly provided evidence of his attributes. "If proof and success elude the leader for long," Weber wrote, "it is likely that his charismatic authority will disappear."[58]

As suggestive as Weber's discussion of charisma is for understanding hero worship in general, the sociologist never adequately explained why an individual's extraordinary qualities inspire people to devote them-selves to him or her, to grant authority and to feel "absolute trust in the leader." He failed to make clear, in other words, why a relationship, an emotional connection, develops between the extraordinary person and those who see him as such. Recently, the philosopher Stephen Turner and the neuroscientist Jaak Panksepp have compellingly taken up where Weber left off.

According to Turner, what makes someone a hero in the eyes of his po-tential following is the capacity to change peoples' expectations.[59] Charisma, Turner writes, is the ability to open new possibilities, to make people be-lieve in the realization of crucial things they have always thought impossi-ble. One way heroes do this is by serving as pioneers, by showing through their actions that something thought prohibitively dangerous can in fact be done without grievous harm. In the 1960s, civil rights leaders, for example, took risky steps by unilaterally integrating segregated facilities, organizing and leading marches, and enduring beatings and prison before ultimately gaining a victorious release. Their achievements gave encouragement by showing that undertakings once believed futile could now produce results. The heroes' actions thus changed the perceptions of others, broadening their horizons and improving their lives.

Even when the trails heroes blaze are too difficult for others to follow, charismatic figures nonetheless open up new possibilities. They do so by demonstrating what can be accomplished and allowing large numbers of people to associate themselves, however indirectly and vicariously, with what they have achieved.[60] When, for example, an explorer travels to uncharted regions, he, or occasionally she, does things practically no one else can repeat. By performing extraordinary feats, the explorer seems to expand the limits of human possibility and broaden everyone's horizons. In sum, the charismatic hero, as opposed to the mere celebrity, blazes new paths.[61] He offers inspiration and the ability to participate indirectly in what he has done. He can offer protection and a feeling of strength, instead of the weakness and vulnerability that may have existed before. In doing these things, the hero fulfills what for Weber lay at the very heart of charisma, the ability to produce change within other people.[62]

If Turner's cognitive psychology provides important clues as to why great explorers of the nineteenth century might have developed charismatic authority and bonded emotionally with a large number of followers, there is perhaps another, newer kind of psychology to consider. The latter comes from the neuroscientific revolution of the past few decades and especially the recent findings of affective neuroscience, the study of emotions and the brain. According to Jaak Panksepp, author of the key synthesis in the field, four basic "command systems for emotionality" are common to all mammals, including human beings: seeking, rage, fear, and panic.[63]

In terms of charisma, the most important of the four is seeking, the vital emotional substructure that "makes animals intensely interested in exploring their world and leads them to become excited when they are about to get what they desire."[64] This system enables animals to find what they need to survive and eagerly to anticipate those essential things: food, water, warmth, and sex. In humans, the seeking system lies at the root of curiosity and intellectual pursuits and produces feelings of interest, excitement, and anticipation. One hypothesis, unprovable but worth considering in relation to our five heroes of empire, is that the actions of certain exciting individuals who undertook courageous forays into the unknown aroused seeking emotions in those aware of their exploits. Such might especially be true of newspaper readers who already felt a need for protection, reassurance, and solace and for that reason had begun to follow the doings of exceptional people in the news. In fact, Panksepp has found neurological evidence that seeking inhibits fear, thus suggesting why those who were worried about their own prospects or about the future of their country might have been drawn emotionally to charismatic figures who seemed immune from fear.[65] The stimulation they provided might account for the emotional connection that ordinary people felt toward them and why daring seekers held particular appeal in the late nineteenth century. This was a time when European societies appeared increasingly "unmanned," mundane, and bureaucratic, when British and French newspapers brimmed with reports of threats to their countries' safety and well-being.

As for the explorers and adventurers themselves, they appear to be paradigmatic examples of people Panksepp would describe as having overactive seeking drives. Such individuals found themselves so moved by what the neuroscientist calls the "foraging/exploration/investigation/curiosity/expectancy/seeking" system that they were willing, even compelled, to place themselves in situations of unimaginable danger and to brave unendurable pain. Individuals like Stanley, Brazza, and Lyautey seemed motivated more by the quest than the goal, itself often ill-defined; more by the desire to plunge into the unknown than by the need to master it. In the late nineteenth century the charisma of such individuals depended little on whether their missions achieved their purported aims or on whether they returned home with measurable gains. The aura inhered in the quest itself.

Ordinary people, those without the same impulse to seek, may have derived vicarious excitement from the plethora of front-page columns narrating the exploits of those who risked life and limb in the heart of Africa. Newspaper readers could look to fearless others for the vicarious thrill of the hunt, for an emotionally liberating quest for new knowledge, new trials, and new acquisitions abroad. Crucial here is the vicariousness of the emotions engaged. In the last decades of the nineteenth century, the emergence of such heroes, like the widespread worries over manliness and national decline, took shape in and through the world's first mass medium, the popular penny press. In these circumstances, images or representations became a crucial element of reality, even when those representations departed from what was actually going on.[66] For this reason, constant talk of national decline and the lack of manliness, of heroic explorers, peaceful conquests, and civilizing missions, could make those phenomena seem palpably real for very large numbers of people—whatever the empirical givens discoverable at the time or later on. The press as a mass medium thus plays a major part in this story. Only when the media paid considerable attention to a particular person, covering his or her deeds and accomplishments, lauding her in editorials, interviewing him, inviting her to contribute articles, did the public gain enough information to endow a given individual with the potential for charisma.

Pivotal as outlets of communication were to the attribution of charisma, nowhere did Weber take up the crucial question of mediation. This lacuna explains in part why he so completely underestimated the continuing relevance, even centrality, of charisma in what he considered the modern rational-bureaucratic world. On the eve of the twentieth century's "age of extremes," an age par excellence of charismatic revolutionaries, Weber predicted that charisma would suffocate "under the weight of material interests" and bureaucratic routine.[67] In making this prediction, the sociologist largely overlooked the eruption of charisma that had marked the late nineteenth century. He missed both the explosion of outsiders into political life and the effort of insiders to spin an aura of charisma around themselves.[68]

These developments stemmed not only from new publishing technologies and means of dissemination but also from fresh journalistic techniques like the interview that allowed editors to advance individuals and personalities over ideas and critique.[69] So did the growing numbers of illustrations and eventually photographs that transformed the newspaper from a solid wall of black ink to the more eye-pleasing publications we know today. Given the low resolution of early newsprint photos, individuals made much better subjects than groups, landscapes, or city scenes. For these reasons, the very structure of the mass press leant itself to the production, amplification, and dissemination of celebrity and charisma.[70]

The bulk of those who figured prominently in newspaper narratives, interviews, and illustrations became celebrities at most, figures who developed a certain reputation, even fame, for who they were or what they had done. It mattered little, then as now, whether they had made genuine accomplishments or were simply "known for [their] well-knownness," in Daniel Boorstin's oft-quoted phrase.[71] Usually the press attended to them for a short time before dropping them for good. Some figures, however, stood out from this pack because they possessed considerably more political, moral, and cultural weight. Such rare individuals distinguished themselves not just as celebrities, though they often became that as well, but as heroes. "The power of charisma," Weber wrote, "rests upon 'heroism.' "[72] What the sociologist overlooked was the mass press's ability to identify and amplify, even create, charisma by focusing on particular individuals and building stories around them.

Two of the heroes studied here, Stanley and Lyautey, published their own accounts of daring colonial exploits, but neither would have had the resonance they achieved without the great echo chamber of newspapers and magazines. Stanley, in particular, sold a great many copies of his books. But sales numbered in the hundreds of thousands, while his renown spread to tens of millions. Book reviews, illustrated weeklies, boys' magazines, and journalistic coverage of his triumphal homecomings, society receptions, lecture tours all repeated and amplified the heroic narratives recounted in his best-selling books.

Although our other heroes published far less—or nothing at all—the media trumpeted their trials and tribulations and framed their work as wondrous, meaningful, and great. Each of the five heroes possessed friends and allies who straddled the worlds of journalism, geography, and politics and deliberately turned the media spotlight toward them. In each instance, journalistic coverage gave the hero a certain renown, and that renown drew crowds to his side. The crowds then became part of the story, a story almost guaranteed to attract ever larger numbers of people eager to see firsthand what the hullabaloo was all about.[73] Reporters now offered the size of crowds as proof of what a great, popular hero the individual in question had become. In diaries and personal correspondence, a large number of people, unknown to the hero, wrote of their efforts to catch a glimpse of the man and of their often-worshipful admiration for him. Given such public endorsement, political officials had no choice but to take these individuals, along with their ideas and demands, into account— often against their better judgment. In some cases, however, political leaders managed to harness the heroes' charisma to their advantage, enhancing their own standing by associating with the charismatic authority the hero had earned.[74]

If mass media made the dissemination and reception of charismatic figures possible, the medium was not, as Marshall McLuhan thought, the message.[75] Only certain kinds of people could evoke the emotional connections that enabled a great many of their countrymen and -women to see them as embodying, as Edward Shils put it, "some *very central* feature of man's existence and the cosmos in which he lives."[76] This formulation might be made more historical by talking not of "existence "and "cosmos" but of the qualities most members of a given society at a particular time consider fundamental to who they are and who they want to be. Between the 1880s and 1914, individuals who appeared to embody the essence of France or Britain and who could thus strengthen feelings of national attachment could be excellent candidates for charisma. Many operated in arduous colonial lands, and the aura that surrounded the most prominent among them gave empire a strong emotional resonance and invested a broad public in its success.

ONE

Henry Morton Stanley and the New Journalism

"DR. LIVINGSTONE, I PRESUME." who doesn't know these words? Only a few other quotations from history class have managed so well to resist the ravages of time and memory. "Four score and seven years ago" and "Let them eat cake" come to mind, as does "Give me liberty or give me death." These other quotations distill certain great moments in the past—the Civil War, the French and American revolutions—and that is perhaps why we remember them. But why "Dr. Livingstone, I presume?" Why do we remember this simple salutation uttered by a Welsh-American journalist in search of a scoop?

Readers will recall that "Dr. Livingstone, I presume?" was the greeting proffered by Henry Morton Stanley when, after an arduous journey, he met the Scottish explorer David Livingstone on the shore of Lake Tanganyika. The likely date was 27 October 1871.[1] James Gordon Bennett, Jr., editor of the *New York Herald,* had sent his ace correspondent Stanley to East Africa to interview the explorer, who had spent some thirty years traveling in the southern half of the continent. Livingstone became a popular mid-Victorian figure in 1857 when he published his widely read *Missionary Travels and Researches in South Africa,* which narrated his African expedition of 1854–56. The Scottish explorer returned to Africa from 1858 to 1864, and on this expedition, his reputation suffered. He quarreled with his European lieutenants, ineptly lost his wife to malaria, and failed to discover a navigable river route to the interior. Faced with heavy journalistic criticism, the British government ordered Livingstone home. By the time of his next African voyage in 1866, his countrymen had largely forgotten him. He likely would have remained obscure, spending the rest of his days wandering unnoticed around the Great Lakes region of Africa. But Bennett and his London bureau chief, Finlay Anderson, decided they could create a journalistic coup by declaring Livingstone "lost" and then having their correspondent meet him on his return to "civilization."[2]

What then has made "Dr. Livingstone, I presume?" such an indelible phrase? Is it the almost absurdly laconic quality of the greeting, its flat commemoration of a moment so manifestly more significant than the words themselves? Is "Dr. Livingstone, I presume?" in other words, the quintessential "English understatement," one that makes Stanley's salutation an emblem of high Victorian culture, with its stiff-upper-lip propriety and emotional restraint?[3] Or is it an example of a certain dry, ironic wit—a stiffly funny comment both on the implausibility of such a meeting and on the unlikelihood that the older white man could be anyone else?

There are doubtless elements of truth in all these possibilities, but problems arise as well. In the first place, neither man was particularly known for his stiff upper lip. Livingstone was given to violent mood swings, and Stanley, when neither angry nor depressed, spoke in the loud, loquacious tones of his own popular journalistic prose.[4] The second problem is that when news of the Livingstone-Stanley meeting first reached London, few commentators found Stanley's salutation particularly English, and no one found it witty. On the contrary, the phrase "Dr Livingstone, I presume?" immediately became an object of ridicule and mirth. Fellow journalists mocked Stanley's listless words, finding the poverty of his language laughable and absurd. In one music hall routine after another, clowns in blackface and African wigs declaimed, "Dr. Livingstone, I presume?" And when Stanley received an honorary doctorate at Oxford in 1890, an undergraduate broke up the house with the cry, "Dr. Stanley, I presume?"[5]

Although British commentators have long found Stanley's salutation a joke, school textbooks, especially in the United States, have leant it a certain dignity, just as the explorer had intended. "What I would not have given," Stanley confided to his diary, to "vent my joy [on finding Livingstone] in some mad freaks ... twisting a somersault, slashing at trees."[6] But his sense of "the dignity that a white man ... ought to possess" and "the presence of the grave-looking Arab dignitaries of Ujiji restrained me, and suggested me to say with a shake of the hand, 'Dr. Livingstone, I presume?'"[7]

Of course, the Swahili Arabs whose dignity Stanley wanted to exceed were appalled by the impoverished emotions he and Livingstone displayed.[8] And had they known Stanley's reasons for behaving so strangely, they doubtless would have been equally dismayed by the tone of racial superiority so characteristic of the Europeans they met. Late in life, Stanley told an interviewer, "I couldn't think what else to say."[9]

These considerations add a certain thickness to the phrase "Dr. Livingstone, I presume?" But they do not fully explain its uncannily secure place in our historical memory. It may be that these words represent considerably more than an enduring Victorian joke, stripped in some quarters of the ironic commentary that made people laugh. Could they signal a historical juncture nearly as important as the Civil War or the French Revolution, a cultural turning point central to the history of the modern world?

Part of the reason we remember Stanley's greeting doubtless stems from the charisma attributed to him. But his personal charisma developed only later in his life, not until the spring of 1890 when he returned home in apparent triumph from what would be his final African voyage. Twenty years earlier, what counted was the transmission worldwide of a perhaps invented greeting uttered in a place until then unknown. The message, not the messenger, held extraordinary appeal. When Stanley and Livingstone shook hands in Ujiji (Kigoma-Ujiji in present-day Tanzania), thousands of miles from London and New York, news of their greeting marked the ascendancy of the world's first mass medium, the industrially produced penny press. This new cultural force possessed the ability to bring even those places most distant and least familiar to Europeans and Americans into the realm of everyday knowledge and rapid communication. Stanley's sensational reports of his search for Livingstone and their dramatic meeting gave his readers the feeling of gazing at a region of the world utterly mysterious to them. His dispatches made the globe seem much smaller than it had ever been.

When Lewis and Clark took their landmark voyage to the west coast of North America early in the century, no one was surprised that they remained incommunicado for long periods of time. No one, that is, thought they were lost. There were legitimate fears that they might have died, but people interested in their explorations did not expect to know where they were.[10] By the late 1860s, however, the Western press had developed to the point that it seemed nothing existed outside its domain, and people had become accustomed to learning about events almost immediately after they occurred. Correspondents reported on wars in distant places and on politics, crimes, and tragedies at home. Railroads and telegraph lines allowed accounts of such events to reach millions of people within two days or less, compared to weeks or months just a decade earlier.[11] The world not only appeared to be shrinking in the late 1860s but also seemed to hold fewer and fewer mysteries and offer fewer places to hide. If no one in London had heard from Livingstone in over a year, he must be lost—lost in one of the increasingly rare parts of the world still beyond the reach of a newly powerful press.

By finding Livingstone in a once unknown part of Africa, Stanley promised—or threatened—to open even the remotest corners of Africa to the scrutiny of "civilization." In the 1920s, Ernst Jünger would look back on Stanley's explorations as marking the eminently depressing closure of the final frontier, the obliteration of untamed, unknown, uncultivated spaces of the globe. "That's most likely the reason I felt so little sympathy for this character Stanley," Jünger wrote. "To illuminate the dark continent, discover the sources of legendary rivers, map once-wild territories— all that seems repugnant to me. Repugnant as well was the eruption of Americano-European energy in such lands. . . . It is as if the immense Congo were now enslaved to the clock."[12] The French writer Antoine de Saint-Exupéry expressed similar sentiments when he said that thanks to Stanley, whom he admired, "there are no more mysteries. The brilliant horizons toward which we have raced have been extinguished one after the other." Explorers like Stanley, added André Malraux, have made us "lose the feeling that we distance ourselves in time as we distance ourselves in space."[13] These are comments of individuals writing after the disillusionment of the First World War and do not reflect views of Stanley held in 1871. But they suggest how later generations would see him and why his meeting with Livingstone might have assumed great significance for those worried about the rationalization and bureaucratization of modern life. For men like Jünger, the vanquishing of the unknown represented the end of a radical freedom found only in uncharted realms of the planet.

Beyond the ability to encapsulate a shrunken world, to make its unknown, unexplored regions wither away, the Stanley-Livingstone meeting provided a spectacular occasion for a new kind of journalism, a reportorial style first developed in the United States and rapidly adopted in France. Only in Great Britain did the new, emotional, sensationalist approach to journalism lag behind.[14] British journalism's resistance to the new "American" ways until the final years of the century would complicate the reception of Stanley's writings in his native country, sapping them of legitimacy and credibility among those accustomed to a sober, high-toned journalistic mode. But across the Atlantic and the English Channel, Stanley's account of the Livingstone event represented a dramatic, perhaps paradigmatic example of the new form of journalism, one that told stirring and often sensational stories focused on individuals while eschewing overt political argument and debate. His kind of reportage lay behind the eruption of charisma in the late nineteenth century and ultimately helped make Stanley himself a charismatic man.[15]

When newspaper editors turned to the sensational, popular mode, first in New York (1830s) and then in Paris three decades later, they distanced their journals from political parties, trade unions, and other polarizing institutions. Their goal was to attract as many readers as possible; to do so, they focused on topics and phenomena that would bring people together rather than split them apart. Accounts of crime and scandal attracted great interest, and the most successful journalists perfected the ability to exploit such stories' voyeuristic appeal.

Working people had long been exposed to such *faits divers* (miscellaneous facts), as the French called them, first through oral storytelling and later through printed canards, chapbooks, ballads, and *libelles*. Until the nineteenth century, most of these narratives focused on miraculous and supernatural events. It was only in the more secular postrevolutionary age that the fait divers became preoccupied with crime.[16] And during the course of the nineteenth century, the narrative style of the fait divers shifted dramatically as the technology of journalism progressed. Thanks to the advent of instantaneous communication first via telegraph and then telephone in the latter part of the century, journalists could for the first time report a story as it was happening, conveying the immediacy of an ongoing, unfinished situation. The static depiction of the crime itself, on which the traditional crime story had focused, gave way to an unfolding story of a criminal, judicial, or journalistic investigation.[17] The narrative, therefore, became inscribed in time, inscribed in an extended present that melded into an uncertain future. Readers were invited first to witness the story and then to participate in it as events played themselves out.

Because crimes occurred every day, the crime story became the staple of the new journalism in France and the United States, its dominance such that the fait divers' distinctive style, with its dialogue, characters, action, suspense, and progression of events, would spill over into most other forms of reportage.[18] Articles concerning national politics and international affairs, social problems and intellectual dilemmas, took on an anecdotal narrative form. Journalists no longer analyzed events and issues in detail but refracted them through descriptions of people and personalities, recounted in a style designed to create suspense, stimulate emotions, and pique the reader's curiosity.

What made the new journalistic mode so popular? Historians have emphasized the extent to which urban life became a spectacle, a shimmering, fast-moving tableau of people and events. People of different social classes and regional and national origins mixed promiscuously on sidewalks bordered on one side by surging traffic and on the other by shop windows enticing strollers to come in. Goods were on display, and so were the people hurrying or sauntering by. Newspapers packaged and reproduced that sensational reality and turned it into yet another commodity to be consumed.[19]

Suggestive as this portrait is, it fails to explain why the mass press found as many readers outside the cities as within them or why many of the scenes of crime and disaster took place in the rural sphere. The crime that launched France's *Le petit journal* into the stratosphere of commercial success, Jean-Baptiste Troppmann's brutal murder of a family of eight (1869), took place in the woody Paris surrounds. The quest for a spectacular version of reality was thus not an urban phenomenon but a democratic one, the result of growing public participation in politics, schooling, the army, and cultural life. By the last third of the nineteenth century (earlier in the United States), ordinary people knew more about the world than ever before, and the knowledge they had acquired made them hunger for even more. It was a hunger incapable of satisfaction, a hunger that could make people aware both of the limits of their lives and the possibility that those limits could be overcome—even if in the form of voyeuristic identification with individuals who seemed to loom above ordinary life. The newspaper brought a large, exciting world into millions of homes, allowing a glimpse of extraordinary people and events to readers safely ensconced in their daily routines. As the French commentator Henry du Roure put it at the time, mass journalism "gave readers what their own lives did not provide them: . . . a life of romance . . . of incredible adventures and overwhelming sentiments, of blood, sex, and death."[20]

Henry Morton Stanley was the first major overseas correspondent to adopt the new sensationalist, voyeuristic style, emphasizing as he did his dangerous, suspenseful adventures, violent battles with "savage" peoples, and the awe and mystery of uncharted, exotic terrain. He took his readers to far-off locales, narrating his escapades as he experienced them, leaving his audience in breathless anticipation as to what would happen in the next dispatch. By 1872, when Stanley's accounts of finding Livingstone began to appear, American readers were accustomed to his brand of journalism and had no trouble believing in the reality of his tale. But British readers, especially those of the middle and upper classes, had little experience of such reportage and relegated it to the realm of fantasy and make-believe.[21]

Nothing in Stanley's early life marked him as a man destined for charisma and fame. Henry Morton Stanley, registered at birth in 1841 as "John Rowlands, bastard," had a nineteen-year-old Welsh housemaid for a mother and three different men who might have been his father. After growing up in a workhouse for poor orphans, Rowlands, age seventeen, moved to Liverpool, where he signed on as cabin boy on a ship bound for New Orleans.[22] Already, Rowlands had distinguished himself as intelligent, persistent, and resourceful, but as a young man with some serious flaws of character and personality. One distant relative summed him up as a "full faced, stubborn, self-willed, round-headed, uncompromising, deep fellow. In conversation with you, his large black eyes would roll away from you as if he was really in deep meditation about half-a-dozen things besides the subject of conversation. . . . His temperament was unusually sensitive; he could stand no chaff, nor the least bit of humor."[23]

Stanley had, at best, a sporadic commitment to the truth and the deep insecurity of an individual who had grown up without the love of his parents or the haven of a family home. Whatever the psychological or biological roots of his personality problems—there is some evidence he suffered from a condition known today as bipolar disorder or manic depression—Stanley was rarely happy, frequently morose, extraordinarily sensitive, and prone to explosive anger.[24] His will was keen, however, and his self-discipline and ability to endure extreme suffering and physical deprivation almost unimaginably strong. But he was socially awkward, reluctant to form emotional bonds with other people, and possessed a streak of cruelty that could turn his anger into self-punishment or violent attacks.

Once in New Orleans, Rowlands went to work for a shopkeeper named James Speake, who became a surrogate father and mentor to the young Welshman. Although Rowlands developed a strong emotional attachment to the shopkeeper, the future explorer would later claim an even deeper tie to a wealthy cotton broker named Henry Hope Stanley. Most biographers have accepted this story and especially the claim that H. H. Stanley had informally adopted the young man, who eventually assumed his first and last name and became an American citizen. Hence the transformation of John Rowlands into Henry Stanley; he added the middle name "Morton" later on.[25]

In his biography, Tim Jeal convincingly shows that Stanley/Rowlands wholly invented this account. In reality, Rowlands had never known Henry Hope Stanley, let alone become his honorary son. The young man assumed Stanley's name purely because the cotton broker ranked high in New Orleans society and Rowlands wanted to identify with him.[26] Having concocted this adoption story early on, Stanley stuck with it throughout his life, piling one fabrication on another until the web of falsehoods became so thick that even Stanley himself couldn't untangle it. For this reason and others he never completed the autobiography his wife ardently wanted him to write.[27]

In any event, when Rowlands left New Orleans in 1860, he identified himself as Henry Stanley. After brief stints on both sides of the Civil War, the Welshman traveled six hundred miles down the Platte River in a homemade vessel and then made his way by riverboat and train to New York. From there he and two companions set sail for Turkey, where they narrowly escaped death and avoided imprisonment thanks only to the intervention of American officials in Constantinople. Back in the United States in 1867, Stanley turned to freelance reporting, covering a series of military expeditions against the Plains Indians. Bennett's *New York Herald* picked up some of these accounts and, impressed by the vivid writing, sent Stanley to Abyssinia, where England had undertaken a nasty colonial war in 1868. His success in scooping all the other reporters soon landed him a salaried berth on the *Herald.* So pleased were Stanley's employers with his African reportage that Bennett and his London bureau chief decided he was the journalist to interview Livingstone, should the explorer appear.

At the *Herald,* Stanley learned what historians have called the "objectivist" mode of reportage, a form of writing developed in early-nineteenth-century America, the country that invented much of what would become modern journalism. After the American Revolution, the fledgling United States already boasted widespread newspaper circulation. The emotionally charged partisan politics of the 1790s moved both Federalists and Jeffersonians to found their own newspapers, whose shrill denunciations of the other side attracted readers and maintained their loyalty.[28] The absence of taxes, caution money, censorship, and seditious libel laws—all ruled out during the eighteenth century—kept newspaper prices lower and news fresher than in Europe, where editors remained plagued by per-page taxes and de facto censorship. Thanks to early America's Protestant traditions, which fostered literacy by insisting on a direct encounter with the Bible, the new republic possessed more readers per capita than anywhere else. And an extensive postal system, which subsidized newspapers, enabled the press to reach into even tiny, remote villages. In 1830 Alexis de Tocqueville famously noted the "astonishing circulation of letters and newspapers in [the] savage woods" of Kentucky and Tennessee.[29]

The result was a new American nation awash in print. A British writer estimated that by 1840, total weekly newspaper circulation in the United States (population 17 million) exceeded that of Europe as a whole (population 233 million).[30] Although only a few papers achieved print runs greater than one thousand, hundreds of localities possessed their own journals, giving readers everywhere access to the news. And not just local news: since the post office allowed editors to exchange newspapers for free, they reprinted articles from distant towns and villages, guaranteeing that village papers would include state and national reports.[31] By the 1830s when two New Yorkers, James Gordon Bennett of the *Herald* and Benjamin Day of the *Sun,* created an innovative penny press, Americans ranked as the best-informed people on the planet, at least in terms of ongoing events.

Although the penny papers did not yet spawn a mass readership—in 1837, Bennett's best-selling *Herald* hawked 20,000 copies a day—they succeeded in attracting an urban clientele of clerks, artisans, petty tradesmen, and others of modest means.[32] This penny press, like its more expensive competitors (six cents as issue), devoted considerable space to politics, but in less overtly partisan ways. Its great innovation was to open its columns to events and phenomena that traditional papers had ignored or played down: crime, natural disaster, exotic places, and individuals deemed worthy of fame or notoriety.[33]

The *Herald*'s most skillful writers could take a relatively common crime and turn it into a lurid story whose narrative stretched over weeks or even months following the event.[34] These tales often embellished the facts at hand and obeyed the conventions of fictional works popular at the time. But they always based their (unacknowledged) inventions on events that really took place, events occurring in the world outside the press. American journalists of the mid-nineteenth century saw themselves as scientists of the pen, as writers whose responsibility was to observe what was taking place in the natural world.

This commitment to "reality," even in the face of narrative strategies that fictionalized events, underlay a growing allegiance to "objectivity"—rather than the "opinion" journalism of the past—among writers for the penny press. During the middle of the nineteenth century, American journalists developed the conviction that what they published needed "to be engaged in a great cause," as Bennett put it in 1840, "the cause of truth, public faith, and science, against falsehood, fraud, and ignorance."[35] This allegiance to truth came from a post-Enlightenment faith in science and a populist belief that facts protected ordinary people from the injustices of power. The quest for objectivity also resulted from the penny press's competition with the older newspapers, most of them allied with political parties, papers whose partisanship, editors like Bennett claimed, prevented them from publishing the unvarnished truth. Even if "objectivity" did not prevent what critics of the penny press called "sensationalism," objectivity did long ensure that journalists would base their reports on real events. Reality, in fact, became the raison d'être of this new commercial press, whose journalists were "reporters" charged with recording the facts. Journalists saw themselves as separate from the events they "covered"—a position, they believed, that gave them the ability to write unbiased accounts.

Having been schooled in this objectivist style of journalism, Stanley made himself a pioneer of a new kind of newspaper writing, one that broke in crucial ways with the now classic American mode. Beginning with his quest for Livingstone, Stanley made two pivotal innovations: he openly placed himself at the center of events rather than appearing to stand apart from then, and more radically, he undertook to create the events he would cover.[36] As cheap mass production and rapid, widespread delivery by rail made newspapers accessible to everyone in the last decades of the nineteenth century, Stanley understood that individual journalists could become as famous as the people they covered. To develop such notoriety, a journalist needed to find ways to stand out. Stanley did so by making himself the hero of his own stories; other writers would soon follow his lead.

In one oft-cited passage from Stanley's *How I Found Livingstone* (1872), the best-selling book based on his *Herald* dispatches, the journalist gave the following account of James G. Bennett, Jr.'s order in October 1869 to find the British explorer:

> "Where do you think Livingstone is?" [Bennett asked.]
> "I really do not know, sir!"
> "Do you think he is alive?"
> "He may be and he may not be," I answered.

"Well, I think he is alive, and that he can be found, and I am going to send you to find him."

"What!" said I? "Do you really think I can find Dr. Livingstone? Do you mean me to go to Central Africa?"

"Yes; I mean that you shall go and find him wherever you may hear that he is, and to get what news you can of him. . . . Of course, you will act according to your own plans, and do what you think best—BUT FIND LIVINGSTONE!"[37]

This is a richly embellished version of a far more equivocal effort by the *New York Herald* to establish contact with David Livingstone. In early 1868 the *Herald*'s London bureau chief, Finlay Anderson, sent Stanley to Aden, a British protectorate at the base of the Arabian peninsula, after rumors surfaced that the British explorer was about to "return to civilization." Anderson had heard that the explorer would emerge either on the east coast of Africa or on the island of Zanzibar. By waiting in Aden, roughly halfway between Sudan and Zanzibar, Stanley would be in a position to interview Livingstone shortly after he appeared. This plan, adventurous as it was, still represented the *objectivist* form of journalism. Livingstone's emergence would be a major event that the *Herald* would cover by sending its reporter to meet him. When the explorer failed to appear, Anderson decided there would be no event, and he withdrew his correspondent.[38] Stanley spent much of 1869 covering the civil war in Spain, where he contributed some fine reportage.

What happened next has long baffled Stanley's biographers. After summoning the reporter to Paris in October 1869 for the urgent—at least in Stanley's telling—"find Livingstone" assignment, Bennett did not send him directly to Zanzibar or East Africa. Instead, the editor had Stanley take a long tour of Egypt, the Middle East, and parts of Asia, asking him to write a series of pieces on "whatever is interesting for tourists." On the final leg of his journey, Stanley was to cross the Caucasus to the Caspian Sea and then travel via Baghdad to India, after which he would return to Zanzibar and wait for Livingstone to appear.[39]

Biographers sympathetic to Stanley and Bennett have explained the apparent contradiction between the order to FIND LIVINGSTONE! and the lengthy Afro-Asian tour that diverted him from that task by claiming the editor had extraordinary journalistic instincts. Frank McLynn wrote that Bennett somehow intuited that a year would pass before Livingstone surfaced and, in the meantime, Stanley could visit a large number of exotic places fascinating to readers of the *Herald*.[40] Biographers unsympathetic to Stanley and his editor find the contradiction between what Stanley claimed and what he did so egregious as to undermine the former's credibility altogether. The "find Livingstone" story, maintains John Bierman, must be a pure fabrication.[41]

The problem with both explanations is that they anachronistically apply the standards of late-twentieth-century journalism according to which writers commonly go out and find their stories, do investigative reporting, and even create the events they recount. In 1869, editors still assumed that journalists had to wait for an event to happen before they could cover it. Thus, until Livingstone appeared on the coast or in Zanzibar, there would be nothing to report. Under those circumstances, it made sense for Bennett to keep Stanley close enough to East Africa to allow him to scoop competing journalists if Livingstone surfaced, but not to idle him for an indefinite period in Aden or Zanzibar. Bennett had no intention to send Stanley into the heart of Africa in search of Livingstone. Stanley's great journalistic innovation was his ultimate decision to create the event himself.

A long letter from Stanley to Bennett, buried until 2001 at Stanley's country estate southeast of London, makes clear that Stanley resolved on his own—and against Bennett's instructions—to plunge into Africa to find Livingstone.[42] Here, Stanley tells his editor that having traveled throughout the Middle East on an assignment "so vague, so unsatisfactory . . . that I could not . . . venture to do anything," he went to Zanzibar to see Dr. John Kirk, Britain's distinguished representative there. Kirk had traveled with Livingstone and knew him well, having remained in regular, if sporadic, contact with him long after the explorer had been declared lost. Stanley questioned Kirk "as to where Livingstone was; Dr. Kirk replied in these words. 'Dr. Livingstone is on the western side of Lake Tanganyika. He expects shortly to come to Ujiji—which is about 4 months travel from here [Zanzibar].'" Stanley then ascertained from Kirk that no European was likely to find Livingstone—not Samuel Baker, stationed on the Upper Nile but interested only in the ivory trade, nor the explorers John Speke or Richard Burton, whom Livingstone "hates like poison." According to Kirk, the Scotsman would almost certainly remain at Ujiji or between there and the east coast on regular caravan routes. "This was the news," Stanley wrote, "I desired to hear. This is what I came for, and the conclusion arrived at is this: that having arrived at Zanzibar . . . through all that round about route of over 18,000 miles . . . that as Livingstone is at Ujiji waiting for his supplies [sent by Kirk] . . . it is my duty to go after him to meet him, to *interview* him [Stanley's emphasis] and to do something in the way of exploration myself."

Stanley, that is, would not wait for Livingstone to appear, as a good nineteenth-century journalist should do. Rather, the Welsh-American reporter would step outside the professional conventions of his time to become a historical actor in his own right. He would "do something in the way of exploration myself"—not for its own sake, but in the interest of a new and better form of reportage. The search for Livingstone—and all its attendant adventures—would become the event to be covered. If Stanley actually found the explorer, so much the better. In that case, he would have made a genuine journalistic coup. But "even if my mission proves unsuccessful, it will have been great glory—glory enough to last a century."[43]

As Stanley placed himself at the center of a Livingstone story he did so much to invent, Bennett too stretched the boundaries of the era's journalistic conventions. It was the *Herald*'s editor, after all, who concocted the idea that the explorer was lost. The doctor, of course, knew where he was, as did residents of the region around Lake Tanganyika where the explorer had toured between mid-1869 and mid-1871. So too did the British government, regularly informed about Livingstone by its consul in Zanzibar, John Kirk. The consul had expressed no worries to officials in London that Livingstone had vanished or died.[44] The explorer was lost, therefore, only to a Euro-American world increasingly saturated by the press.

If Bennett stretched journalistic standards by inventing a lost Livingstone, he did not go so far as to order Stanley into Africa. Even a journalist as tough and adventurous as Stanley hardly possessed the skills and experience needed to survive in the African interior.[45] Horses and mules died so quickly in most of Africa's midsection that travelers had to make the strenuous journey on foot and depend on Africans to carry their supplies. The high heat, torrential rains, and often unnavigable rivers added to the difficulties of African movement, as did a widespread hostility to outsiders caused, in large measure, by the brutalities of the East African slave trade.[46] Stanley knew that Bennett did not approve a foray into the continent, which explains why the reporter kept secret his intention to search for Livingstone. He told only one person, Francis Webb, the American consul in Zanzibar, and swore him to silence. Once Bennett learned that his reporter had set off in search of Livingstone, the editor refused to honor the debts Stanley had contracted to equip and staff his expedition.[47] The odds, after all, were that Stanley would not survive the ordeal of traveling seven hundred miles over difficult malaria-ridden terrain to the eastern shore of Lake Tanganyika and that none of his stories would ever be read.

Virtually all we know of Stanley's journey from Zanzibar to Ujiji comes from his own dispatches.[48] Stanley told his readers that during the four months he spent en route to Zanzibar in late 1870, he perused every account of African exploration he could find—Livingstone's *Missionary Travels and Researches in South Africa* (1857), Burton's *The Lake Regions of Central Africa* (1860), and Speke's *Journal of the Discovery of the Source of the Nile,* as well as books by Samuel Baker and Paul Du Chaillu.[49] This literature taught him the genre of African travel writing, many of whose narrative conventions he reproduced in his own work. These conventions included ethnographic observation thickly laced with inherited stereotypes of African peoples; "scientific" details about topography and climate; descriptions of disease and other hardships; scenes of battle and confrontation; and condemnation of slave traders, especially those of "Arab" origins. As an experienced journalist, Stanley wrote better and far more vividly than his predecessors, giving his work a popular appeal that enabled him to shape Europeans' perceptions of Africa well into the twentieth century.[50]

Beyond their literary influence, the writings of Livingstone, Burton, and other travelers showed Stanley how to mount and conduct an expedition into the African interior. Stanley learned perhaps even more from talking with Swahili Arab merchants and slave traders in Zanzibar, who for centuries had traversed Central and eastern Africa. In particular, Stanley adopted the slavers' militaristic model of travel based on a "caravan" of soldiers and porters.[51] His would be the largest African expedition ever. He recruited some two hundred people and carried eight tons of supplies, including two boats, a variety of tools and medicines, and a small arsenal of weapons. Stanley also hired the experienced African commander Bombay, who had served both Burton and Speke.[52] Bombay's knowledge of the people and terrain would help Stanley find his way.

The trip from Zanzibar to Ujiji took more than eight months; the cost in human terms was extraordinarily high. Both of Stanley's British assistants died from diseases en route, and three-quarters of the caravan's other members succumbed to illness, exhaustion, malnutrition, and dehydration or to peoples opposed to Stanley's advance.[53] The journalist himself suffered frequent bouts of malaria, the worst of which rendered him physically incapacitated and delirious for nearly two weeks. "From a stout and fleshy

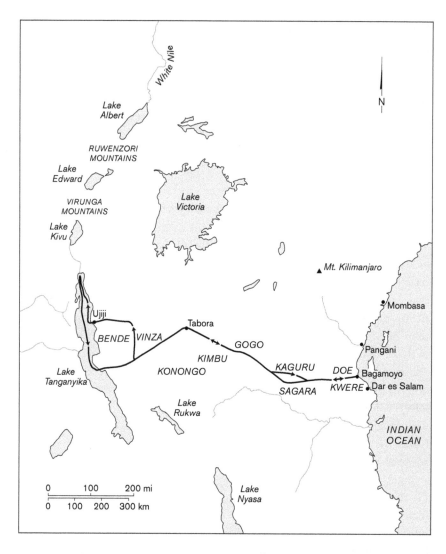

Map 1. Stanley's first journey: The search for Livingstone, 1870–71.

person, weighing 170 pounds," Stanley wrote in his first dispatch to the *Herald*, "I was reduced to a skeleton, a mere frame of bone and skin, weighing 130 pounds."[54] Soon his horses and mules began to drop, for Stanley had not heeded warnings that pack animals would fail to survive. Experienced African travelers knew it was risky to bring animals into the interior, though not until years later did people understand the cause: tsetse flies.[55]

With the animals gone, porters had to carry all the supplies. Rejecting the added burden, many of Stanley's men fled into the bush. To staunch the flow, the journalist hunted down the deserters and brought them back for severe public floggings. Himself possessed of an almost inhuman capacity to endure pain and suffering, Stanley held all those who traveled with him, whites as well as blacks, to his own nearly impossible standards. His intractable desire to press on, combined with a willingness to push others to their limits of endurance, helps explain how this journalist, untested as an African explorer, could have succeeded as well as he did. Stanley's stubbornness, however, cut both ways. By compelling him to "prove himself" at every turn, obstinacy gave him the strength and persistence to overpower obstacles, human and otherwise, that would have made a more reasonable man give up. But it also led him to ignore others' warnings and advice, causing avoidable troubles that threatened the expedition as a whole.

At times, Stanley's stubbornness verged on insanity as he pushed his men beyond the breaking point. Unlike virtually all other African travelers, Stanley insisted on setting out during the rainy season in an effort to save time. But doing so forced his caravan to trek through mud, swamps, swollen rivers, and flooded plains. The constant dampness worsened the agony of the fevers, smallpox, and dysentery that tortured Stanley's cortege; even so, the journalist forced his followers on when he should have allowed them to rest. "The virtue of a good whip," Stanley wrote, "was well tested by me . . . and I was compelled to observe that when mud and wet sapped the physical energy of the lazily-inclined, a dog-whip became their backs, restoring them to a sound—and sometimes to an extravagant activity."[56]

Stanley wrote these words while still on the relatively easy part of his journey. The first half of the route to Ujiji regularly accommodated Swahili Arab traders and featured villages with friendly inhabitants whose leaders did not demand exorbitant "tributes" of passing caravans. Stanley was able to barter for food and, trigger-happy as he was, mostly avoided violent confrontations. But as he headed toward the substantial town of Tabora, the obstacles multiplied. The dry season brought searing heat and lack of water, followed by a smallpox epidemic that further thinned the caravan's ranks. More seriously, a war between the Swahili Arabs of Tabora and the powerful Myamwezi chief Mirambo blocked the route to Ujiji. But having marched 525 miles in eighty-four days, Stanley did not consider turning back. He was moving very fast, fifty days faster than it had taken the professional explorers Burton and Speake to cover the same route in 1857–58. To press on as quickly as possible, Stanley decided to lend men and firepower to the war against Mirambo. This decision proved a disastrous mistake. The well-armed Mirambo, whom Stanley later dubbed the Black Napoleon, outsmarted the combined forces opposing him and, in a brilliant stroke of deception, lured the major part of the Arab-*Herald* fighters into an ambush from which not a single man escaped.

After this fiasco, Stanley resolved to spare his expedition further combat against the Black Napoleon. He charted a route to Lake Tanganyika well south of the main caravan trails, where he hoped to steer clear of the ongoing conflict.[57] Tabora's leaders warned Stanley against continuing, but he ignored them despite an alarming desertion rate. To make an example of those he recaptured, he clapped them in the neck chains that notoriously symbolized Africa's commerce in slaves. During the rest of the march, Stanley and his troops had to endure near-starvation, neck-high mud, crocodiles, smallpox, malaria, dysentery, midnight marches, confrontation with the dangerous Ha people, and extraordinarily high tribute payments. At one point, Stanley narrowly escaped death at the hands of mutineers, after which he resorted to pure sadism in an effort to keep his people in line. When a female porter began to scream so loud that Stanley feared she would alert the Ha, he whipped her until the screaming ceased.

Stanley received some welcome news when a traveling Arab told him that an elderly white man had recently returned to Ujiji. The Welsh-American did not yet know it, but Livingstone's arrival in that Lake Tanganyika town had come after two years of roaming throughout the region. Had Stanley not been halted for three months by the war against Mirambo, or had Livingstone been delayed another month, the two might never have met. Stanley's personal travail and the hardships he imposed on his flock would have made a good story, but nothing more. But the journalist's luck was to hold. As he entered Ujiji dressed in his best white flannels, his boots oiled and his helmet well chalked, he met Livingstone's English-speaking servant, who led him to the great man. The explorer and the journalist tipped their hats.

"Dr. Livingstone, I presume?"

"Yes."

"Doctor, I thank God I have been permitted to shake hands with you."[58]

Despite Stanley's fears to the contrary, the notoriously misanthropic Livingstone was extremely happy to see him. The American had brought a huge sack of mail for the explorer, but before opening it, Livingstone wanted to hear the headlines of the past five years. He was as starved for information about the "civilized" world as that world had been starved for information about him. Stanley's first service to the famous explorer was thus to exercise his journalistic talents and supply all the news Livingstone had missed—the Franco-Prussian War, the opening of the Suez Canal, the election of U. S. Grant, the completion of the American transcontinental railroad, the Carlist wars, and many other events. "I never fancied myself more like a newspaperman," Stanley confided to his diary, "than I did when at Ujiji with such an attentive listener as Livingstone."[59] Stanley's report, Livingstone later wrote, "had an immediate and beneficial effect on my health."[60]

The explorer was perturbed when Stanley revealed that he worked for the *New York Herald,* "that despicable newspaper," as Livingstone put it. But the latter softened when Stanley told him (falsely) that his editor had been willing to spend huge sums not only to find Livingstone but to shower him with needed food and supplies. All the paper asked in return was an interview with the explorer and a formal letter of thanks from him to James Gordon Bennett. Not only did Livingstone readily agree to these requests, but he also volunteered to contribute some dispatches of his own. These contributions, as well as the letter of thanks, would prove central to the later debate over the authenticity of Stanley's reports.

Although Stanley had worried that Livingstone would be cold and dismissive, as he had found so many other British men of note, the journalist and the explorer took to each other immediately. The one fulfilled an important need of the other.[61] Livingstone had long lived apart from his children, and he expressed disappointment with his sons. Stanley, some thirty years his junior, seemed to him the manly and adventurous but nonetheless respectful son he had always wanted. For the younger man, Livingstone—accomplished, religious, moral, and unpretentious—could substitute for the unknown father who had sired him and then abandoned mother and baby to an unhappy fate. Livingstone may also have fulfilled Stanley's wish to be the son of a prominent, highly respected man. It is not unlikely that the Scotsman served as an emotional replacement for Henry Hope Stanley, the esteemed New Orleans cotton broker whom John Rowlands had falsely claimed as his adoptive father. After their famous meeting, Stanley and Livingstone explored the northern reaches of

Lake Tanganyika together, and as they spent several weeks in close company, their bond tightened. They became so close that Livingstone wrote warmly of Stanley to his influential friends in London; as for the reporter, his dispatches formed the nucleus of what would become a powerful and long-lasting Livingstone myth.[62]

Although Stanley met Livingstone in late October 1871, the journalist's initial article about the expedition, written nearly four months before the encounter, did not reach New York until two months after it.[63] By the time Europeans and Americans learned of Stanley's foray into the African interior, it had long since reached a successful conclusion. The industrialized world, along with parts of its colonial fringe—Bombay, Suez, Algiers—was now closely linked by telegraph cables that transmitted information almost instantaneously, turning what was new into "news." But large swatches of territory including most of Africa and South America and much of China and India still lay outside the rapidly expanding network of global communications.[64] A dispatch originating in Bombay could reach newspaper and government offices throughout Europe and the eastern United States in a matter of hours; it took months for that same dispatch to travel from Kwihara (Tanzania), where Stanley wrote his first report, to the closest telegraph station. Although rumors that Stanley had found Livingstone reached London in May 1872, more than six months after the event, the first articles based on Stanley's actual reports did not see print until July, nearly three-quarters of a year after their encounter had taken place.[65]

Bennett's view of the Stanley expedition changed dramatically after his reporter had achieved the amazing feat of meeting Livingstone in the heart of Africa. "You are now famous as Livingstone," the editor telegraphed Stanley, "having discovered the discoverer. Accept my thanks, and whole world." The *Herald*'s London bureau chief added, "Accept in addition assurance, fellow correspondent, that more splendid achievement, energetic devotion and generous gallantry not in history human endeavor."[66] Now Bennett not only made good the reporter's debts but spared no expense to trumpet his accomplishments.[67] Already in December 1871, the *Herald* boasted that the Stanley mission had not only changed the face of modern journalism but advanced civilization itself. "An African exploring expedition is a new thing in the enterprises of modern journalism, and in this, as in many other great achievements of 'the third estate,' to the *New York Herald* will belong the credit of the first bold adventure in the cause of humanity, civilization, and science."[68]

Other American papers agreed. The *Herald* of Frederick Maryland called Stanley's work, "the greatest achievement of modern journalistic enterprise that has ever been recorded." Meanwhile, the *Indianapolis News* effused that the expedition "is in the history of journalism what great battles, the founding of new nations or the completion of great public works are in the history of the world."[69] The *Memphis Appeal,* for its part, praised the *New York Herald* for its success in "defying parties, news associations and political combinations," such that "now it supplants governments."[70] Beneath this hyperbole and self-congratulation lay the recognition that the *New York Herald* represented something new, that it formed the vanguard of mass journalism with the potential to wield extraordinary power and sway. With its vast readership and mounting revenues—the Bennetts ranked among the richest families in the United States—the penny press could now do more than merely shape public opinion. It had become a cultural, political, and economic power in its own right.

In trumpeting its accomplishment, the *Herald* used the Stanley story both to assert the superiority of the American press over its European rivals and to celebrate the dynamism of a nation just beginning to flex its muscles as a world economic force. Stanley's achievement, the *Herald* proclaimed, "is distinctively the work of the American press, whose aspirations and ambitions have grown with the majesty of the land, and whose enterprise has been molded [sic] on the national character." Bennett also touted his paper's role in the civilizing mission abroad, writing that Stanley's defeat of the barbaric Mirambo "is the emblem of the modern Christian crusade under the lead of the great newspaper press. It is the accomplishment, as well as the foreshadowing of the work of peaceful civilization in the future"— unlike any exploit of the British, who waved the "blood-red banner of conquest, division of caste, and general despair."[71]

The *Daily Telegraph,* England's best-selling penny paper, doubtless did not share the *Herald*'s sense of American superiority, but the London editors agreed that Stanley and others like him "will turn the eyes of civilized nations to a part of the globe that has been like a sealed book through all the ages of history. The native tribes will be brought in contact with modern civilization, and it will not be long before that vast and well watered tableland will be reached by the enterprise and commerce of the white man."[72] Here, in these lines, is that staple of modern imperial ideology—the notion that the work of "civilization" goes hand in hand with Europe's economic penetration of untamed and barbarous lands.[73] The newspaper would be crucial to that penetration because it would provide the road map to Africa's unexploited wealth.

The *Daily Telegraph* aspired both to master Africa through the knowledge journalists would spread and to unlock the mysteries of the planet as a whole. "The press will spread the information broadcast over the civilized world. . . . Nothing can be hid long in this age from the researches of enterprise and science. The burning equator and the frozen poles alike must give up their secrets."[74] Echoing these notions, the *Manchester Guardian* proclaimed "that a single resolute man, with unlimited command of money, can find any one he chooses to look for, even in the very heart of Africa."[75] As these commentaries suggest, the success of the *Herald*'s expedition and Stanley's ability to spread his story far and wide gave a newly confident mass press the belief that nothing could escape its gaze. That self-assurance would soon transform itself into a widely shared sense that Europeans and Americans constituted the dominant race and that their superior "civilization" was destined to shape the entire world in its image.[76]

The growing intellectual confidence of the press found its match in a mounting fascination with the knowledge that newspapers now displayed of what had long been mysterious and obscure. "Stanley," wrote the *London Daily News, "is like a man returning with the story of another universe."[77] Imaginative fiction had long been replete with tales of lost worlds, and for Europeans of the late nineteenth century Central Africa had remained one of those worlds. Only, it was a lost world that really existed. In "finding" Livingstone, Stanley had uncovered a whole new realm. Stanley's ability not only to go there and back but to vividly describe what he saw gave newspaper readers the vicarious thrill of being there with him as he unmasked the unknown and illuminated the very heart of the "Dark Continent."

Even as American journalists—and some of their British colleagues—marveled over their power and emphasized the press's commitment to knowledge and truth, a large number of English papers expressed skepticism over the veracity, even the reality, of Stanley's accounts. The triumphal tone in New York sounded against a London register of ridicule and disbelief.[78] Shortly before Stanley's return to Europe, Sir Henry Rawlinson, president of England's snobbish Royal Geographical Society (RGS), claimed, "If there has been any discovery and relief it is Dr. Livingstone who had discovered and relieved Mr. Stanley. Dr. Livingstone, indeed, is in clover while Mr. Stanley is nearly destitute."[79] While Rawlinson merely insinuated that Stanley had falsified his story, another prominent RGS member, the explorer James Grant, called the American's account an outright lie. "No one," Grant wrote the assistant secretary of the RGS, "believes Stanley found Livingstone."[80]

Shortly after the first account of Stanley's success saw print in early July 1872, skeptical remarks from the RGS leadership found their way into the *Times,* which began to publish letters from others who doubted the American's veracity. J. E. Gray of the British Museum wondered whether "any of your readers . . . have received any letters from Dr Livingstone. It is curious if Mr. Stanley was with him some time, he did not write to someone."[81] The *Pall Mall Gazette,* a self-consciously sophisticated journal of commentary and opinion, took the tack of ridicule. "The summary of Mr. Stanley's dispatches to the *New York Herald,* giving an account of that gentlemen's adventures in search of Dr. Livingstone, is one of the most comical things of its kind ever penned."[82] The *Spectator* too joined the chorus of disbelief, wondering why the sober Dr. Livingstone's letters "are written with an uneasy, or, to speak plainly, a vulgar jocularity as foreign to the great traveler's character as it is possible to conceive."[83] The insinuation was clear: Stanley himself wrote the letters attributed to Livingstone, an austere missionary hardly known for "jocularity."

This controversy reverberated beyond London into the English provinces and across the Channel to Europe. It then quickly bounced back to London as telegraphed copies of foreign articles were translated and published in English papers. Summarizing the British debate, *Le Temps,* France's equivalent of the conservative, establishment-oriented *London Times,* concluded: "It is certain that Livingstone did not write, at least not as they were published, the two letters we translated." The real question, the paper went on to say was "whether these letters were edited, augmented, and corrected by Stanley or whether they are completely false, a pure American fabrication." The editors leaned toward the harsher conclusion, quoting a "celebrated Berlin geographer" who claimed, "It is not absolutely impossible that he [Stanley] never saw Livingstone."[84]

Meanwhile, the *Standard* intensified the skepticism in London against Stanley by raising the following questions: "Why did not Dr. Livingstone return with Mr. Stanley? Why was the great traveler driven to be so uncommunicative to all but the *New York Herald?* Why did not the [Royal Geographical Society's own] relief expedition go on and relieve him?"[85]

No one could mistake the implications of these questions: Stanley was clearly a liar and a charlatan; his reports were an elaborate hoax engineered by the sensationalist *New York Herald* to sell papers.

What is remarkable about this incredulity is that it persisted even after British foreign secretary Lord Granville publicly announced that he had "not the slightest doubt, as to the genuineness of the papers which have been received."[86] As if these words were not enough, Tom Livingstone also confirmed Stanley's account, writing, "We have not the slightest reason to doubt that this is my father's journal, and I certify that the letters he has brought home are my father's letters, and no others."[87] Even so, a widely circulated rumor held that Stanley had never actually met Livingstone but rather encountered an African messenger carrying Livingstone's letters, confiscated the material, and then fabricated the tale of marching to Ujiji and finding the explorer.[88]

Why such persistent incredulity? Why a suspicion of Stanley so widespread that nothing short of seeing Livingstone in the flesh would put it to rest? Stanley's recent biographers agree on two explanations: class prejudice against a lowborn American autodidact who wrote for a New York newspaper; and a repressed national shame that Americans had upstaged England in the search for Livingstone—the Royal Geographical Society had mounted its own unsuccessful mission to find the explorer.[89] There is a measure of truth in both points. Most leading members of the RGS belonged to the well-educated, economically comfortable ranks of society. As a group, these gentleman geographers looked down on journalists, whose profession was not yet considered respectable and who lacked the scientific credentials they claimed for themselves.[90] A general condescension toward journalists shaded into resentment of Stanley, whose American audacity had enabled him to succeed where the British had failed. As the *Daily Telegraph* put it, "It must, no doubt, be a little vexatious to Royal Geographers—who like to receive tidings from their emissaries in the grand, slow, traditional manner—to witness a young New York correspondent 'wiping the eye' of their [own] 'Search Expedition' in the most triumphant manner."[91]

These explanations, plausible as they are, do not account for the extraordinary depth and persistence of the skepticism toward Stanley. After all, English gentlemen did not automatically discount what London journalists wrote, even though they rejected members of that profession socially. Moreover, the nationalistic resentment of Stanley, understandable as an initial reaction to the news from Africa, should not have outlasted all the evidence supporting the veracity of the journalist's claims. The deeper reason for the unwillingness to believe Stanley's reports lies in the kind of journalism he represented. It was not that his profession automatically evoked disbelief, but that the American form of journalism Stanley embodied—popular, colloquial, lowbrow, and audacious—was still essentially unknown in England's respectable society. True, the country had a few penny papers, the oldest dating back to the mid-1850s, but in content and style these journals resembled the staid *London Times* far more than the "sensationalist" *New York Herald.*[92] Penny papers like the *Daily Telegraph* had not yet developed a "tabloid style," nor did they stray very far from the traditional fare of the quotidian press—politics and Parliament in England, and politics and parliament abroad. Crime, fire, scandal, and natural disasters—long staple stories of the *New York Herald* and increasingly prominent in France's *Petit journal*—had yet to make a significant appearance in the British press—except in the Sunday papers, disparaged in polite society for their lowbrow readers.[93] In the United States, the widespread belief in journalism's "objectivity," the notion that it narrated true events, kept skepticism of Stanley to a minimum. But in Great Britain's main public sphere, the absence of the new journalistic mode made Stanley's style of reportage immediately suspect.

The *Herald*'s issue of 2 July 1872 devoted the lion's share of its news space—nearly half of the paper consisted of ads—to the Stanley-Livingstone story. There was a two-page map of east-central Africa, two more pages summarizing Stanley's dispatch, and column after column of editorials and commentary praising the *Herald*'s initiative, Stanley's heroism, and Livingstone's discoveries. The long summary of Stanley's letters had been written in London and then telegraphed to New York at enormous cost. The story's many subheadings gave a vivid flavor of its writing style and made it almost unnecessary to read the text: "The Thrilling Narrative," "The Terrible Climate," "The Incessant Rains," "The Total Loss," The Herald Goes to War," "In a High Fever," "The Ambush of Mirambo," "A Terrific Slaughter," "The Astonished Natives," "A Historic Meeting." The article itself read much more like an adventure story or romanticized history, like the immensely popular tales of George Henty, than the sober political reports that filled English newspapers.[94] One typical paragraph narrated the "Ambush of Mirambo," in which "a superior body of natives, armed with muskets, assegais (spears) and poisoned arrows, had suddenly burst upon the Arabs. A TERRIFIC SLAUGHTER ENSUED."

The tone of the *Herald*'s summary matched that of Stanley's own dispatch, finally published on 15 July 1872. "The Arabs were so confident of easy victory over the African King [Mirambo] . . . that I was tempted in an unlucky moment to promise them my aid. . . . On the first day we burned three of his villages, captured, killed, or drove away the inhabitants. On the second I was taken down with the ever-remitting fever of the country. On the third a detachment was sent out and audaciously attacked [Mirambo's] fenced village, [producing] a great slaughter of the Arabs."

Although newspaper readers were accustomed to war correspondents' dispatches, English reporters rarely wrote as vividly as this. Stanley's innovation, as we have seen, was to structure his story around himself, liberally using the first person and emphasizing his own point of view. These journalistic departures fascinated readers from New York to Paris, Havana to Bombay.[95] And most reactions to the Stanley story, whether the writers believed it or not, emphasized its vivid, romantic, fictional style. London's *Daily News* described the American journalist as if he were a hero from Greek mythology. "Mr. Stanley made his way from the sea, over deserts and through fiercely hostile tribes, until, after adventures that almost seem incredible, he came upon the object of his search." After a fierce battle with Mirambo, Stanley finally resumed his quest: "In many a romantic story the hero who has lost his way, and sees no chance of otherwise finding it again, escapes from every difficulty." These and other actions made the American journalist "a conquering hero," an individual larger than life whose daring ranged from the ridiculous to the sublime. "Nothing more heroic and more ludicrous, more oddly suggestive of Pizarro, and of Astley, has been carried out and described in the history of modern adventure."[96] Although Stanley was as yet too little known to emerge from this expedition a charismatic figure, writings such as these set the stage for his later charismatic renown.

As these commentaries suggest, readers could identify Stanley's dispatches as adventure stories because he clearly obeyed the conventions of the genre, so much so that the editors of the *Daily News* described the American's accounts as if they were works of imaginative fiction.[97] Fictionalized they clearly were, but no serious historian or biographer has ever suggested he made them up.[98] It's just that the narrative forms he used reminded especially his English readers more of novels and mythology than journalism. As one contemporary commentator put it, "The way Stanley wrote . . . led people to believe that [his reports] had the same standing as a novel by Alexander Dumas and that the only place Stanley had seen Livingstone was in his dreams."[99]

Viewing the Stanley dispatches in this way makes it understandable that members of the Royal Geographical Society, upset over the claim that an American got to Livingstone first, would have disbelieved his story. Henry Rawlinson had sneered in May 1872 that Stanley was neither "a simple tourist, nor even an explorer," but a journalist "sent out by our Transatlantic cousins, among whom the science of advertising has reached a far higher stage of development than in this benighted country."[100] His implication was clear: the *Herald* was capable of inventing the story. Or perhaps even worse, it was likely to use that story for its own commercial purposes rather than in the service of science. As John Kirk had written Rawlinson the previous March, "I doubt not if in possession of real news of Dr. Livingstone he [Stanley] would try to pass it on directly to New York in order that it might first be published in the *Herald*."[101] Such a prospect horrified key members of the British establishment. Explaining its own unwillingness to believe the Stanley account, the elite *Pall Mall Gazette* wrote, "It is impossible to place the same amount of confidence in reports thus obtained [by a sensationalist American newspaper] and diluted before they reached our hands, which we should feel if the Doctor's traveling experiences were communicated to us in something more resembling an official shape."[102] In other words, stories appearing in the populist *New York Herald* could not be trusted—at least not until they had been vetted by the *Times*.

The middlebrow *Daily Telegraph,* relatively staid as it was, sided with its "transatlantic cousin." "We are afraid that the learned President [Rawlinson] can scarcely forgive this new and energetic modern spirit of journalism which does what Royal Societies and Search Expeditions only talk about." The gentlemen's mistrust of the new American journalism, the sense that it had overstepped the press's proper role, underlay the refusal to believe Stanley's story, even in the face of powerful evidence that he had indeed "found" Livingstone. For Sir Henry Rawlinson, as for the *Pall Mall Gazette,* journalism's role was to report official news, news filtered through established authorities. The last thing it should do was to create what it reported and then present those creations in the style of popular fiction. The British elite was not yet ready for the brave new mediated world to come, a world in which mass-circulation newspapers wielded growing political and economic power and journalists sought to entertain as well as inform.

Such was far less true of Britain's middle and lower social ranks, whose members increasingly found themselves drawn to the new journalism. By the late 1880s many would forget about Stanley's American interlude and extol him for embodying the best characteristics of the British "race." They would endorse the notion, already advanced in 1871, that Stanley resembled the mythic heroes whose courage and manly abilities provided models for contemporary men.

TWO

Pierre Savorgnan de Brazza and the Making of the French Third Republic

WHEN HENRY MORTON STANLEY took the podium at the Hotel Continental in Paris, the room was palpably tense. His fellow Congo explorer, the French naval officer of Italian birth, Pierre (Pietro) Savorgnan de Brazza, had been attacking him, and the audience knew Stanley had prepared a blistering response.[1] The date was 19 October 1882, and members of the American elite in Paris had invited Stanley to address a banquet given in his honor at a club named for him. That evening the crowd included the American ambassador to France, the consul general, an assortment of well-to-do expatriates, and reporters from the *Times, Daily Telegraph, Standard, Daily News, New York Herald, Boston Journal,* and many other prominent papers. The French press was amply represented as well.

As a former journalist for the *New York Herald,* Stanley would ordinarily have felt very much at home, using the occasion to recount his most recent adventures. But the Stanley Club speech was different. The American meant to challenge what Brazza had been saying about him, and that required a more political kind of talk. But to criticize Brazza in the heart of Paris, albeit in an American setting, was not an easy thing to do.

During the summer and fall of 1882, no French man or woman was more visible than the explorer Pierre Savorgnan de Brazza. At a time when France confronted armed resistance to its imperial efforts in North Africa and Indochina, Brazza's "pacific conquest" of extensive lands along the Congo River made him a national hero. Parisian journalists lauded him for winning the Congo "without spilling a drop of blood"—unlike other imperialists who seemed to do nothing but. Brazza's stature was enhanced all the more by his widely publicized rivalry with Stanley, whose current employer, King Leopold II of Belgium, had sent him to seize the same lands. Brazza's view was that the Congo should belong to France, and the Parisian press, almost without a dissenting voice, cheered him on. So, even though Stanley appeared at a club that bore his name, he found himself behind enemy lines, where the French press lay in wait.

"When I met M. de Brazza in 1880," Stanley began, "The last thing in the world I thought was that I was in the presence of a man who, before too long, would exercise such a powerful influence. A man, without shoes, re-markable only for his threadbare tunic and his unruly hair . . . was not, as you can imagine, an imposing figure."[2] But little did Stanley know that "this man without shoes . . . would become the phenomenon of the year. . . . According to the newspapers [this man] was not just an angel," declared a now thickly sarcastic Stanley, "but an apostle of liberty, the new apostle of Africa . . . who delivered the coup de grace against West African slavery," something the British had not been able to do with a half century of effort and the expenditure of millions. Stanley continued for some time in this vein, ridiculing the French press for its fantasy portrait of Brazza as a lib-erator so beloved by the natives that their king voluntarily ceded to this European—and his heirs—extensive amounts of land.

Stanley was referring here to a treaty with the Makoko, or hereditary ruler of the Bateke people, signed in October 1880. The treaty placed un-der France's protection a huge swath of Congolese territory.[3] Stanley ridi-culed the notion that a monarch as powerful as the Makoko could have in-tended anything of the sort. "I have often wondered," Stanley declared, "whether M. de Brazza indicated to Makoko the meaning and the signifi-cance of this piece of paper written in such strange hieroglyphics."

This treaty would play a major role in Brazza's emergence as a charis-matic hero and French media celebrity in the early 1880s. And Stanley, jealously but not without justice, ridiculed this development as well. "This shoeless traveler, lost and poor, has become . . . a brilliant diplomat, a ge-ographical strategist, and agent of French annexations. He's feted at the Sorbonne; applauded by the whole of France. . . . At this moment, gold medals are being cast in his honor and painters can now immortalize him on canvas so that posterity can admire him."

Envious as Stanley was of this "French upstart," he had put his finger on several crucial phenomena: the ability of a newly ascendant mass press to represent, even create, a national community along with charismatic figures believed to incarnate that community; the hold of Africa and African exploration on the popular imagination, thanks in large part to the new journalism; the national chauvinism of France's media campaign for the annexation of African lands; and Brazza's emergence as a hero who could unify "the whole of France."

Stanley attributed these developments to Brazza's Machiavellian charm. But the French fascination with Brazza and with the remote parts of Africa he explored and ultimately "gave" to his adopted homeland are considerably more complicated than Stanley could have suspected. These developments are crucial to any understanding of the early Third Republic and to the pivotal role played by mass journalism and France's colonial empire in shaping how the new regime was represented and understood. By turning Brazza into a hero-celebrity in the 1880s and helping him personify a new French standing in Africa and the world at large, the French press used Brazza's image to rally French men and women around a fledgling republic in need of great men and great deeds. Journalists encouraged leaders of the Third Republic, long averse to territorial annexation, to plant the French flag in equatorial Africa. In doing so, they helped transform the image—or at least the self-image—of the new regime.

In the aftermath of the disastrous Franco-Prussian War (1870–71), prominent French commentators and political figures responded to their country's humiliating loss by fashioning what Wolfgang Schivelbusch has called a "culture of defeat." This culture, he argues, allowed opinion makers, political leaders, and ordinary citizens to erect a set of emotional defenses against the trauma of defeat by redefining military losses both as moral victories and as the first, necessary stage in the inevitable triumph to come.[4] Although Schivelbusch goes too far in calling this apologetic discourse of the 1870s a "culture," the set of emotional defenses he identifies held considerable sway during the decade following the Franco-Prussian War. It would be revived after France's humiliating defeat at Fashoda in 1898.[5] (See chapter 5.)

With the advent in 1879 of a solidly democratic centrist republic, one led by optimistic, forward-looking men, the defensiveness of the 1870s subsided in favor of more straightforwardly confident views. No longer would the fledgling Third Republic be the beaten, humiliated nation of 1871; it would now be a great colonial power, a player on the world stage whose territorial holdings rivaled those of Great Britain and vastly surpassed those of its enemy to the east. But the new colonial France, its republican advocates maintained, would not mirror the British Empire in being largely a business enterprise. Leaders of France's new democratic Third Republic, heir to the liberal and liberating aspirations of the French Revolution, would construe the new imperialism as a humanitarian and civilizing mission.[6] Not unlike the revolutionary armies of the 1790s, French colonists of the Third Republic would conquer in order to liberate. If necessary, the republic would use force to spread the ideals, values, and achievements of France's superior civilization to less favored regions of the world. But even truer to its ideals would be the *conquête pacifique,* soon the trademark of Brazza. In pursuing this civilizing mission, the republic's leaders, touting Brazza's accomplishments, directed attention away from the two provinces, Alsace and Lorraine, lost to Germany in 1871 and toward the new provinces of Africa and Asia.[7] In the process, the centrality of empire became a crucial part of an emerging national-republican message.

Throughout the 1880s, the republican government tried to instill a commitment not solely to the new regime as such but to the values and institutions it enshrined: secularism, rationalism, free enterprise, moderate democracy, public schools, and the *mission civilisatrice.* To accomplish these goals, leaders created a system of secular public schools; commissioned statues, busts, and images of the republican goddess Marianne and installed them throughout the country; and enshrined Bastille Day as a national holiday, urging the mayors of France's 36,000 communes to celebrate the 14th of July through festivals and other public events.[8]

Although these efforts eventually achieved a measure of success, it took time for the republican educational system to bear political and ideological fruit; in some regions, ordinary people and members of the upper classes fiercely resisted the encroachment of the new system on traditional religious education. As for the Mariannes, their diffusion proceeded slowly, and those built in the early years languished unnoticed in public gardens, indistinguishable from other classical statuary. The Mariannes were not, therefore, particularly visible as representations of the new Republic, especially since their gender distanced them from the very idea of politics and political power. Never in French history had formal political authority resided in the body of a woman. Salic law had required that only men could inherit the throne, and the French Revolution retained the culture, if not the specific form, of Salic law by excluding women from citizenship and thus from the possibility of exercising power in any formal way.[9]

If the Mariannes could not exactly stand in for the republic or help transmit its values, what could? The French Revolution had produced no George Washingtons, no founding fathers around whose memory and mythology almost everyone could rally. The memory of absolutist kings, Robespierre, and two Napoleon Bonapartes (I and III) placed the idea of political fathers beyond the pale. Rather than individuals, republicans turned to symbols—the tricolor flag, the Marseillaise, the Bastille successfully overcome.[10] But compelling as these symbols could be, they remained too abstract, mobilized too few emotions, and appeared too secular to create the kind of civil religion that could satisfy a widespread hunger for spirituality that the new republic, hostile to Catholicism, left unfulfilled.

What did succeed in instilling republican values and a measure of national solidarity was the new regime's effort to venerate deceased republican leaders, to endow them with charisma at the moment of their death. The Third Republic's large number of state funerals—eighty-two over seventy years— with their solemn processions, religious imagery, and soaring eulogies helped give republican France the elements of spirituality that its official opposition to Catholicism and the Church otherwise foreclosed.[11] Since a man safely in his coffin posed no threat to the regime, he could become a kind of republican saint, his life story told as a narrative of republican virtue, as a concrete example of what the regime represented and how its citizens should behave. Beginning in the late 1870s, one newly deceased notable after the other emerged in funeral celebrations as incarnations of the regime: Adolphe Thiers (1877), Louis Blanc (1882), Gambetta (1883), Victor Hugo (1885), Jules Grévy (1891), Jules Ferry (1892), Louis Pasteur (1895).

The most extraordinary of these events was doubtless the commemoration of Hugo, which drew a million people into the streets of Paris.[12] Although the state, unwilling to recognize living heroes, waited until the poet's death to endow him with the aura of sanctity, the press had accomplished his beatification years earlier. Beginning with Hugo's return to France in September 1870, journalists played a key role in making him one of the very charismatic heroes that the new state had failed to provide. Part of the writer's exalted standing at the moment of his death stemmed from his coronation by the press as a living hero during the fifteen years before he died. A dead saint begins to fade away as soon as the funeral orations end; a living hero can project ideas and values and inspire action every day. But even Hugo's heroism had its limits. The more republicans feted him, especially in the militant form their celebrations often took, the less Hugo appeared to represent the nation as a whole. He became so identified with zealous republicanism that moderate and conservative French men and women no longer saw themselves in him. What the Third Republic needed even more than republican heroes were national heroes, individuals who unified in themselves the nation and the republic. This still-contested form of government needed the modern equivalent of the king's two bodies, one body to represent the stable, eternal France (the nation) and the other to represent the changing, modern France (the Republic).[13] If the Republic was to achieve the near-unanimous acceptance it had thus far lacked, it needed to establish itself as the legitimate heir of the country's prior regimes.

Given the Republic's squeamishness about the fabrication of living heroes, its leaders and publicists often turned to heroes of the past. The state did not, however, serve as the key medium for accomplishing this crucial goal—for anointing heroes who melded the nation and the republic into one. That medium became the newly ascendant popular press, whose main organs in the 1880s were the *Petit journal, Petit parisien,* and *Matin.* In the late 1890s, one of France's top sociologists, Gabriel Tarde, attempted to theorize the unifying role of the popular press, and his ideas remain useful today. For Tarde, the new mass press, a medium born with and nurtured by the Third Republic, possessed the ability to forge community and create solidarity as no other institution could.[14]

In an extraordinary pair of essays published in 1898 and 1899, Tarde argued that mass journalism had emerged after 1860, when the effects of nineteenth-century inventions—the railroad, the telegraph, and the high-speed printing press—came together to create "perfected means of locomotion and instantaneous transmission of thought over long distances."[15] Such instantaneous transmission created a vast national community of readers brought together by the common experience of imbibing the same material at the same time. The existence of such a community was unprecedented and had profound cultural and political implications.

Members of this community, Tarde wrote, "do not rub shoulders, nor do they see or hear one another." They are bound together by the "simultaneity of their convictions or their passions," shaped by the press.[16] Tarde called this community a public. In general, he wrote, different newspapers created different publics, though readership and thus publics overlapped. But under certain circumstances, these once divergent publics would become "a single unified public as a result of [every member's] common agreement on a few important points."[17] The great engine of such agreement was the mass press, a medium with the ability to overcome differences of "class, profession, union membership, political party" to create a unified *"public français."*[18] Their common ideas formed what Tarde called Opinion, certain widely shared attitudes or beliefs that emerged from the simultaneous reading of the press.[19] Such accord was not incompatible with individualism and democracy, Tarde added, because it was based on the ideas readers come to hold in common, which need not encompass the sum total of each individual's beliefs. Members of a large national public draw together not by "flattening diversity and people's special qualities" but by expressing a "communion of ideas and passions that does not inhibit their individual differences."[20]

With this analysis, Tarde anticipated by nearly a century the ideas of Benedict Anderson, whose imagined national communities are rooted in simultaneous reading of the press. Each reader in a given nation, Anderson writes, performs a ceremony "replicated simultaneously by thousands (or millions) of others of whose existence he is confident, yet of whose identity he has not the slightest notion."[21] Anderson does not join Tarde in claiming that such parallel reading leads to a partial unanimity of belief, but maintains nonetheless that the common reading of newspapers by people dispersed in space both helps make a national community possible and provides evidence that such a community exists.

In the case of Brazza, the widespread simultaneous reading of press commentary on his pacific conquests in Africa both shaped and reflected a nascent national community defined in part through the explorer's colonial exploits. In Tarde's terms, attitudes about Brazza reveal the emergence of Opinion, of certain shared beliefs held by people who otherwise differed in a great many ways. The flowering of such shared beliefs was crucial to the legitimacy of the Third Republic and its perceived rootedness in France's national past. It is, of course, easier to demonstrate a near-unanimity about Brazza among a multitude of ideologically diverse newspapers than among their even more diverse readers. But there is considerable evidence that large numbers of ordinary people, all influenced by the press, overcame differences of class, profession, and gender to rally both to Brazza's support and to the colonial republic he came, charismatically, to represent.

Brazza was not, of course, the only explorer who sought to claim territory for France, but he may have been the most successful. His version of imperial conquest had the great virtue of being relatively nonviolent and inexpensive. It was, for that reason, uncontroversial—or at least much less controversial than France's interventions in Tunisia and Tonkin, where many French soldiers died. Brazza's imperialism leant itself to exactly the kind of unifying story newspaper editors wanted to tell.

Not only could Brazza's version of imperialism bring French men and women together; so could the man himself. As a recently naturalized citizen of Italian noble origins, Brazza had participated in none of the conflicts that had fragmented French society, dividing republicans from monarchists, secularists from Catholics, workers from bourgeois. As a man without a history—at least a French history—Brazza could represent anyone and everyone. That he chose to become French in the aftermath of the Franco-Prussian War, having fought on the French side, gave him an especially patriotic allure. As the Gambettist *République française* declared, "Brazza was one of those who responded to Victor Hugo's magnificent wish . . . that he were not born French so he could ask to become one of France's soldiers and citizens at precisely the moment" the country needed him most.[22] The editorialist might have added that Brazza enjoyed certain political advantages that Hugo did not possess. The explorer's apparently pure patriotism, unmarked by any overt ideological positions, distanced him from Hugo's archrepublican stance. Brazza could become everyone's hero—not, like Hugo, solely a hero of the left. For this reason, French men and women of all political stripes could see Brazza as an embodiment of their nation however it was defined.

Crucial as well for journalists' interest in Brazza as symbol of a resurgent French nation and unifier of a long-divided country was the kind of explorer image he so assiduously cultivated. Brazza was quick to comprehend the power and importance of the new mass journalism. With a subtle command of the medium's rules, the explorer fashioned for himself an image of manliness, virility, and power—an image tempered by the grace of aristocracy and the kindness of noblesse oblige. Although the standard allegorical symbols of the republic were female, the heroes of a supposedly eternal France, its living embodiments, its kings and emperors, had virtually all been male.[23] To become consonant with the nation as a whole, the Republic had to find its embodiment in a man. But that man had to possess a particular set of qualities. He could not be a purely military figure, given the army's monarchist and aristocratic reputation, but he had to exude enough strength and virility to represent France's desire to maintain its standing as a world power.

The question of masculinity and male identity was extraordinarily vexed in the aftermath of the Franco-Prussian War. An array of journalists

and other commentators saw that war as an emasculating event, as an ig-
noble defeat that had stripped French fighters of their manhood just as it
had stripped France of Alsace and Lorraine.[24] Writers such as Alexandre
Dumas, fils, sought to restore virility by keeping women firmly in their
place, while others hoped to democratize the male culture of honor so
pronounced during the decades before 1848.[25] Whatever their prescription
for success, commentators of all stripes sought a revised image of masculinity, one both consistent with the new republic's egalitarian values and
capable of projecting a sense of strength, confidence, and power.

As a manly but gentle explorer, a modest aristocrat who sacrificed his
fortune for France, Brazza seemed to represent precisely this kind of male.
He fashioned himself as a military man, but one with an uncommonly delicate touch. He was a conqueror, but one who seized territory without violence, a manly adventurer equally devoted to the pursuit of knowledge and
the betterment of humankind. Brazza was, in short, a man's man, but one
with prominent "feminine" features (as defined at the time): patience, tact,
gentleness, subtlety, and charm. He thus stood out as the perfect male embodiment of a new French republic built on tempered imperial strength—
a manly man with the best qualities of women. Such a man could be the
hero who embodied a *nation* determined to remain a world power and a
republic devoted to the rights of man.

Roman born in 1852, Pietro Savorgnan de Brazza was the seventh son of
an old Udine noble family. His father was a liberal nationalist of the Romantic school whose own passion for geography and faraway places apparently inspired his son. According to Brazza's biographers, even as a young
man, Pietro (later changed to "Pierre") expressed interest in travel and exploration.[26] After meeting a French admiral, the marquis de Montaignac,
Brazza decided to join the French navy; thanks to Montaignac's support,
he gained admission to the school for naval cadets at Brest. While study-
ing there, he read books by David Livingstone, Sir Richard Burton, Paul
Du Chaillu, and other well-known explorers of Africa. Brazza also became
an ardent French patriot. His parents, at once liberal and skeptical of Italy's
violence-prone unification movement, taught him as an adolescent to see
France as an orderly alternative to their own tumultuous land. And it may
be that the young nobleman rejected the closed, increasingly restrictive
aristocratic society of his Italian youth. With the zeal of a convert, he
embraced his adoptive country.[27]

After receiving his naval commission in 1870, Brazza applied for active
duty during the Franco-Prussian War. He also requested naturalization as

a French citizen, granted in 1874, and was sent in 1871 to Algeria, where he witnessed the machine-gunning of Berber insurgents. Between 1871 and 1874, Brazza was posted to a ship that sailed regularly to France's small Gabon colony, and there he developed an interest in exploring interior regions of Central Africa via the Ogooué and Gabon rivers. In June 1874, he devised a plan to explore the Ogooué, submitting it to the French minister of the navy, who was none other than his patron, Admiral Montaignac. The latter endorsed the plan on grounds that it not only would provide geographic and ethnographic information but might also open new and potentially lucrative markets. A year later, Brazza's small, modestly funded (10,000 francs) expedition left for Gabon, to the total indifference of the French press.

Unlike Stanley, who had at about the same time begun his pioneering trip down the Congo, Brazza was lightly armed and accompanied by a tiny group of men.[28] Brazza's meager stock of weapons prevented him from using force against the Africans who opposed his advance, and in any event, his temperament was more suited to negotiation than to combat. Whether he avoided violence by necessity, choice, or both, Brazza frequently had to employ his not inconsiderable diplomatic skills. And he was not above using trickery and showmanship to get his way. The explorer had equipped himself with a supply of fireworks, which he used to dazzle—and doubtless intimidate—the Africans he encountered.

Short on presents to offer his African hosts, many of whom were loath to receive him, Brazza inched up the Ogooué River. He and his men found themselves slowed as well by frequent bouts of malaria, dysentery, exhaustion, and injury. Travel in Central Africa was especially difficult for Europeans, who lacked resistance to local diseases. But those who accompanied Brazza and later wrote about their experiences unanimously praised him for his kindness to those who fell ill and for his own ability to press on even while sick and wounded.[29] His ability to endure deprivation, illness, and injury would figure prominently in Brazza's budding heroic myth.

In July 1877, after nearly two years on the Ogooué, Brazza found, to his great disappointment, that the waterway petered out without emptying into the Congo or one of the great African lakes; the Ogooué proved a dead end. Undaunted, Brazza headed out on foot toward what the Batekes, a large ethnic group that inhabited the region, called "big water" (the Congo). He found the narrow Alima River, which seemed to flow in a promising direction. Once on the river, Brazza and his men encountered violent opposition from the Apfourus, who attacked his canoes. The

European party fought back, felling the outgunned Apfourus in a hail of bullets. Here, Brazza's tactics mirrored Stanley's, except that the American carried a larger supply of arms. But faced with Aphouru reinforcements and dwindling ammunition, Brazza decided to retreat. Three years later, he learned that he had turned back just a short distance from the point where the Alima empties into the Congo, providing a relatively good route from the Atlantic coast to the navigable part of the great trans-African river and thus to the center of the continent. (So many rapids and cataracts punctuate the lower Congo that it is impossible to travel down the river to the estuary.)

When Brazza finally straggled back to the Gabon coast, French soldiers and settlers greeted him as a hero for having ventured as far as he had. But that welcome paled in comparison to the reception he received on his return to Paris at the end of 1878. He had been gone for three and a half years, and during that time the press had begun to take note of Central Africa. France's Universal Exposition of 1878 had been the first to highlight the country's colonial possessions.[30] And if Brazza's exploits had inspired French reporters, they found themselves dazzled by Henry Morton Stanley's even more spectacular feat. During his three-year chute down the entire length of the Congo River (1875–78), the Welsh-American explorer seemed to defy impossible odds. Stanley's unprecedented voyage had been financed and elaborately covered by two of the largest-selling newspapers in the world, the *New York Herald* and the *London Daily Telegraph*. The first was Stanley's old employer, America's leading penny paper, populist in tone and conservative in politics. The second was London's most popular penny journal, a third the price of the *Times* and, in the early years at least, considerably to its left. As in the Livingstone expedition, Stanley penned his own highly colorful dispatches, which appeared regularly in both papers from 1875 to 1878.[31] And like his earlier accounts, the new ones read like adventure stories and appealed to readers excited by the journalist's vivid writing style and by his skillful blending of the familiar and the unknown, a technique that made Stanley's Africa seem palpably real.[32] To add to the drama, he emphasized his sometimes violent encounters with the Africans whose territory he traversed.

But popular at it was, Stanley's vivid journalism gave French commentators ammunition against him. They touted Brazza, emphasizing the contrast between the Frenchman's pacific methods and the apparent brutality and violence of his rival. Brazza and his supporters met in the Paris Geographical Society (PGS), which brought together gentlemen geographers,

Africa-hardened explorers, journalists, and intellectuals who all shared an interest in the uncharted regions of the globe and in claiming those regions for France.[33] Having joined Stanley in placing Central Africa on the journalistic map, Brazza sought to deepen the renascent national sentiment of the 1870s and to direct it toward his own imperial designs. In doing so, he would help build the prestige of France's new republican regime while rallying its long-divided population around the bloodless colonial conquest he sought to represent.

When Brazza returned from his first African voyage in early 1879, he faced a country still largely hostile or indifferent to colonization. France's recent colonial experiences in Algeria and elsewhere had been costly in men and money without achieving measurable results. Part of the problem was that military officials and even local commanders controlled the country's imperial policy, often defying orders from Paris; their actions usually took the form of violent conquest and fierce repression of local opposition. After 1870, republican leaders opposed further colonial expansion, partly in an effort to restrain these overly independent generals. And in the wake of the country's military defeat in 1870–71 and the loss to Germany of Alsace and Lorraine, a great many French leaders and commentators wanted to focus not on foreign adventure but on restoring the conquered provinces to France. The final issue was money. The enormous reparations payments France owed Germany after the war and the cost of rebuilding the country ruled out substantial expenditures abroad.[34]

This colonial reticence began to give way after Stanley's voyage down the Congo. By then (1877), a once wobbly republic had been firmly established and new leaders had taken power, leaders who believed in science, progress, and the future of France. To assure that future, a small but influential group of journalists, politicians, and members of the national and provincial geographic societies created a "colonial lobby" whose pivotal organization became the Committee for a French Africa.[35] Although some members of the lobby had investments and economic interests overseas, most belonged for political and cultural reasons. They maintained that a policy of active colonial expansion would restore French grandeur and rejuvenate a culture facing decline.

The French colonialists' bible was Anatole Prévost-Paradol's best-selling *La France nouvelle* (1868), which went through eleven editions in its first year on the market and several more in the 1870s and 1880s.[36] The noted French liberal argued that France was in danger of becoming "as Greece is now—an ancient though dead civilization, an historical and cultural

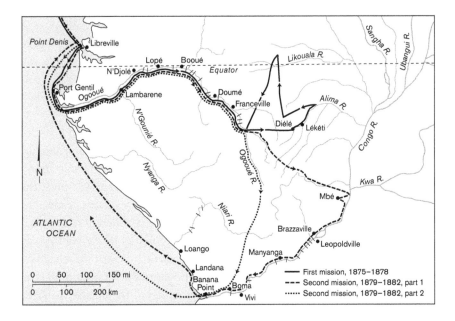

Map 2. Brazza's exploration of the Congo, 1877–82.

artifact." The antidote to such decay was imperial expansion, an effort that would restore France's cultural and national vigor and reverse its demographic slide. Through colonization, Prévost-Paradol wrote, France could extend its language and civilization throughout the world, creating a greater France that would stretch from Calais to Chad and encompass "one hundred million Frenchmen."[37]

In the wake of the Franco-Prussian War, a variety of other commentators took up Prévost-Paradol's message, now with greater urgency. "One must collaborate," declared Alfred Babaud, president of the Geographic Society of Marseille, "with the manly effort of those who explore, describe and exploit the earth. To do so, would be to heal France's wound and recover its place in the world."[38] Babaud's idea that empire would enable France to regain its prestige and standing became a common theme, as did the notion that colonization would allow the country to challenge English hegemony and demonstrate the superiority of France's motives. "England has set foot in no country," wrote Pierre Foncin, founder of the Alliance française, without establishing her counting houses; France has nowhere passed without leaving the perfume of her spirituality."[39] To these cultural justifications, other commentators added an economic rationale. A new empire, maintained men like Eugene Azam, head of Bordeaux's geographic society, would vastly expand the market for French goods and supply the raw materials so crucial to France's own industrial development.[40] Such arguments found support mainly in port towns like Bordeaux, Marseille, and Lyon.

By the late 1870s, these positions coalesced in a generalized imperial ideology that emphasized three main points: colonization as antidote to French national decline; France's responsibility to spread its "civilization" to "backward" parts of the world; and the economic benefits, both for France and for the colonized, of French-controlled overseas trade and commerce.[41] It was one thing, however, to develop a coherent ideological position, and quite another, as members of the colonial lobby realized, to convince a largely indifferent parliament and public to adopt these views.

Fortunately for the advocates of French expansionism, two of the country's most prominent republican leaders rallied to their cause. In 1878, Léon Gambetta—journalist, cabinet minister, and orator extraordinaire— decided that France could restore itself as a great power only by developing a new colonial empire. The effort to retake Alsace and Lorraine, he now maintained, should no longer divert his country from its imperial destiny. Gambetta's new position influenced Jules Ferry, the uncharismatic but effective centrist destined to be *président du conseil* for three crucial years in the early 1880s.[42]

During his tenure as council president, Ferry presided over the transformation of a largely moribund French Empire (save for Algeria, colonized in 1830) into a far-flung colonial domain covering more than 3 million square miles and substantial parts of two continents. France expanded into Tunisia, Tonkin, Madagascar, the Congo basin, Upper Senegal, the Western Sudan (parts of present-day Mali, Ghana, and the Ivory Coast), Somalia, and several Pacific islands.[43] But the new republican government achieved these gains with considerable difficulty—both at home and abroad. Virtually every effort to seize new territory evoked armed resistance from the local population. And a series of humiliating military reverses in Tunisia (1881), Madagascar (1883–84), and Tonkin (1883–85) inflamed domestic opposition to colonial expansion, uniting the extreme left and monarchist right in an unholy alliance against Ferry and the moderate republic.

Given the depth of the indigenous resistance to French expansion in Asia and North Africa and the roar of domestic opposition such resistance helped to produce, Brazza was a godsend to the colonial movement. As a peaceful conqueror and paragon of the mission civilisatrice, a charismatic character who fostered the public's emotional involvement with him, he promised to achieve what no other French political or military leader had been able to do. He would bequeath to his country a huge colonial empire at a fraction of the human and material cost of other imperial ventures.

Back in Africa in early 1880, Brazza resolved to push as fast as he could to Malebo Pool, later renamed Stanley Pool, after the Frenchman's rival. There, on the shores of the Congo's broad, lakelike expanse, just up-stream from the rapids, Brazza intended to "plant the French flag." The French explorer knew that Stanley, now employed by the Belgian king, had returned to the region, and Brazza wanted to get to the pool first. Brazza succeeded in this goal, although Stanley, governed by personal and pecuniary motives rather than nationalistic ones, had no idea there was a race.[44]

It was just upriver from the pool, at the village of Mbé, that Brazza en-countered the Makoko Ilo, king of the Bateke people. Their kingdom can be traced back to 1600; its sparsely populated villages clustered north and east of the pool, where the Batekes grew tobacco, corn, and manioc while engaging in trade, often over relatively long distances.[45] The meaning of Brazza's original encounter with the Makoko has long been contested, though the basic facts are clear. On 10 September 1880, after two weeks of talks, Ilo put his mark on several copies of a document written by Brazza. The document declared that the king ceded to Brazza all hereditary rights to his lands and placed himself under the protection of the French. Brazza then took this "treaty" to a series of other local chiefs loyal to the Makoko, who allowed the explorer to establish a fort on the right bank of Stanley Pool, soon to be known as Brazzaville.[46]

Although Stanley argued that Ilo could not have known what he was signing and that no chief of his stature would simply give away his lands, Brazza and his many publicists—as well as most later biographers—disagreed. They maintained that the Makoko had ceded his domains and placed himself under French protection because he feared Stanley's vio-lence. The Bateke king turned to the gentle, compassionate Brazza as his rightful white chief and the lone European capable of protecting his people.[47] Though the Makoko clearly preferred Brazza to Stanley, it is un-likely that he intended to cede any territory to France. African custom sharply distinguished between the possession and use of land, and the Makoko doubtless thought he had agreed only to give Brazza its use.

Whatever the monarch's reasons for signing, the treaty's announcement in the French press in the spring of 1881 sharply accelerated Brazza's rise to heroic status, encouraging colonialists to tie their efforts all the more to the explorer's growing reputation. At this time, the Paris Geographical Society decided to make public correspondence from Brazza that seemed to reveal an extraordinary degree of self-sacrifice in the service of a patriotic ideal. "Despite the severely compromised state of my health," Brazza wrote, "I have made an unflinching effort to carry out the task I had taken on. I will continue as long as I have the strength to keep me going, and if I fall I shall not get up again."[48] Always the propagandist, the explorer added the following coda to his letter: "If I have spoken so much of myself, something I rarely do, it is because I want to push you [members of the PGS] by my own example to act more effectively" on behalf of our common goals.[49] This letter, which also detailed a series of debilitating illnesses and injuries, did much to root the story of France's colonial efforts in the person of Savorgnan de Brazza, the martyr who suffered for the salvation of France. Citing the document, leaders of the PGS extolled the explorer as a "messenger of peace" and "apostle of liberty," taking pains to distinguish Brazza's personal travails from those Stanley was said to inflict on the African people.[50] Two decades later, Jean-Baptiste Marchand, the "hero of Fashoda," would become a different kind of martyr, one who saved France by enduring glorious defeat, a defeat that would ensure the country's victories to come. Such martyrs became saints for a secularizing age, individuals who helped endow the nation-state with a sacredness once reserved for religion and the Church.[51]

Having cultivated the image of a manly but gentle explorer, a charismatic Italian nobleman devoted to France, Brazza returned to Paris in early June 1882 to great public acclaim. Referring to his recently concluded African expedition, the *Petit parisien* declared, "Brazza has had the flag of the fatherland accepted as a sign of peace and friendship by all the peoples he visited." The paper urged its readers to pay homage "to all those who extend nonviolently the prestige of the fatherland by fraternally linking faraway peoples to France."[52] The normally sober *Le Temps* spoke in the same tones as the sensationalist *Petit parisien*. "Everywhere he has gone, [Brazza] has appeared as an agent of peace, an enemy of slavery, and as an intermediary between peoples in a state of war. . . . His conduct, inspired by the most noble feelings, has enabled him to acquire among the blacks of the Ogooué and the Congo a prestige and a moral authority that, alone, can explain how he was able to achieve so much with such feeble resources."[53]

As other newspapers echoed such sentiments, Brazza prepared for his first public speech in three years, an event carefully organized by the PGS. The occasion was too important to the future of French colonialism for Brazza's friends and patrons to trust him to compose the speech himself. The Italian-born explorer possessed great personal magnetism, but he wrote very poor French. Charles Maunoir, general secretary of the PGS, penned Brazza's text.[54]

On the appointed evening, Brazza stood in the amphitheater of the Sorbonne before a crowd of ten thousand people who spilled into the aisles and onto the street. Lectures sponsored by the Paris Geographical Society had once been purely "scientific" events, attracting an audience of experts and receiving little attention from the press.[55] With Brazza, geographic knowledge melded into journalistic sensationalism and colonial advocacy, as the line between scientist and celebrity, geographer and propagandist, withered away. His presentation became a notable public event, attended by the fashionable *Tout-Paris* and extensively covered by both the "serious" and the penny press. As he took the stage, a small army of journalists and sketch artists readied their pens.

"When I abruptly left Europe on 27 December 1879," Brazza began, "with nothing more than the promise of 100,000 francs, I thrust myself, still sick but full of ardor, toward the Ogooué River." Once again, he emphasized the contrast with Stanley, whom he had met in a chance encounter on the lower Congo: "Two men, two antitheses: speed and slowness, boldness and caution, strength and weakness." Brazza is David to Stanley's Goliath, a male Joan of Arc representing France against a ruthless, seemingly superior English foe. Brazza's greatness lay in his apparent weakness and poverty, which he either overcomes or uses to his advantage as he achieves his dramatic results.[56] Unlike Stanley, who for all his money and power alienates the Makoko with his "terrible guns" and maniacal speed, the Frenchman uses "pacific methods" and a "humanitarian approach to create an unshakable influence in these regions."

Stanley's impressive speed, dramatic as it is, leaves him in "absolute ignorance about the immense region bathed by the Congo and about its numerous tribes." The Anglo-American, in short, does nothing for science or civilization; his heroism is superficial at best. Brazza's languid pace, by contrast, enables him to extend geographic knowledge, learn local languages, and come to know the peoples of the region. The example Brazza gave of his ethnographic wisdom is telling, designed as it was to titillate his audience and exalt himself.

The observer notices that morality varies inversely with the size of the *pagnes* [waist cloths] that are about the only things native [women] wear. As one advances toward the interior, the pagnes shrink from the top and the bottom until they are no larger than the size of your hand. Even so, morality is not as lax as one might think, especially considering that, as with the veils of Turkish women, the more transparent the material, the higher the wearer's social rank. No less curious is the custom of considering the highest chief as the husband of the wives of all the lesser chiefs. I hasten to add that this position is more or less platonic and that the wife's principal duty is to cook for her putative spouse. As the great white chief, I had no shortage of cooks of all ages and all pagnes.

This comment, with its image of near-naked African women, doubtless evoked chuckles from his audience. It also emphasized the explorer's status as a great man. By European standards, Brazza may not have been rich and powerful, but in Africa he was the great white chief, and that standing radiated back to Europe, where Brazza subtly ranked himself among the kings. The sexual innuendo is interesting as well, for Brazza's anecdote conveyed an allegiance to European moral standards while strongly suggesting that, as a great white chief, he had plenty of opportunities to stray. Brazza could therefore be heroic in a double sense: heroic for resisting sexual temptation and heroic for his ability to possess a great many women, every one of them a queen.

This image of Brazza inspired a drawing in the pictorial weekly *L'Illustration* that emphasized the explorer's access to near-naked African women. A half-page woodcut, published shortly after Brazza's speech, shows a bare-breasted woman on her knees bowing before a seated Brazza. A long line of other women clad only in waist cloths snakes behind her, each member presumably waiting to take a turn bowing before him as well. A second half-page drawing in the same issue depicts an extremely shapely African woman with a pagne that looks like a miniskirt and a side view of her naked breast.[57]

Another notable feature of Brazza's speech is that for all his talk of peaceful methods and humanitarian aims, the threat of violence was always there. Brazza told a group of Congolese chiefs that he was giving them a choice "between the cartridge and the flag . . . the one will be a sign of war without mercy, the other, the symbol of a peace as profitable to your interests as to ours." In some ways, the violent image of Stanley that Brazza obsessively painted worked as a threat as well: cooperate with us or Stanley

Figure 1. Congolese women bowing before Brazza (*L'Illustration*, 8 July 1882).

will be your fate! Brazza's nonviolent stance is, therefore, relative and conditional, something Ilo well understood. Brazza quotes the Congolese king as saying that he decided to sign a treaty with the Frenchman because "we did not want to fight against two parties [Stanley and Brazza], so I resolved to guarantee the peace by becoming the friend of the one who inspired confidence."

This reasoning stands as perhaps the best explanation for the Makoko's decision to sign this document, especially since he did not believe he was actually giving up the territory. It also helps clarify the meaning of the oxymoronic sobriquet that soon became attached to Brazza's name: "pacific conqueror" *(conquérant pacifique)*. Brazza understood that he could conquer without violence as long as the threat of violence hovered subtly around him. In fairness to the French explorer, he was certainly more temperamentally suited to negotiation than to force, more the diplomat than the soldier. He possessed none of the explosive anger that plagued Stanley's personal relations. And although Brazza shared the general European condescension toward Africans, he seems to have genuinely cared about them as human beings—as, in fact, did Stanley as well.[58] Brazza bought a number of people out of slavery and was loyal to the Africans who served him. Still, there were occasions when he shot and killed Africans and even when he kept individuals in slavery until he no longer needed their labor.[59]

It goes without saying that few of these subtleties came through in the Sorbonne speech. The dominant image was of Brazza the pacific conqueror, the martyred man of peace who gave France an empire without risking lives and costing money. What remained to be done, Brazza concluded, was to give him the political support necessary to finish the work for which he had martyred himself. "Exhausted and wracked with fever, I gave my fortune, my youth, and my health. . . . You who know me . . . understand the sacrifices that duty imposes. But you also understand the mute and horrible suffering that tortures the man who fears that all his efforts might come to naught."

Ferdinand de Lesseps, president of the Paris Geographical Society, ended the meeting by endorsing the image of Brazza as self-sacrificing hero of the colonial cause and by urging France's political leaders to reap what Brazza had sown. "Your applause will tell the Chambers and the high administrators that in helping M. de Brazza they genuinely serve the interests of the country." The next step was to have them ratify the Makoko treaty and make the Congo officially part of France.

Over the following six months, the French press, normally at daggers drawn, came together in a rare burst of unanimity over Brazza. "The entire French press," declared the editors of Le Temps, has supported Brazza "with a warmth that we have never seen in connection with colonial affairs."[60] "The entire press," echoed La République française, "is favorable to him."[61] Journalists ratified the explorer's standing as national hero and unifier, urging in unison that his treaty be ratified as well. "On this [treaty] question," proclaimed L'Illustration, "the apparent unanimity is absolutely astonishing. In the entire French press, from L'Intransigeant to journals of the right . . . we are hard-pressed to find a single discordant voice."[62] Brazza's national stature preempted all debate over the wisdom of annexing the Congo, as the entire country seemed to come together in adulation of its hero. "There was no examination, no rational debate over the pros and cons," concluded the historian Jean Stengers. "There was simply applause. To question anything Brazza said . . . would have been considered an act of treason."[63]

Amid the press's unrelenting praise and the hero-worship of "La Conquête Pacifique," Brazza decided to take advantage of Stanley's well-publicized intervention at the Hotel Continental, the incident with which this chapter begins. As the Welsh-American was concluding his speech, having condemned Brazza again for his "immense need to be a celebrity" and for "introducing an immoral diplomacy into a virgin continent," a commotion drew attention to the back of the room. Brazza had entered uninvited and requested the right to speak.[64] The Frenchman calmly strode toward the dais and made the following statement, in English:

> This reception of M. Stanley having been held in Paris, I have wished to appear among those who offered him this welcome. . . . Those flags I gave there [in the Congo] to the native Chiefs as symbols of protection are . . . announcing that a new and pacific era is now beginning for those unfortunate populations. Gentlemen, as a Frenchman and as an officer in the French Navy, I raise my glass to the civilization of Africa by simultaneous efforts of all nations under all flags.[65]

Brazza had perhaps just heard Stanley's heavily sarcastic remarks about Brazza's use of the French flag, accusing him of "covering his personal ambitions with that noble tricolor flag, symbol, as we knew, of civilization in Europe and everywhere else." That comment allowed Brazza to highlight the contrast he wanted to make between Stanley's vindictive, narrow-minded talk and his own ecumenical toast to the "civilization of Africa by . . . all flags." Then, as he was about to leave, Brazza twisted the knife. Shaking Stanley's hand, he declared, "I understand, cher collègue, that you have roughly attacked me in your speech. Before I learn what you actually said, let me shake your hand."

Words of admiration Brazza received from the president of the Stanley Club, a former colleague of Stanley's at the *New York Herald,* made it clear that the Frenchman's savvy intervention had worked. The following day, French editorialists used the occasion to heap contempt on Stanley and lavish Brazza with near-unanimous praise. The French explorer had known full well that the press would be heavily represented at the meeting, and having been warned by Stanley himself of his impending *"coup mortel,"* Brazza had staged his response accordingly.[66] Brazza, who did not speak English, had a friend compose his statement for the Stanley Club, which he then rehearsed several times.[67] It is not unlikely that he also alerted several of the pro-colonial journalists with whom he regularly socialized at the Petite Vache, the café that served as the unofficial headquarters of the Paris Geographical Society.[68]

Brazza and his friends had been working for months to create a groundswell of support for annexation of the Congo, and Stanley served their purposes very well—especially now that he had attacked the popular French explorer at home. Stanley's speech highlighted his rivalry with Brazza, and the Frenchman's theatrical intervention at the Stanley Club turned the rivalry into a symbolic joust between France and Britain, whose ambitions the Welsh-born Stanley was seen to represent. The Stanley Club incident took place against the backdrop of mounting colonial tensions between the two cross-Channel neighbors. In August 1882, British forces had occupied the strategic centers of Egypt, a country over which England and France had, until then, informally exercised joint economic control.[69] That incident produced an outburst of anti-English sentiment among French journalists, many of whom now argued that France needed to seize territory elsewhere in Africa in compensation for the "loss" of Egypt. As *Le Constitutionnel* put it, "Our conquest [of the Congo] would be the best and most certain revenge for the reverses we have just suffered in Africa." Such a "marvelous conquest" would allow France to regain "something of its tarnished luster and its diminished grandeur."[70]

In this nationalistic context, the French press seized the opportunity to throttle the Welsh-American Stanley, a man who "spread terror everywhere he went," for daring "to speak with a certain irony about 'that noble French flag' . . . right in the capital of France."[71] In their commentaries on the Stanley-Brazza conflict, French journalists turned Stanley—a man they portrayed as brutal, ruthless, and arrogant—into a foil for their own African explorer, a gentle Frenchman, whose very gentleness qualified him to be precisely the kind of hero France seemed to require. The new French Republic needed a charismatic figure to embody both the virtues of the new order and the strengths of traditional France. It needed a fresh national hero who could bring together conservatives and republicans, Catholics and anticlericals, the nation and the republic, the eternal France and the modern regime.

From late September to early November 1882, one newspaper after the other echoed these sentiments, arguing that the parliament needed to confirm Brazza's gift of the Congo by ratifying the Makoko treaty.[72] And virtually every paper maintained that the politicians would have to act favorably because "opinion" was unanimous—as if the press simply reported opinion rather than shaping it. Journalists had played so skillfully on the rivalry between Stanley and Brazza, between the rapacious British-American villain and the pacific French hero, that to oppose the acquisition of the

Congo would be to side with the villain against the hero. "M. de Brazza," declared the *Petit journal,* was a "French hero who had given France new lands," an accomplishment achieved in the wake of a "battle between MM. de Brazza and Stanley, a battle from which the Frenchman had emerged victorious."[73] In this context, journalists warned the government that if it failed to take advantage of "this exceptionally favorable occasion to extend our colonial power, it would have a hard time defending itself before the Chambers and before 'opinion.' "[74]

Completely forgotten in the press's beatification of Brazza was his Italian birth. At a time of mounting hostility toward foreigners, Brazza's example shows that it was still possible for certain individuals to "become French." Despite Brazza's Italian origins, his strong accent, and Mediterranean looks, public adulation had mounted to the point that after his dramatic intervention at the Stanley Club, he could go nowhere without being saluted on the street. His long, taciturn face now stared down from shop windows everywhere, as cheap portraits of Brazza flooded Paris and the provinces. Clubs begged his presence, and he was honored at one public ceremony after the other. Despite such extraordinary support, Brazza and his friends persisted in their campaign.[75] In late October he spoke again to an overflowing audience at the Sorbonne, where he received the Société historique's highest honor and boasted again of having "planted the French flag in the middle of Africa." He claimed to have freed so many slaves that the Africans now called him "Le père des esclaves."[76]

Brazza's most important event was a reception by the Paris city council, where he would receive the capital's gold medal. For this occasion, Brazza's friends left nothing to chance. "You would do well," wrote Charles Maunoir in a *pneumatique,* "to prepare *very carefully* [Maunoir's emphasis] your speech in response to the one the President [of the city council] will give." Try to find out what he plans to say, the general secretary advised, and then write your talk accordingly. Above all, "do your best to have your speech ready in time to hand it out to the journalists who will be present at the meeting." A second *pneumatique* added still more advice: "The President will read his speech, so you can read yours as well. . . . Write it in large characters and practice it again and again paying careful attention to your intonation. . . . Beware of memory lapses, which could cause you to ad lib and get you into trouble."[77] These instructions make clear that Maunoir was concerned above all about the impression Brazza would leave with the journalists so crucial to the image-making machine.

He need not have worried. The city council members showed Brazza such deference and adulation that he could have said almost anything. And the pomp and circumstance of the event could only have enhanced the explorer's stature. Uniformed members of the *gardes républicaines* escorted his carriage as he rode to the Hotel de Ville. In this historic place, Brazza heard one dignitary after the other rehearse the themes now familiar to any reader of the popular press: the successful struggle with Stanley, the "conquête pacifique," the lack of resources, the disinterested service to France. "I do not know what material advantages your work will bring," concluded the prefect of the Seine. "But I know of no conquest more pure. You have made that conquest without shedding a single tear or spilling a drop of blood. Your achievement is the expression of the greatest qualities of our national character."[78]

By the eve of the vote to ratify the Makoko treaty, Brazza, the nation, and the republic seemed to have become one and the same. The government, long reluctant to acquire new African territory, now called for parliament to rally to the explorer's support. Without any debate, right, left, and center united in a patriotic embrace, endorsing the treaty with just three dissenting votes.[79] As the colonial advocate Gabriel de Charmes wrote, the extraordinary "public support for Brazza's enterprise in the Congo" has meant that "for the first time in our contemporary history, we have seen all political parties, from the extreme right to the extreme left, burn with the same zeal for the same cause."[80] Thanks to Brazza's heroic work, added *Le Temps,* the parliament has "abdicated all dissent; it has become truly French."[81]

If Parisian journalists reveled in jubilant zeal, their colleagues elsewhere in Europe expressed amazement and concern. The *Times*'s commentary was not unjust: "Never has a government submitted to parliamentary ratification a treaty of the reality and results of which it knew so little. . . . The Cabinet [has committed itself to] protecting at haphazard, without any precise preliminary information, under the mere unreasoning pressure of the public, a foreign adventure, of which it has ascertained neither the utility nor the consequences."[82]

The Chambers not only ratified the treaty without debate but even agreed to award Brazza 1.2 million francs for his next expedition. This sum represented more than a twelvefold increase over what had been appropriated for the earlier mission, and it made Brazza at once a charismatic hero and a quasi-official representative of the state. In both guises, Brazza became one of the most visible personalities in France, endlessly drawn and photographed for the country's widely circulated illustrated press.

Perhaps the most influential and enduring image of Brazza was a publicity photograph taken by Félix Nadar, nineteenth-century France's celebrity photographer who became just as celebrated as those whose portraits he took: George Clemenceau, Sarah Bernhardt, Charles Baudelaire, George Sand, and many others.[83] What was destined to become his iconic portrayal of Brazza appeared as an engraving in L'Illustration's November 1882 issue (fig. 2). Among other things, this picture comments ironically on Stanley's dismissal of Brazza as a shoeless nobody dressed in rags.[84] As we have seen, Brazza used that image of poverty and lack of support to enhance his stature as a hero. His apparent neediness also helped qualify him as a kind of secular saint by advertising the extent of his self-sacrifice: the ragged pants, torn at the knee; the bare feet; the dark beard; the purposeful but dour expression. There are no weapons of any kind in this photograph, only a walking stick designed to make him look like a barefoot prophet, a modern-day Moses doing the Republic's work in the wilds of Africa.

A second widely circulated photograph shows Brazza looking, as one biographer put it, "more like an apostle than a conqueror" (fig. 3).[85] He seems possessed with religious fervor, a wide-eyed visionary whose facial expression has an unkempt intensity that makes him look either like a madman or a prophet. His clothes are worn and wrinkled, signifying poverty and self-sacrifice. The explorer seems to care not at all for worldly goods; he is an apostle of humanity and civilization who brings enlightenment to the Dark Continent. Everyone knew that Brazza came from Italian noble stock; he owed his poverty, the image seemed to say, to sacrifices he had made for France, a willingness to devote his once considerable personal fortune to the country's conquêtes pacifiques.

Another Nadar photograph shows Brazza dressed in somber civilian dress (fig. 4).[86] He has a cigarette in his hand and appears unarmed once again. Flanking him are two African boys in naval garb. As in the images mentioned above, Brazza's facial expression is serious, even dour. He gazes into the distance, as if to keep Africa in sight. In posing this picture, Nadar seems to have transferred Brazza's naval identity onto the boys while giving the explorer an aura of neutrality, as if he could represent anyone or anything, even the nation as a whole. The young African men are subordinate to the hero, but there is nothing servile or savage about them. Brazza's work of "civilization," the photograph seems to say, has humanized the boys and redeemed them from their once primitive state.

At a time of considerable animosity between Catholics and anticlericals, images such as these reinforced Brazza's standing as a hero for the nation

Figure 2. Savorgnan de Brazza. Engraving after a photograph by Nadar (*L'Illustration*, 25 November 1882).

as a whole, not just for its republican incarnation. The religious imagery emphasized poverty, sacrifice, and redemption, recalling the prints of saints and Jesus that had circulated in France for centuries, as well as portraits of famous clergymen. Although there is no direct evidence that these illustrations appealed to devout Catholics, many of whom remained hostile to the newly established republic, it is clear that Catholics held Brazza himself in high esteem. The conservative Catholic paper *L'Univers* applauded the explorer as both a secular and a religious hero, for having "enabled France to penetrate into the center of Africa and bring to these

Figure 3. Brazza, apostle of empire (Nadar Photo Collection).

savage populations . . . the life of the soul."[87] It is likely that these images of Brazza spoke to Catholic believers and that they did so without alienating secular men and women: his religiosity was confined to the images; it rarely became manifest in text. No captions called Brazza a saint, nor did the commentaries surrounding the pictures make direct religious allusions. The public imagery of Brazza thus made him one of the few Frenchmen capable of uniting his religious and secular compatriots. Thanks to his charismatic allure, he could bring the two groups together around the nationalistic theme of French exploration and expansion oversees.[88]

Only rarely did Brazza have himself photographed in military garb, preferring to portray himself as more "pacifique" than "conquérant." The picture in figure 5 reminded his compatriots of his military status, although

Figure 4. Brazza with two African boys (Nadar Photo Collection).

as a gentle naval man rather than a member of the colonial army, known for its brutality.[89] His rifle is at rest, ready for action but not in use. The explorer appears considerably more prosperous in this image than in the earlier ones, and though undated, it was doubtless taken after he had received his 1.2 million francs. No longer a poverty-stricken apostle, he now represents the French Republic in the newest phase of its budding empire. He stands as a respected, important man whose handsome coat, well-polished boots, and shiny weapon all suggest that he has become an authority in his own right. Once a purely popular and journalistic hero, he has now become an official one as well.

Figure 5. Brazza with weapon at rest (*Journal des voyages,* 23 July 1882).

A final illustration brings together the images of popular hero and official hero, charismatic outsider and paragon of republican France. Here, he is well dressed in an untattered safari suit, the official uniform of white men in Africa (fig. 6).[90] He has abandoned the barefoot raggedness of the earlier photos to don a suit with a hint of the military in it, but only a hint. To suggest strength of will and character rather than physical strength, the artist has Brazza sitting atop the world rather than holding it up, Atlas-like, on his shoulders. Like Atlas, Brazza is larger than life, acting on the whole of the globe. But unlike the mythical figure, the French explorer distinguishes

Figure 6. Brazza on top of the world (*Les hommes d'aujourd'hui* 289 [1886]).

himself not by his brute physical force but by his calm mastery of the world. His face determined, his gaze fixed on the distance, Brazza is the "conquérant pacifique."

Beyond this proliferation of images, merchants introduced an array of Brazza paraphernalia, creating a veritable *"mode Brazza"* in the 1880s.[91] It did not take long for France's budding consumer culture to appropriate the hero, exploiting the popular veneration that surrounded him to sell products.

People could buy Brazza writing paper, pens, vases, commemorative medals, and books. Gentlemen dueled with swords made in honor of Brazza, and restaurants created menus celebrating the great man. Those who wanted to experience Brazza's presence more directly could visit the Musée Grévin, France's answer to Madame Tussaud's, where the explorer joined France's greatest celebrities in having his likeness immortalized in wax.[92]

We do not know exactly how many Brazza pens or vases were sold, though it is clear that many tens of thousands of people gazed at his waxen form in the Musée Grévin (fig. 7).[93] And there is good evidence that substantial numbers of people from all walks of life identified with him, looked up to him, and saw him as a hero to whom they could appeal. When Brazza announced he was looking for a small number of men to join his third expedition in 1883, he found himself deluged with more than fifteen hundred applications.[94] One man wanted to participate because the expedition's "goal was to complete the pacific conquest that you have made for France."[95] His words suggest that the term "conquête pacifique," so prominent in Brazza's speeches and newspaper reports about him, had resonated with the public. Charles de Chavannes, who ultimately succeeded in joining the expedition as Brazza's private secretary, wrote of having to wait for days to see the explorer, as he competed with scores of others for the hero's attention.[96]

Brazza's mail was full of letters from people he did not know, letters offering praise and asking for jobs, advice, favors, and money. This one-way correspondence suggested that a great many people felt an emotional attachment to him. An unemployed journalist in desperate straits wrote begging the explorer to take him along on the next trip. Attached was a poem he had composed:

> You, Monsieur Savorgnan, so full of goodness,
> Bear the glorious title named generosity!
> Take pity on me, relieve my distress,
> . . . .
> For this time, at least, be my protector.[97]

If Brazza could help the poor savages of Africa, this secular prayer seemed to say, he could surely do something for a countryman down on his luck.

Some writers became angry when Brazza appeared to ignore their appeals or the concierge barred them from seeing him when they called at his

Figure 7. Wax figure of Brazza in the Musée Grévin (Musée Grévin, Paris).

hotel. These followers of the charismatic Brazza felt an intimate connection with him, an "intimacy at a distance" that convinced them that this man they looked up to and followed vicariously should notice them and respond to their needs. The relationship was complex and ambiguous, since readers interacted with newspapers and magazines but not Brazza himself. This situation allowed individual readers to construct versions of the hero that suited their needs, images of the charismatic personality uncontrolled by any direct intervention from him.[98]

Still, the overwhelming majority of the unsolicited letters to Brazza came from people who wanted nothing.[99] A surprising number composed poems, some printed, some in script. One printed verse by a Jules Blancard, member of the International League for Universal Peace, celebrated Brazza as a "genuine hero" who "outshines all the Cesars." Another poem by the same author paid homage to all the Italian heroes whose "male virtues" presaged those of Savorgnan de Brazza.[100] One amateur poet, Roseline Caumel Decazès, sent two copies, the second a corrected version of the first, of a handwritten verse. "Oh Brazza!" she wrote,

Who at this moment all France acclaims!
Permit the poet, inspired by the radiance of your soul,
To praise your sublime works!
Which have allowed you to surpass the honor of your rivals!
. . . .
On a young people you impose yourself as king.
But mild in your triumph and great in your conquest,
Under your scepter falls not a single head.
Soothing their terror by your serenity,
You bring forth from them songs of liberty.
By presenting Progress as a deliverance,
You have them salute the flag of France.[101]

Yet another verse, dedicated to "Monsieur de Brazza, L'Illustre Explorateur, Le Grand Français," came from "an admirer of your generous initiative and your enormous courage . . . who wants to congratulate you for your glorious civilizing exploits in the name of France."[102]

Taken together, these amateur poems imply a popular endorsement of the Brazza portrait sketched by the explorer himself and by his friends and supporters in the press. Savorgnan de Brazza, the poems confirm, was a charismatic man around whom French men and women could unite, an extraordinary individual who inspired others with his exemplary commitment to France as a nation, republic, and generous imperial power. These writings, like the other varieties of hero-worship, suggest that Brazza's personal qualities, his heroic yet pacific exploits, formed the core of what attracted his compatriots to Africa. His charisma outweighed the lure of any particular imperial project defined in traditional political and economic terms.

For this reason, France's political leaders had to take Brazza's image and popularity into account in policy discussions and negotiations over African lands. During the Conference of Berlin (1884–85), convened by Bismarck to resolve European conflicts over African territory, Jules Ferry, France's president du conseil, wrote his representative at the talks, "Even the most recalcitrant centers of opinion will approve of our arrangements at Berlin as long as we can ensure that those arrangements do not result in an indirect victory of the Association [i.e., Belgian King Leopold and Stanley] over M. de Brazza. Brazza is popular; he has an enormous following, and he has come to represent the national honor."[103]

As Ferry wrote these words, his British counterpart, William Gladstone, also found himself subject to the charismatic authority of his country's reigning colonial hero, General Charles Gordon. But if Ferry drew a measure of strength from Brazza's popularity, Gladstone would confront a Gordon fully capable of bringing him down.

THREE

───────────

Charles Gordon, Imperial Saint

ON 13 FEBRUARY 1885, THE *London Times* broke the terrible news: General Charles George "Chinese" Gordon was dead. He had perished, so the editors said, defending British civilization from Islamic fanatics. For more than a year, the newspaper declared, Gordon had single-handedly protected Khartoum from a Muslim savior (the Mahdi) intent on imposing his barbarous rule over the Sudan, and then over Egypt and the rest of the Ottoman world. The announcement of Gordon's death produced an outpouring of public grief unlike anything in recent memory. From one end of the political spectrum to the other, journalists, clergymen, schoolmasters, and many others manifested sorrow and regret, while the moderates and conservatives among them flashed with anger, bitterness, and wounded pride.[1]

More than any other episode in the history of Victorian Britain, the Gordon campaign revealed the newfound power of the press. Among many other things, the press now possessed the power to transform a reclusive military officer like Gordon into a great colonial hero, one whose exemplary qualities served to build support for imperial ventures among both ordinary people and policy-oriented elites. Beginning in 1884, journalists used the heroic figure of Gordon to put such pressure on Prime Minister William Gladstone, pressure believed to have widespread public support, that the Grand Old Man approved a series of interventions in the Sudan

83

that violated his own, oft-stated principles. Gladstone prided himself on his anti-imperialist ideals, on his refusal to seize overseas territories by force. But after a powerful press campaign spearheaded by the *Pall Mall Gazette* and the *Times,* the Liberal government agreed to send Gordon to the Sudan in January 1884. Seven months later, after Khartoum fell under a Mahdist siege, the cabinet dispatched an army commanded by General Sir Garnett Wolseley to "rescue" Gordon. And after reports announced Gordon's death, Gladstone approved a military mission designed to exact revenge.

It is true that influential members of Gladstone's cabinet, especially Secretary of State for War Lord Hartington, felt far more sympathy for imperial ventures than did the prime minister.[2] But without the massive journalistic campaign for Gordon, and the widespread reverence for the hero it both created and revealed, it is unlikely that Hartington or his ally Wolseley could have overcome Gladstone's resistance to direct British involvement in the Egyptian colony. In 1881, Hartington had not persuaded Gladstone to intervene in South Africa after the Boers humiliated British forces at Majuba Hill. Nor had Gladstone seen fit to commit British forces after a British-led Egyptian expedition suffered annihilation at Mahdist hands in November 1883. In those moments, no hero emerged, or was advanced, to personify British honor and enlist popular support to reverse Britain's losses.[3]

Why, then, did journalists and editors fly Gordon's flag in 1884 and 1885? Although the military maverick had achieved fame two decades earlier in China, where he helped end the fourteen-year-long Taiping Rebellion, he had deliberately avoided the limelight since then and enjoyed nothing like the prominence associated with Livingstone and Stanley, or Wolseley himself. Still, certain journalists and military men saw Gordon as a master of irregular warfare in colonial settings, as a man who could preserve and even extend the empire at relatively little cost. In the mid-1880s these and other influential people sought a more active imperial role for Britain than the country had played since the late 1850s. The grueling stalemate slaughter of the Crimean War (1854–56), followed by the Indian rebellion of 1857, with its worrisome threats to British hegemony and shocking atrocities on both sides, made British governments of the 1860s and early 1870s wary of foreign interventions.[4] Political leaders kept the British army small, and conscription remained politically impossible, recruitment difficult.[5] The government did send gunboats to China in 1860 and approved Gordon's service there for the Manchu government; but in general, successive cabinets, whether Liberal or Conservative, shied away from imperial ventures.

These hesitations began to dissipate in the late 1860s, but especially after 1874, when Benjamin Disraeli became prime minister.[6] He had run for office on a mildly jingoistic platform and, once elected, adopted a relatively forward foreign policy. He intervened in the Ottoman Empire's conflicts with Russia, took the major symbolic step of making Queen Victoria empress of India, and in 1875, hastened to buy the Egyptian ruler's stock holdings in the Suez Canal. This purchase made Britain the principal owner of the waterway, with 44 percent of the shares. Still, Disraeli showed no interest in political control of Egypt, nor did he seek to intervene elsewhere in Africa. Wars against the Zulus in South Africa (1879) and against tribal fighters in Afghanistan (1878–80) originated with British proconsuls in the two regions. In both cases, British forces suffered costly losses before emerging with solid, if tainted, victories.[7]

These setbacks raised fears about England's world standing and helped produce a shift within the British political class and commentariat—and perhaps the public at large—toward a more active imperial policy. Already in 1868, the same year as the French writer Anatole Prévost-Paradol published his pro-imperial *La France nouvelle,* Sir Charles Dilke, a Radical politician and future British government minister, brought out his own colonialist *Greater Britain.* Like Prevost-Paradol's work, Dilke's extolled empire as a means of stemming national decline. Two years later, the critic John Ruskin lectured a packed Oxford audience on the country's "Imperial Duty." The don argued that England must "reign or die." Its government and people "must found colonies as fast and as far as she is able, formed of her most energetic and worthiest men;—seizing every piece of fruitful waste ground she can set her foot on." Colonies, Ruskin said, would be schools of patriotism, where men will volunteer to "cast themselves against cannon-mouths for love of England."[8] The imagery here is striking: British soldiers had retaliated against Indian insurgents thirteen years earlier by strapping them to the mouths of cannons and blasting their bodies to bits.[9] As if to assuage a lingering guilt, Ruskin seemed to require voluntary sacrifices from British citizens akin to those imposed as punishment on people subjected to its colonial rule.

Views such as Ruskin's horrified Gladstone, who asked his countrymen to "remember the rights of the savage" and to pursue "justice, peace, and liberty," not empire.[10] Even so, the Grand Old Man presided over a series of imperial engagements in South Africa (1880), Egypt (1882), and the Sudan (1884–85) that revealed a slide toward more active intervention abroad. Except for a small number of diehard Little Englanders, the minimalist position on empire had now become one of imperial defense, advocating the protection of overseas possessions against encroachment from European rivals. An emerging maximalist position took its cues from Ruskin in championing the acquisition of new territories, not just the preservation of existing ones.[11]

Increasingly, maximalists and minimalists alike expressed concern over what the *Pall Mall Gazette* called "the dethronement of England."[12] Having achieved unprecedented economic, military, and political power during the decades after the Napoleonic Wars, the country appeared to head downhill not long after commemorating its ascendancy with the Great Exhibition of 1851.[13] By the 1870s, the United States had surpassed Britain as the workshop of the world, and before long the new German empire would as well. Both of these newcomers developed strong banking systems and powerful navies, and both would challenge Britain's domination of world markets.

If Britain's relative economic vulnerability revealed itself gradually over the second half of the nineteenth century, its supremacy as an imperial power faced more abrupt challenges. "If we annex a single acre of Africa," wrote the *Pall Mall Gazette* in February 1885, "we have to give notice to all the Powers, [and] we now find every ocean highway furrowed by European ironclads, while over many a colonial frontier frowns the cannon of Continental rivals."[14] Under these circumstances, growing numbers of British commentators reacted vigorously against any perceived threats to Britain's standing in the world.[15] Still, the Gladstonian wing of the Liberal Party remained opposed to imperial expansion, promising to withdraw from Egypt at the earliest realistic moment.[16] Such Liberals concerned themselves more with home rule for Ireland and a further expansion of suffrage than with competing for real estate in Africa. The result of these conflicting developments was a polarized public discourse over the wisdom of territorial expansion, but against the backdrop of widespread agreement over the need to protect and maintain existing colonies, commercial installations, and international influence.[17] Only the most advanced imperialists wished to devote sizable armies and resources to their cause. Most others, Gladstonian Liberals included, hoped to maintain empire on the cheap and to do so as a civilizing, Christian mission rather than as a series of military assaults. Gladstone himself did not oppose the projection of

British power and influence, just the violence and destruction often associated with it.[18]

In this context, Charles Gordon promised to reconcile the different positions on empire, to embody a middle ground between advanced and reluctant imperialists. He was a frank colonialist, but one guided by religious and civilizing motives rather than aggressive, mercenary aims.[19] Although by reputation a successful military leader, he was said to go into battle unarmed and to prefer calm persuasion to violent assault. "There are numberless instances," wrote Licurgo Alois Santoni, an early Gordon companion, "in which with gentleness and good manners and with gifts he succeeded in . . . retain[ing] the friendship of those people who . . . had been hostile."[20] Individuals who knew him commonly emphasized his soft feminine qualities as much as his aggressive masculine ones. "He appeared to be as gentle as he was strong," wrote a family friend, "for there was a certain tenderness in the tones of his rich, unworn voice and in the glance of his delicately expressive blue eyes."[21] Another friend, Laurence Oliphant, found "extraordinarily attractive" his "underlying meekness . . . this intense desire for service however humble [that] made me feel him to be the most Christ-like man I ever knew."[22]

Even his physical appearance suggested humility and, at most, a quiet hint of force. Everyone described him as small and slight, "a little quite unmilitary man," as the Orientalist Wilfrid Blunt put it, who would give no "stranger the idea of his being a leader of men."[23] Britain's army leaders apparently did not think he could command; only foreign governments gave him the military reigns. Altogether, such qualities—his pious Christianity, his meek, humble demeanor, his feminine grace—reassured British commentators, and doubtless their readers, that Gordon would defend the British Empire gently and without undue violence. Like France's Savorgnan de Brazza, Gordon would aim for civilization and enlightenment rather the kind of assertive military conquest that still, in the early and mid-1880s, made a great many people uncomfortable.

Twenty-five years earlier, the public beatification of General Henry Havelock as selfless savior of innocents martyred during the Sepoy Rebellion (or Indian Mutiny) had accustomed journalists and readers alike to personify the army and, through it, the country in an individual hero.[24] The Havelock narrative anticipated many of the themes that made Chinese Gordon an even greater colonial hero three decades later. Like Havelock, Gordon went to a far-off land to relieve his besieged countrymen and their allies held hostage by "rebels" believed until then loyal to British rule. And like Havelock, Gordon distinguished himself as a pious Christian soldier. Both appeared to be modest, self-effacing men more interested in serving others than in earning fame and fortune for themselves. Gordon, like Havelock, achieved not just heroism but martyrdom in service to his queen. And both found themselves tragic protagonists in a narrative of rescuers who arrived just hours "too late." Through no fault of his own, Havelock got to the besieged Indian city of Cawnpore while the blood of innocents was still fresh; Gordon's assassination took place just two days before a relief column appeared.

After 1857, the need to rescue innocents from subject peoples that no longer knew their place would become a key justification of new colonial ventures. Gordon was sent to Khartoum to open a besieged city and lead its residents to safety; a year later he would need rescue himself. The failure to save Gordon in 1885 would justify a new invasion of the Sudan in 1896. Meanwhile, Stanley billed his final African expedition (1887–89) as an effort to rescue an Anglo-Egyptian administrator said to be under siege in the southernmost province of the Sudan. In each case, however, the rescuer served a different purpose. Havelock's was to preserve a key imperial possession threatened from within. There was little thought as yet to expand the empire into fresh new domains. Thirty years later, Gordon's mission stood ambivalently at the cusp of a new British effort to enlarge its imperial dominions in dramatic ways. Partly as a result of his demise, there would be less ambivalence in the future. When Stanley returned from his Emin Pasha Relief Expedition in 1890, some journalists criticized his methods, but few denied Britain's right to extend its empire further into the African continent.[25]

If Havelock attained fame and hero-worship only posthumously, and Stanley became one of history's most famous men, Gordon ranked in between. As Lytton Strachey famously understood, his greatest renown came after his death.[26] But thanks to the press's steady growth and the advent of the interview and journalistic portrait, he could command far more attention during his lifetime than Havelock had decades earlier. Magnifying Gordon's visibility was the near-uniformity of foreign coverage in the 1880s. In those years, the *Times* and *Daily Telegraph* so completely dominated overseas news—partly because they alone could afford its extremely high costs—that other papers, even those with diametrically opposing points of view, pirated or purchased their telegraphic dispatches.[27] Although

Gordon eschewed publicity, the *Times* and *Telegraph* sought him out and made him a hero even before his martyrdom came.

Born in January 1833, Charlie Gordon hailed from a solid middle-class family, the son of a career officer and a woman from prosperous merchant stock. As a young boy he lived the itinerant life of an army offspring until arriving at boarding school at age ten and the Royal Military Academy, Woolwich, five years later.[28] His biographers all portray his early years in essentially the same broad strokes. An indifferent student, except in geography and mapmaking, Charlie was a high-spirited, resourceful young man who enjoyed practical jokes. He showed aggression early on and refused to bow to school authorities, who viewed him as a behavior problem. Toward the end of his school career, Gordon found himself disciplined for bullying other students, and his punishment made him inadmissible to the Royal Artillery, in which his father and brothers served. Instead, he had to content himself with the Royal Engineers, which, the biographers say, suited him better. The Engineers rewarded energy and tolerated unconventional behavior much better than the Artillery and opened the way to much swifter promotion.

Sent to the Crimea in 1854, Gordon fought fearlessly, if with reckless abandon. He became fast friends with Garnett Wolseley, the future field marshal, who described him in 1855 as "a good-looking curly-headed young man [whose] bright blue eyes seemed to court scrutiny, whilst at the same time they searched into your inner soul."[29] Wolseley observed Gordon's "indifference to danger of all sorts," and biographers have commonly noted Gordon's utter fearlessness in the face of death, a fearlessness born of a religious desire for the afterlife. "When I was ordered to the Crimea," Gordon wrote in 1880, "my sincere hope [was] that I should die there."[30] The more religious he became, the more fervently he claimed to wish for death. It is impossible to know how seriously to take his claim, though, death wish or no, the bravery he exhibited in battle was unusual even for such a seasoned officer.

Although periods of inactivity punctuated Gordon's career, he jumped at almost any opportunity for military engagement, the riskier the better. Sent to China to help quell the Taiping Rebellion in 1860, he assumed command of the Ever Victorious Army three years later.[31] The EVA was a Beijing defense force whose officers all came from the West. Gordon did not single-handedly suppress the Taiping movement, as British contemporaries and future biographers maintained.[32] But his mercenary army played a major role in the Manchu commander Tseng Kuo-fun's successful efforts to finish off the rebellion and keep China open to the West.

British journalists searching for post-Crimean heroes to vindicate the national standing discovered in Charles Gordon a new exemplary man.[33] By the time the freshly promoted colonel returned to England in January 1865, he had acquired considerable renown as "Chinese" Gordon.[34] Even so, he could have achieved more fame than he did. In this age, twenty-five years before the Stanley apotheosis and the advent of a full-fledged "hero industry," those who became famous usually had to publish books. A book generated publicity in the form of reviews, invitations to give lectures—which themselves attracted press coverage—medals from the Royal Geographical Society (more coverage), keys to the city, and the like. Although Gordon wrote a great many letters, he published virtually nothing—unlike the prolific, sensationalist Stanley.

The contrast with Stanley highlights the limits to Gordon's fame in other ways as well. While Stanley expressed discomfort with the demands of polite society, he nonetheless sought the limelight, writing one book after the other, agreeing to lucrative and well-covered lecture tours, accepting a plethora of awards and medals. Gordon not only denounced society and its demands but shunned them as well. "I hate and abhor being complimented or having speeches made," he wrote Colonel Harness of the Royal Engineers. "There is nothing I would not go through sooner than [be lionized over dinner]."[35] Rather than a seat at a lavishly endowed table, his goal was to earn a "seat at the right hand or left of the Savior."[36] He wanted to see himself as but a tiny speck of matter, an insignificant creature with no will of his own. "A man glories in some act he has performed," Gordon wrote his sister Augusta. "I say he has nothing to do with it; that God used him, as we use any instrument; that God could have worked with the smallest insect as well as with him."[37] How then could he accept the public adulation offered him, when he bore no responsibility, for good or ill, over what he did?

Although famous people often claim to eschew publicity and praise, Gordon appeared to mean it.[38] His refusal to accept dinner invitations frustrated many a society hostess, and his general unwillingness to appear in public made it difficult for editors to keep him in the news. *Vanity Fair* may have called Gordon "the grandest man now alive" (19 February 1881), but journalists had to create a legend of Chinese Gordon largely on their own. They succeeded in linking his name with heroism but often had to remind people who he was. His absence from public life permitted the government and army, both wary of his independence and odd religious zeal, to overlook him. In 1873, when the British decided to teach the incompliant Ashanti king a lesson, a great many newspapers clamored for an invasion of West Africa with Gordon in command, calling him the era's "finest soldier for irregular warfare."[39] The Cabinet chose the safer, more reliable Wolseley instead.

The first to employ Gordon (after the Chinese) was Ismail, the khedive or viceroy of Egypt. Although officially a province of the Ottoman Empire, Egypt had achieved considerable independence in the early nineteenth century. Ismail's grandfather, the Albanian-born Muhammad 'Ali, sought to preserve his newfound autonomy and add to his domains by colonizing the Sudan in the 1820s. What he mainly accomplished was to impose on the vast territory an Ottoman-Egyptian elite composed of Turks, Circassians, Albanians, and Armenians who had little in common with the peasants and tribesmen they ruled. Corrupt and ineffective, hated by the locals, the governing pashas did little to make the Sudan pay—except to encourage a slave trade from which they profited handsomely.[40] When Ismail became Egypt's ruler in 1863, these unpopular pashas opposed his efforts to modernize the Sudan. He looked elsewhere for people to rule in his name, fixing his attention on Europeans experienced in Africa or Asia.[41]

He selected as his first European deputy the British explorer and big-game hunter Sir Samuel Baker, whom he named an Ottoman pasha. Ismail ordered Baker to claim for Egypt the vast region stretching from the upper reaches of the Nile just north of the equator to the huge inland seas of Central Africa. Ismail called this territory Equatoria; with it, he hoped to extend his power deep into the continent, making himself the greatest African ruler. Baker became Equatoria's first governor. To get there, he had to hack his way through the Sudd, a dense tangle of plant life that grows wildly and shifts unpredictably in the nearly stagnant Nile waters south of Khartoum. Hundreds of Baker's men died of disease and sunstroke as they battled the morass; when the pasha finally emerged, he created a small base at Gondokoro, about five degrees north of the equator and a thousand arduous miles from Khartoum.[42] One of Baker's tasks was to create a series of secure settlements along the river all the way to Lake Victoria. The other involved the slave trade, which Baker, supported by humanitarian organizations in Britain, aimed to suppress. But rather than embracing Baker as their savior, the region's residents saw this unknown European, bedecked in Ottoman garb, as yet another Turkish slave-raider. The pasha found himself attacked on all fronts and his efforts to claim the Upper Nile of Egypt turned into a series of local wars. After three years, he resigned, exhausted, having made only a small dent in the slave trade. Equatoria consisted of little more than a handful of forts along the Nile.

With Equatoria's governorship open, Ismail's prime minister, Nubar Pasha, offered the position to Gordon, who hastened to accept. He was eager for religious reasons to join the battle against slavery. Gordon had become an evangelical Christian after returning home from China, developing an intense, if idiosyncratic, devotion to Christ. He nurtured his spirituality through an almost daily correspondence with his older, unmarried sister, Augusta, who published a carefully selected collection of his letters after he died.[43] He told Augusta that he aimed to submit himself completely to the will of God and that he could serve Him only by renouncing all earthly pleasures and temptations. He understood his body as nothing more or less than the transitory host of a soul that had always existed, though in many different forms. His flesh was meaningless, except as a kind of conduit between an eternal soul and its Maker.[44]

Gordon contemplated Christ and God so many hours a day that he came to feel the enlightened "knowledge that God dwells in our bodies." He sought to be entirely "filled by our Lord" so he could find a complete union with Him.[45] With no remaining self, he would become the pure embodiment of God's will, which, he soon discovered, pointed him toward Africa. There, he would become a latter-day Moses ready to sacrifice his life to free those whom "Egypt has always enslaved." Despite such self-denying views, he wasn't altogether without ambition of his own and admitted, somewhat guiltily, that in addition to freeing slaves he wanted to be a great explorer. "I feel that I *wish it* to be God's will that the river may be navigable to the lake. . . . I do trust Him that if [the Nile] is navigable, He will save me from being puffed up."[46]

Once in Equatoria, Gordon labored mightily to block slave-trading routes along the Nile, shield tribes threatened by slavers, and capture or kill those involved in the unholy commerce. But slave traders enjoyed protection in high places, especially from the Sudan's governor-general in Khartoum. Slavery had existed for centuries in the Sudan, and its traders in human flesh had long supplied Egypt, Arabia, and other regions of the Middle East with black Africans to serve as soldiers, domestic servants, and members of a powerful man's harem. Islam allowed slavery as long as its victims did not belong to the faith; hence the interest in those Sudanese who remained outside the Dar al-Islam, the Land of Islam. In the nineteenth century, slavers and slave owners justified the practice as a civilizing mission; once in a Muslim household, a slave would be exposed to the true religion.[47]

Although Gordon marginally reduced the commerce in human beings, he possessed neither the manpower nor the firepower to pursue major actors like Suleiman Zubayr of Darfur, who owned some 4,000 slaves. Gordon faced an even more difficult situation in the Bahr el Ghazal, whose 10,000-man slave army had nothing but suspicion for a European pasha's promise to liberate them.[48] Even after Britain and Egypt signed the Slave Trade Convention of 1877, which outlawed the Egyptian commerce as of 1884 and the Sudanese one five years later, Gordon recognized the durability of the slave regime. As he wrote his sister, "no government, either British or Khedivial, could enforce [an anti-slavery pact] *without militantly occupying the whole country, even Darfur.*"[49]

After three years as governor of Equatoria, Gordon—sick, disheartened, and exhausted—had had enough. Not only did the slave trade continue largely unabated, but he discovered the impossibility of navigating up the Nile to the Great Lakes. River traffic reached a dead end at the Fola Falls, where ten miles of foaming rapids and steep cascades foreclosed any direct water link between the Great Lakes and the Mediterranean Sea. In 1877 he sent Ismail his resignation, but the khedive refused it. Gordon agreed to remain, but under two conditions, both granted: that he be named governor-general of the whole of the Sudan and that the governors of each of the Sudan's provinces, some of them notorious slave-traders, report to him rather than directly to the khedive, as in the past. Gordon now enjoyed absolute authority over the Sudan.[50]

While Gordon worked to strengthen the khedive's Sudanese empire, Ismail's Egypt slid further and further under British and French control. The colonizer was being colonized.[51] The khedive had borrowed so heavily from British and French banks that when the Egyptian economy sank in the late 1860s, his government found itself without the revenue to meet its mounting obligations. European bankers and diplomats stepped in, taking effective control of the country. They replaced Ismail with his more prudent son Tawfiq but, in doing so, sparked a protonationalist rebellion in Cairo. Egyptian officers led by Colonel Ahmad Urabi seized the War Ministry in what amounted to a coup d'état. Urabi hoped an internal show of strength would deter a European invasion of his country. It did just the opposite, as British bankers and bondholders successfully pressured Gladstone to send warships to Alexandria.[52]

French vessels steamed in as well, and the presence of a European flotilla in Alexandria's harbor sparked a violent uprising in the city. The Paris government forbade its navy to intervene, but British ships opened fire, ultimately flattening much of the ancient Egyptian town. Urabi vowed to fight on, defying orders from both Tawfiq and the Ottoman sultan to stand down. The British responded by landing near the Suez Canal some twenty thousand troops commanded by General Wolseley. In September 1882 Wolseley routed Urabi's forces at Tel-el-Khebir, sixty-five miles outside Cairo. The British claimed interest only in protecting the canal, along with the investments of European bondholders. But rather than leaving, they remained in force under the leadership of Sir Evelyn Baring (Lord Cromer as of 1892), who as British Agent and consul-general, directly or indirectly ruled Egypt until after the turn of the century. Baring also presided over the reorganization of the Egyptian army, all of whose top officers, including then-captain Herbert Kitchener, would hail from the British Isles.

Colonialists in France, meanwhile, felt betrayed by both the British and their own government for effectively ending French influence in Egypt. The annexation of the Congo in November 1882 helped soothe a wounded national pride, but growing numbers of influential Frenchmen nursed a desire for revenge against perfidious Albion. By the mid-1880s, the post-1870 passion to avenge Germany's annexation of Alsace and Lorraine had given way in many quarters to a quest for vengeance against the hereditary enemy across the Channel.[53] Increasingly, French leaders and opinion makers paid more attention to the Nile and Congo than to the Rhine.

The situation around the two great African rivers had become enormously complicated. The Congress of Berlin of late 1884–early 1885 was to outline clear European spheres of influence in Africa, but geographic ignorance and the resistance of indigenous peoples and states foiled this attempt.[54] Many of the territories in question remained unknown to outsiders, a situation that encouraged the various powers to seek new "facts on the ground" through exploration, treaties, and strings of military posts flying the national flag. The French and the Belgians were most active in this respect, as they each sought to expand their Congolese possessions at the other's expense.[55] The British played a powerful defensive role, doing everything in their power to keep all European rivals away from the Nile. Since Baring enjoyed solid control of Egypt proper, it was the Sudan that the British needed above all to defend.[56]

Before concerning themselves with French and Belgian designs on the Nile, the British had to confront powerful indigenous opposition in Egypt's colony to the south. At the behest of slave traders and other Sudanese elites, Tawfiq had dismissed Gordon in January 1880. This action revealed weakness rather than strength in Cairo, encouraging Sudanese forces to rebel against their Egyptian masters, themselves confronted with Urabi's coup and Britain's military response. The rebellion spread quickly, as the slave traders' commercial networks facilitated political organization. So did a long-standing undercurrent of popular Islam organized by Sufi guides hostile to infidels, whether formally Muslim or not.

Since the twelfth century, members of religious orders and other missionaries had spread unorthodox strains of Islam into the Sudan, where they often developed into intense forms of popular piety. From the beginning, millenarian or eschatological beliefs underpinned this popular Islam, creating expectations of a "Deliverer" who would purify religion and society and usher in a golden age.[57] During periods of economic difficulty or political strife, Sudanese peoples were especially receptive to missionaries and prophets who promised deliverance from their ills. Egypt's nineteenth-century conquest of the Sudan constituted one of these periods, for not only did new, oppressive foreign rulers arrive in the region but they brought with them an orthodox, and therefore alien, set of Islamic practices and beliefs. Such orthodoxy conflicted with local ways and means, creating a widespread desire to purify the faith. When a young Sufi ascetic named Muhammad Ahmad, a spiritual man with a gift for preaching and mobilizing support, declared himself the Mahdi, or Expected Deliverer, in 1881, a new religious movement was born. Ahmad drew on the belief that the Mahdi would appear at the low point of Muslim civilization, destined to come in the year 1300 after the Hegira, Muhammad's flight from Mecca to Medina. That year was said to be 1882 on the Christian calendar.[58]

Ahmad claimed to be the Prophet's descendent, endowed with holiness and extraordinary powers. His growing reputation as a mystic and teacher together with his charismatic ability to gather a huge following enabled him to overcome tribal divisions, regional difference, and rivalries between village and town. Ahmad united political elites and ordinary people, slave traders and petty merchants, under the banner of a pure, pristine Islam, unsullied by Ottoman-Egyptians and Christians alike.[59] As the Mahdi himself would write: "Religion fell into the hands of the Turks, who . . . annulled the laws of the Merciful and revived the ways of Satan after his own inclinations. When God determined to cut short such a state of things, he called me forth as Mahdi. . . . We are promised the possession of all the earth."[60]

By 1882 the Mahdi had seized the central and southern regions of his country, threatening Egyptian rule and British influence over the Sudan. Against Gladstone's wishes, Tawfiq moved to reassert his colonial control, sending Colonel William Hicks, a retired Indian Army officer, up the Nile accompanied by 8,000 men. The Mahdist forces, as Ahmad's followers now were known, amassed 50,000 fighters, who proceeded to wipe out virtually all of Hicks's troops. In doing so, the Mahdists effectively made the lands once governed by Gordon an independent Islamic state. Khartoum alone remained firmly in Egyptian hands, although the soldiers, administrators, and civilians stranded there appeared highly vulnerable to a Mahdist assault.[61]

The British government, still officially committed to withdrawing from Egypt, refused to intervene to reverse Hicks's defeat. Gladstone described the Mahdists, not incorrectly, as a movement of "people struggling to be free," and Baring considered the desert country worthless economically and of little strategic importance.[62] But ardent imperialists together with anti-slavery organizations opposed the idea of leaving Sudan to its fate. So did the editors of the *Times* and *Pall Mall Gazette,* who mounted a powerful press campaign, endorsed by many other papers, to intervene in the Sudan. Their efforts showed that the "public sphere," at least in part, favored imperial policies considerably more aggressive than those of the government.[63]

On January 9, 1884, the *Pall Mall Gazette* published a front-page editorial and long interview with Gordon. The editorial urged the government to address the "crisis" in the Sudan by sending the recently promoted general to Khartoum. Since the mid-1860s when journalists dubbed him Chinese Gordon, he had existed largely beyond the radar screen of British public life. His six years in the Sudan kept him out of the news, as had several out-of-the-way assignments. When he returned to England after leaving Sudan and Egypt in early 1880, his renown dipped to the point that only a few old friends met him at the dock.[64] Brazza, by contrast, had been feted and thronged when he returned from Africa in 1879, as had Stanley two years earlier. As always, Gordon shunned the limelight, avoiding London, high society, and the press. Between his return home in 1880 and his death five years later, he spent only a single steady period in the British capital, and that lasted only four months.[65]

During those months, *Vanity Fair* tried to revive his reputation by publishing a worshipful profile of him and adding his caricature to the list of luminaries elegantly portrayed in the magazine's Men of the Day series.[66]

Gordon had resisted the effort to include him in the issue, protesting, "I *do not like* to be put before the world in any way." But the magazine founder and editor, Thomas Gibson Bowles, an ardent imperialist fascinated by Africa, won him over, both for the articles and two sittings with the caricaturist Ape (Carlo Pellegrini). Gordon disliked publicity, but not entirely. If he shunned crowds and society dinners, he apparently could not resist being counted among people like Sir F. Phillips, Lord Mayor of London; Sir Henry Rawlinson, head of the Royal Geographical Society; Lord Alverstone, Lord Chief Justice of England; Sarah Bernhardt; and the other "sovereigns, statesmen, and men of the day" deemed worthy of *Vanity Fair*.[67]

"'Chinese Gordon,'" Bowles declared in the article framing Ape's drawing, "is the most notable of living Englishmen." He single-handedly "reconquered China . . . for the Manchoo *[sic]* dynasty," showing such heroism, indeed near-magical powers, that "he never himself went armed with more than a bamboo stick." Once in the Sudan, Gordon "governed, fought, and conquered, showing himself a true master of men." The article stressed Gordon's "complete contempt for money," his saintly status as "a poor man with nothing in the world but his sword and his honor." He not only knew no greed but was "entirely without vanity or self-assertion." At once manly and "very modest and very gentle," he cared only for "what he holds to be right." The "official mind," Bowles said, could not comprehend such disinterestedness, finding him "cracky" and "unsafe to employ." But for *Vanity Fair*, Gordon stood tall as "the grandest Englishman alive . . . a fine, noble, knightly gentleman, such as is found but once in many generations."

Ape's caricature represents the modesty more than the grandeur (fig. 8). Pellegrini pictured Gordon as simply, if properly, dressed, though far better than he actually looked. Meeting Gordon on the Pall Mall, George Curzon, the future viceroy of India, noted his "seedy black frock coat, trousers that did not come down to the boots, and a very dilapidated black silk topper."[68] The caricature portrays Gordon in civilian, not military clothes, and no medals or insignias adorn the sketch. We see no weapons of any kind. If Brazza appeared as a pacific conqueror, Gordon seems to present himself as no conqueror at all. His face shows in profile, his eyes glancing down. It is as if he's too modest to gaze back at the portraitist. His demeanor exudes no hint of power or pride or even self-confidence. He's a shoulder-slumped man who does his duty and expects nobody's thanks.

Gordon's own self-portrait resembles the caricature more than the article. Asked to describe himself, the general wrote: "Gifted with instinct of a woman without judgment; impulsive to the right path, or the wrong, as

Figure 8. Gordon caricature by Ape (Carlo Pellegrini) for the Men of the Day series in *Vanity Fair,*
19 February 1881.

moved by emotions; practically, and with reason, preferring to gain the
hearts of men than £'s sterling."[69] It is notable that Gordon saw himself as
having feminine as well as masculine characteristics—a view widely shared.
It may be that part of Gordon's reason for avoiding the limelight had to
do with shyness, his lack of assertiveness, a certain awkwardness in public.
Crucial as well were his religious convictions, especially the belief that he
acted purely as God's instrument and possessed no significance of his own.
Still, as Strachey famously asked, how could Gordon know where God's

will ended and his own began? "In the depths of Gordon's soul, there were intertwining contradictions—intricate recesses where egoism and renunciation melted into one another, where the flesh lost itself in the spirit, and the spirit in the flesh."[70] Those ambiguities could allow ambition to creep in, as it did not only in the case of *Vanity Fair* but also when he allowed one George Birkbeck Hill to publish a collection of his letters from the Sudan. If Gordon claimed he did "not care a jot about whether the book [of letters] comes out or not," he nonetheless made no effort to prevent its publication. A book of correspondence does not, of course, possess the same narrative effect as, say, the stirring, dramatized, accounts Stanley wrote. For this reason, interest in *Colonel Gordon in Central Africa* (1881) remained slight. We had "looked for a gale," wrote Birkbeck Hill; "there was not more than a breeze."[71]

When W. T. Stead decided to advance Gordon's candidacy as savior of the Sudan, he and other journalists who favored intervention there needed to revive the Gordon myth. The *Pall Mall Gazette* editor, who had already made himself master of the interview, chose this technique to focus attention on Chinese Gordon. Although the general "did not wish to press [his] opinions upon the public" and later wrote that the *Gazette* had "invaded" his sanctuary, he quickly agreed to the meeting, which took place in his sister Augusta's sitting room in Southampton. He had things "to say about the Sudan."[72] Without a campaign to retain this land, Gordon warned, "the spectacle of a conquering Mahommedan Power [the Mahdi], established close to your frontiers [Egypt]," could easily incite rebellion in Cairo and other Egyptian cities, "where it will be felt what the Mahdi has done, they may do; and, as he has driven out the infidel, they may do the same." An anti-British rebellion in Egypt, Gordon added, would inevitably have a domino effect, exciting "dangerous fermentation in Arabia and Syria" and causing "Arab tribes on both sides [of] the Red Sea [to] take fire."[73] Eventually, an unchecked Mahdi would embolden Arabs everywhere to throw off Ottoman rule, upsetting the delicate European balance of power maintained by keeping the old Eastern Empire alive.

Ostensibly religious as Mahdism was, Gordon considered it a purely political, protonationalist movement. "It is an entire mistake," he told Stead, "to regard the Mahdi as in any sense a religious leader. . . . He has assumed a religious title to give color to his defense of the popular rights." The Mahdi, Gordon declared, was "a mere puppet put forward by . . . the largest slave-owner in Obeid." The Mahdists wanted to throw off the Ottoman-Egyptian yoke, not to establish an Islamic paradise. In part, Gordon said, the Sudanese discontent was his own fault; as governor-general, he had "taught them something of the meaning of liberty and justice and accustomed them to a higher ideal of government than that with which they had previously been acquainted. As soon as I had gone, the Turks and Circassians returned in full force . . . and a population which had begun to appreciate something like decent government was flung back to suffer the worst excesses of Turkish rule." Many British readers would have known full well from travel writings and other materials what those "excesses" involved: moral and religious depravity, cruelty, irrationality, effeminacy, and avarice.[74] Only the British, Gordon said, could provide the good government that would diffuse the revolt and eliminate the Mahdist threat.

Despite his long experience in the Sudan, the general's diagnosis of the situation could not have been further from the mark. Gordon had indeed helped cause the rebellion, but not by creating rising expectations. He had, rather, stirred widespread anger among the Sudanese by attacking their elites, menacing their livelihoods, and embodying the very foreign, Christian rule against which the Mahdi, waving the banner of Sufi-style Islam, could rally the Sudan's disparate population. Religion alone enjoyed the potential to unify the country's diverse tribes and competing elites, stretched as they were over a land as large as India; no nationalist appeal could mobilize the people of this vast territory. They spoke different dialects; had no newspapers to create cultural commonalities or imagine a national community; possessed no common history, invented or otherwise; and competed, often mercilessly, for scarce water, ivory, slaves, and arable land. The lone intellectual and cultural resource with the force to galvanize a successful anticolonial movement was popular Islam, a malleable set of beliefs grounded in local knowledge and practice and linking individuals to one another through God.[75]

Once the Mahdi had harnessed the power of popular religion in this way, no effort to impose "benign" British rule could possibly diffuse it. Gordon's idea that he could "make an arrangement with the Mahdi" was doomed in advance. But such realities did not trouble British imperialists, who decided that the dashing officer could "save" Egypt and the Sudan as he had supposedly saved China and the Manchu dynasty. "We cannot send a regiment to Khartoum," Stead wrote, "but we can send a man who on more than one occasion has proved himself more valuable in similar circumstances than an entire army."[76]

The *Pall Mall Gazette* disputed the government's stated policy of evacuating all Egyptian troops, administrators, and other foreigners from the

Sudan, claiming it would be impossible to do so without first securing Khartoum and negotiating with the Mahdi. Only Gordon could accomplish such a task. Stead did not say precisely how Gordon might reduce the Sudan's "raging chaos to order," and he ignored the contradiction between competing intents. On the one hand, Stead hoped the general would "assume absolute control of the territory"; on the other, he wanted him to arrange for the safe and orderly evacuation of troops and civilian personnel. But if Gordon could take complete control of the Sudan, no withdrawal would be necessary. And how, Stead neglected to ask, would he achieve control without any new troops? Did Stead believe that Gordon's military and leadership talents were such that he could single-handedly turn the disparate, demoralized Egyptian soldiers trapped there into a potent fighting force, one capable of battling its way out of the country or of reclaiming Egyptian control?

That the *Gazette* failed to dispel these confusions and contradictions did nothing to prevent a great many other newspapers from endorsing the cry to send Gordon to the Sudan. One paper after the other recalled the legend of Chinese Gordon, who as Stead put it, had "crushed the Taipings and saved China." The Chinese believed Gordon possessed magical powers, and Stead suggested they might have been right. "He always led his troops into action himself, armed with no weapon save a small cane, but the superstition of his soldiers transformed it into a magic wand of victory, and an almost perfect immunity from wounds established a belief that he had a charmed life." Perhaps "such marvels in China" would occur in Khartoum as well?[77]

In the wake of Stead's interview, journalists throughout the country depicted Gordon as if he did in fact possess magical powers, as if he was a hero of ancient and modern myth. Since Havelock had saved India and Gordon China, why couldn't he rescue the Sudan as well? In any event, two days after the *Gazette* interview, the *London Times* published a correspondence between Gordon and Baker, arguing that the British must intervene to "secure those Sudanese their liberty." To abandon the Sudan, Baker claimed, "will of necessity drive every tribe . . . into the arms of the victorious Mahdi."[78] The argument here was not that Gordon should organize an orderly evacuation of the Sudan but that he should confront the Mahdi and deprive him of tribal support.

The relationship, if any, between British government officials and the pro-Gordon press campaign has never been clear. Strachey suggested that Lord Hartington, Gladstone's secretary of state for war, and Wolseley, the adjutant-general of the army, advocated "the very policy which had been outlined by General Gordon in his interview with Mr. Stead and his letter to Sir Samuel Baker." Hartington and Wolseley anticipated that if "a popular agitation in the Press" resulted in a Gordon mission to the Sudan, that mission might blossom into a military effort to wrest the country from the Mahdi's grasp.[79] Such an outcome would have pleased the two ardent imperialists. As for their relationship with Stead, Strachey asked two questions whose implied answers are clear: "Was the movement in the Press during that second week of January a genuine movement, expressing a spontaneous wave of popular feeling? Or was it a cause of that feeling, rather than an effect? The engineering of a newspaper agitation may not have been an impossibility—even so long ago as 1884."[80]

The problem with such either-or questions is that successful press campaigns rarely fit completely into one category or the other. A campaign that represents the machinations of government officials (or, say, business interests) but stands outside the ideas, attitudes, or beliefs of a sizable segment of the population is unlikely to gain much purchase. At the same time, it is unusual for ideas or issues simply to well up from below without any conscious organization and seize the media as a "spontaneous wave of popular feeling." Gordon and Wolseley had long been friends, and they and their intimates inside and outside the government knew leading journalists. We can thus assume contact among influential politicians and journalists on the Sudan situation in general and on whether to send Gordon in particular. Perhaps someone in government advised Stead to seek out Gordon, or perhaps the editor's journalistic instincts led him to the officer on his own. In any event, no amount of political and journalistic collusion could have guaranteed the extraordinary public resonance of the pro-Gordon campaign, nor could such collusion have guaranteed that dozens of newspapers would republish Stead's interview and comment favorably on it. Gordon had, in short, become a charismatic personality, an individual capable of moving journalists and readers alike, of making them believe he possessed extraordinary qualities. What is unusual about Gordon is the relatively small role he himself played in creating the aura that surrounded him. If Stanley and Brazza had done a great deal to fashion their own charismatic myths, the British officer did very little. In Gordon's case, journalists worked largely on their own to make him the Victorian hero he became, a man widely deemed capable of doing what nobody else could do.

Earlier press attention to Havelock, Livingstone, Stanley, and Gordon himself had centered coverage of empire on individual heroes, identifying

India with Havelock, the Congo with Stanley, China with Gordon. A great many newspaper readers thus found themselves well prepared to believe that Gordon, and Gordon alone, could save the day in the Sudan. "The expectation of General Gordon's success in this apparently desperate enterprise," declared the *Illustrated London News*, "is amply justified by his past career. . . . His extraordinary combination of tact, energy, and courage triumphed over all obstacles, brought every savage tribe into subjection, enabled him to suppress the slave trade, and established order and peace throughout the vast territory." The new assignment, "gigantic though it seems, is trivial compared with what he accomplished in the same region a few years ago."[81] As the *Birmingham Post* concluded, "Rarely has there been such striking testimony to the magic of a name."[82]

In none of these editorials was Gordon's mission presented as primarily a military venture. Like Brazza's African explorations, his was a peaceful conquest, a labor of almost womanly love, a selfless humanitarian gesture designed to liberate the enslaved and relieve the oppressed. As the *Illustrated London News* put it, "This simple-minded, God-fearing man, who combines dauntless courage with womanly tenderness . . . has gone out to fulfill his destiny [by] rescuing the beleaguered garrisons in the Soudan, rescuing the Arab tribes from oppression, and extirpating the slave trade in Equatorial Africa."[83]

Although the press commentary emphasized Gordon's humanitarian objectives and nonaggressive designs, some admitted that economic interests and national standing counted as well. The *Manchester Examiner,* a radical paper, wanted Gordon to retain Khartoum, not give it up, and anticipated the time when "a cheap railway may be laid down between Souakim [on the Red Sea] and some point on the Nile."[84] And since the geopolitics of Africa figured with growing prominence in the geopolitics of Europe, several papers, including the *Times,* spoke of the need to maintain England's prestige by teaching the Mahdi a lesson. Still, the underlying and pivotal objective was a white man's burden. "The weary [English] Titan," wrote the *Spectator,* "is heavily burdened already, but . . . it looks very much as if Providence intended once more to use Englishmen in the work which they do best—the maintenance of peace, order, and justice among dark races too weak of themselves to be anything but prey."[85] The Catholic weekly *Tablet* stood out as one of the rare voices cautioning against "the acceptance of responsibilities . . . which are not English at all."[86]

Inevitably, the press's clamor for Gordon in January 1884 drew the government's attention, whether cabinet members wanted to focus on him or not. They had already decided to withdraw completely from the Sudan, forcing a reluctant khedive to go along. But the question of how precisely to leave this huge country remained. Without some kind of orderly, protected retreat, the 21,000 Egyptian soldiers stationed there, along with their British officers and civilian personnel, risked being slaughtered by the Mahdist army. Gordon believed he could prevent such an outcome and "come to terms with the rebels" by placing them under the benign protection of an Englishman like himself. "The Mahdi's kingdom will fall to pieces ere long," he wrote Northbrook, first lord of the Admiralty.[87] Gladstone and Baring disagreed with Gordon's assessment, and in any event, the last thing the two British leaders wanted was an Englishmen at the Sudanese helm. Even so, in mid-January, Baring called for a British officer "to go to Khartoum with full powers, civil and military, to conduct the retreat."[88] This call opened a Pandora's box.

With the journalistic fever for Gordon continuing to mount, the queen herself weighed in, urging his appointment to the Sudan. Gladstone still appeared reluctant to send him but worried about the pressure of "public opinion."[89] He and his colleagues compromised by ordering the hero to Khartoum, but only as an observer—or so Gladstone thought. But with the prime minister away on holiday, Lord Granville, the foreign secretary, added significantly to Gordon's responsibilities when he instructed him by cable to "consider the best mode of evacuating the interior of the Sudan . . . and perform such other duties as may be entrusted . . . by the Egyptian Government through Sir Evelyn Baring."[90] Given Gordon's penchant for acting on his own authority, the license to "perform other . . . duties" likely told him that he enjoyed a carte blanche.[91]

Whatever Granville and Baring's precise intentions, it made no operational sense to send Gordon, of all people, on any Sudanese mission other than to organize a military campaign. Gordon's forte had always been daring assignments and irregular warfare.[92] He was a man of action, not a diplomat or intelligence analyst. As noted, Strachey concluded, without direct evidence, that government hawks had intended a military venture all along, and that they allowed Gladstone to believe they had sent Gordon to Sudan merely to placate public opinion, not actually to do anything. Perhaps Strachey is right, but if so, why did a general of Wolseley's experience believe Gordon could organize an effective military campaign by going to the Sudan alone, without so much as a single soldier in tow? Strachey suggests that Wolseley anticipated that once in Khartoum, Gordon himself would require rescue. The inevitable clamor to retrieve him would force Gladstone to launch a British column up the Nile. This, of course, is what would eventually happen, but the idea that Wolseley had planned such a series of events seems plausible only in retrospect. Wolseley could not have known in January 1884 that Mahdist forces would besiege Khartoum with Gordon inside, nor could he have been confident that Gladstone would send a posse after his friend. The prime minister not only opposed British intervention in the Sudan but, as everyone knew, he also wanted to withdraw from Egypt.

The more likely explanation for the otherwise incomprehensible decision to order Gordon to Africa was that British cabinet members, including Gladstone himself, found themselves swept up in the same mass enthusiasm of hero worship of and magical thinking about Gordon that had affected so many of their countrymen. Government officials, like millions of ordinary people, had attributed to the general charismatic authority and, with it, extraordinary powers. If Chinese Gordon could single-handedly save the Manchu dynasty, why couldn't he restore order in the Sudan? In popular belief, he had, after all, turned a motley crew of drunken mercenaries into an Ever Victorious Army. Certainly, he could transform a 6,000-man Khartoum garrison into a mighty anti-Mahdist machine. And wasn't his standing and influence among the Sudanese people such that his simple presence in their country would stop the Mahdi in his tracks?

There is no reason to assume that politicians develop immunities to the cultural phenomena that affect almost everyone else. And in this case, Gladstone and his colleagues had their own, additional reasons for wishful thinking about Gordon. A great many influential British voices expressed the desire to remain involved in the Sudan: humanitarians who sought to quell slavery; imperialists who believed that the Sudan protected Egypt and that Egypt protected the path to India; soldiers allergic to withdrawal and retreat. Many of those voices came from within Gladstone's own Liberal Party, voices he could not ignore. By sending Gordon, he could hope to quiet dissent and escape undamaged politically from the Sudan. As for his cabinet colleagues, more willing to intervene there if only to prevent another humiliating loss of British officers, Gordon allowed them to indulge the wish that his heroism and military genius would make things right.

Gordon had made clear in his interview with Stead that he didn't believe in evacuating Egypt's colony to the south; even before arriving there, he announced far more ambitious plans. He had himself declared governor-general of the Sudan and vowed to rule with the aid of traditional, not

Ottoman-Egyptian, elites.[93] At home, meanwhile, the *Times, Pall Mall Gazette,* and other papers argued against any retreat from the Sudan, maintaining instead that Gordon should be "supported," as Baker wrote to the *Times,* "by troops forwarded [there] as rapidly as possible." Baker expressed incredulity over the prospect of the general's arriving "at Berber [the key city between the Egyptian border and the Sudanese capital] and Khartoum without an army." "Unprotected and alone," Gordon would be powerless to act.[94] Baker's appraisal of Gordon's prospects made a great deal of sense, but no government official and few journalists appeared to share his view. Somehow, Gordon would single-handedly untangle the Sudanese knot.

While Gordon made his way slowly up the Nile in January and February 1884, Mahdist forces won a series of military victories and attracted growing numbers of tribes into their fold. Gordon blundered by announcing at Berber that the Egyptians planned to evacuate their colony. This news destroyed what remained of the Egyptian officials' authority in that crucial region between the mother country and Khartoum. The announcement also revealed that no army waited in the wings to back the new governor-general and that he could offer neither protection from the Mahdi nor rewards for supporting him rather than the "rebels."[95]

As for the Mahdi himself, he could now appreciate Gordon's weakness. The general had hoped to convince the Islamic leader to halt his insurrection in exchange for being named a regional sultan; Ahmad rejected Gordon's offer out of hand. As "the Expected Mahdi," the revolutionary leader wrote, "the Successor of the Apostle of God . . . I have no need of the sultanate . . . nor of the wealth of this world and its vanity. I am but the slave of God, guiding unto God and to what is with Him."[96] This statement might have reminded Gordon of things he himself professed to believe. In any event, he now understood that the Mahdi intended to take the Sudan as a whole.

By the time the general reached Khartoum on 18 February, the Mahdi succeeded in placing tens of thousands of men in the field, many armed with weapons captured from defeated Egyptian troops. Those Egyptians who acted quickly to return home arrived safely; meanwhile, most Sudanese tribes declared allegiance to the Islamic guide. Ignoring these realities, Gordon professed the same belief in his charismatic abilities as his compatriots back home: "I come [to Khartoum] without soldiers, but with God on my side, to redress the evils of the Soudan."[97] Despite such faith, the general made no serious effort to organize an evacuation from the city. He must have realized that he had grievously underestimated his opponent's military strength. The Egyptian garrisons and the civilians who wanted to leave with them would now have to fight their way out. "The Mahdi," Gordon declared, "must be smashed up."[98] The British Cabinet, officially committed to evacuating the Sudan and avoiding war, expressed horror over the general's new rhetorical escalation. But such was the price government leaders had to pay for sending Gordon to the Sudan and believing either that he could do no harm there or that he could magically resolve a situation whose dangers and complexities they did not begin to grasp.

Once Gordon had reorganized Khartoum's defenses and stockpiled food and other supplies, he found himself with time on his hands. He befriended the *Times*' correspondent in Khartoum, Frank Power, a journalist without rivals among hero-worshipers of Gordon. On arriving in Khartoum, Power had cabled, "General Gordon is perfectly confident that he will accomplish the pacification of the Soudan without firing a shot." The governor-general rewarded the correspondent with a steady stream of newsworthy tidbits, one of which prompted a *Times* leader to declare, "The coming of one noble hearted Englishman, resolute, righteous, and fearless, [showed] the people of Khartoum . . . that their protector and deliverer had once more come among them."[99] In fact, the city's residents lived in growing fear of a Mahdist siege; by early March, Gordon and Power had no choice but to report a deteriorating situation. With the Mahdi winning crucial tribes to his side, his burgeoning forces closed in on Khartoum.[100]

As news of what now amounted to a Mahdist revolution reached Great Britain, the press commentary became urgent, even hysterical. If the dominant narrative in January and early February had brimmed with hope and confidence, the mood now turned dark, the prognosis increasingly pessimistic. Part of the reason for this dramatic change in tone, as Gladstone told the queen, turned on Gordon's "too free communications with persons who act as correspondents of the public journals."[101] Assimilating the grim news, Conservative commentators flatly accused the Liberal government of sacrificing Gordon, of abandoning him as it had abandoned the Sudan. Tories in Parliament raised the specter of a no-confidence vote, and a journalistic chorus pressured Gladstone to approve a British-led expedition to rescue the endangered hero. At the same time, leaders of the antislavery lobby, close politically to Gladstone, reacted angrily to news of Gordon's efforts to conclude a military alliance with Zubayr Pasha, notorious in Britain as the Sudan's leading slave-trader.

Once again, Gladstone found himself pressured from all sides. He had not wanted to send Gordon to the Sudan or intervene there in any way, and now his erstwhile allies raised a furor over Zubayr, while his enraged opponents blamed him for sending the hero into a trap. The *Pall Mall Gazette,* the *Times,* and other papers began to publish letters, ostensibly from Liberals, denouncing Gladstone and demanding British military intervention to rescue Gordon. In its letters column, the *Gazette* printed a poem by a "Scottish working man" lamenting that Chinese Gordon has been stranded in "The desert, unarmed and alone, / [Without] Britain's best "blood" at his back. / [We must save him] For with Gordon our glory and honor must die!"[102] The paper's lead editorial that day claimed the workingman's verse "undoubtedly expresses a very general feeling," but declared it premature to condemn the government for failing to send troops. Gordon, the editors said, wielded "more power than a large standing army could confer." As late as mid-February, the *Pall Mall Gazette* still indulged in the magical thinking, the charismatic hero worship, that had led to Gordon's misguided assignment in the first place.

A crucial turning point in the press coverage of Gordon came when Mahdist forces cut the telegraph line between Khartoum and Berber on March 10. No longer could the governor-general communicate with Cairo or London, save for occasional letters smuggled out of town, most of which never reached their destinations.[103] Like Livingstone before him, Gordon was now lost to the "civilized" world. The paucity and irregularity of information about him raised anxiety levels and sharpened criticism of Gladstone's government. Queen Victoria expressed a widespread sentiment when she telegraphed Hartington: "Gordon is in danger. You are bound to try to save him."[104] The government put her off, and Gladstone persisted in his refusal to commit British troops to the Sudan. He denied that the general faced any real danger and that the Mahdist movement represented anything other than a legitimate fight for Sudan's freedom.[105]

Meanwhile, the most widely read newspapers, especially the *Daily Telegraph* and the *Times,* pressed the government to intervene on Gordon's behalf. By May, the domestic uproar was such that the Conservatives proposed a censure motion in Parliament, and mass meetings took place throughout the country to demand Gordon's rescue. Virtually every conservative paper, along with many liberal ones, vilified the government for failing to act. On May 8, the Baroness Burdett-Coutts wrote the *Times* saying she had received a large number of private contributions for a Gordon relief expedition, many of them from poor workers who "raise their voices in unison with their wealthier fellow-countrymen against a base surrender of a nation's good faith and honor, as well as of a gallant and Christian life."[106] Significant numbers of Britons doubtless remained unmoved by Gordon's fate or agreed on principle with Gladstone's anti-interventionist stance. Still, the *Times* did not err in writing: "The anxiety as to General Gordon's safety is not confined to London, or fomented by Opposition prints. . . . It is discernible in the organs of all classes, those of the working men not excepted, and is plainly manifested in the North of England and Scotland, the strongholds of Liberalism." Workers, the *Times* declared, like "the great mass of General Gordon's countrymen are persuaded that there is a sacred duty to relieve him from his peril" and avoid a "national humiliation." The pro-Gordon views of Sunday papers like *Lloyd's* suggest the *Times* was right.[107]

Such journalistic pressure, combined with entreaties from powerful men such as Hartington, leader of the Liberals' Whig faction, and Wolseley, himself a popular hero, forced Gladstone to act. Having opposed sending Gordon to the Sudan, the prime minister now found himself forced to commit British troops to rescue him. The Mahdists' hold on the region had tightened to the point that any effort on Gordon's behalf would bring British troops into direct conflict with a swelling army of Islamic fighters. In late May, the Mahdists took Berber, the pivotal town linking Khartoum, Egypt, and the Red Sea. Now the revolutionaries blocked both routes out of the Sudan, the one leading north via the Nile and the other east via Suakin and the Suez Canal. Meanwhile, the bulk of Mahdist forces closed in on Khartoum, with the Mahdi himself reaching Omdurman, just across the Nile, on 23 October. By November, the capital was surrounded and under siege.[108]

Back in England, the press, starved for information about the besieged hero, made the most of what news came in. On August 8 the *Daily Telegraph* exulted in its first solid information since the previous April, indulging in magical, wishful thinking about Gordon's situation. "History, ancient or modern, can show no parallel to the feat which this single Englishman has accomplished. Alone in the beleaguered city . . . he has struck blow after blow at his enemy, and with every blow . . . his weapon has grown stronger and keener in his hand." The legend of Chinese Gordon inspired faith in "Gordon of Khartoum," the "born leader of Oriental races" who would transform "faint-hearted Egyptian[s]" into an "'ever victorious army.'"

Under mounting pressure to launch the Gordon rescue, the government nonetheless proceeded slowly, prompting the *Telegraph* to warn, "The honor of England" is at stake, "and no Government which failed to re-deem it would be forgiven." Finally, in early September 1884, Gladstone sent Wolseley to Cairo, ordering him to lead 10,000 men up the Nile to Khartoum. Logistical problems, sluggish decision making, and the dip-ping Nile waters slowed the column's progress. Wolseley's men did not reach the vicinity of the Sudanese capital until mid-January 1885. As the British army crossed the desert en route to Khartoum, Mahdist warriors attacked it in human waves. The Muslims swept toward the foreign forces, who desperately sprayed them with machine-gun fire. Mahdist soldiers, climb-ing over mounds of fallen bodies, soon breeched the British military formations arrayed into traditional fighting squares. Rudyard Kipling narrates this battle in *The Light That Failed,* having his hero, a military sketch artist named Dick Heldar, slashed with a Mahdist sword. Nearly fatal, the wound causes an injury that ultimately makes him blind.[109] British-led forces had themselves blindly pushed into the Sudan unpre-pared for the difficult desert conditions and unfamiliar with Mahdist mil-itary tactics. By the time the British reached the Nile near Metemma, 10 percent of their men lay dead, the wounded too numerous to count.[110] With the naval contingent also badly mauled, Gordon's would-be rescuers found themselves unable to launch their planned invasion of Khartoum. A small reconnaissance force reported that the Egyptian flag had come down and that the Mahdists now controlled the capital of Sudan.

The Mahdist army had easily taken the city on January 25, killing Gor-don as he vainly defended the governor's palace. One assailant cut off his head and wrapped it in a cloth (or put it in a leather bag, depending on the account), apparently intending to take it to the Mahdi as a trophy. Rudolf Slatin, the former governor of Darfur captured by the Mahdists, was the first to see it. As Slatin told the story, the Mahdist soldier unwrapped the cloth, asking, "Is not this the head of your uncle the unbeliever?" Gor-don's blue eyes were wide open.[111]

In Khartoum, the victorious Mahdist Ansar killed a great many people, looted homes and shops, and captured and enslaved women and children. After Wolseley's broken British army limped back to Egypt, an incipient Mahdist state controlled the entire Sudan, except for the southern part of Equatoria province. To break symbolically from the legacy of Turkish and Egyptian rule, the Mahdi established a new capital for his revolutionary state near the fort of Omdurman, opposite the now-abandoned Khartoum. Muhammad Ahmad was not, however, destined to rule; he died almost exactly five months after seizing Khartoum.[112] His successor, Mohammad Abdallahi, known as the Khalifa, governed Mahdist Sudan until 1898, when a new British invading force restored the Sudan to the much-expanded British Empire.

When the *Daily Telegraph* broke the story of Khartoum's fall on February 5, 1885, "the disastrous tidings . . . spread like wildfire through the West-end of the town." The interest and consternation was such that "men and youths, and even ladies stood at the street corners and upon the pavements, papers in hand, eagerly devouring the substance of the telegrams." The great hero had been unable to save the day; his very survival was in doubt. "A sentiment of universal sorrow for the fate of the heroic Gordon was manifestly the uppermost feeling in all men's minds."[113] The Mahdi's victory, the *Daily News* and *Morning Advertiser* declared, represented "a national calamity," a disaster "as grave as any country has had to encounter since the darkest days of the Indian Mutiny."[114] This tragedy, the *Times* added, "has no parallel in the experience of the present generation."[115]

Despite this widely shared feeling, it did not take journalists long to transform Gordon's defeat and death into a de facto victory by eulogizing him as a hero, martyr, and saint. It didn't matter, they said, that he had not prevailed, that the magical abilities expected of him had not born fruit. He had shown extraordinary, exemplary courage in the face of overwhelming odds against him, and that was what counted. "Never has the figure of an English general," the *Daily Chronicle* said, "loomed through the storm-wrack of disaster surrounded by a brighter halo of glory. A hundred English armies may in years to come win a hundred victories on many stricken fields of battle, but no feat of theirs will do more to gild with honor the great name of England than that which Charles Gordon has achieved, almost single-handed, on the battlements of Khartoum."[116] His defeat was thus a victory, a victory of "English manhood" as the *Daily Telegraph* put it, of the "matchless courage, noble disinterestedness, and sublime recognition of duty" that have made the country what it is.[117] Gordon's heroic sacrifice, the *Telegraph* added, points confidently to future successes, because it gives us "proof that the power of great personalities has not passed away." The hero's "courage and genius . . . the force of that one solitary British spirit, [worked] like a breakwater across the fierce rebellion . . . performing for his Sovereign and his country as much as a corps d'armée does elsewhere."[118] His ability to hold out for nearly a year against overwhelming odds convinced a great many commentators that had the government sent British troops to his aid several months sooner, he could have stopped the insurrection in its tracks.

Earlier, commentators had mocked, ignored, or dismissed Gordon's messianic, fundamentalist Christianity. Now they extolled the Christian virtues that had moved the great general to martyr himself on England's behalf, to die so that his people could be saved. According to Professor Benjamin Jowett, master of Balliol College, Oxford, Gordon's religious "fancies or meditations" were of the kind "entertained by almost every saint of mediaeval times, Catholic or Protestant [sic]." What is important about his religiosity is his "intensity of self-devotion, [his] abnegation of all things which men hold dear . . . if he might serve God and his fellow-men." This is why "there never has been a public calamity (not [even] the death of Nelson . . .) affecting so deeply the hearts and minds of England" as the death of Charles Gordon.[119] He was a "soldier with the spirit of the saint," wrote the *Morning Advertiser.* "He perished in his mission; and the Christian hero is a Christian martyr."[120] He showed that "death may be more potent than life, [that] there is something which succeeds even better than success—heroic, unmerited failure."[121] We pray, concluded Professor Jowett, "that the lesson of a great man's death may not be lost upon us, but that . . . we may gather [inspiration] from his courage and firmness and wisdom and self sacrifice and strength in all the trials which the English people may have to undergo in generations to come."[122]

The worry underlying these comments was that in an age of modernity, masses, and machines, British men, more accustomed to the shop and office than to the barracks and battlefield, lacked the fortitude to prevail over determined foes. Gordon reassured the commentators against such doubts; his simplicity, religious devotion, dashing heroism, and willingness to take matters into his own hands recalled the romance and glory of earlier, more robust times. "The age of chivalry is not gone," declared the *Daily News.* "It revives again in Gordon's history. . . . He was Lancelot and Galahad both in one, [having] brought something of the glamour and brightness of the heroic ages into the dull realities of these prosaic times."[123] The *Times* echoed these comments about chivalry and heroism, maintaining that Gordon "has proved, too, that the English race is in no sense degenerate."[124] If certain writers had begun to highlight Britain's supposed degeneration, Gordon's example, and the popular endorsement it received, appeared to challenge their claims.[125] "Had all been true," declared the *Daily Telegraph,* "which has been said of the selfish materialism, the perverted aspirations, the corrupted instincts of our age, it would have been impossible for the glow of generous emotion which has been felt throughout England and Europe at Gordon's crowning act of self-sacrifice to be enkindled at all."[126] It was as if Gordon's martyrdom resulted in the dispersion of his charisma throughout the land, endowing his countrymen with a measure of the heroic manly qualities once seen as unique to him.

Such sentiments united virtually all commentators, except that it was mainly the conservative ones who made an explicit contrast between base (liberal) politics and heroic action, "between Mr. Gladstone and General Gordon, between the man of words and the man of deeds, the hero and the rhetorician."[127] Gordon stood out as Gladstone's manly, genuinely English foil. Responsibility for the hero's death, wrote the *Pall Mall Gazette,* rested "entirely on [the prime minister's] shoulders"; a great many English men and women agreed.[128] For weeks after the fall of Khartoum, crowds besieged 10 Downing Street, where Gladstone, long known as the Grand Old Man, or simply the GOM, now found himself jeered as the MOG, Murderer of Gordon. He could not go to the theater without being booed and hissed by the crowd.[129] Queen Victoria led the chorus of vilification, writing, "The government is alone to blame, by refusing to send the expedition before it was too late."[130] In a letter to Gordon's sister, the queen extolled her "noble heroic brother, who served his country and his Queen so truly, so heroically with a self-sacrifice so edifying to the world." That promises of rescue and reinforcement were unfulfilled left the queen with a "grief inexpressible."[131]

The most serious political recriminations would come soon enough, with censure votes and, ultimately, Gladstone's political defeat and replacement by Salisbury's Tories, less squeamish about imperialism than the Liberals. In the immediate wake of Gordon's death, a great many editorialists called for revenge against the Mahdi, for a tough military lesson to "teach the poor brave fanatics of the desert what is the length of England's arm, and what the weight of England's sword."[132] The only question was when to attack. Although some writers thought Wolseley needed time to regroup, the *Times* and *Telegraph* wanted him to retaliate immediately, fearing that any hesitation or retreat would have an extravagant domino effect. As the *Times* put it: "It is not Egypt alone that is concerned. The countries of North Africa along the Mediterranean seaboard, the dominions of the Sultan in Europe and Asia Minor, the East African coast down to Zanzibar, Arabia, Persia, Afghanistan, and even British India, may be easily brought within the reach of the Mahdi's authority, if only his title be consecrated and affirmed by victory."[133] To prevent such a victory, the working-class *Lloyd's Newspaper* declared, "It is incumbent on us not to relieve, but to re-conquer Khartoum, and in such a way as to inflict a defeat that the whole world shall witness upon the Mahdi, and prove to the Mussulman [sic] tribes of Africa that the might of England is irresistible."[134]

Although a great many newspapers expressed similarly aggressive views, some raised voices of dissent. For the *Manchester Examiner,* a liberal paper, it was "absurd to talk of putting down a revolt, or of chastising the rebels. These men, in our eyes, are engaged in no revolt, and are not rebels."[135] For the *Scotsman,* "the danger of the moment" turns not on any Mahdist aggression, but on "warlike spirit aroused throughout the country by the fall of Khartoum, [which] may hurry [the government] into measures which will commit us to the stupendous futility of conquering the Soudan."[136] Despite such liberal sentiments, the general outcry led the government to decide that for reasons of domestic politics it had no choice but to go "smash" the Mahdi. A deafening public chorus demanded vengeance for the man whom even Gladstone called "a hero of heroes." "He being dead," declared the *Daily Telegraph,* "yet speaketh, and in a voice [that] silences all others, or leaves the nation with no ear for them." Gordon's once-contested desire to rule the Sudan had been, "in a moment, elevated into a legacy of national duty by his self-sought martyrdom."[137]

Although Wolseley agreed in principle with these views, he advised against attacking the Mahdist Ansar in the near future. He understood that his damaged army lacked both the manpower and the equipment to wrest Sudan from the Mahdist forces that now controlled it.[138] Wolseley's realistic assessment suited Gladstone, eager once again to rid himself of the Sudanese albatross. In late April 1885, Hartington ordered the general to withdraw, thereby relinquishing the entire Sudan save for Suakin, the strategic Red Sea port seized in a rare victory over Mahdist forces.

Amid the outpouring of anger and grief over Gordon's fate at Khartoum, Britain's religious leaders conducted a Protestant beatification of the martyred hero. The archbishop of Canterbury, himself shaken by Gordon's death, wrote in his diary, "There never has been so universal a sense of loss and danger in England." He declared 13 February a day of national mourning, and religious services, overflowing with grief-stricken people, were held throughout the country.[139] At the elite Harrow School, the Reverend

Dr. Butler's eulogy voiced the widespread perception of Gordon as at once a religious and military figure, an imperial "hero and a saint—the most soldier-like of saints, the most saintly of soldiers."[140] In the 1880s, Gordon represented a still-common understanding of the empire as devoted to the conquest of souls as well as the conquest of land.[141] His imperial service made him not just a saint but a modern-day Christ. Comparing Gordon's entry into Khartoum to Christ's entry into Jerusalem, an Anglican preacher evoked a Sudanese people "crowded around Gordon, kissing his very feet, and hailing him as their savior."[142] The popular writer and lecturer Sir Arthur Quiller-Couch (widely known as "Q"), proclaimed Gordon "the noblest Briton of our times," the "nearest approach to Christ of any man who ever lived."[143]

The sermons in Gordon's memory were legion. In a typical oration, William MacDonald Sinclair, vicar of St. Stephen's, Westminster, spoke of Gordon's charisma in religious terms: "The secret of [Gordon's] miraculous power was that, in an age of doubt and worldliness, his faith was the faith which removes mountains, and his surrender of himself to Christ complete, entire, and absolute."[144] With these comments, Sinclair anticipated Weber's understanding of the charismatic prophet, an individual whose authority stemmed from his connection to the divine.[145] In Gordon's case, that divine gift of grace endowed him with a "courage such as never was equaled, the highest possible skill in war, a magical insight into human character, and an inspired knowledge of the right thing to be done at the right moment."[146] Fifteen years later, just after the "reconquest" of the Sudan, another bishop, William Boyd Carpenter, explained the reasons for Gordon's—or any individual's—charismatic appeal. "We may admire a man's achievements, but we are drawn by an irresistible fascination to the *man* who achieves; we want to be near, and to understand if we can, the hidden life power—whether of brain or character—which has made these achievements possible."[147]

Judging from the tall stack of letters—most written in verse—addressed to Augusta and to Gordon's brother, Sir Henry, it seems clear that Gordon's charisma derived in part from a popular Protestant religiosity focused on him.[148] This religiosity expressed many of the evangelical impulses that had swept through Britain beginning in the mid-eighteenth century. Evangelicalism, both in its Methodist and Anglican varieties, challenged the cold formalities of High Church tradition. It energized religious practice and belief by encouraging individual conversion experiences and vibrantly emotional forms of worship. Both fostered a deeply personal commitment to God, family, and the community of believers.[149] The pulpit was of course central to the evangelical enterprise, but beyond it, religious writers spread its message through stories of "exemplary lives," hagiographic accounts of individuals whose piety and service to God and country invited others to follow their lead.[150] After the mid-nineteenth century, such evangelical stories blended with calls for a more "muscular" Christianity by centering on the heroism of pious soldiers and chivalrous fighters for whom no sacrifice was too great. No one fit this description better than Charles Gordon, the hero and now the martyr of Khartoum.

Those who wrote to Gordon's brother and sister, most anonymously and emphasizing their modest social rank, doubtless chose poetry as the noblest form of writing, the means of expression that seemed at once prayerful and grand. As one described Gordon's exemplary life: "No braver soldier e'er drew human breath / No prouder, Christlier Christian ever passed / Within the dark veiled aperture of death . . . / But not in vain he died: his glorious name / Emblazoned with the autograph of Heaven / Shall burn in history a holy flame / To highest hope and aspiration gain."

Virtually every poem expressed such themes: Gordon's heroism, bravery, self-sacrifice, self-abnegation, and devotion to God—even a quasi-divinity of his own. The amateur poets often spoke of England's shame in failing to rescue Gordon, but also of the lessons learned from the failure to stand behind the hero:

O noblest son of England's race
Hero of heroes, saint of God,
Looking for months in death's pale face
Sworn never to deny his lord:
Weep, weep O Britain for thy slain,
And weep yet one more time our own deep shame!

Beyond such sentiments, letter writers presented Gordon as "the grandest life for centuries known," the paragon of "True Christian manhood." They extolled him as a model for British men and boys: "Mark his life. . . . Live like him." Gordon not only exemplified heroism, wrote one Francis H. Doyle, but revived a long-dormant heroic spirit in a country gone soft through corruption, commerce, and ease.

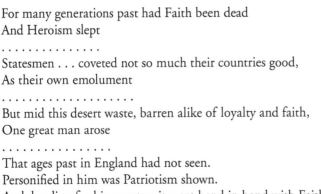

For many generations past had Faith been dead
And Heroism slept
. . . .
Statesmen . . . coveted not so much their countries good,
As their own emolument
. . . .
But mid this desert waste, barren alike of loyalty and faith,
One great man arose
. . . .
That ages past in England had not seen.
Personified in him was Patriotism shown.
And, battling for his country, it went hand in hand with Faith.

In several letters, the poor (those who "Exist in cottage and ken") asserted their right to worship Gordon alongside the rich. George W. Levack sent a handwritten poem because "this is the only contribution I can send towards the memorial of your deceased brother, as gold and silver I have none, moving in the humblest ranks of life." Another writer, more prosperous than most, had 1,000 copies of his poem printed. Still, in a short preface, he wrote: "No death has affected the nation so powerfully as that of General Gordon, and while men of name and fame have expressed their sorrow, men, humble and unknown, have none the less felt deeply the loss of one who was indeed a grand character, reminding us of the Chivalry of the Middle Ages."

These verses reflect a powerful emotional attachment to Gordon, one with religious overtones and expressions of profound personal loss. "Every night and morning during the past fortnight," wrote Maggie Cecil Ryner, "I have prayed that General Gordon might be alive." But on hearing definitively of his death, "I never felt so miserable in my life before." For one writer after the other, Gordon's death had deprived them of a hero imagined at once as a friend, model, mentor, and god. "It is the privilege of very few indeed," declared E. J. Sale, "to soar away to the sublime heights upon which rested the late George Charles Gordon. [I extol] one so superlatively higher than myself."

Such sentiments helped at once to fashion and represent a process of mythmaking that made the memory of Gordon a key element in what James Morris has called the late century's "craze of empire."[151] The era's "hero industry" placed Gordon's statue in Trafalgar Square (1888) and produced more than seventy biographies of the British proconsul within months of his death. Eyewitness accounts of Gordon's demise, as retold by F. R. Wingate, director of military intelligence in Egypt, sold many thousands of copies in one edition after the other, as did the various hagiographies. Seton Churchill's portrait of Gordon as Christian knight attained 41,000 copies printed and its thirteenth edition by 1907.[152] Perhaps most important, Gordon's likeness enjoyed a prominent place at Madame Tussaud's Wax Museum. Between 1885 and 1901 the museum displayed eight panoramic scenes, all focused on the empire and three of the eight on Gordon. The first, on view from 1885 to 1909, depicted the hero's "betrayal" and death and Britain's revenge against the Sudan. The second (1891–1902) showed the daring rescue of Sir Charles Wilson, one of the officers sent to save Gordon. It suggested the extent to which Britain had snatched victory from the jaws of defeat. And the third, a panorama exhibited for nearly a half century (1897–1941) reproduced G. W. Joy's celebrated painting *General Gordon's Last Stand* (1885).[153]

In what became an iconic image of Victorian Britain, Joy's hero looks down on a band of turbaned, spear-carrying fighters creeping toward his uniformed figure perched atop a flight of stairs. The Mahdists are barefoot and bloody, while Gordon stands unscathed, his sword hanging at his side, his pistol pointing down and away from his assailants. It appears as though he could have killed several of the men crouching before him. But peaceful civilizer that he is, a Christian man with no fear of death, Gordon throws the Mahdists a resolute and slightly disdainful look. One bloodied Mahdist points his spear toward the martyr-to-be. This painting, like the waxwork exhibit it inspired, emphasized the religious, spiritual quality of Gordon's (and England's) imperial mission, depicting Gordon as a Christian hero-martyr who had succumbed bravely and without resistance to the Islamic hordes. It is much more likely that Gordon died a soldier's death, fighting ferociously before Mahdist soldiers cut him down.[154] But the desire to portray him as a transcendent, Christian knight required beatific passivity in the face of Islamic violence. Wingate's supposed eyewitness accounts reinforced such imagery, as did the poet John Greenleaf Whittier, who proclaimed Gordon "the nearest approach to that one Man, Christ Jesus, of any man that ever lived."[155]

Between 1896 and 1898 Gordon's unresisting martyrdom served to justify a new imperial war of reconquest and revenge. As Churchill wrote in *The River War,* his famous account of Kitchener's 1898 victory over the Mahdist state, Gordon's blood left a "dark stain which was not immediately effaced; it became an invitation for Gordon's death to be

Figure 9. *General Gordon's Last Stand* (oil on canvas) by G. W. (George William) Joy (1844–1925). © Leeds Museums and Galleries (City Art Gallery) UK/The Bridgeman Art Library Nationality.

avenged."[156] Like Wingate before him, Churchill highlighted the contrast between the savage brutality of the Mahdists and Gordon's apparent unwillingness to take a single human life, even in self-defense. That contrast revealed the gulf that separated civilization from barbarism, a gulf that only a new British intervention in the Sudan could close. But Gordon's death, Christian and noble as it was, showed that civilization could not be restored without violence. If the martyr revealed the goodness of the nation he represented and the benevolence of its imperial rule, England's military prowess would demonstrate its power to make things right. The Sudan, Wingate said, cried out for the "delivery of her enslaved and decimated peoples," while Britain called for the restoration of its national honor.[157]

Such ideas served not only to justify the "reconquest" of the Sudan but to silence an already meager opposition to it, an opposition loudly condemned for its "utter want of patriotic feeling," complicity with Madhism's "odious tyranny," and worst of all, its "betrayal of the heroic Gordon."[158] In this context, an increasingly nationalistic imperial discourse complemented at the popular level a new post-Gladstonian aggressiveness among British elites.[159] The memory of Gordon and the aura of saintly martyrdom that surrounded him thus did much to propel British forces back into the Sudan, into those "large tracts of useless territory" that Cromer had once dismissed as too "difficult and costly to administer properly."[160] But with both the French and Leopold's Congolese increasingly active in Central and East Africa, cost seemed increasingly beside the point; England's very standing as a Great Power appeared at risk. As the *Times* put it, "Whatever the commercial and economical value of Central Africa may be, there are other reasons why England should keep herself well to the front in its partition. We cannot . . . afford to allow any section even of the Dark Continent to believe that our Imperial prestige is on the wane."[161]

Such new thinking convinced British leaders to consolidate their de facto protectorate over Egypt and, despite Gordon's defeat, to continue to regard the Sudan as territory within its sphere of influence.[162] The French rejected that view, deciding in the wake of Britain's 1885 withdrawal from Khartoum that the Sudan had become unclaimed territory. The Mahdists, with their elaborate, if dysfunctional, state, didn't count.[163] In the second half of the 1880s, French colonialists turned toward the Upper Nile, setting the stage for the Franco-British collision at Fashoda in 1898. But before that famous confrontation took place, Britain became involved in yet another failed rescue effort in the Sudan. The hero of this new adventure was Henry Morton Stanley. His own effort, the Emin Pasha Relief Expedition, took shape amid the culture of Gordon worship and martyrdom that made the Upper Nile the unlikely focus of British imperial designs and of the popular enthusiasms that helped make them what they were.

FOUR

The "Stanley Craze"

IF HENRY MORTON STANLEY ACHIEVED fame and celebrity in the wake of his "find Livingstone" mission, he became a charismatic hero in 1890 after returning to Britain from the Emin Pasha Rescue Expedition (1887–89). The press treated him as a conquering idol, lauding him and his apparent accomplishments in almost unprecedented terms. Queen Victoria sent him a personal greeting, and the prince of Wales presided over a mammoth welcome-home reception at London's cavernous Royal Albert Hall. Other members of the royal family, aristocrats, and numerous dignitaries populated the front rows. More than twenty-five hundred people, many of whom Stanley did not know, sent him telegrams and letters of congratulation, and his portrait graced the cover of every illustrated magazine. Medals were cast in his honor, biographies written, photographs taken, his wax likeness featured at Madame Tussaud's. Beginning with London, virtually every municipality in Great Britain offered him the "freedom of the city," and the Royal Geographical Society, along with practically every provincial affiliate, invited him to speak. Admirers, fans, and "celebrity tourists" mobbed him everywhere he went, grabbing him, jostling him, demanding his autograph, and just trying to glimpse the famous man. Stanley's two-volume book narrating the Emin Pasha expedition, *In Darkest Africa,* appeared simultaneously in English, French, German, Spanish, and several other languages. The England-language original sold 150,000 copies within the first few months. Already wealthy from his earlier books, Stanley now became as affluent as the aristocrats, bankers, and businessmen who extolled his heroism and manly strength.

How to explain such extraordinary popularity? What was it about Stanley and his accomplishments that gave him charisma? Unlike his quest for Dr. Livingstone and his chute down the Congo, the Emin Pasha Rescue Expedition had not, after all, been a success.[1] Emin Pasha (né Eduard Schnitzler), governor of Sudan's Equatoria province and putative object of Stanley's rescue effort, not only refused to return home with the explorer but defected to the other side, declaring his allegiance to his native Germany. Worse, Stanley came home with not a single ounce of the vast stock of valuable ivory Emin was said to possess. And his long three-year journey left behind it a well-publicized trail of cruelty, violence, and death. This grim record served only to confirm the reputation of a trigger-happy plunderer that had dogged Stanley since his Congolese expedition of the 1870s. The explorer did succeed in establishing a British commercial claim to vast areas of East Africa, but much of this region proved inaccessible to Europeans, and, besides, Germans believed the same territory belonged to them. The Anglo-German competition for these lands would soon produce a major diplomatic headache for Britain's careful Tory prime minister, Lord Salisbury.

Overall, then, Stanley's mission was an abject failure, a bitter and grueling wild goose chase that needlessly cost hundreds, perhaps thousands, of lives. By rights, Stanley should have been lucky to escape widespread condemnation in the press; instead he became the object of a worshipful "Stanley craze."[2] Stanley's biographers have tended to emphasize the short-lived nature of his fame and the criticism that followed closely on its heels.[3] But Britain's—indeed, the world's—adulation was such that it cannot be passed over so quickly, especially since it was the condemnation that did not last. Beginning in December 1889, while Stanley was still in Africa, a wave of hero worship washed over England, Scotland, and Wales, and that wave continued for nearly a year. Not until November 1890 did mainstream journalists begin to attack Stanley for his harsh comments about the two European lieutenants, Edmund Barttelot and James Jameson, who had died during the expedition. Both men had belonged to prominent families, Barttelot the son of a baronet and Jameson the scion of an Irish whiskey distiller. In each case, close relatives published books that denounced Stanley and defended the names of kinsmen they believed unfairly besmirched.[4] Although his reputation sank for a time, Stanley bounced back with the help of a loyal underling, William Bonny, who appeared to confirm Stanley's side of the story.[5] If the explorer would never regain his godlike status—and it is difficult to see how any living person could have enjoyed such adulation indefinitely—Stanley nonetheless retained his enormous fame. After a narrow electoral defeat in 1892, he won election to Parliament three years later as a Liberal-Unionist in a district traditionally hostile to this group's views. Three years after that, Queen Victoria made him a knight.

As with our other colonial heroes, we can understand Stanley's extraordinary standing as a form of charisma. Weber mostly applied this term to political and religious leaders (Napoleon, Jesus) who mesmerize their followers by virtue of quasi-divine or magical natural gifts. But the sociologist also meant it to describe individuals who "earn" their charisma through heroism, through "trials of courage, tortures, gradations of holiness and honor . . . and preparation for battle." This form of charisma, Weber wrote, is not an already existing natural endowment, "a personal gift that can be tested and proven but not transmitted and acquired," but a quality learned through an elaborate process of "education." This process usually involves "isolation from the familiar environment and from all family ties . . . asceticism, physical and psychic exercises of the most diverse forms [and] continuous testing of the level of charismatic perfection through shock, torture and mutilation."[6] The Emin Pasha Rescue Expedition appeared to fulfill all of these conditions. Press accounts emphasized the superhuman trials Stanley appeared to undergo, the tortures and deprivation, the long isolation from "civilization," the unimaginable feats of endurance and perseverance, the sheer physical prowess he seemed to display.

Although Weber does not locate this form of charisma in particular historical experiences, except to say that some ancient Hebrew warriors underwent such an education in charisma, we can see how certain widely shared perceptions in late Victorian Britain made charismatic the forms of heroism Weber describes. This was a society whose leading commentators worried about "degeneration," about the decline of the English "race" and the unraveling of British manhood in the face of a wide variety of threats. The relative peacefulness of the years after 1815, combined with growing prosperity, the feminization of family life, and the advent of emancipated women—all these phenomena appeared to threaten male power, independence, initiative, and even sexual potency. Virility itself seemed at risk and, with it, the strength and international standing of the countries for which weakened men would someday have to fight.[7] Commentators thus considered it imperative to reverse this masculine decline. One way to do so was through the charisma of manly men—soldiers, adventurers, explorers—who would inspire their male counterparts at home. Many such characters emerged from a new and highly popular literature of adventure produced by writers like Robert Louis Stevenson, Henry Rider Haggard, and Rudyard Kipling.[8] But even more important were images of real adventurers, men whose exploits took them to lands marked for imperial conquest.

Contemporary personalities like Livingstone, Gordon, and especially Stanley, European trailblazers who disappeared into the dangerous, unknown heart of Africa, loomed large as modern-day successors to the heroes of ancient and medieval myth. The references to mythical heroes resonated widely in Britain, where the Victorian era saw a revival of ancient Roman legends, chivalry, and Arthurian myths, along with a vogue for Scandinavian and Germanic folktales featuring supernatural saviors and saints. Such stories figured prominently in poetry, painting, sculpture, music, opera, and the theater.[9] The association of ancient myth and modern publicity enabled certain colonial personalities to capture the public imagination, giving them a charismatic aura that made them stand out. In the wake of the Emin Pasha expedition, Stanley returned to Britain endowed with such blinding charisma that he seemed to eclipse everyone else.

A key ingredient of that aura was a tough, fierce version of masculinity at odds with the image of male domesticity typical of British middle-class men during the early and mid-Victorian periods.[10] Throughout the first half of the nineteenth century, legions of bourgeois men, their values shaped by evangelical Protestantism, had seen the family as a "haven in a heartless world," a place of nurture and comfort to which they could retreat from the competitive, amoral marketplace of capitalist life.[11] Their wives, dubbed "angels of the home," helped them restore the moral values that the world of business had undermined. Women were thus central to that private domestic sphere, but men remained in charge. Their manliness came from their power in the home and from the seriousness, self-denial, and rectitude with which they maintained their dominant place.

In the second half of the century, male domesticity and the values that sustained it gradually evaporated, as post-Napoleonic peace and middle-class prosperity began to give way. The Crimean War and Indian Rebellion of the late 1850s revealed the potential vulnerability of the empire and even the British Isles themselves. By the 1880s, competition from France, Germany, and Russia forced Britain to aggressively defend its once unshakable standing in the world. The new, more dangerous circumstances of the late century seemed to require a different kind of man, a man endowed with the robustness, perseverance, and stoicism needed to face up to these growing threats, a man no longer defined by gentle family life but by a fierce engagement with the world.[12]

No one seemed to embody these traits more than Stanley. Thanks to his best-selling books and colorfully written newspaper dispatches, his robustness was legendary even before he went to Africa to rescue Emin Pasha. When his first newspaper dispatches from the EPRE reached British readers in 1888, they were reminded of the hero's plucky adventurousness and his superhuman ability to survive the attacks of fierce African tribes, the ravages of tropical disease, the jungle's searing heat, the terrifying dangers of the unknown. As for Stanley's perseverance, that too was the stuff of legend. He owed a large measure of his fame to the extraordinary feat of having navigated the entire length of the Congo River, an accomplishment long believed impossible.[13] During his travels of 1887–89, he seemed to top even his Congo exploit, persevering through dangers that many commentators said he would never survive. So robust was this manly man that Africans had dubbed him Bula Matari, the "breaker of rocks." Stanley was no effete intellectual, no armchair geographer idly staring at his maps. For him, geography "was ever a military and manly science, dedicated to the subjugation of wild nature; its books and maps were weapons of conquest rather than objects of contemplation."[14] Such ideas fit perfectly with notions espoused in late-nineteenth-century British public schools, namely that action, adventure, and the spirit of organized games vastly outweighed sedentary academic work.[15] By 1890, much of the press and public was ready to embrace a great new national hero, one whose manliness would set an example for the regeneration to come.[16] For a time, Henry Morton Stanley seemed perfectly to embody that role, which explains why the Emin Pasha expedition stands as the most notable voyage of his career.

Having spent the early 1880s in the Congo leading King Leopold's effort to establish a personal colony there, Stanley found himself at loose ends once the monarch no longer needed his services. He accepted a series of speaking engagements in the United States but remained ready for a new African expedition. Such an opportunity presented itself in 1886 when British journalists, joined by Stanley's businessman friend William Mackinnon, took up the cause of Emin Pasha, widely presented as a last, vulnerable holdout against a tide of Islamic fanaticism and the expansion of East African slavery.

Emin Pasha, or Eduard Schnitzler, belonged to the small stratum of nineteenth-century Europeans receptive to Turkish and Islamic societies and capable of adapting to them. A middle-class Prussian from Silesia, Emin mastered Arabic—along with several other languages—and as a young adult found himself practicing medicine in the Ottoman province of Albania in 1864. His integration, he wrote his sister, was such that "I have turned so brown that I no longer look at all like a European, and the fez and clothing of course add to my foreign appearance."[17] Schnitzler had "gone native," as British commentators would have said, "crossing over" to a non-Occidental society where he found himself more at home than he had in Germany.[18] Eventually, the ex-Silesian meandered to Khartoum in 1875, and from there to Sudan's Equatoria province a year later, when Charles "Chinese" Gordon invited him to serve as chief medical officer in Lado, the provincial capital.

Overlapping present-day Sudan, Uganda, and the Democratic Republic of Congo, Equatoria formed an oval of land flanking the uppermost reaches of the Nile. The region became known in the mid-nineteenth century for its ivory—the soft, opaque, easily fashioned kind much in demand in prosperous Victorian England.[19] If European commercial interests coveted Equatoria's ivory, British humanitarians vowed to eradicate slavery and the slave trade long central to the region's economy. These objectives dovetailed with the long-standing interest of Egypt's rulers in colonizing the Sudan. When Gordon became governor-general of that country in 1878, Emin/Schnitzler succeeded him as governor of Equatoria. By then, the province boasted a capital, Lado, with several hundred buildings, a mosque, a school, and a hospital. Agriculture prospered in the relatively mild climate, and the local peoples drawn to Lado and the other settlements began to assimilate elements of Middle Eastern culture, language, and religious observance. Still, the areas under Egyptian administration clung precariously to a narrow territory along the Nile; all traces of Emin's rule faded to nothing as the broad waters receded from view.[20]

When the Mahdists seized Khartoum in January 1885, severing all connection between Equatoria and the Lower Nile, Emin told missionaries in Buganda (Uganda today) that he was eager to join his province to the British Empire in exchange for protection from the Islamic army. This proposal received no official response, though journalists for the *Times* and other papers took it up.[21] Beginning in October 1886, a journalistic chorus, encouraged by the Royal Geographical Society and its Scottish counterpart, tried to endow Emin with some of Gordon's charismatic aura, forgetting the pasha's German origins and emphasizing his potential service to the British Empire. The *Times* dubbed the ex-Silesian "a second Gordon" whose "true heroism" would help rid the region of slavery.[22] Since large sectors of the British public and much of the press had blamed Gladstone for Gordon's death, the Liberal lion's Tory successor, Lord Salisbury, felt intense pressure to protect Emin from Gordon's fate. It is difficult to know how deeply this budding campaign resonated with the public at large, though it is likely that little had changed since huge crowds demonstrating outside 10 Downing Street had held Gladstone responsible for Gordon's "murder."[23]

The sentiments surrounding Gordon and his "noblest" lieutenant, Emin Bey (Pasha), genuine as they doubtless were, do not fully explain the interest among Britons in the governor of Equatoria. The Scottish businessman and philanthropist William Mackinnon, who ardently opposed African slavery, was eager at the same time to exploit the commercial possibilities of East Africa.[24] Mackinnon had established a successful steamship company in India, and his boats also operated in and out of Zanzibar. From there, he hoped to develop profitable commercial relations with the African interior.[25]

An effort to aid Emin Bey seemed an ideal way to do just that. Amid the loud journalistic campaign that Mackinnon and others had helped create, the "Mackinnon clan," as Stanley called it, worked through sympathizers in the Foreign Office to organize a mission on Emin's behalf. The clan argued that British interests needed to stake out an economic claim to the Great Lakes region of East Africa before the Germans did so first. The best way to accomplish this goal, Mackinnon maintained, was to have Stanley lead an expedition to Equatoria with two objectives—the protection or "rescue" of Emin and the signing of commercial treaties with local rulers between Mombasa on the coast and Equatoria in the interior.[26]

Although Salisbury's government persisted in its refusal to sponsor such an expedition, fearing a reprise of the Gordon fiasco, a compromise solution took shape. The Egyptian government, nominally independent of Great Britain, would finance half of the expedition's cost, with private investors covering the other half. (The latter hoped to recoup their initial outlay by claiming a large share of the ivory Emin was said to possess.) Under these circumstances, Salisbury could present the project as an Egyptian matter, not a British one, while giving Stanley's expedition his tacit support.[27] In this way, the government could appear mindful of public opinion while bearing no direct responsibility either for the mission itself or for Stanley's fate, should it fail. As for the Mackinnon clan, it now enjoyed the prospect of extending "British influence" across a wide swath of East Africa while laying the groundwork for the Imperial British East Africa Company, which the clan intended to set up. Modeled after the East India Company, the IBEAC would be a commercial concern with political prerogatives and an effective monopoly in the region. It would "peg out" an area the British government wanted to keep out of German hands without requiring the Foreign Office to establish a colonial administration it was unwilling to finance or defend.[28]

By early December 1886, everything seemed set, except for the route Stanley would take. Mackinnon's Emin Pasha Relief Committee assumed that the explorer would cross to the mainland from Zanzibar and then take one of three or four possible overland routes to Lake Victoria before entering Equatoria. Stanley, however, intended nothing of the kind. Ever the adventurer, he wanted to traverse uncharted territory between the Congo River and Lake Albert. Stanley thus favored a route from west to east that would take him up the Congo and then due east through a dense rain forest unknown to Europeans. This itinerary possessed the virtue for Stanley, still in King Leopold's service, of passing almost entirely through the Congo state. The monarch applauded this idea, since he hoped to attach Emin and Equatoria to his already huge colony. But the Congo route presented several problems. It was much longer and far more difficult than any eastern one, and it required an expensive boat trip from Zanzibar (which offered an ample supply of porters) around the cape and up to the Congo's mouth. This, however, is what Stanley wanted, and as leader of the operation, he had negotiated complete control. After recruiting a cadre of European officers and conducting lengthy negotiations for supplies, ammunition, and porters, first in Cairo and then in Zanzibar, Stanley set out for West Africa on February 25, 1887. The Emin Pasha Relief Expedition was under way.

Arriving at Zanzibar, the same island from which he had begun his quest for Dr. Livingstone, Stanley met with the sultan Barghash and recruited some 620 Zanzibaris to serve as porters for the mission. As for his European officers, the explorer enjoyed what seemed an embarrassment of riches. He had received more than four hundred applications for what everyone knew would be an arduous voyage. From this large pool, Stanley selected six military men and two civilians, most with experience in the colonies. The officers included Major Edmund Barttelot, Captain Robert Nelson,

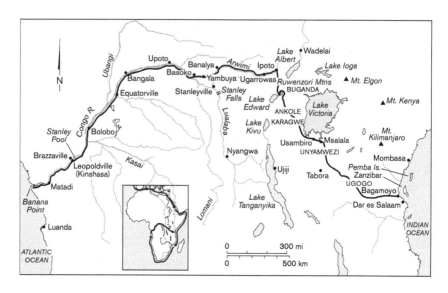

Map 3. The Emin Pasha Relief Expedition: Stanley's last African journey.

Lieutenant William Grant Stairs, and Lieutenant John Rose Troup, who had served three years in Leopold's Congo and spoke fluent Swahili. To handle the inevitable medical problems connected with African travel—malarial fevers, gastrointestinal illness, insects bites, bullet and arrow wounds, poisoning, and all the rest—Stanley engaged Dr. Thomas H. Parke, an army surgeon, and William Bonny, a former sergeant in the army medical corps. Rounding out the group were civilians James Sligo Jameson and Arthur J. Mounteney-Jephson, both of whom had bought their way into the expedition by contributing £1,000 to the Emin Pasha relief fund. Whereas Jameson had traveled extensively in South Africa, hunting big game and collecting specimens of flora and fauna, Jephson could boast no such qualifications. This young Anglo-Irish aristocrat owed his acceptance to the wealth and connections of his aunt, the countess de Noaille.[29]

The other "officer" of note was the powerful Swahili Arab ivory trader and political leader Tippu Tip.[30] Born on Zanzibar in 1840, Hamed bin Muhammed el Murjebi, also known as Tippu Tip, was the son of an Arab merchant and his Arab wife whose families had migrated in the late eighteenth century from Oman (southeastern end of the Arabian peninsula) to Zanzibar. On the island and in coastal cities like Mogadishu and Dar es Salaam, Arabs mixed with the native African peoples, creating a hybrid

Afro-Arab culture whose language was Swahili and religion Islam.[31] Tippu's grandfather had been one of the first Arabs to push into the African interior. He helped establish an Arab settlement at Tabora in present-day Tanzania, about three-quarters of the way from Zanzibar to Lake Tanganyika. Tippu's father, Muhammed bin Juma, established his own commercial base in that town, and he brought his son there in 1858, just after his eighteenth birthday.

As a young man, Tippu Tip fanned out from Tabora, trading in ivory and slaves and ultimately establishing himself as a major political force in the area between Lake Tanganyika and the Congo River. He erected his headquarters at Kasongo, in the far eastern region of what is now the Democratic Republic of Congo. When King Leopold created the Congo state in the mid-1880s, Tippu became his main African rival. In many ways the stability, even the persistence, of Leopold's colony depended on the goodwill of this "Arab potentate."[32]

Tippu Tip was equally crucial to the success of Stanley's new mission, and when the two men met in Zanzibar in February 1887, the African leader held the upper hand. In one of his often-brilliant verbal portraits, Stanley described him as

a tall, black-bearded man, of negro complexion, in the prime of life, straight and quick in his movements, a picture of energy and strength. He had a fine, intelligent face, with a nervous twitching of the eyes, and gleaming white and perfectly formed teeth. . . . This Arab was a remarkable man. . . . He was neat in his person; his clothes were of spotless white; his fez cap brand new; his waist was encircled by a rich dowel; his dagger was splendid with silver filigree work; and his tout ensemble was that of an Arab gentleman in very comfortable circumstances.[33]

The success of Stanley's expedition depended on the Arab leader's ability to procure porters to transport the mission's huge stock of supplies—largely weapons and ammunition destined for Emin Pasha's defense. In exchange for porters, Tippu would receive a healthy share of the ivory Emin was said to possess. Since Stanley intended a military-style mission, he put together an impressive arsenal: 510 Remington rifles and 100,000 rounds of ammunition; 50 Winchester repeaters with 50,000 cartridges; two tons of gunpowder; 350,000 percussion caps; and another 65,000 machine gun cartridges. In addition, the explorer became the proud owner of a Maxim Automatic Gun donated by its inventor, Hiram Maxim. This state-of-the-art machine gun could fire six hundred rounds per minute, a rate three times greater than that of any other weapon.[34] To organize the mass of people and equipment, Stanley divided his men into companies, each commanded by a British officer. As in European armies at the time, discipline would be severe, with floggings for a variety of infractions and the prospect of execution for desertion, the latter destined to be a major problem as the mission dragged on.

Beyond the arms and ammunition, Stanley purchased 27,000 yards of cloth, one and a half tons of beads, and a ton of brass, copper, and steel wire. With these items, he would buy the supplies his small army needed to survive. But if native peoples refused to sell him food at what he considered a reasonable price, or if they threatened to slow his progress, Stanley planned, as in the past, to use his superior weaponry to bend them to his will. Such tactics had earned Stanley the hostility of certain influential people back home, but this opposition would do nothing to prevent the Emin Pasha Relief Expedition from being seen as a great and noble enterprise, complete with cheering crowds to see him off.[35] Stanley's fame and status as a celebrity largely trumped the moral reservations that many of his countrymen often vocally expressed.

Setting off from Zanzibar on 24 February 1887, Stanley commanded a chartered ship loaded with many tons of weapons and supplies plus a huge and diverse personnel. In addition to 620 Zanzibari porters, the expedition included Tippu Tip and his 96-person retinue, including 35 wives and their children; 74 Sudanese and Somali soldiers; and the European officers and their personal servants. Before leaving, Stanley had telegraphed King Leopold requesting that he have a flotilla of small river steamers waiting when Stanley's ocean vessel reached the mouth of the Congo. The steamers would take the expedition one hundred miles upriver to where the Congo's cataracts begin. Apparently, the monarch never received the cables; no ships met Stanley when he arrived at Banana on the Atlantic coast. He had to cobble together water transport, forcing him to split up the expedition and delay his ascent. The voyage was off to a wobbly start.

When the crowd of more than eight hundred men, women, and children finally reassembled at Stanley Pool, the explorer learned that, contrary to Leopold's promises, the Congo state had provided not a single steamer for Stanley's use. There were no vessels to move the expedition and its cumbersome baggage up the long, wide navigable part of the Congo River, which arcs north and east for 1,000 miles. This setback, coming on the heels of the earlier one, frayed Stanley's always volatile temper, to which he subjected his European officers. Stanley took a particular disliking to Bart-telot, his second-in-command, whom he found, with some justice, unequal to his responsibilities. Stanley publicly insulted his other officers, under-mining their authority over the men they commanded, and neglected to consult them when important decisions had to be made.[36] "What sickens one of the whole thing," Jameson recorded in his diary, "is the utter dis-trust which Mr. Stanley plainly tells us he has of us all . . . it is frightfully disheartening.[37]

Stanley's bitter childhood experiences and the resulting deep scars of in-security distanced him emotionally from the Africans he encountered, as from the Europeans in his entourage. Lacking empathy and compassion, he could coolly gun down those in his way and treat harshly even those who made sacrifices on his behalf. "I never permitted myself in Africa to indulge in laudation of any act however well done."[38] Stanley's own vicious-ness set the example for his men. As Barttelot wrote, "I felt like a brute, flogging the men to get them on. . . . We have been nothing but slave-drivers since we started."[39] Still, Stanley's subordinates were military men, accustomed to harsh treatment, and, except for Barttelot, they respected— and feared—Stanley enough to give his mission a semblance of order, de-spite the early setbacks it received.

Finding no means of water transport awaiting him at Stanley Pool, the explorer had to improvise. Local missionaries possessed three steamers and four barges in various states of disrepair, all of which Stanley comman-deered over the vehement opposition of their owners. But this ragtag flotilla proved grossly inadequate to the size of his expedition, laden with heavy baggage as it was. Stanley had no choice but to divide his traveling army into several sections and deposit them along the Congo from Leopoldville to the point where the Aruwimi River branches off to the east. The com-mandeered steamers then spent the next two months, from mid-April to mid-June, ferrying hundreds of men and a measure of supplies on a nearly 1,000-mile journey each way. The ships paddled up the Congo and the Aruwimi to a fortified base station Stanley had his men build at Yambuya, a hundred miles east of the Aruwimi's juncture with the Congo (north-eastern Democratic Republic of Congo today). Small and feeble and sprout-ing with leaks, the steamers lacked the capacity to carry Stanley's heavy loads of ammunition and supplies against the river's swift current. This crucial equipment, destined for the rescue of Emin Pasha, had to be left in Leopoldville, to be transported later, Stanley hoped, to the Yambuya camp. Meanwhile, the people of this tiny village, already short of food, had no interest in sharing it with several hundred newcomers. When they resisted Stanley's efforts to settle there, he ordered his soldiers to attack. The villagers fled into the countryside, and the invaders occupied their abandoned homes.

At this point, Stanley faced a serious dilemma. He had promised to provide Tippu Tip ammunition in exchange for six hundred additional porters who would make the round-trip from the Upper Congo to Lake Albert, where he expected to meet Emin Pasha. But most of his ammunition was stranded in Leopoldville, along with many of the porters Tippu had promised. With porters and firepower in short supply and his matériel stuck 1,000 miles downriver in Leopoldville, Stanley devised a new plan for the remainder of his expedition. He decided to leave the growing number of weak, sick, and disabled people at the Yambuya base camp under Barttelot's command. This contingent would become the infamous Rear Column, whose terrible story would partly inspire Joseph Conrad's *Heart of Darkness*.[40] According to Stanley's new plan, the expedition members deposited along the Congo between Stanley Pool and the Aruwimi would gradually find their way to Yambuya, where they would join the Rear Column. While these stragglers came together, Stanley would speed on toward Lake Albert in an Advance Column composed of the fittest soldiers and carriers laden with light loads of essential goods.

In a long letter to Barttelot (24 June 1887), Stanley ordered his second-in-command to remain at the base camp until the supplies and men left in Leopoldville and other places arrived via steamer at Yambuya.[41] By that time, Stanley hoped, Tippu Tip's promised porters would also appear, and the Rear Column would set out along the trail Stanley would blaze. It could move fast, the explorer suggested, because the path would have been cut and the obstacles cleared. Barttelot could thus get to Lake Albert in time to reinforce the Advance Column and rescue Emin. Stanley appeared obsessed with the notion that he had to reach Emin Pasha as soon as possible. He feared a repeat of the Gordon debacle, when the troops sent to rescue the general arrived too late to save him from the Mahdist attack.[42] In the event that Tippu Tip failed to supply the porters, Barttelot was instructed to remain at the base camp until Stanley returned.

These instructions reassured Jameson, though not Barttelot, who adamantly protested being left behind.[43] And though more willing than his colleague to trust Stanley, Jameson was far from happy being stranded in the Congo basin. "It is peculiar," he wrote, "what a feeling of hatred the river inspires one with. One hates it as if it were a living thing—it is so treacherous and crafty, so overpowering and relentless in its force and overwhelming strength. . . . The Congo river god is an evil one."[44] Both men were right to be upset. Stanley' plan proved to be little more than wishful thinking, especially in wildly overestimating the number of porters Tippu Tip could provide. Given the paucity of carriers, it is difficult to see how Stanley would ever have been able to transport to Lake Albert the ammunition, weapons, and supplies stranded downriver at Leopoldville. Stanley's second error of judgment was to underestimate the difficulties of feeding the several hundred men confined to the base camp at Yambuya. Game had all but vanished from the region, and the lone reliable crop was manioc, a tuber with good nutritional value but poisonous when eaten uncooked. Starving members of the Rear Column often did just that, especially since they suffered from the lack of meat. The final problem was the sheer inactivity of this group. With nothing to do and no place to go—at least not until Tippu Tip's phantom porters arrived (which they never did)—demoralization set in among people already plagued by uncertainty and want. Had the Rear Column been endowed with an excellent leader, its situation might not have become as dire as it did. But Barttelot was unequal to the responsibilities Stanley had given him; his hot temper, his overt hatred of the blacks and Arabs, his festering anger over having been left behind all conspired to make a terrible situation even worse.[45]

While the horror of the Rear Column unfolded unbeknownst to Stanley, his own Advance Column pressed on toward Lake Albert. To get there from the lower Aruwimi required him to traverse the vast Ituri rain forest, a dense jungle that no European had ever explored. Stanley loved to accumulate firsts, and this would be one of his most memorable feats. The problem was that Stanley thought he could cross the forest and reach Emin Pasha within two months. Instead, it took half a year to reach the lake and another four months to encounter Emin. The crossing proved so arduous that of the 389 men who set out with Stanley in June 1887, only 169 remained when the Advance Column reached Lake Albert in December.[46] Once again, Stanley had grievously underestimated the obstacles he would face. The forest turned out to be twice as wide as he expected, its foliage thicker and more menacing than in any jungle he knew. Worse, the canopy of giant trees proved so dense that sunlight could never burn through. To enter this forest was to plunge into a twilight world of steamy tropical heat where violent rains soaked the traveler without cooling him, poisonous insects lurked behind every bush, and hidden thorns shredded the flesh, causing infection, ulcers, and death. Within this forest lived small groups of pygmies quick to defend themselves with poisoned arrows and poisoned spikes camouflaged in the tangled jungle floor. Dozens of Stanley's men succumbed to the pygmies' attacks, as a great many more pygmies fell to the bullets of his troops.

The Advance Column had left Yambuya with only a small supply of food; once in the forest, the sources of nourishment vanished almost entirely. Arab slavers had destroyed villages and forced the locals to abandon their fields. In one clearing after the other, Stanley found not a single edible crop. When he chanced upon a settlement, he was so desperate for food that he did exactly what the slavers had done, capturing women and children and holding them hostage until the men provided something to eat. Although Stanley seemed to take such tactics for granted, his officers were horrified, even sickened, by the casual cruelty he displayed. When one expedition member shot two unarmed natives attempting to flee the onslaught, Jephson wrote, "I felt sickenly *[sic]* sorry for them. . . . It was such a cruel, ruthless, unnecessary thing."[47]

As Stanley and his men penetrated further into the forest, such raids became routine. As the explorer wrote, "Even the white man does not endure hunger patiently. . . . Despite education and breeding, the white man is seldom more than twenty-four hours ahead of his black brother and barely one hundred hours in advance of the cannibal."[48] When several Africans sold their weapons for a few morsels to eat, Stanley sentenced the culprits to death, shooting one as an example to the rest. Finally, the Advance Column reached an Arab settlement, composed mainly of ivory hunters, where Stanley bargained for food and arranged to leave some fifty sick and dying men behind—despite clearly inadequate provisions to support them. Most would perish before he returned.

Stanley pressed on, his men weak with hunger and totally demoralized. He left more of the sick and dying at a second Arab village, as he and his still-healthy followers scoured desperately for food. They came so close to starvation that Stanley contemplated suicide.[49] Finally, at the end of November, the Advance Column emerged from the forest. Glimpsing sunlight for the first time in more than five months, Stanley wrote: "We emerged upon the plains, and the deadly gloomy forest was behind us. After one hundred and sixty days' continuous gloom, we saw the light of the broad day shining all around us and making all things beautiful. . . . The men literally yelled and leaped with joy."[50]

Better even than sunlight was the food. There, on the grassy plain, the Advance Column found populated villages and cultivated fields. The survivors would live, and Lake Albert loomed just two weeks' journey away. Stanley rejoiced over the prospect of finally meeting Emin Pasha, but when he arrived at the western shore, the governor did not appear. None of the locals knew his whereabouts, and no one had seen him in ages. Deeply disappointed, Stanley had to wait another four months before making contact with Emin Pasha, whom he met on 27 April 1888, with a tepid reprise of the Livingstone handshake now two decades in the past. Stanley found the governor "a small spare figure in a well-kept fez and a clean suit of snowy cotton drilling, well-ironed and of perfect fit. . . . There was not a trace . . . of ill-health or anxiety; it rather indicated good condition of body and peace of mind."[51] In fact, the contrast between Stanley's band and Emin's followers was striking. The "rescuers" had arrived half starved, dirty, and in rags, while the "rescued" seemed the picture of health and well-being. Whereas, on Stanley's first African voyage, British skeptics had claimed Livingstone had rescued him rather than vice versa, this time the reversal appeared closer to the truth. Emin issued Stanley and his men new clothing and treated them to European-quality food, drink, and tobacco of which they had been deprived since leaving Zanzibar more than a year earlier.

Despite appearances, Emin's power and authority lay in ruins. In the early 1880s, Mahdist incursions had sent Emin and his forces fleeing to the south, and subsequent rebellions and dissension among the inhabitants of Equatoria had shrunk the territory under his control even further. By 1887, when Stanley's relief expedition began, Equatoria had been reduced to a series of fragile settlements along the southernmost banks of the Nile. The huge, prosperous central African colony of Mackinnon and Leopold's dreams had all but disappeared. Although Emin enjoyed a certain comfort in his headquarters just north of Lake Albert, he had lost control over most of Equatoria; the arrival of Stanley's expedition would cost him the rest.

Legendary throughout Central Africa for his power and brutality, Stanley aroused fears of a European colonial takeover among Emin's Egyptian and Sudanese troops, whose leaders accused the pasha of collaborating in such a venture. These accusations soon reduced Emin's authority to nothing, effectively leaving him in Stanley's hands. But before ushering the deposed governor out of Africa, as the trophy of his long and grueling expedition, Stanley needed to retrieve the several hundred men he had left behind. He thus headed back toward the immense rain forest, with its menace of gloomy heat, hunger, illness, and death. En route, he caught sight of the Ruwenzori Mountains, the legendary snow-capped "Mountains of the Moon" that Ptolemy first mentioned in ancient times. No European had ever seen them—or at least realized he had. The Ruwenzoris, with several peaks more than 16,000 feet high, are cloaked in mist most of the year. They are invisible even to people close by. Although Stanley claimed to have discovered these mountains, Parke actually saw them first. The medical officer declined to contradict Stanley, and the explorer received the credit. This discovery resolved once and for all the mystery of the Nile's sources. The river's origins resided not in Lake Albert or Lake Victoria, as earlier explorers had thought, but in these snow-capped mountains, whose runoff emptied into a network of lakes and rivers out of which the great river springs.[52]

It took Stanley three full months to retrace his steps back through the forest and down the Aruwimi, where he finally rejoined the Rear Column in mid-August 1888. He had been gone fourteen months. Stanley's description of what he found there needs to be quoted in full:

> Pen cannot picture nor tongue relate the full horrors witnessed within that dreadful pest-hold. [I saw] many a hideous-looking human being, who, disfigured, bloated, marred and scarred, came, impelled by curiosity, to hear and see us who had come from the forest land east. . . . There were six dead bodies lying unburied, and the smitten living with their festers lounged in front of us by the dozen. Others worn to thin skin and staring bone from dysentery and fell anaemia, and ulcers as large as saucers, crawled about and hollowly sounded their dismal welcome. . . . I scarcely know how I endured the first few hours. . . . I heard of murder and death, of sickness and sorrow, anguish and grief. . . . I sat stupefied under a suffocating sense of despondency. . . . If I were to record all that I saw at Banalya [where he found the Rear Column] in its deep intensity of unqualified misery, it would be like stripping the bandages off a vast sloughing ulcer, striated with bleeding arteries, to the public gaze.[53]

The fourteen months the Rear Column languished at Yambuya turned out to be one of the most awful episodes in the history of European exploration. The endless sojourn there resulted in the deaths of about half of the original 271 members of the column, with many more too unfit to carry on. As for the European officers stationed there, Barttelot was shot to death as he threatened to kill an African woman; Jameson died of hematuric fever; Troup was sent home an invalid; and Ward frittered his time away on a needless 1,000-mile trip to the nearest telegraph station. Only Bonny remained. Stanley, of course, bore much of the responsibility for this disaster, though he heaped the blame on Barttelot.[54] It is extraordinary that the British press and public would not, for the most part, criticize Stanley until he had the bad grace to openly attack the two dead men, Barttelot and Jameson, not long after returning home. And even then, Stanley ultimately emerged with his reputation tarnished but still largely intact.

Having reassembled his Advance and Rear columns, Stanley set out yet again—for the third time in just over a year—to cross the Ituri rain forest. On this harrowing march, the expedition lost yet another hundred-odd men, with 124 more so sick they could barely walk. He himself lost almost a third of his body weight, dropping to a mere 127 pounds. Parke described him as "cadaverous and ragged to an extreme degree," but as a man whose intense suffering made him a hero. "I never felt so forcibly as now how much this man was sacrificing in the carrying out of a terribly heavy duty. . . . He might very well have been living in luxury" in London, but "here he was. . . . I had never before so fully believed in Stanley's unflinching earnestness of purpose and unswerving sense of duty."[55]

By mid-January 1889, Stanley had once again reached Lake Albert, only to find that Emin and Jephson had been taken captive and that Mahdists and the pasha's mutinous troops had seized much of what remained of Equatoria province. Stanley succeeded in releasing the two men, but at the cost of abandoning Equatoria for good.[56]

The denouement of this story involved another 1,200-mile trek, a three-month-long journey south and eastward from Lake Albert to the bottom of Lake Victoria, east to Tabora, and finally to Bagamoyo on the coast. On this part of the trip, which took Stanley through lands uncharted by Europeans, he signed several "treaties" on which the IBEAC would later base its claim to this region.[57] The casualties, as throughout the expedition, were horrendous. Nearly half of Emin's people died or disappeared en route, and many more would eventually succumb to illnesses and injuries they owed to the trip. As for the EPRE itself, only 210 of the 708 Zanzibaris, Somalis, and Sudanese who had set out with Stanley in February 1887 returned home thirty-four months later.[58] Many of these losses were to desertion, but most of the deserters surely died, unable to survive on their own in a Central African landscape short on food and hostile to outsiders, whether Arab, African, or European. This is, of course, to say nothing of the large number of indigenous people killed in skirmishes with Stanley's columns, their villages burned, livestock slaughtered, and cultivated fields stripped to the naked soil.

Meanwhile, Emin Pasha's Equatoria province lay in ruins, and the former governor himself literally collapsed in a heap shortly after the expedition reached Bagamoyo. Mistaking a window for a door, the nearsighted Emin fell from a second-story opening during a banquet in his and Stanley's honor. He fractured his skull and remained unconscious for twenty-four hours. After a long recovery, during which he found himself feted and lionized by representatives of his native Germany, and even by the kaiser himself, he accepted a position with a German chartered company that hoped to profit from the East African trade. The huge stock of ivory once in his possession had been looted or destroyed, ensuring that the EPRE would return to Europe empty-handed. If Emin eventually recovered physically from his fall, he never recovered emotionally from the collapse of Equatoria and of the African Eldorado he hoped it would be. Demoralized and disillusioned, he lived only another two years.

As for Stanley, he was perhaps one of the greatest survivors of all time. Not only did he complete the journey largely intact, but the news it generated made him, for a time, the most famous man in the British Isles and perhaps the world. What is more, Stanley's fame was grounded not in a superficial celebrity status, in being famous for being famous. His fame was rooted in a widespread sense of his heroism, of a manly greatness that made him an example of the courage, perseverance, and strength that British commentators widely deemed their country to need. This status became increasingly impervious to reports of the excessive violence and needless killing long associated with his African exploits and widely publicized midway through the EPRE.

Already in the mid-1870s, the influential humanitarian organizations known as Exeter Hall denounced "the murderous acts of retaliation" Stanley had committed as "unworthy of a man who went to Africa professedly as a pioneer of civilization."[59] The influential *Saturday Review* called Stanley's first Congo expedition an "outrage on a peaceful and comparatively unarmed people."[60] While under way, the EPRE evoked similarly hostile comments that alerted readers to its violence and brutality. Disgusted, the *Spectator*'s editors concluded, "It is high time, [to] insist on a radical change in the present method of exploring and settling East Africa."[61] Perhaps the most critical periodical was Henry Labouchere's *Truth*, which asked, "What benefit . . . is it to the cause of civilization that a white man should hire a vast number of carriers and undertake an expedition in which half of them die of fatigue, and some are hanged for wishing to desert, in order to force his way through tribes by burning their villages and shooting them?"[62]

When Stanley finally surfaced in Bagamoyo in December 1889, the British press widely reported the massive toll the EPRE had taken. Given this information and the attacks on the mission circulating for more than a year, it was reasonable to expect that his accomplishment, such as it was, would be greeted with at best mixed reviews. But the reality was otherwise. Almost without dissent, the press represented Stanley as a national hero, a great and extraordinary man who embodied Britain at its best. The thousands of letters Stanley received suggest that the public at large shared this view.

"Why do we revere Stanley?" as much as we do, asked an editorial in the *Morning Post*. It was because, the editor went on, the British public saw in him "the best embodiment of qualities which, while they exist in every race, are, as we hope and as we believe, more distinctive of the Anglo-Saxon strain than of any other."[63] There was no mention of the shooting of natives, the whipping and execution of porters, the horrors of the Rear Column. Rather, "the story of the enterprise of Briton's sons contains no nobler or more interesting chapter than that of the rescue of Emin Pasha by Henry Morton Stanley, the poor Welsh boy, who has already done more, with less means, than any other explorer." For this reason, "Stanley's career has a lesson in it for every British man and every British boy. That lesson is best expressed in two familiar phrases: 'Dare and do!' and 'Suffer and be strong.'" Here was the prescription for manliness that Stanley would come to represent: courageous action, endurance, and strength.[64] Stanley's greatness, added the *Leeds Mercury* four months later, resided in his "chivalrous devotion to a set purpose, [his] undaunted, indomitable courage [and] absolute disregard of what to the great mass of men are causes of failure."[65]

This is what made Stanley so important in the last years of the nineteenth century, a time of growing international rivalry, economic competition, and mounting threats to the British Empire. "The country will feel," said the *Mercury*, "that in the mere potentiality of the prestige of Stanley's name and presence, he possesses a reserve force of strength which would certainly be forthcoming in an emergency such as might not inconceivably arise at any time. It is no slight advantage for a nation engaged so deeply as

THE
EMIN PASHA RELIEF EXPEDITION

MR. H. M. STANLEY'S MARCH THROUGH THE GREAT FOREST REGION OF CENTRAL AFRICA
FROM THE CONGO TO THE NILE LAKES.
WITH SKETCHES AND DESCRIPTIONS BY OFFICERS OF THE EXPEDITION.

Figure 10. Depiction of Stanley leading the Emin Pasha Relief Expedition (*The Graphic*, 30 April 1890).

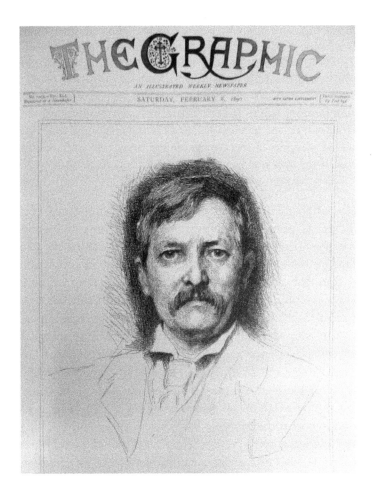

Figure 11. Portrait of H. M. Stanley (*The Graphic*, 8 February 1890).

we are in the competition for civilizing and commercial influence . . . to feel that we have Mr. Stanley on our side."[66]

The *London Times,* the paper that did not merely represent the establishment but embodied it, also sounded the theme of Stanley's exemplary power in a time of danger and uncertainty:

Men of common fiber would have been overwhelmed by such an accumulation of difficulty and disaster; but for Mr. Stanley and his gallant followers difficulties seem to have been regarded merely as incentives to fresh exertion, while disaster and suffering were powerless to daunt the indomitable spirit of men who were led by one who had never known fail-ure. It is not so much the rescue of Emin Pasha that Englishmen admire. . . . It is the magnificent display of all those qualities which men recognize as truly heroic whether they are seen on the field of battle or in the longer and more deadly conflict which these men have waged with the relentless forces of nature and of barbarism. . . . Englishmen would cease to be Englishmen and to take a just pride in the nobler and more heroic qualities of their race, if their recognition of deeds such as these and their welcome of the men who have done them did not rise to the level of a genuine national enthusiasm.[67]

While lionizing Stanley in this way, comparing him to Napoleon and Alexander, the British press took pains to emphasize not just the journalists' fervor for him but also the passionate, apparently spontaneous acclaim he received from the public at large.[68] When Stanley returned to England after a three-month detour to Cairo (January–April 1890), where he wrote his best-seller-to-be, the popular newspapers paid a great deal of attention to the crowds—crowds awaiting him at the docks of Dover, crowds lining his route to London, crowds greeting him at Victoria Station. "The streets are deserted, wrote the *Daily Telegraph*'s special correspondent, "and no wonder, for all Dover is down by the waterside, [where the hero] stands, welcomed as few foreign potentates would be hailed."[69] On Stanley's arrival in London, reported the *Morning Post,* there was "an enthusiastic popular demonstration [and] every point where observation of his movements was possible, large bodies of spectators had gathered." At Victoria Station and the surrounding streets, "some difficulty was experienced in keeping back the excited throng," which applauded Stanley with "one of the heartiest demonstrations that London has witnessed for a considerable time."[70]

Such descriptions surely depicted a reality, but they helped create one as well.[71] Newspaper readers noted the existence and apparent importance of these crowds, so elaborately and approvingly discussed that they wanted to be part of them too. As the *Morning Post*'s writer explained, "There are probably few Englishmen, or, for that matter, English-women either, who have not been stirred . . . by the news that Mr. Stanley is with us once more. Of course, we have all of us known, except that section of the com-munity if such section there be, which never sees a newspaper in this the newspaper age, that Mr. Stanley's arrival was close at hand."[72] Newspapers made Stanley's return a great event, and readers responded by rushing to witness it.

Figure 12. "The Return of Mr. H. M. Stanley" (*Illustrated London News*, 3 May 1890).

Large as the crowds became, they did not, of course, include everyone. Journalists nonetheless represented these throngs as standing in for the country as a whole. Stanley's arrival, wrote the *Daily Chronicle,* brought out a "crowd that was truly representative of the general community."[73] Or as another paper put it, "The unanimity and the sincerity [of the acclaim for Stanley] are beyond all question."[74] As we have seen with other colonial figures, the crowning of national heroes enabled the popular press not just to bring people into the streets but also to represent the public's "spontaneous, unorganized, and unsolicited expressions of popular admiration for [Stanley]" as an occasion for, and sign of, national unity.[75] These representations depicted, and perhaps evoked, Stanley's ability to counteract divisions of class, party, ideology, age, and gender.

Once the explorer installed himself in freshly appointed London rooms, he prepared for the next round of frenzied attention. Like Hollywood stars of later times, Stanley found himself surrounded by fans everywhere he went. People tried to see him, touch him, shake his hand, obtain his autograph and pieces of his clothing. He was deluged with mail, business propositions, invitations to dinner, and lucrative speaking engagements throughout the British Isles.[76] But before traveling to other parts of the realm, the first order of business was for Stanley to be officially consecrated a national hero and "lion of the season" in a series of huge receptions occupying London's largest and most prestigious locales.[77]

The first reception belonged to the Emin Pasha Relief Committee, headed by Stanley's friend and patron William Mackinnon. Held at St. James Hall, the meeting featured the prince of Wales as its chair, elaborate press coverage, and the presence "of the nobility and persons of rank and fashion."[78] A woman journalist reported that though "as a rule, ladies do not appear in full dress when they attend lectures," on this occasion "every lady wore evening dress. It was an imposing sight."[79] The *Times* called the event "a brilliant and striking scene and a display of popular enthusiasm that has been rarely paralleled."[80] When Stanley mounted the stage, his "appearance was hailed with prolonged cheering," a "loud and long display of enthusiasm" so deafening that it nearly drowned out the marching song "See the Conquering Hero Comes" vibrating on the organ.[81] His speech, a narrative account of the EPRE, evoked frequent shouts and cheers from the audience. Two nights later, it was the Royal Geographical Society's turn to fete the new national hero. The RGS had engaged the Royal Albert Hall, by far London's largest, with all 7,000 seats taken for the event. Once again, the prince of Wales and other members of the royal family joined in the celebration.[82] Behind the speaker's podium stood a huge map of Central Africa, showing the territory Stanley had covered during the grueling three-year expedition. This meeting and the one preceding it had produced such widespread interest that Stanley found himself besieged with requests for tickets—most of which he couldn't fulfill.[83]

Following these two events came several more, the excitement building each time. On 6 May, Queen Victoria received Stanley at Windsor Castle, and though she didn't broach the subject, discussions regarding a knighthood were under way.[84] The next week, London dignitaries conferred the Freedom of the City on Stanley for the second time in three years. When Stanley accepted his award, "every man and woman leapt to their feet and the kerchief waving and the cheering were renewed again and again." This welcome, wrote the *Telegraph*, "must have convinced him that pluck and perseverance are qualities as dear as ever to the inhabitants of London," dazzled by "deeds of daring such as no knight-errant of legend, no paladin of history had accomplished."[85]

Figure 13. Stanley speaking in Royal Albert Hall (*The Graphic*, 10 May 1890).

Meanwhile, Stanley received word of his selection as an honorary doctor of letters at Oxford; he would soon pocket honorary doctorates from Cambridge and the University of Edinburgh as well. At Cambridge, Stanley delivered the prestigious Rede Lecture, endowed in 1524 and given each year "by some distinguished man on some subject of science, literature, or art."[86] Such distinctions were not bad for a lowborn, semi-orphaned Welshman who had grown up in a workhouse and enjoyed very little formal schooling. "And perchance in this hour of triumph," wrote the *Daily Telegraph,* "his thoughts went back, not to the deserts and the dangers of the darkest Africa, but to that humble birthplace in Wales whence the lad with a will set forth, resolved to become a man of the world."[87] In addition to everything else, Stanley was a "self-made man," one likely even to impress the Victorian icon and author of *Self Help,* Samuel Smiles.[88]

Sandwiched among such prestigious honors and awards were several other notable events. At a banquet in Stanley's honor, the president of the Turners' Company declared: "One man like this fires the imagination of a whole century. . . . There is nothing like example to inspire the youth, and strengthen the manhood of a nation for great resolve and noble undertaking."[89] Stanley also enjoyed an exclusive dinner at the Savage Club, hosted by the adventure writer George Henty.[90] The menu for the dinner featured an image of Stanley wearing a military uniform and carrying a rifle. Next to him is a white woman representing Africa. Her breasts are naked, and Stanley reveals them by lifting up a large sheet or blanket covering her. She's wearing a long loincloth open on the side all the way to her waist. Her waistband reads AFRICA. She looks apprehensive, but not uninterested, as Stanley gazes at her, seemingly contemplating an advance.[91] The sexual imagery here requires no commentary, though it is significant that Africa takes the form of a white woman. This racial transformation suggests, perhaps, the perceived desirability of the African continent. That desire was mostly political and economic, but so powerful was the longing to possess Africa that it could seem almost erotic.

Although the British press mainly reported Stanley worship as if it had emerged completely and spontaneously from the will of the people, a great deal of evidence suggests that the quality of the reception had not been left to chance. If people from all over the British Isles responded enthusiastically to Stanley and genuinely thought him a hero and a celebrity, their responses were prompted by a sophisticated publicity campaign carefully organized before the explorer's return to England. It is unlikely that those close to Stanley deliberately delayed his return to Britain in order to whet the public appetite for him, but the three months he spent in Cairo did just that.

During the period from January to April 1890, when Stanley "returned to civilization" but not yet to the British Isles, his friends encouraged journalists and editors to build anticipation among their readers for his return. Newspaper editors received and dutifully published copies of Stanley's dispatches from the EPRE, and they narrated his adventures in one article after the other. Already in December 1889, the *Illustrated London News* ran a huge, two-page drawing of the expedition, and two months later the popular journal published a lengthy supplement devoted to the voyage.[92] The *Penny Illustrated Paper* did likewise, as did the *Daily Graphic* and its weekly cousin, the *Graphic*, which put Stanley's portrait on its cover on 8 February 1890. The *Illustrated London News*'s next special supplement was itself the focus of a newspaper article, "How I Got Stanley's Sketches"— one of myriad headlines recalling the title of Stanley's first book, *How I Found Livingstone*.[93] Not to be outdone by its illustrated competitor, the *Graphic* ran a huge double issue on the EPRE, timed to coincide with Stanley's arrival back in England.[94] This thirty-page supplement, including eighteen full or half-page drawings, sold out in two days.[95] The price was one shilling, twelve times the cost of a typical penny paper.

Meanwhile, Stanley's friends busied themselves organizing the receptions honoring him and welcoming him home. In February 1890 Francis de Winton, Stanley's former colleague in the Congo state, wrote from London asking him to say privately when he planned to come back. To build maximum interest, "we want as much time as possible, not only to make the necessary arrangements [for our events] but also to send out our invitations and arrange our seats."[96] The prince of Wales, Winton said, was eager to preside over the principal event but needed to know the dates, and the RGS hoped to book the Royal Albert Hall, "the largest place we can find."[97] The Emin Pasha Relief Committee proposed, Winton wrote, "to fill that building and give you such a reception as can be equaled by few and excelled by none." Meanwhile, provincial geographical societies prepared their own receptions and medals, always in consultation with their hero, and Moberly Bell, managing director of the *Times*, arranged for Stanley to dine with the paper's powerful owner, A. F. Walter.[98]

While these negotiations proceeded, Stanley's editor, Edward Marston, undertook elaborate preparations for the publication of the explorer's book, for which the editor had very large plans. Marston traveled to Cairo in late January 1890, when Stanley began writing and stayed there almost until the explorer finished two months later. The editor hoped to profit not just from the sales of Stanley's book but also from a volume of his own, *How Stanley Wrote "In Darkest Africa."*[99] In this account, Marston describes his author's extraordinary endurance in writing his book, endurance he likens, not without some justice, to Stanley's African feats. The explorer sat down to write on 25 January and worked at the rate of 8,000 words, or about thirty typescript pages, a day. After fifty days, the two-volume, 1,000-page book was done. During this time, Stanley labored from 8 A.M. until midnight, rarely stopping, even to eat, and sleeping just five hours a night.[100] His only breaks were to respond to the hundreds of telegrams and letters he received every week. "Every mail," Marston wrote, "brought Stanley shoals of letters from all sorts and conditions of men, women, and children, and from all parts of the world; and his courier was besieged by numbers of total strangers ready to bribe him to any extent if only he could arrange for them to get even a glance at him."[101]

Although the editor complained that Stanley's marathon pace would ruin his health, both men wanted the book to come out quickly. Before the EPRE began, Stanley had required each of his European officers to sign an agreement promising not to publish anything about the expedition until six months after the leader's own book appeared. Both the explorer and his editor knew that the faster their book came out, the more likely others would respect the letter of this agreement. Marston also understood the importance of having the volume appear shortly after Stanley returned to Britain, when his fame was likely to be at its height. And while neither man admitted as much, both had to know that given the controversies that had already erupted over the Rear Column, the violence and death toll of the expedition, and its meager practical results, Stanley's reputation might suffer when other narratives came out. Speed was therefore of the essence, and Marston moved heaven and earth to publish the volumes in record time. An international army of copyeditors, typesetters, pressmen, bookbinders, and translators, among many others, worked round the clock to have tens of thousands of books in twelve languages ready for the marketplace on exactly the same date, 28 June 1890. This was just two months after Stanley finished writing his work.[102]

Marston's strategy of simultaneous publication maximized sales by preempting bootleg translations and unauthorized versions of the book.[103] The first edition, thought to be the largest ever in British publishing history, sold out within a week, as did a fancy two-guinea (£2.1) printing, whose price exceeded the weekly earnings of Britain's best-paid working-men.[104] A deluxe version priced at £10 doubled in value on the secondary market after just a few days. All told, readers in Britain and the United States bought a record 150,000 copies within the first several weeks.[105] We have no sales numbers for the nine different continental European editions, or the ones published in Russian or Arabic, but the widespread commentary about the book throughout the continent suggests that it did unusually well.[106]

Once published, *In Darkest Africa* enjoyed adulatory attention from reviewers almost everywhere. Although the various commentaries dutifully summarized Stanley's narrative, most focused on the author-adventurer himself—as if the man loomed so large that he overshadowed even his own book. "Large as the subject is," wrote the reviewer for *Blackwood's Magazine,* "our attention is constantly diverted to the commanding figure of the explorer himself, whose indomitable energy, decision of character, and rigid will have achieved such a victory over nature's sternest and most primitive forces." The man himself, added the writer, "provokes an enthusiasm which, casting a glamour over sober criticism, makes us diffident of dealing with such a personality according to the ordinary canons of judgment." For this reviewer, Stanley "is a Napoleon" whose only flaw, and it is a large one, is his intolerance of error and failure and of any obstacles he sees. This intolerance extends, the writer says, to his own shortcomings, which he cannot acknowledge and for which others are made to suffer.[107] Like many other commentators, the *Blackwood's* writer suggested that such flaws were part and parcel of what made Stanley great; without them, he would not have fashioned himself "the strongest man of our day," a man "to whose future the world cannot but look with a special hopefulness."[108] For, despite Stanley's harsh intolerance, his rash will to act regardless of the consequences—or because of those qualities—Stanley held "the unrivalled honor of being, among living men, the one who has done most to bring millions of the oppressed into helpful communication with their more favored brethren."[109] The ends of civilization, the reviewer maintained, justify the often-brutal means Stanley employed—a position not uncommon, even among those highly critical of Stanley's methods.

Virtually all of Stanley's reviewers joined their *Blackwood's* colleague in emphasizing the explorer's manliness, his Napoleonic "will of steel and personal courage." What a *Times* commentator liked best of all was the virility of Stanley's literary style, the "direct, vigorous, and incisive" narrative, which exuded the confidence of a "man of action rather than a man of letters."[110]

Even Stanley's religiosity, much on display in his book, mirrored the manly "muscular Christianity" popular among imperialists of the late nineteenth century. Stanley's was "the religion of a fighting, confident people, reverencing duty, as they conceive it, fearless of all else, by no means willing to turn the [other] cheek."[111] Emin Pasha, by contrast, unchristian and irreligious, "erred through amiability," declared *Queen, the Lady's Newspaper.* He ignored "the fact that semi-barbarous races cannot be ruled by kindness alone."[112] Stanley had himself contrasted his own manly bearing with Emin's feminine airs. The pasha reminded him of a "model housewife," with his "painfully clean and dainty . . . habits," his "delicate and slender fingers . . . naturally fitted for delicate and dainty tasks."[113]

Although it was not uncommon for Stanley's reviewers to mention his flaws of character and personality, if only to downplay them as essential to his greatness, a *Times* critic restricted himself to hyperbolic praise: Stanley told his tale "with so genuine a modesty of temper, so transparent a fidelity to fact, so generous and eager a desire [to give] praise and recognition to each and all of his subordinates," including the Africans, "that the critic's task becomes merely one of unstinted admiration." This comment is almost laughably false. With Stanley's long history of putting himself at the center of every story, "modesty of temper" hardly stood as one of his attributes. As to "fidelity of fact" and "recognition of his subordinates," they rank among the last of Stanley's qualities. These realities should have been clear from early reports published in the *Times,* which, by themselves, might have encouraged the reviewer to moderate his conclusion that Stanley's "inexhaustible patience, forbearance, and consideration for the feelings and failings of others [have] placed him high in the ranks of heroes and leaders of men."[114]

If all this extravagant praise and all the receptions, dinners, speeches, medals, and honorary degrees had not already made Stanley famous enough, with his engagement to Dorothy Tennant, announced just two weeks after his return from Africa, he eclipsed every other star in the firmament of celebrity. If anything, the media frenzy over the explorer's impending marriage promised to overshadow even his African exploits.

Like most of those who explored Africa and other distant lands, Stanley was hardly a ladies' man. His gnawing insecurity made him tongue-tied around women and uncomfortable at dinners or other gatherings where he might have attracted members of the opposite sex. Besides, as Stanley's recent biographers have pointed out, it is difficult to find evidence of any physical attraction to women, though there are ample indications of his interest in men and especially boys.[115] No writer has found evidence of sexual relations with men, and the greatest likelihood is that, like many a good Victorian, he repressed or sublimated his homosexual tendencies and lived an uncarnal life. But Stanley, a loner by nature rather than choice, wanted companionship, and for that he needed a wife.

At a dinner party in 1885, he met Dorothy Tennant, who hailed from an artistic and intellectual family and claimed Oliver Cromwell as one of her ancestors. When Stanley first proposed to her—in writing—she turned him down. But while he was away in Africa from 1887 to 1890, Dolly changed her mind. Her letter asking to renew their relationship awaited him at home. Still smarting from the earlier rejection, however, Stanley took up bachelor quarters in London and coldly refused. Dolly persisted, and on 16 May the unlikely couple—he a misanthropic traveler of humble origins, she a cultivated artist of good family—announced their engagement.[116] With it, the press's obsession over Stanley, already slackening a bit, received a new and sensational jolt. The lion of Africa and hero of the civilized world now became a leading man and romantic hero as well. London's journalists, eager for fresh copy on Stanley, went to town. The actual facts mattered little; it was the romance that counted.

The *Pall Mall Gazette,* long the paper of record for London's clubbable elite, quickly made the story its own. "Few people would suspect," an editorial writer declared, "that Mr. Stanley, the man of iron, could be the hero of a romance as touching as anything in fiction. But the true story of Miss Dorothy Tennant's engagement to Mr. Stanley will appeal to the heart of every woman in the land, for it is a veritable romance in real life."[117] This romance the *Gazette* hastened to invent. The couple, it said, had fallen in love and become secretly engaged before Stanley left on the EPRE. "During those terrible three years Miss Tennant has waited for her lover. Times without number came the news of his death, and for many dreary months, the news was full of terrible rumors of his fate. Now he had died like a dog in a fetid African swamp, now he had been slain by blacks, now he was caged up in Khartoum. Such was the only news which came to this courageous woman, whose sufferings in all this terrible time may be left to the imagination."

This concocted, romanticized story of the Stanley-Tennant courtship gained wide acceptance for reasons the *Scotsman* explained:

The public is a kindly and warm-hearted creature. It dearly loves a romance, especially a romance through which there is drawn the golden thread of love, and which ends in a peal of wedding bells. . . . This has been the orthodox ending of tales of real and feigned romance and the ideal recompense of valor and of constancy ever since it has been the nature of men to go forth in search of adventure, and of women to love them for the dangers they have passed. There is every reason to believe that he has won what has been described as the chief prize of life—a wife worthy of a man's utmost love, honor, and cherishing—a "perfect woman nobly planned."[118]

At the end of the nineteenth century, British newspaper readers were far from immune to seeing their heroes as chivalrous knights, valiant men whose daring deeds and selfless service won them the fair maiden's hand. If critics routinely found "the fiction of Mr. Rider Haggard . . . less exciting than [Stanley's] true tale," now they and their readers could see the explorer's quest for Dolly Tennant as an even better, real-life version of Robert Louis Stevenson's most romantic work. His enormously popular medieval romance, *The Black Arrow,* had appeared just two years earlier.[119] Such medieval resonances figured prominently in poems written to Stanley, especially those submitted for a contest sponsored by the *New York Herald*'s London edition and by the *Globe.* In "Welcome to H. M. Stanley," an amateur poet wrote:

> Welcome, hero, traveler, sage
> . . . .
> From the darkest African gloom,
> Where the stoutest well might quail,
> Fearless, stainless, "Wanderer-Knight,"
> Proudly now we bid you hail!
> . . . .
> An honest, valiant, kindred heart,
> A kingly hero of the crowd.[120]

As soon as Stanley and Tennant announced their engagement, telegrams and letters of congratulations began to pour in. Many, of course, came from their friends and acquaintances, but hundreds of people unknown to either wrote them as well.[121] A huge number asked for tickets to the wedding, which, like the marriages of princes and noblemen, would be held at Westminster Abbey. Large as the Abbey is, some five thousand ticket requests had to be denied.[122] Accompanying these letters was a vast array of wedding gifts, the majority from people the couple didn't know.[123]

Figure 14. "Mr. Stanley's Wedding—The Ceremony in Westminster Abbey" (*Illustrated London News,* 19 July 1890).

Coverage of the wedding began almost as soon as the engagement was announced. Journalists endlessly described Dorothy Tennant, usually making her younger and prettier than she was.[124] As for the marriage itself, newspapers routinely likened it to a royal wedding, calling Dolly "a queenly bride."[125] Everyone knew that the queen had given Dolly a bejeweled locket as her present. And journalists marveled at the stature of the guests—"many of the most notable people in the land." Not even "royalty," it was said, "could have been more observed on its marriage day."[126] The event became, wrote *Country Gentleman,* "the apotheosis of Stanley worship."[127]

As usual, the newspapers focused on the crowds—the crowds blocking the streets surrounding the Abbey, the crowds trying to get inside, the crowds craning a collective neck to catch a glimpse of the bride and groom. "The public," explained the *Scotsman,* "has insisted on being present, in spirit, and, as far as space could admit, in body. . . . It has made Mr. Stanley's private happiness and good fortune its own concern."[128] Stanley's fame was such that a great many people from all walks of life, people "of high and low degree," wanted to participate in his life.[129]

If they had enjoyed an "intimacy at a distance" with Stanley, they now wanted that distance to shrink—by force, if necessary: "When the north transept, which was given over to the general public, was thrown open, the crowd moved forward like an irresistible torrent, and in a very short time not an inch of space remained unoccupied."[130] Reporters described the hordes of spectators blocking the path of people holding tickets and the pushing and shoving that ensued. Even the best-dressed ladies tried to elbow their competition aside. "Into this space [the north transept]," wrote the *Scotsman*, "the fashionable ladies outside made the most determined efforts to come." Overwhelmed, police officers "had literally to turn their backs upon the ladies to prevent an utter collapse of discipline." Only with great difficulty did the bobbies begin to clear a path, soon to be stymied once again. One "stout middle-aged lady in purple . . . proved an insurmountable obstacle," and the "unhappy officer . . . had to retire beaten from the field."[131]

This popular mania for the celebrated explorer, this "Stanley craze," expressed itself not only in the crowds assembled at his public events but also in the thousands of unsolicited letters he received. A great many people participated vicariously and often emotionally in Stanley's life; they thought about him, worried about him, prayed for him, and exalted in his fame. "Not once," wrote one G. Mont, "but a thousand times we spoke of you, and prayed for you, when countless hearts throbbed with fear at your possible fate . . . but we are glad and rejoice again at your triumphal return and glorious success, proving yourself as always a Man, a Christian, and a hero. . . . We rank you with Bonaparte and Columbus and we greedily devour every scrap of information published about you."[132] Stanley's correspondents regularly identified him with the French emperor and other legendary men; as a Mr. Burt commented, "One feels inclined somehow to leave out the *Mr* . . . when speaking of the immortals."[133] In letter after letter, Stanley's fans told him how much he meant to them. "We are personally unknown to you," wrote H. S. Burcombe. "Still, we take—and have taken—a very very deep interest in your welfare and career past, present, and future."[134] Although Stanley's correspondents seldom explicitly praised his role in extending the British Empire, they routinely extolled his service to "civilization," his "great and glorious work for England and the English race."[135]

Many of the letters are religious in tone. Correspondents had prayed for Stanley's safe return, and God had answered their prayers, thus confirming their faith. "No one thanked God more heartily [than I] when at last you arrived safely from all those perils."[136] Or, as another "stranger" wrote: "Whilst you have been away this time in the Dark Continent, it has been my usual custom, particularly during the last year or two, that I pray for you (often by name) every Sunday morning in our family worship. . . . Rest assured that in any work which may yet lie before you, you will be supported by the prayers of many whom you do not know."[137] More than a few religiously oriented writers saw Stanley as a martyr who "suffered and endured for Africa" at God's behest.[138]

Amid this vast pile of letters, there were many whose writers saw Stanley simply and primarily as a star, albeit one that shined very bright. Beyond tickets to his speeches and wedding, people wanted his autograph, his portrait, or something belonging to him. "I have never forgotten," wrote Amy Skirm, "the splendid photograph you so kindly gave me with your autograph in 1886. I greet it *daily,* as it has never been out of our sight."[139] One Thomas Minton had made a sculpture of Stanley, which he wanted him to autograph, and another writer offered him a "fancy price" for the actual "cap you wore through Africa."[140] Meanwhile, several correspondents said they had named newborn sons after him, and others would have, had they not given birth to a girl.[141] Some wrote on behalf of their children, as did J. E. Viles, whose eleven-year-old daughter Violet said on witnessing Stanley's arrival at Victoria Station, "Seeing Mr. Stanley was better than all we had seen at the South Kensington National History Museum (where we had been that same afternoon)."[142] Another eleven-year-old girl wrote Stanley on her own: "It was very kind of you to go through such perils to rescue Emin Pasha."[143] Other correspondents sent poetry, asked to meet the explorer, wanted him to endorse their products, or simply expressed admiration. His acquaintances asked to see him, hear from him, and deluged him with dinner invitations. Those who knew him best promised to spare him the demands of society by not inviting anyone else.[144]

Stanley had become so famous that friends and sympathetic journalists worried that the demands of his fans and admirers would wear him out. A leader (editorial) in the *Daily Telegraph* complained: "He is never, apparently, during his waking hours left to himself. . . . [His admirers] should remember, in the fervor of their hero worship, that the hero, after all, is a man—even though he be a Stanley."[145] We know from the explorer's unpublished journals that he himself possessed mixed feelings about his fame. On the one hand, he clearly sought it, since he wrote his books to sell widely and appeared frequently in public, giving speeches, accepting awards, and cooperating actively with those who sought to gain maximum publicity for his views. Stanley's humble origins and the slights he had endured after finding Livingstone doubtless impelled him to prove his worth, both to himself and others. But powerful as these impulses were, he suffered from them. The limelight made him uncomfortable, for he was oversensitive and feared new forms of dismissal and contempt. He lacked basic social graces, especially the ability to banter and chat. He knew how to command, but not to persuade, preferring monologue to dialogue, and he found himself ill at ease when surrounded by people whose standing equaled or exceeded his own.

Shortly after completing the EPRE, having received telegrams of congratulations from Queen Victoria, Kaiser Wilhelm II, the president of the United States, the khedive of Egypt, and many other dignitaries, Stanley composed a long, rambling journal entry on the perils of fame.[146] This entry, never published and clearly not intended for publication, reveals a great deal about him—his blinding self-deception, his misanthropic contempt for other people, his inability to overcome what Freudians would call his "narcissistic wounds," even those inflicted decades in the past.[147] "I dread," he wrote, "undergoing what the above cablegrams [from the queen, the president, and the others] portend. Some men are born with a taste for this kind of glory. Nature, education, habit have fitted them to receive it gratefully. But my feelings are decidedly averse from it." He explains how much he dislikes the receptions and banquets to which he will have to submit, the need to sip wine and gorge himself on fancy meals, "to listen to talk which has no interest for me, smile and bow to the reiterated compliments a hundred times," to waste money on elegant clothes and travel by cab. All this burdens him to no end, but "Society says with a smile 'you must bear the penalties of greatness' . . . and throws a silken leash round my neck."[148]

Reading these lines, one would think Stanley had no choice but to submit to an endless number of banquets and receptions in his honor. But as Gordon's example shows, nothing compelled him to attend so many events or to write "sensational" books that attracted a great deal of attention while inevitably evoking a measure of anger, hostility, and contempt. (Florence Nightingale famously called his Livingstone volume "the very worst book on the very best subject.")[149] In fact, Stanley found himself at once drawn to the attention his countrymen offered and repelled by it. He craved the recognition, praise, and encouragement denied him early in his life, but that very denial had lodged in him the feeling that he did not deserve, or could not live up to, the compliments raining down on him. As Stanley confided to his diary, "[A] reference to me from any Geographer [upper case in orig.] . . . or jealous journalist, however disguised by words, [betrayed] a strange undercurrent of hostility." These people "blew the trumpet of my fame loudly, but I had an intimate conviction it was disdain" that they truly felt.[150]

He goes on to rehearse the indignities he suffered nearly twenty years earlier following the Livingstone mission, when English commentators turned his "fame into the vulgarist disgrace," when the newspapers called him a "villain, forger, and pirate."[151] Tellingly, he neglects to mention the extent to which powerful, important people took his side, ultimately vindicating him and setting the stage for his brilliant career as an explorer. In the end, Stanley vanquished the gentlemen geographers of the RGS who had belittled him and refused, at first, to acknowledge his accomplishment. But in Stanley's psyche, only the original insult counted; it appeared to confirm what Stanley most feared about himself, namely that he was indeed unworthy of praise and incapable of genuine success. Why else would the slights he had experienced so long ago still be so fresh in his mind—especially given the vast recognition he had earned in the intervening years?

The contempt that Stanley perceived in others was an emotion in which he himself frequently indulged. People, he said, wrote to him, came up to him, stalked him on the street, not because they admired him but because they wanted something from him, usually money. "My life was made a torment by the heaps of letters brought by each post [from people who] appeared to know me, and would give me no peace until I had appeased their itching palms with silver, frequently with gold." Speaking of women, this lonely man who craved their companionship if perhaps not their sexual attentions, heaped contempt on "these women [who] haunted me for years," forcing him to "request the hotel people to eject them, so fierce were they for my embraces." On the street, his life "was made a burden for the photographers. Shop windows were littered with my portraits, and some sharp fellows were certain to recognize me, [making] the street no longer possible for me."[152]

Contemptuous as Stanley was, his complaints about the perils of fame do not seem entirely out of place. Celebrated men and women have often felt haunted by their fame, besieged by their fans.[153] And it is true that fans do indeed desire something from them. But only rarely do they want money; what they crave is exactly what Stanley craved: recognition, acknowledgment, and a sense of appreciation. Stanley's women stalkers sought not to sleep with him, as he feared, but to have him return a measure of the affection they felt for him.[154] The same is true of most of the others who sought his notice. As we have seen from the plethora of letters he received, Stanley played a large role in the emotional lives of a great many people. Most expected no reciprocity, but more than a few wanted some emotional engagement from him in return.

In his long soliloquy on fame, Stanley reserved his most bitter remarks for the press, the institution that arguably made him what he was. "In my younger days," he writes, "I used to think that it would be sufficient fame to see my name in print in the *New York Herald,* but now that I am close on 50, I have been able to fill 14 large volumes of newspaper cuttings on myself. I would willingly give them all for a day of that boyhood when I was blissfully obscure. I once thought that a Press notice of me was 'Immortality,' but alas! I have found that that kind of 'Immortality' means only abject slavery."[155] What an amazing comment from someone about to be hero-worshipped by the press, his earlier sins all but ignored, the failure and disappointment—to say nothing of the violence and cruelty—of the EPRE largely overlooked! And if those newspaper clippings were so painful to him, so much the sign of his "abject slavery," why did he continue to fill volume after volume with them, including several large ones on the EPRE?[156] It is true that a part of the press would ultimately turn on him, at least for a time, but it did so largely because of the "scandal" he himself would needlessly create.

While Stanley fulminated in private about the problem of fame and the press, several prominent newspapers and journalists examined the issue in their columns. The "Stanley craze" was so all-embracing, so widespread, and so rare for someone of his humble background that it seemed to say something important about modern life—or at least about what we now call the mass media. Stanley, himself a product of modern journalism in more ways than one, moved the press to reflect on itself. The most interesting reflections came from William Stead's *Pall Mall Gazette,* whose editorials ranked among the most influential of any British newspaper. "Though Mr. Stanley's strength of purpose and devotion to duty have been the main factors in his success, he nevertheless owes much to an agency which is one of the peculiar forces of the present age. Mr. Stanley is essentially a newspaper man. He is a hero in his own right; but he is also a celebrity by grace of the newspapers."[157] The distinction here between heroism and celebrity is interesting. It suggests that heroism is a quality an individual attains for himself, something objective and clear, while celebrity comes from sources outside the man or woman; it is an invention of the modern world and, in particular, of the press. Still, no sooner did the *Gazette* distinguish heroism from celebrity than it blurred the difference. Stanley "has done things, great in themselves; but he has always had the breath of the public prints to spread the report of them abroad. He himself has always been the centre, so to say, of what he has done." Stanley's greatness, the *Gazette* suggested, had always been linked to publicity about it, publicity his own journalism had helped create. Stanley's skill in spinning news narratives around himself constituted his most distinctive contribution to modern journalism. Some twenty years after he pioneered this approach, the *Pall Mall Gazette* invoked it to explain the "Stanley craze."

Stanley's celebrity wasn't just his own doing, of course. It required the complicity of his fellow journalists, who, the *Gazette* said, "have seized on the man so mercilessly that his personality has sometimes been in danger of overshadowing his deeds." With this comment, we come to an apt understanding of celebrity, for the nineteenth century as for the twenty-first. Celebrities are people who have often done noteworthy, even great, things but whose deeds have shrunk in importance relative to the "frenzy of renown" that diverts attention away from their accomplishments and toward their personalities and personal lives.[158] It was precisely this diversion that Stanley's own journalism helped to produce, even as he deplored its effects.

If the *Pall Mall Gazette* reveled in the newfound power of the press, especially as arbiter of celebrity and fame, some of its writers wearied of the Stanley craze. A verse entitled "The Old, Old Strain (Or too much Stanley)" expressed the exasperation certain sophisticates felt:

> From the breaking of the morning till the setting of the sun,
> [The Constant Reader]
> Sees and hears of nothing but what Stanley's said or done.
> He takes the morning paper, and he searches it for news—
> He learns that Mr. Stanley must some social feed refuse.
> . . . .
> He opens then a "monthly" that for favor makes a bid—
> Its pages but relate the things that Mr. Stanley did.
> Enraged, he buys a "weekly" that by politics is led—
> Its columns simply catalogue what Mr. Stanley said.[159]

After a solid month of all Stanley all the time, some dissenters had had enough. "We are heartedly tired of the Stanley craze," announced the satirical journal *Moonshine,* while *Truth,* long a critic of Stanley's methods, declared it time to "Ring down the curtain!"[160] Anticipating Andy Warhol, *Punch* reassured these critics that Stanley's star would quickly fade. "Mr. Stanley, Mr. Stanley, / You have been a nine days' wonder / But already it would seem, sir, / You are destined to go under."[161] The ditty was droll, but Stanley would not go away. When the press finally tired of feting him, he gave it the delicious opportunity to skin him alive. In October 1890, the "Stanley craze" turned into the "Stanley Scandal."[162] Indulging their dislike of Stanley, most recent historians and biographers have emphasized the scandal and downplayed the fete. In fact, both constitute the two-sided coin of Stanley's fame.[163]

Until October 1890, Stanley enjoyed the exclusive right to tell the EPRE story in print.[164] *In Darkest Africa* blames Barttelot and the other Europeans left behind at Yambuya for the Rear Column disaster. Perusing Stanley's book, John Rose Troup found himself "much pained by reading most inaccurate accounts." So was Barttelot's family, who published the major's posthumous memoir in late October, shortly before Troup's own book came out. Both accounts charged Stanley with a major error of judgment in dividing his expedition into two columns and leaving the sick and disabled behind. Both Barttelot and Troup claimed Stanley had negligently sacrificed hundreds of lives in an effort to reserve all the glory for himself while fraudulently enriching his friend William Mackinnon.

The publication of these two volumes produced a whole new Stanley sensation, and now the different newspapers insisted that Stanley respond. What could be better than a huge dustup over Stanley and a press scandal that threatened to bring the hero down? The machinery of scandal resembled the production of celebrity, only with scandal, the famous and powerful no longer held the upper hand. Celebrity status was a fragile thing; what "public opinion" could give, it could just as easily take away.[165]

Situations like these showed Stanley at his worst. He had always been thin-skinned, and he responded to criticism with anger and contempt. His curt, hostile answers to the Barttelot family's charges earned him further condemnation for attacking a dead man. Journalists demanded that the explorer cancel the lucrative American lecture tour scheduled for the winter and spring of 1890–91; with Stanley far away, it would be difficult to keep the scandal alive. But the explorer had no intention of forfeiting a tour that would ultimately earn him $60,000, or about 1.2 million in today's dollars. Before leaving London, Stanley told the *New York Herald* that he knew what had really happened to the Rear Column but had refrained from revealing it in his book out of consideration for Barttelot's and Jameson's families. He hinted that both men had been guilty of terrible crimes and that they had sought to protect themselves by blaming him.

These remarks kept the press in high lather as the different newspapers summarized the charges and countercharges, criticizing Stanley anew for impugning the honor of two men who could do no more than turn in their graves.[166] The attacks confirmed Stanley's hostile feeling toward the press and his belief that "society" would never accept him. As he confided to his journal, "I could scarcely have expected anything else than abuse from the English Press. . . . Throughout the length of Great Britain no name is more reviled than mine."[167]

Stanley exaggerates here, especially since much of the press would soon return to his side. It would do so thanks to the one EPRE member who had yet to speak in public, William Bonny. After the expedition, Stanley had befriended Bonny, whom he hadn't much appreciated during the journey itself. In return, the junior officer leapt to his leader's defense. He told journalists that Stanley was right to blame Barttelot and Jameson, since both had behaved with sadistic cruelty, beating and stabbing Africans to death and showing nothing but contempt for those in their charge. Barttelot, Bonny declared, had caused his own death by pointing a gun at an African soldier's wife. The man, Sanga, shot the major to prevent her from being killed.[168] Turning to Jameson, Bonny resurrected the story of his deceased colleague's role in an act of cannibalism and Jameson's coldly dispassionate account of the killing and eating of a ten-year-old girl. At this point the *Times* piled it on, reprinting an 1888 account of Jameson's behavior written by Assad Farran, the expedition's Syrian interpreter.[169] Commentators had mostly dismissed that account when it first appeared, but now they took it seriously. The result of these new testimonies was to discredit Barttelot and Jameson and restore the balance of journalistic judgment in Stanley's favor. Papers like the *Globe* that had harshly condemned Stanley in October, now, three weeks later, took his side. If the explorer had acted rashly and made some mistakes, the editor said, nothing he did could be compared with Jameson's role in a cannibals' feast.[170]

The result, as one paper put it, was that "Mr. Stanley has come out of his squabble with Major Barttelot's family with flying colors."[171] Although Stanley's reputation would never quite return to its pre-scandal heights, he remained an immensely popular—and celebrated—personality. Over the next two years, his journal notes again and again the public's fervent interest in him, the audiences "very kindly disposed," "extremely appreciative," "splendid and kindly," "enthusiastic." Never inclined to exaggerate the quality of his reception, he reported packed lecture halls and good net earnings.[172] Invited to Wales, he found the crowds so enthusiastic that he feared for his safety. "I felt hands touch my coat, then, getting bolder, they rubbed me on the back, stroked my hair, and, finally, thumped me hard, until I felt that the honors were getting so weighty I should die if they continued long." When he spoke near his birthplace in June 1891, the popular frenzy reached such proportions that officials had to charter eight special trains to bring ticket holders to his talk.[173] Such experiences evoked another long journal entry on the "'penalties of fame'—Curious lookers-on [who] keep incessant watch over our car," the crowds that "mob me at the stage door every night," the fans who "follow me in the street," the "fellow who will dart forward and clutch my hand."[174] If Stanley hated and feared the crowds he always drew, he clearly depended on them and craved their applause. Though he didn't need the money, he continued to lecture at a frenetic pace. His fans wanted to get close to him, while he sought to keep them at arm's length. But he wanted them there just the same and traveled great distances to bask in their love.

There would never be another Stanley craze, but in 1895 the prematurely aged explorer won election to Parliament, and in 1898 the queen made him a knight.[175] His fellow Victorians proved far more drawn to him than repelled by his violent methods and disregard for African lives. And even if most Britons did not explicitly link him to their expanding empire, evidence strongly suggests that Stanley's fame directly affected British colonial policy. After the Emin Pasha expedition, the explorer enjoyed such public support that Prime Minister Salisbury found himself forced to confront Germany over African lands the Tory leader considered of little interest but that Stanley sought to bring under British rule.[176]

More than perhaps any British political figure or intellectual proponent of empire, Stanley turned his compatriots toward Africa, a continent he had opened to Britain's colonial embrace. In doing so, he had helped focus his compatriots' attention on the mounting conflict with France while forging a kind of social unity at home. If his rivalry with Brazza had personified the cross-Channel competition, a new opposition between the Englishman Herbert Horatio Kitchener and the Frenchman Jean-Baptiste Marchand would show just how central—both for foreign and domestic politics—the scramble for Africa had become. Such was especially true of France, a country threatened in the late 1890s with civil war.

FIVE

Jean-Baptiste Marchand, Fashoda, and the Dreyfus Affair

DURING ONE "BLOODY WEEK" IN the late spring of 1899, the Dreyfus Affair threatened to split France apart.[1] Two apparently contradictory judicial decisions placed France's highest courts on both sides of the case, widening the gulf between Dreyfusards and anti-Dreyfusards and sending both groups into the streets. The case had agitated the country since Captain Alfred Dreyfus, a rare Jewish member of the army's General Staff, found himself sentenced to Devil's Island for espionage. The charges against Dreyfus were false, and anti-Semitism had played no small part in both the accusation of treason and the solitary confinement and other harsh punishments he endured. By 1899, impartial observers could see that the Jewish captain had been framed and that the actual spy was another man. Even so, most military leaders, government officials, and pundits of the right opposed all efforts to absolve Dreyfus of guilt.[2]

On 29 May the presiding justice of the combined civil and criminal courts, Ballot-Beaupré, recommended to the High Court of Appeals (Cour de Cassation) that the Dreyfus case be reopened. The courts, he said, could no longer ignore evidence that the document long believed to incriminate the Jewish officer had been forged. Two days later, the assize court, meeting across the hall, exonerated the notorious anti-Dreyfusard Paul Déroulède for having fomented a coup d'état. Speaking in his own defense, Déroulède told the jury that, if acquitted, he would immediately go out and try his coup again. "If you approve of what I did and of what I have to do, set me free. It's the only form of liberty I'll accept."[3] The good citizens declared him not guilty after only a few minutes' discussion.

Meanwhile, the forty-odd justices of the High Court of Appeals began their deliberations over Ballot-Beaupré's recommendation. After a long and stormy debate, Chief Presiding Justice Mazeau declared on 3 June that the Appeals Court "rescinds and annuls the verdict rendered on 28 December 1894 against Alfred Dreyfus."[4] The Dreyfusards wept with joy; the nationalists erupted with rage. This was the first time an official organ of the Republic had questioned Dreyfus's guilt, and those questions galvanized the captain's supporters and opponents alike. On 4 June an impeccably dressed young baron named Fernand Chevreau de Christiani entered President Loubet's box at the Auteuil racetrack and tried to batter him with his cane. The president was unhurt, but the baron's arrest moved a group of royalist demonstrators to attack the police. A few days later, some one hundred thousand Dreyfusards, taking their cue from the cane-wielding baron, armed themselves with sticks and marched menacingly through the streets. The anti-Semitic demagogue Edouard Drumont needed little provocation, but these incidents stirred him all the more. He urged his supporters "to start up again"—that is, to prepare another coup—and certain ranking military officers threatened to use armed force "against the army's insulters."[5] In the face of such right-wing agitation, republicans and socialists in the National Assembly managed to pass—but just barely—a resolution calling for the Appeals Court's decision to be posted throughout the country. Rarely had the country seemed so divided.

These events should have worsened France's domestic crisis. But the politics of empire intervened at this moment not just to divert attention from the Dreyfus case but to soothe the deep political, moral, and philosophical divisions it had caused. While the Déroulède and Dreyfus cases were being decided in late May and early June 1899, a third element entered France's highly charged political mix. Jean-Baptiste Marchand, the "hero of Fashoda," returned from his long African trip. Nationalists hoped Marchand's immense popularity and African military experience would make him the ideal leader of a rightist counterrevolution. The republican government took Marchand's potential threat very seriously; police agents followed him around the Hexagon and reported on his every move.[6] But even as they kept the charismatic hero under watch, France's political leaders publicly associated themselves with the "national sentiment" Marchand had come to represent. Thanks to an almost obsessive interest in him by the popular press, Marchand now seemed to embody the glories of the French Empire. By praising Marchand and basking in his heroic aura, the government could rally support for an embattled Republic, whose "national" credentials were now fortified by a renewed emphasis on its recent imperial past. As for Marchand himself, once seen as a danger to the Republic, he now unwittingly served its political needs.[7] His heroic image helped submerge the Dreyfus crisis beneath a thick layer of patriotic and fraternal consent.

Like Brazza before him, Marchand found himself elevated to the status of colonial hero in the aftermath of a long and spectacular voyage across Africa, one that made him the first European to traverse the continent at its widest point.[8] The popular pictorial weekly *L'Illustration* had sent the journalist and sketch artist Charles Castellani to follow the trip, and Castellani's reports extolled the explorer's valiant efforts on behalf of France. The only precedent for such newspaper coverage of an African expedition was the series of dispatches Henry Morton Stanley had filed about his own exploration of Central and East Africa two decades before.

Though Castellani did not get on with Marchand, who sent him home after a year, the journalist would do more than anyone to create a hero cult of Marchand.[9] "From the moment he came into the world," Castellani wrote, Marchand was destined to save France. He stood as "a hero and a Frenchman of the purest kind," a valiant military leader like those of the French Revolution whose victories over English and German armies had made France great.[10] For Castellani, Marchand was a male Joan of Arc, a simple soldier destined for illustrious deeds.

From the first reports of Marchand's presence at Fashoda in September 1898 until his evacuation order ten weeks later, countless journalists, writing for the most widely read newspapers, would echo Castellani's words. But the way commentators represented Marchand's heroism would depend on the political positions they held and especially their views of the Dreyfus Affair. Nationalists used Marchand's image as virile fighter and intrepid explorer to thrash the government for its supposed cowardice in the face of British "provocation" and to blame such cowardice on Dreyfusards and the Jews.[11] Déroulède was particularly scathing, calling Minister of Foreign Affairs Théophile Delcassé a "foreigners'" minister for supposedly favoring British claims over those for which Marchand had risked life and limb.[12] Committed Dreyfusards took the opposite view; they stood alone among leading commentators in refusing to join the chorus of hero worship. Clemenceau's *L'Aurore* rejected Marchand's African expedition as futile, even immoral, fearing his heroic image would strengthen the "militarists" who had unjustly condemned Alfred Dreyfus.[13]

As for the centrist and mass-circulation press, its editors endorsed the view of Marchand as national hero and virile fighter, but they saw his image as an antidote to the divisions opened by the Dreyfus Affair, not as a wedge for making them even wider. "The more complicated this lamentable Dreyfus Affair becomes," wrote Jean Frollo, the editorial nom de plume of the *Petit parisien*, "the more we want to divert our attention to the soldiers of the Marchand mission. . . . France is united in embracing these brave men."[14]

The idea of Marchand as agent of French unity increasingly took hold during the months between the French evacuation of Fashoda in early November 1898 and the commander's triumphal return to France in May of the following year. Dreyfusards and republicans muted their criticism, as commentators of the left and the right came together in reshaping the myth of Marchand. Journalists now portrayed him as a heroic *martyr*, as a kind of national saint who had sacrificed himself for the future of France. Although Delcassé's decision to withdraw Marchand from Fashoda represented an abject political and military defeat, very few commentators chose to portray it that way. For most French writers, Fashoda became a moral victory, a momentary setback on the road to great colonial successes to come. Marchand became a hero who had snatched a moral victory from the jaws of an only apparent military defeat.

In ultimately portraying Marchand as a martyr-hero rather than as a hero *tout court*, French commentators represented the French humiliation at Fashoda in much the same way their predecessors in the 1870s had depicted the French debacle of the Franco-Prussian War. They returned, that is, to the "glorious defeat," to the set of emotional defenses that had redefined military losses both as moral victories and as the necessary first stage in the inevitable triumph to come.[15] By century's end, the Third Republic had come full circle, as the forward-looking optimism characteristic of the 1880s—already shadowed by political scandal, anarchist attacks, and the ferocious battles of the Dreyfus Affair—gave way to a new failure on the international front.[16] Having helped explain away the disaster of 1870–71, the idea of the "glorious defeat" returned to offer emotional solace in Fashoda's wake. Earlier commentators had accomplished their postwar emotional work largely through the medium of national heroes, and, after Fashoda, analysts and observers would do the same.

What is notable about the heroes of the early Third Republic is their status as martyrs to the nation rather than victors of war. This is especially true of Joan of Arc, whose image permeated the popular culture of the 1870s and united the left and the right. But central as well were Roland, immortalized in the medieval *Song of Roland,* and the Roman-era fighter Vercingetorix. Theatrical productions, public lectures, wax museums, and a shelfful of schoolbooks structured historical lessons around these and other notables said to represent the essential, if not immediately apparent, greatness of France.[17]

No one did more to promote Joan's image as martyr and heroine than the historian Jules Michelet. "The pious tears," Michelet wrote, "of *La Pucelle* (Joan) regenerated France. . . . Joan of Arc, the last of martyrs, is also the first patriotic figure."[18] Here, in the immediate aftermath of the French debacle of 1870–71, Michelet downplayed Joan's military victories to exalt her heroic sacrifice for France. It was a sacrifice widely seen as leading to the ultimate victory of her country, something that boded well for the defeated French of the 1870s and helps explain the bipartisan interest in Joan.[19]

As Wolfgang Schivelbusch shows, the legends of Roland and Vercingetorix did at least as much as that of Joan to help the French cope with their humiliating defeat. As understood in the early Third Republic, the *Song of Roland* turned a great defeat for France into a demonstration of the nation's moral superiority over its enemies and showed that today's defeat was little more than a prelude to tomorrow's victory. This chanson de geste written at the end of the eleventh century recounted an apocalyptic confrontation between the Christian forces of Charlemagne and the infidel Muslim Saracens of Spain. A personal rivalry with one of Charlemagne's lieutenants ensnares Roland, the king's lead vassal, in a fatal military trap. Roland's levelheaded companion Olivier urges him to blow his elephant-tusk horn to call Charlemagne's army back to the scene of Roland's ambush in the pass of Rencesvals. But the proud and valiant Roland resolves to take the Saracens on himself, claiming he and his men can defeat them without Charlemagne's help. The Franks fight with extraordinary bravery, but they are outnumbered and overpowered by the Muslim horde. Roland does not himself fall to the enemy's sword. After killing as many as he can, he finally decides to give his horn one mighty blow, bursting his own temples from the blast. His death is thus more a self-sacrifice than a defeat, a martyrdom whose bravery puts the Muslims to shame. In the end, Roland's sacrifice prepares France's ultimate victory and national salvation. Charlemagne hears his vassal's horn and returns to avenge Roland's defeat. A new battle is joined at Rencesvals, with the enemy routed and Roland's loss erased. The Saracens' capital of Saragossa now belongs to the French.

It is not difficult to understand the appeal of this story in 1870s France. Roland's defeat was more apparent than real; the valiant soldier symbolized a country too morally superior to win quick and easy victories. But French forces bounced back from defeat by barbarians, overcoming the disastrous outcome of the original battle with a glorious new victory. The quest for such a reversal, or *revanche,* permeated the political rhetoric of the 1870s and 1880s and became a powerful cultural trope.[20] As the medievalist Leon Gautier wrote at the time, "we have [in the *Song of Roland*] the story of a great defeat for France out of which the nation emerged not only glorious but having settled old scores. What could be more topical today? Defeat may be all we see at the moment, but . . . perhaps before we know it we will be celebrating a new Saragossa."[21]

A third hero-martyr widely lionized in school textbooks and the object of many a republican lesson was Vercingetorix, who led the doomed Gallic resistance against the Roman conquest of France.[22] Rediscovered early in the Third Republic, Vercingetorix became a hero in the French revolutionary tradition. He was said to represent a plebeian Gallic France against the "Frankish" France of a blue-blooded elite. In the eighteenth century, pamphleteers had distinguished a Gallic Third Estate from a Frankish nobility, and the French Revolution was said to mark the victory of France's plebeian "race."[23] After 1871, republican writers maintained this social and racial distinction, but they did so in an interesting way. Textbook authors, in particular, portrayed the Frankish descendents of the Roman conquerors as the bearers of a technology and know-how superior to that of the valiant but backward Gauls. Vercingetorix's defeat was thus a cultural necessity; it permitted the modernization of the Gauls and, with it, the birth of what would become the great nation of France. Like Joan and Rolland, Vercingetorix had suffered an only apparent defeat. In an account of Vercingetorix's martyrdom written in 1888, Francois Corréard explained, "The Gauls lacked the quality of discipline essential to national greatness. They were . . . destined . . . to fall prey to a better organized and more disciplined nation." As Schivelbusch writes, this was a fundamental lesson of France's defeat in 1870–71. The nation needed to retain the cultural and moral attributes that led to the glorious martyrdom of Joan and Rolland, while adopting and adapting the discipline and orderliness that had permitted the Germans to win in 1871.[24]

These stories permeated the culture of the early Third Republic. They would predispose French writers, politicians, and their audiences to contemporary personalities who could be represented as at once heroes and martyrs, as individuals who embodied France's cultural superiority while sacrificing themselves for the long-term interests of their country. Since France was at peace in Europe between 1871 and 1914, its *military* heroes were drawn almost exclusively from those who conducted missions of exploration and conquest abroad. The heroes of the Third Republic were thus above all colonial heroes, and the extraordinary dangers they faced in Africa made it easy to portray them as martyring themselves for France. Jean-Baptiste Marchand, hero of the lost cause of Fashoda, is a case in point.

Although Marchand became a great favorite of French journalists in the 1890s, we lack detailed knowledge of his life. Unlike most other notable African explorers, Marchand published nothing—no memoir or autobiography, not even a full narrative account of his famous expedition to Fashoda. He did write a fair number of reports, which reveal something of his character and political views, but these official writings tell us little about his early life or about his ideas and experiences outside the context of his various African missions.[25] What we know comes from a series of biographies written long ago.[26]

Jean-Baptiste Marchand was born in 1863, the oldest of five children. His father worked as a carpenter in the town of Thoissey, a small commune about forty miles north of Lyon. Jean-Baptiste attended the Christian Brothers' elementary school and won a scholarship to the town's private junior high *(collège)*. But his family needed him to work, and at age thirteen he signed on as clerk for a local notary. All his biographers say that while performing his routine clerical tasks, he dreamt of becoming an adventurer and avidly read about Stanley, Livingstone, and Brazza. We have no direct evidence for such an early interest in African exploration, but we know that a great many French boys of Marchand's age possessed an unquenchable thirst for the adventure tales that flooded the bookstalls around this time.[27] His biographers also say he had promised his mother that he would remain ensconced in the safety and stability of his clerical job.

Shortly after Mme. Marchand's death in 1883, Jean-Baptiste joined the Fourth Regiment of the Marine Infantry. At a time when most army officers still belonged to the upper classes, Marchand had to begin as a private and move through the ranks. This he did with extraordinary dispatch, earning the Legion of Honor within seven years and his captain's bars within nine. He would be promoted to lieutenant colonel after Fashoda, and he became a general during the Great War. He died in 1934 at age seventy-one—an extraordinarily long life for a European who had spent many years in Africa, with its harsh climate and often-fatal disease.

Marchand's biographers characterize him as a born patriot, "destined to serve the Motherland," a man who could "think only of France."[28] Such remarks are doubtless hyperbolic, but as an adult, he expressed an ardent patriotism again and again. On joining the marines, Marchand requested to serve in the colonies, the only late-nineteenth-century theater in which a young soldier could distinguish himself and achieve rapid promotion.[29] After the French debacle at Tonkin and the fall of Jules Ferry in 1885, France's colonial spotlight shifted definitively to Africa; the young Marchand found himself assigned to the Western Sudan (present-day Mali). There, he quickly attracted the attention of Colonel Louis Archinard, the military commander of what the French took to be a crucial stretch of territory potentially linking their old Senegal colony with Algeria to the north, the Ivory Coast to the south and the Nile region to the east. The Western Sudan was central to the French desire to contain Britain's colonial aspirations in West Africa and establish a French presence from the Atlantic to the Indian Ocean. This presence, French strategists believed, would checkmate the British effort to control eastern Africa "from Cairo to the Cape."

Such beliefs were the stuff of French colonial dreams. The reality would embroil France in a decade of difficult and costly wars with two of West Africa's most powerful leaders, the sultan Ahmadu, whose Islamic Tukulor people had built a prosperous commercial state, and Samori Turé, leader of the Mandinka and long-standing rival of the Tukulor.[30] The French used the already classic colonial strategy of divide and conquer, sometimes supporting Ahmadu and sometimes Samori. Although Archinard largely succeeded in defeating Ahmadu by 1893, Samori proved much more difficult. The Islamic *almamy*, or "leader of the faith," proved a brilliant military strategist and savvy politician who did not hesitate to mobilize British commercial agents and their local political representatives against the French.[31]

In 1888 Archinard resolved to chip away at Ahmadu's empire by attacking one city at a time. Marchand led a charge into the Tukulor town of Koundian, and the bravery and bravado he showed there both impressed the colonel and launched the younger man's military career. Marchand's own reports on the battle, copies of which reached friendly journalists, helped feed what would become his legend. Wounded in battle, Marchand emphasized a stoic bravery that allowed him to persevere: "A corporal poured his gourd over my head to stop the blood running down my forehead. I no longer felt anything." After an hour and a half of battle in which his command turned the tide against the Tukulor fighters and ulti-mately took their city, Marchand "lost consciousness . . . [and] dropped in a heap against the wall."[32] This report and others like it added Marchand to the short list of those believed willing to sacrifice themselves and risk death for the good of France.

In 1893 Marchand, now a captain, won authorization directly from Paris to search for a route linking the Western Sudan to the Ivory Coast. The ul-timate goal of this mission of exploration was to enlist Ivorian peoples in the fight to eliminate Samori. The region was unknown to Europeans, and Mar-chand found himself required to cover some four thousand kilometers, mostly on foot. The captain traveled this terrain so expeditiously that the locals dubbed him Kpakibo, or "he who crashes through the forest."[33] Mar-chand's successful mission to the Ivory Coast added to his growing reputa-tion in France. Newspaper readers followed his battles and came to know him as "Marchand l'Africain." France's elite pro-colonial organization, the Comité de l'Afrique française, recognized his work, and its members invited him to speak.[34] In 1895, he obtained an audience with Gabriel Hanotaux, the foreign minister, who had earlier said of Marchand and his fellow officer Charles Mangin, "Both of them already had the faces of heroes."[35]

Marchand's face attracted a good deal of attention in the 1890s; by the end of the decade it would be everywhere. Journalists focused on the cap-tain's eyes, said to be piercingly intense and to reflect a steely purposefulness lacking in the soft culture of mainland France.[36] Marchand's chin, too, at-tracted notice. Writers described it as strong and forceful, elongated by a carefully trimmed beard and topped by the moustache de rigueur among virile military men.[37] The eyes, chin, and no-nonsense cut of his hair were all said to reveal a level of fortitude and determination far beyond the norm. Leon Daudet, who dedicated an entire worshipful chapter to Marchand, wrote that when the hero walked into a room, "glory, honor, and virtue en-tered with him. . . . He was an exceptional human being, a man who stood out above the rest . . . a natural born leader . . . who inspired confidence and great devotion."[38] Daudet extolled Marchand's "taste for action, . . . his thirst for risk and the unknown," his ability to defy death through sheer will and the "moral and physical force that resided in him." Here was a man, Daudet said, of such "limitless resolution" that he "knew neither fatigue, nor obstacles, nor impediments." Because he possessed not an ounce of van-ity, a feminine quality, he was indifferent to his "overwhelming fame," though he found himself bothered by the "noisy adulation surrounding his name." All he had was a masculine pride.[39]

Figure 15. Portrait of Marchand (*L'Illustration*, 3 June 1899).

Like Daudet, Marchand's fellow officers emphasized his immense physical energy, iron constitution, and uncanny ability to persevere even when overcome by malarial fever. Hard on himself, the captain was equally hard on his men. "You've got to work quickly," he wrote Mangin, "surmount all difficulties, overcome the impossible, and not spend a dime."[40] Marchand, in short, appeared to be one of those rare "professors of energy" extolled by the nationalist writer Maurice Barrès—a "real man" who could help restore a fin-de-siècle manliness widely believed in decline.[41] In an urbanized, bureaucratic, and commercial landscape, a realm haunted by the New Woman and spooked by Germany's technical and military superiority, French commentators saw in Marchand a powerful masculine ideal.[42] Unlike General Georges Boulanger, who had renounced a nationalist coup d'état at his mistress's behest, Marchand, the budding colonizer, "never submitted to any woman's empire"—or so Castellani would write.[43]

Marchand was not unaware of the imagery surrounding him and used it to advance his goals. Working with leaders of the colonial lobby, the captain hatched an audacious plan to challenge Britain's supremacy in Egypt by leading a small French force to the Upper Nile. Marchand proposed to travel there not via the Nile itself, something the British would never allow, but via France's colony on the Congo. Once on the Upper Nile, Marchand would sign treaties with Menelik, emperor of Abyssinia, and the Mahdists' Khalifa. The captain considered Sudan's Islamic rulers France's "natural allies" because they too opposed England's occupation of Egypt.[44] His African diplomacy achieved, Marchand would then negotiate with Britain from a position of strength. Before meeting with Hanotaux, Marchand leaked his plan to several top journalists, many of whom wrote for the mass-circulation press and gave the proposed expedition and its virile, charismatic leader wide publicity.[45] Under these circumstances, Hanotaux had to give Marchand a sympathetic hearing.[46]

Despite the credence given it at the highest levels, the project devised by Marchand and his colonialist allies made little geopolitical, military, or economic sense. First and most important, the British government had warned against such an undertaking in the clearest possible terms. In March 1895, Edward Grey, then under-secretary for foreign affairs, declared that "the advance of a French expedition under secret instructions . . . into a territory over which our claims have been known for so long . . . would be an unfriendly act, and would be so viewed by England."[47] This was highly menacing language for a diplomat, and as a deliberately public statement, it would be difficult to take back. French embassy officials in London called Grey's statement "a quasi-declaration of war against France."[48] Hanotaux understood its gravity and privately sought to mollify Britain's Liberal government. Even so, French officials at the Ministry of Colonies quietly put the finishing touches on their plans for the "Mission Marchand."[49]

Given the pro-imperial premises of French foreign policy, such a risky venture might have been worth undertaking had the chances of success been strong. But this was not the case. African expeditions as ambitious as Marchand's rarely achieved their goals, and essentially never when led by French explorers.[50] The most reasonable expectation was that a small band of French officers and African men would prove unable to make it to Fashoda intact—at least not in a reasonable time. And even if Marchand were to reach his goal, it strained credulity to assert that he would be well positioned to challenge a large, well-equipped Anglo-Egyptian force ordered to advance up the Nile. Worse, there was no evidence whatever that the Mahdists would agree to ally with one European power against another. In reality, the Khalifa amalgamated all Europeans with the hated "Turks" who had brutally ruled the Sudan. For him there was no such thing as a good—or even a better—European.[51]

If the political and military situation promised the French little enough, there were no good economic reasons for colonizing the Sudan. The region around Fashoda offered scant economic potential; Salisbury had dismissed its landscape as "wretched stuff." Any effort to capture it, wrote France's economically oriented *La Politique coloniale,* would be "a crazy adventure that will lead to disaster."[52] And even if the area had had some economic potential, it is difficult to see how the French, lacking control of the Lower Nile, could have exploited it.

But this was not an issue decided on pragmatic, coolly strategic grounds. Although economically oriented colonialists argued against the project, they found themselves without influence given the primacy of "prestige and national honor."[53] Marchand's plan was explicitly anti-British. It appealed to a not-so-latent Anglophobia simmering among France's politicians and publicists since Britain's seizure, against French wishes, of effective political and economic control over Egypt in 1882.[54] By the mid-1890s, French writers and politicians clamored, as the *Petit parisien* put it, for a "revenge" against Great Britain for its "most odious spoliation" of Egypt. Such revenge would be "fully legitimate but morally pure." Even right-wing nationalists like Paul de Cassagnac, ardent Germanophobes in the 1870s and '80s, now turned their ire against Britain. As Cassagnac wrote, "People are beginning to weigh deliberately the two hatreds; that of the German, a little cooled with time; that of the English suddenly revived and burning."[55] No longer did Germany monopolize evil and brutality and serve as the main candidate for revenge.[56]

By the 1890s, left-wing republicans also made the shift from anti-German to anti-British hostility. And since, for them, France had distinguished itself as "the veritable pioneer of civilization," it stood alone as the only country capable of establishing "peace on the banks of the Nile."[57] For these reasons, anti-British colonial ventures enjoyed widespread support in the 1890s on patriotic, national grounds. Even the socialist leader Jean Jaurès, later a critic of French imperialism, employed a textbook example of "nation-talk" to justify his vote to pay for the Marchand mission. "It is not a *political* vote that we are casting," Jaurès declared, "but a *national* one."[58]

Endorsement of an "imperialism of prestige" was so self-evident, so "national," even to socialists, that it seemed to have nothing to do with politics. The Chamber of Deputies voted 482–22 to finance the expedition.[59]

Underlying these considerations was a set of representations about France and its history that shaped how officials and members of the public alike would understand the government's policy choices and the people who carried them out. Marchand was crucial in this respect. He was a charismatic hero, one of those classic French saviors who not only turn defeat into victory but even rule out the very idea of defeat—at least in the longer run of time. No matter what the odds, Marchand would succeed in advancing the cause of France, because that is what French heroes did.[60] As Maurice Barrès would later write, Marchand was a hero engaged in "an incessant struggle against the impossible," a great man who rendered the impossible possible.[61] In trying to understand how experienced politicians could have authorized Marchand's improbable plan, we must keep in mind the emotional power of cultural representations that seemed to shield France from the prospect of defeat.

Leaving from Bordeaux and Marseille between April and June 1898, the Mission Marchand trekked overland from Loango on the West African coast to the colonial capital Brazzaville. The mission included a dozen French officers and some 150 Africans, mostly inhabitants of the Western Sudan. Though billed as another French "conquête pacifique," much like Brazza's expedition of the early 1880s, Marchand's voyage cost a great many African lives. The Bateke and other peoples who lived along the old slave-trading route from Loango to Brazzaville found themselves forced at gunpoint to carry the Mission Marchand's supplies. Those who refused could be shot, and those who ran away had their homes and villages burned to the ground, their crops and livestock destroyed.[62]

From Loango the expedition sailed up the Congo and into the narrow Ubangi River, where Marchand had to dismantle his primitive steamboat and proceed in a fleet of seventy-two dugout canoes. At the tiny French post of Ouango, 450 miles upriver from Bangui, smooth water gave way to impassable rapids. Once again, the expedition had to make its way on foot, hacking into the dense swampland of the Bahr al-Ghazal, the steamboat's 2,000-pound metal hull in tow. Traversing the mosquito-infested swamp proved the most difficult part of the voyage; once on the other side, Marchand and his men sailed into the Bahr al-Ghazal River, which flowed into Lake No and then the White Nile, just 100 miles upriver from Fashoda.[63] Part of the voyage matched the one described by Joseph Conrad's hero Marlow, and like Conrad, L'Illustration's Castellani portrayed it as a descent through unknown dimensions of space and time and into a starkly primitive, barely human world.[64]

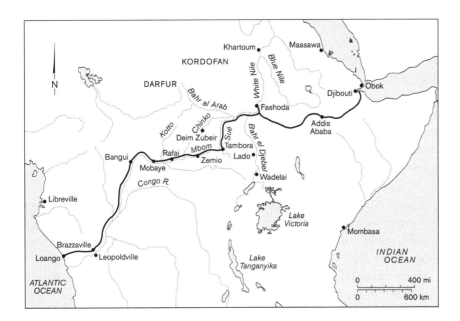

Map 4. Marchand's mission.

In late September 1898, the French government and public learned that Marchand had arrived safely at Fashoda. British reporters covering General Horatio Herbert Kitchener's "reconquest" of the Sudan, his effort to regain control of a country "lost" to the Mahdi in 1885, relayed news of an encounter on 19 September between Kitchener and Jean-Baptiste Marchand. The Sirdar, as the British general was known, discovered the French commander ensconced in an old fort at Fashoda, from which he intended to stake out a claim over the entire Upper Nile. At his government's behest, Kitchener demanded that the French evacuate the fort and give up any claims over the region. A French refusal, Kitchener made clear, could result in war. These British reports evoked a strong response from French journalists, whom Kitchener barred from covering the confrontation directly. As French readers soon understood, Marchand steadfastly refused to abandon Fashoda despite Britain's increasingly urgent demands.

As Marchand dug in, numerous French journalists began to lionize him even more than before. His heroic persistence in the face of a militarily superior but morally inferior British rival testified, they wrote, to the greater glory of France. While the French captain had marched through Africa as a new "conquérant pacifique," intending a "peaceful penetration" of the continent, Kitchener had proved himself a brutal killer in the Stanley mold.[65] On September 2, 1898, the Sirdar had turned his vastly superior weaponry against the 52,000 Mahdist troops arrayed outside the gates of Omdurman. Although the Anglo-Egyptians found themselves outnumbered two to one, the battle quickly turned into a rout. Kitchener's modern weapons, explained the veteran war correspondent George Steevens, enabled the British and Egyptian soldiers to "pour out death as fast as they could load and press the trigger." In the words of another war correspondent, the young Winston Churchill, "It was a matter of machinery," a mechanized slaughter so awful that both he and Steevens, neither known for pro-Arab sympathies, complained that it had gone too far. "It was a terrible sight," wrote the future prime minister; some fifteen thousand Mahdist soldiers lay dead, while "they had not hurt us at all."[66]

Such feelings did not prevent Steevens, Churchill, and most other British journalists from exalting their country's success in winning back the Sudan. Steevens described the Battle of Omdurman as "altogether . . . the most crowded glorious day we shall any of us ever see; the greatest fight of half a generation of Sudan warfare and the most fruitful victory."[67] In the aftermath of Kitchener's "glorious day," most British writers rejected Marchand's right to remain on the Upper Nile or to make territorial claims of any kind. Meanwhile, the majority of French observers disagreed, denying that Britain enjoyed any exclusive control over the region.[68]

Unfortunately for the French, this budding colonial confrontation coincided with a dramatic new turn in the Dreyfus Affair. On August 31, Colonel Hubert Joseph Henry committed suicide following revelations that he had forged crucial documents in the Dreyfus case. Ferdinand Walsin-Esterhazy, now unmasked as the real traitor, fled to England a few days later. And on September 3, Alfred Dreyfus's wife, Lucie, formally requested that the high court reopen her husband's case. These developments produced large-scale defections from the anti-Dreyfusard side, equalizing support for the two camps and creating a political situation in France more polarized than ever before—even including the aftermath of Zola's "J'accuse."[69]

To make matters worse, several hundred construction workers walked off their jobs in mid-September, their numbers swelled when railroad employees joined them in a huge sympathy strike. The government responded by sending 60,000 troops to train stations and other strategic locations in and around Paris. Radicals and socialists feared a coup d'état, and nationalists threatened to carry one out. But no military figure stepped forward to overthrow the government, which seemed ripe for a coup when it lost its parliamentary majority on October 25.[70] At this point, leading nationalists began to see Marchand as a new and improved Boulanger. In keeping with their own representations of this stalwart of colonial war, nationalists dared hope that Marchand possessed the fortitude Boulanger had lacked, that their hero would lead them into a post-republican promised land.[71]

Under these circumstances, the last thing the French government needed was a dangerous international confrontation over Fashoda. With the Dreyfus case now before the Cour de Cassation and unlikely to be quickly resolved, political leaders needed to contain the situation in the Sudan. Responsibility for doing so fell to Théophile Delcassé, the minister of foreign affairs. As colonial minister in the mid-1890s, Delcassé had been one of the original advocates of the Marchand mission, dismissing as empty bluster the Grey declaration threatening a retaliatory war. But amid the heightened Dreyfus conflict, strikes, and domestic troop deployments, Delcassé had to take seriously Britain's claim to the Upper Nile while assessing the realities of the balance of power between the two countries.

In the wake of Kitchener's devastating victory over the Mahdists, Delcassé could see that Marchand's tiny band was no match for the Sirdar's triumphal force. And he knew France's navy could not stand up to the British fleet. There was only one possible course of action: conciliation.[72] But given the French hero worship of Marchand, the foreign minister had to proceed cautiously; a great many influential voices argued that the commander should stay put. In response, Delcassé declared himself guardian of the "national honor" and publicly demanded negotiations with the British before he would consider ordering Marchand home.

British officials understood the foreign minister's dilemma and sympathized with it. "Delcassé has judged quite correctly as to the utter impossibility of the French Government conceding the recall of M. Marchand," wrote Sir Edmund Monson, the British ambassador to France. "The irritation of the Army and of a large portion of the public over the Dreyfus Affair, renders the situation of the Government more than usually delicate; and any symptom of weakness on the Fashoda question would be the signal for their downfall within twenty-four hours of the meeting of the Chamber."[73]

Meanwhile, British prime minister Lord Salisbury confronted pressures of his own. Although he had shown willingness to compromise in the past, he needed now to avoid any appearance of weakness vis-à-vis the "wily French." His minister of colonies, the arch-imperialist Joseph Chamberlain, had publicly criticized him for shortchanging Britain's national interests, and there is evidence that Chamberlain wanted a preventive war against France.[74] The opposition Liberal Party, itself increasingly pro-imperial, responded to Fashoda by taking a much harder line than Salisbury. In mid-October, the former Liberal prime minister Lord Rosebery announced his maximalist position in the pure tones of nation-talk. British policy in the Sudan, declared Rosebery, "is not a matter of the politics of a particular government; it is a matter of the nation itself. . . . [We will] forever defend the rights and the honor of our flag. . . . Any government that tried to renounce our claims wouldn't last a week."[75]

With such "support" from the opposition, and given the "ostentatious criticism and disquisitions of the most influential London newspapers," as Monson described the press's feverous state, "the task of diplomacy, so far as [it] is concerned with keeping the peace, [is] more difficult than ever."[76] M. Geoffray, the French chargé d'affaires in London, strongly agreed. He was convinced that "the British population, regardless of social class, accepts the idea of a war." By the end of October 1898, officials on both sides of the Channel actively worried that the popular press would push them into an unnecessary war; "public opinion" resembled a force of nature beyond their control.

When Delcassé attempted to negotiate some face-saving concessions, hoping for a piece of territory in the Bahr al-Ghazal in exchange for withdrawing Marchand, he met with a flat British refusal. Such obstinacy was unusual in nineteenth-century colonial contests such as this. In the great game of empire, European diplomats generally obeyed a tacit agreement not to humiliate a Great Power, not to risk tipping colonial rivalries into a European war.[77] Based on prior Franco-British negotiations over other parts of Africa, Delcassé's demand for some compensation was not unreasonable, especially since Salisbury was known for pragmatism. But given the widespread belief in Britain that the empire was at risk, political leaders enjoyed less room to maneuver than before—especially after the Grey declaration, when the British government publicly threatened war with France. Grey had issued his threat partly to satisfy the demands of an increasingly vocal mass-circulation press, which now sought a role not just in debating foreign policy but in making it as well.[78] As the *Petit parisien* wrote, "Today, officials can no longer hope to confine discussions of foreign affairs within the walls of chancelleries; such discussions spill out beyond them and invade the public sphere."[79]

Fashoda became the first great European crisis to take place under the full spotlight of a mass medium. The penny press was still in its infancy at the time of the Franco-Prussian War, and during the previous Franco-British war scare, the Pritchard Affair of 1844–45, the print runs of all daily papers combined reached only a few tens of thousands.[80] In the wake of Fashoda, the mass press's tendency to personalize complex issues and reduce difficult problems to simple matters of "Us" versus "Them," heroes versus villains, and most vividly, Kitchener versus Marchand did much to enflame the situation. It was easiest to root unambivalently for your own side when your nation's attributes could find expression in a single man and when journalists framed political phenomena in the language of the fait divers, personalizing the issues of the day and rendering them in all-too-human terms.

For these reasons, both the content and style of mass journalism at the fin-de-siècle constrained diplomatic and other government officials as never before, convincing them of the terrible, uncontrollable power of the press. According to Geoffray, "Here in England, the press acts in an especially powerful way. Every Englishman reads a newspaper, and in general, he reads only one. But he believes what it says as fully and steadfastly as he believes in the Gospel itself. If journalists portray the Frenchman as a kind of hereditary enemy, the English newspaper reader is easily led to believe it true."[81] Geoffray's counterparts in the Foreign Office appeared to agree, complaining that the power of the press made their jobs next to impossible. "The *Daily Mail*," confided one British diplomat, "this newspaper so omnipresent in England nowadays, . . . exercises an absolutely deplorable influence when it come to good relations between [Britain and France]."[82] It enjoyed such influence, bragged Kennedy Jones, editor of the *Mail's* sister paper, the *Evening News,* that it could stymie Salisbury's efforts to contain the jingoistic anti-French and anti-Marchand reaction of a country "still intoxicated by the reconquest of the Sudan."[83] To try to reassert a measure of control, Salisbury met regularly with Alfred Harmsworth, owner of the *Mail* and *Evening News,* throughout the entire Fashoda crisis.[84]

These meetings did little to moderate either paper's editorial tone. "England has said that any invasion of the Nile Valley would be regarded as an unfriendly act," a prominent editorial declared, "and the Englishman keeps his word. The nation will not falter."[85] The *Mail's* main news articles advertised their contents with a series of "decks," a stack of subheadlines that told the story in sharp, clear-cut tones. On 10 October 1898, the decks read:

WE STAND FIRM
GRAVE OUTLOOK
OUR RIGID REFUSAL TO RECOGNIZE MARCHAND[86]

It was impossible to miss these decks, especially the ones in large boldface type. They told readers how to understand the rest of the story and, for many, undid in advance any nuances that might exist in the finer print. Maps served a similar purpose; on 21 October 1898, the *Daily Mail* published a huge illustration showing the strength and deployment of the British and French fleets. The paper had warned in a headline the day before: FRANCE ARMING. To such threats, there was only one possible response: BRITAIN'S FOOT DOWN. The leader that day bore the title "A Grave Situation" and asserted, "The nation may be approaching the hour of trial." After denouncing the French press, the editor went on: "Lord Salisbury . . . cannot surrender; the die is cast. The sympathy and support of all Englishmen will be with him. . . . We feel that in the present question it is not an unhealthy spot on the Nile which is at stake, or even a fertile province, but the whole question of British domination in Egypt, and the vaster and larger question of the right of the British Empire to exist."

The *Daily Mail* may have been the bluntest of the important British dailies, but with the notable exception of the liberal *Manchester Guardian,* the other major papers echoed its views.[87] The *Evening News* translated the Fashoda situation into the apparently simple terms of everyday life. "If a householder finds a man in his back garden, he does not go to arbitration about the matter or enter into elaborate arguments to show that he, the householder, is the owner of that garden. He simply orders the trespasser out, and, if he will not go out of his own accord, he has to go in another fashion."[88] As if to clear up any remaining ambiguity, the *Spectator* announced, "It is quite clear that Fashoda must be retained, even at the cost of war."[89]

The French press displayed more divisions than its British counterpart, thanks in large part to the Dreyfus Affair. But Gallic papers nonetheless echoed British ones in raising the specter of war—blamed, of course, on the other side and especially the British press. The moderate, sober-toned *Le Temps* warned the British government not to follow "the lead of the English newspapers." If it did, British officials risked causing "a complete change in the conciliatory attitude that [French] public opinion has manifested."[90] Over and over, French journalists denounced their British homologues for inflaming an already dangerous situation, for "speak[ing] of nothing but war."[91] The two largest-circulation national papers, the *Petit journal* and the *Petit parisien,* appeared relatively temperate compared to their British counterparts, the *Daily Mail* and *Evening News.* But they joined the explicitly nationalist French press in invoking national honor and dignity and urging the government not to give in, not to compromise the nation's hard-won colonial prestige.[92]

As for the nationalist journals, editors and writers increasingly represented the Dreyfus Affair and the Fashoda crisis as a single unified problem. In their view, the Dreyfusards served, in effect, as domestic agents for the English, as internal enemies determined to undermine the army and prevent the country from protecting its colonial domains. "We recognize," declared *La Patrie*, "that the Dreyfusards, those hypocritical allies of the English, want to minimize the importance of the [Marchand] mission, whose success so troubles our rivals across the Channel." Henri Rochefort upped the ante, maintaining that the "Dreyfusard Party" was doing everything in its power to undermine Marchand and force the government to cede Egypt and the Nile to England.[93] The British enemy had gained ground not because Marchand's position was untenable but because Jews and other traitors had stoked Albion's "outrageous demands."[94]

In France, the roiling emotions of the Dreyfus Affair had turned both right and left against the government, accused by both sides of compromising the nation's honor.[95] The more the right-wing press warned cabinet ministers against a Jewish and Dreyfusard fifth column at home, the more the left warned against a military coup d'état designed at once to resolve the affair and take France to war. This is precisely what Monson feared would happen, reporting as much to Salisbury after a particularly fierce anti-Dreyfusard demonstration on 25 October and the fall of the French government that same day.[96] Under these circumstances, France's council of ministers, weak in constitutional terms, possessed very little room to maneuver. Political leaders found themselves buffeted by an army of polemically practiced journalists and a British and French "public opinion" over which journalists were thought to exercise near-absolute control. It matters little that diplomats and government officials exaggerated the influence of the press or that they tended to conflate editors' beliefs with those of their readers. Unskilled as yet in manipulating the mass press, in using it effectively for their own purposes, European politicians of the fin-de-siècle had no choice but to take very seriously what they imagined public opinion to be. Such was particularly true when a great charismatic hero like Marchand or Kitchener appeared to incarnate the public's beliefs.

Besides, the attitudes of policy makers were themselves fashioned by many of the cultural and political phenomena that helped make "public opinion" what it was.[97] Like members of the public at large, Salisbury and Delcassé were motivated by considerations of honor and prestige, by a belief in the superiority of their respective nations, by reverence for heroes and heroism, and by simple maxims and common sense that seemed so obvious as to be beyond dispute.[98] Salisbury's admission in 1887 that the arousal of "national, or acquisitional feeling" played a large role in Britain's policy toward Egypt likely represented both his acknowledgment of public opinion's growing power ("It has tasted the fleshpots and it will not let them go") and his own not dissimilar national feeling.[99] Likewise, Queen Victoria's statement "Giving up what one has is always a bad thing" doubtless seemed no less reasonable to Salisbury and Rosebery than to large numbers of their fellow citizens.

Given the firmness of British "public opinion," France's domestic turmoil, and a balance of naval and military power that favored Great Britain, Delcassé possessed only a single choice. On 4 November 1898, the French government ordered Marchand to abandon Fashoda. It did so without receiving a shred of compensation, even symbolic, in return. This withdrawal humiliated a French regime already weakened by the Dreyfus Affair. It also transformed Marchand from the "hero of Fashoda" into the "martyr of Fashoda," the martyr who had suffered a "glorious defeat." Nationalists imagined that the Africa-hardened commander would rebound from the martyrdom of his "temporary" loss to win a great new victory over the traitorous Dreyfusard republic. Marchand would exact "revanche" on those who had humiliated and dishonored him, as they had humiliated and dishonored the army's high command. The nationalists' effort to link the Dreyfus and Fashoda affairs guaranteed that there would be no unanimity of press opinion on the meaning of Marchand's withdrawal from the Sudan. But six months later, when the commander returned to France, the republican and Dreyfusard press ceased all criticism of Marchand. The left, like the right, would try to turn the heroic, martyred figure of Marchand to their own advantage, rallying the country around the lost cause of Fashoda.

Because Marchand refused to travel through British-held territory, his return trip took nearly six months; he would not reach French soil until 30 May 1899. In the meantime, nationalists prepared to exploit the Marchand legend to which they had contributed so much. According to police agents, nationalist groups developed a coordinated response to the trial of Déroulède scheduled for late May and the return of Marchand, expected around the same time.[100] Déroulède's Ligue des Patriotes sent Georges Thiebaud to Djibouti to give Marchand a medal of honor and accompany the "the unsullied hero with visionary eyes" back to France.[101] Once the commander arrived in Paris, the *ligue* planned to disseminate 100,000 photographs of Marchand to the huge crowds expected to greet him in the streets.[102] Déroulède's group also decided to send a large contingent of its members from Marseille to Toulon to be at the port when Marchand arrived from Africa. According to the Marseille police, the ligue's objective was to disrupt the official welcoming ceremony organized by the municipality of Toulon.[103]

Toulon's plans suggest that the government had decided not to allow nationalists to have Marchand all to themselves. City officials worked with the ministry of the interior in Paris as they organized Toulon's "civic festival" welcoming Marchand. And the city's *commissaire spéciale* assured the interior minister that "all demonstrations in preparation will have a completely patriotic character."[104] The plan, in other words, was to drown out any nationalist disruption and claim Marchand for the republic as a whole. There is no direct evidence that the government in Paris coordinated with localities along the route of Marchand's railroad journey from Toulon to Paris—the trip took two days and nights—but a series of official celebrations suggests some cooperation. At each whistle-stop, Marchand received greetings from the local prefect and mayor, who welcomed him back to France on behalf not of any political group but of the population as a whole. Elaborately covered by the press, Marchand's leisurely journey up the middle of France recalled Napoleon's dramatic return from Elbe eighty-five years earlier.

Even in regions not on the train route from Toulon to Paris, towns staged official celebrations of the hero's return. The municipality of Remiremont in the Vosges illuminated its town hall as Marchand's train passed by a few hundred kilometers to the west. The firemen, sports club, and local band all joined the festivities. A placard posted in the town square contained a patriotic, but not nationalistic, message: "Let us all express in unison our common enthusiasm. . . . We ask everyone to join in. . . . Marchand has given a great service to France. All Frenchmen should pay homage to Marchand."[105]

As the commander traveled up the spine of France, nationalist and republican journalists vied with increasing urgency to claim the hero as their own. No one tried harder than Edouard Drumont. The anti-Semitic demagogue opened the media extravaganza over Marchand with an enormous "Illustrated Supplement" published on 29 May, twenty-four hours before the commander docked at Toulon. The page-one headline read: "The

Marchand Mission: A Fistful of Heroes." In the center was a large drawing of the commander, with the caption "Le héros de Fachoda." Surrounding his visage were smaller drawings of Marchand's officers, a portrait of the hero's father, and sketches of the modest dwelling where he grew up. Page two featured a map of the mission's long trek across Africa and portraits of the other Frenchmen belonging to the expedition. There were even two African faces, those of Menelik, the emperor of Abyssinia, and a member of the now famous "*tirailleurs sénégalais*," or West African soldiers who formed the bulk of Marchand's troop. Parallel with the map was a reproduction of the "sword of honor," presented to Marchand by leaders of the nationalist right. On the third page, readers could see a drawing of the fort at Fashoda that made it look far more imposing than it was. Also included here was a view of Marchand's steamboat, *La Faidherbe,* a portrait of Kitchener, and a reproduction of *L'Illustration*'s cover showing Marchand, Napoleon-like, communing with pyramids and the Sphinx (fig. 17). The final page featured a drawing of the Sirdar's steamboat flotilla advancing toward Fashoda and the fateful meeting with Marchand. Altogether, there were twenty-nine illustrations, a huge number even for an illustrated supplement. It was enormously expensive to print.

In the accompanying article, Drumont's talented writer Lucien Pemjean depicted the boat carrying Marchand toward Toulon as the sign of a new France purged of the decadence and corruption wrought by the Jews. For Pemjean, the hero of Fashoda was the very antithesis of Alfred Dreyfus, a spoiled Jewish intellectual born to opulence and an easy upward path. Marchand had enjoyed no such privileges, succeeding only by dint of a "prodigious will" and extraordinary perseverance. He was the "real" Frenchman, a real hero, a man of the people who represented the true France of soil and blood: "The professional defenders of Dreyfus can glorify their 'hero' all they want. As for France, France acclaims another." Pemjean focused a great deal of attention on Marchand's masculinity, which he distinguished from the effeminacy of the Jews and the Dreyfusard elite.[106] Marchand, Pemjean said, was too active to spend his time writing, and what reading he did was limited to books about war, dangerous voyages of exploration, and the manly subjects of history and geography. Mostly, the hero devoted himself to physical exercise: running, horseback riding, swimming, and swordsmanship. Even the games he played as a child were "perilous and violent."

Once in Africa, Marchand endured unimaginable suffering, Pamjean went on, willingly accepted any sacrifice—all for the good and glory of the

Figure 16. La Mission Marchand (*La libre parole*, 29 May 1899).

L'ILLUSTRATION

Prix du numéro : 75 centimes.   SAMEDI 26 NOVEMBRE 1898   56ᵉ Année. — Nᵒ 2909.

Figure 17. Marchand and the Sphinx (*L'Illustration*, 26 November 1898).

Fatherland. The writer then told the story of Marchand's African journey, a story indeed quite extraordinary, even if not as peaceful and selfless as the journalist maintained. In Pemjean's hands, Marchand's expedition became a tale of "superhuman effort, a colossal travail, [a] Herculean tour de force," a chronicle of sheer physical endurance, of hunger, heat, pestilence, and disease overcome, of savages vanquished, and finally, a story of patriotism triumphant. Against all the odds, against the naysayers and Dreyfusards and cowards, Marchand succeeded in "planting the French flag" in that crucial, now legendary spot on the Upper Nile.

But like all those brave souls who belonged to the bedrock France that Marchand embodied, the hero had been betrayed. Pemjean quoted a letter the commander had written the previous fall just after meeting Kitchener for the first time. The British had allowed some French newspapers to reach the French troops at Fashoda, and after reading them for an hour, "the ten French officers," Marchand wrote, "trembled and cried. It was not until then that we learned that the Dreyfus Affair had been reopened, with its horrible campaign of infamy. We remained speechless for a day and a half." How, Pemjean asked, could a Frenchman read Marchand's "simple and vibrant letter without suffering, without crying?" Only one thing could have been worse, and that happened a few weeks later when France's traitorous government ordered Marchand's surrender and defeat. The great hero was thus a martyr too, but his martyrdom came at the hands of his own government.

> By forcing this heroic officer to hand Fashoda, his glorious conquest, over to the English, by inflicting on him this torture and humiliation in the eyes of the enemy, THEY should have known that . . . the France of Joan of Arc and Napoleon, oppressed, abased and blackened by a band of politicians [and] the barons of finance . . . would recognize itself in Marchand and embrace him as the very image of the Fatherland. Too bad for the Dreyfusards if the cry 'Vive Marchand' erupts over the entire breadth of our land, as the revanche of Frenchness itself, the emblem of our disgust and our hopes.[107]

With this peroration, Pemjean put the final touches on his right-wing rendition of France's discourse of defeat. In the journalist's narrative, France did not genuinely lose at Fashoda. What actually happened was something else altogether: a real France found itself martyred to a false France, a false France in league with the enemy. And because the real France did not lose, the hero-martyr Marchand would soon turn this apparent defeat into a great victory, into a "revanche of Frenchness itself." The martyrdom of the hero would precede, as it always did in glorious defeats, the ultimate triumph of France.

In presenting Marchand this way, Pemjean and Drumont joined all the other spokesmen of the nationalist right—Rochefort, Barrès, Déroulède—in claiming Marchand for themselves. They not only denied him to the republicans but also argued that the republicans, true to their traitorous, anti-military inclinations, were doing everything in their power to dissociate themselves from the hero and to dampen the groundswell of popular enthusiasm he had inspired.[108] Had this assessment been true, the nationalists might have achieved greater success in wrapping themselves in Marchand's flag. Unfortunately for them, republicans, no less than nationalists, could view Marchand as a hero and martyr who could turn an apparent defeat into victory. It was a victory around which the entire nation could unite. When a nationalist member of the Chamber of Deputies proposed a motion of congratulations to Marchand, a group of republicans introduced a similar measure of their own. It was the republican motion that came before the Chamber as a whole, and the nationalists could hardly vote no. The result was a unanimous declaration of praise not only for Marchand but for all the "soldiers and administrators who, in Africa, have extended French influence or assured French domination."[109] The republicans thus succeeded in making themselves the spokesmen of a unanimous parliament, erasing the country's divisions, at least momentarily, by invoking the image of Marchand.

By the time the hero arrived in Paris, the republican papers spoke of nothing else. On 2 June, *Le Matin,* a mass-circulation paper and quasi-official voice of the regime, blanketed every square inch of its front page with news of Marchand's ecstatic popular reception in Paris the previous day. The big banner headline read:

LA FETE DE L'ARMEE — VIVE MARCHAND!

This republican, moderately Dreyfusard paper now wanted to celebrate the army. But *Le Matin*'s army was not that of Henry, General Mercier, and the Dreyfus Affair; it was a different army, a colonial army, an army of imperial heroes like Marchand, Gallieni, and Lyautey. The leaders of this more activist army, one that worked for the prestige and glory of France, had all cut their teeth fighting the endless and often brutal colonial wars of the past decade and a half. They would lead French forces in the Great War to come.

Below the banner headline, *Le Matin* printed a series of decks:

LES HEROS DE FACHODA
La foule à la gare de Lyon
Les ovations succèdent aux ovations
Une journée d'enthousiasme.

"The Commander Marchand," exclaimed *Le Matin's* reporter, "has arrived amid an indescribable enthusiasm. . . . The streets surrounding the Lyon Train Station have been invaded by a crowd so dense as to make all movement impossible."[110] There is no way to know exactly how many people made up that crowd; estimates ranged from several tens of thousands to several hundreds of thousands. Photographs of the scene depict an immense assembly of men and women packed tightly together and extending past the edge of the frame. Those who could not get close enough to the Gare de Lyon parked themselves all along the parade route Marchand was supposed to take. It seemed as though every Parisian had descended into the streets.

One eyewitness, a little-known jeweler and art collector named Henri Vever, recorded the following account of Marchand's reception in his handwritten diary: "Finally, Marchand came into view. Everyone waved their hats in the air, and the huge crowd overwhelmed the tight cordon of police officers. An immense clamor rose up . . . and the vast crowd spilled out of the Place de l'Opera and onto the *grands boulevards*. . . . Unceasingly, we acclaimed Marchand, singing the Marseillaise and demanding to see the hero once again . . . [The celebration] lasted until midnight; it was impossible to go to sleep. . . . What a wonderful day for the hero of Fashoda."[111]

Since no one could know exactly who was in the crowd or how large it was, different newspapers construed it in different ways. For the pro-government *Le Matin,* it was a festive crowd, an enthusiastic patriotic gathering of no particular political hue. According to the right-wing *Le Gaulois* (2 June 1899), "The people in the streets of Paris were anti-Dreyfusard to a man." The mass of journalistic accounts suggests that *Le Matin* had it right.[112] The near-absence of pro- and anti-Dreyfusard cries indicates that most people had come out not to demonstrate but to glimpse the hero, to bask in the presence of "Marchand l'Africain." "The enthusiasm is unbelievable," wrote the journalist for *Le Matin,* "everyone is intent on seeing, even touching" Marchand

Figure 18. A huge Parisian crowd welcomes Marchand (*L'Illustration,* 10 June 1899).

and his men.[113] The immense crowd seemed united in a patriotic endorsement of the charismatic personality—precisely the outcome government leaders had sought.

The republican orators and government officials who addressed this Parisian throng took pains not only to associate themselves with the heroic Marchand but to redefine his defeat as a victory, just as Schivelbusch has led us to
expect. The minister of the navy called Fashoda "a victory brought home . . .
by French arms in the service of the civilization of laws."[114] For Georges Du-
ruy of the pro-Dreyfusard *Figaro,* Marchand's "triumphal return" showed
both France's persistent strength and its ability to remain invincible in the
face of "suffering, sickness, and death."[115] Writing in the mass-circulation *Le
Journal,* the historian and former minister of foreign affairs Gabriel Hanotaux maintained that Marchand represented a France so morally superior, so
indifferent to economic gain, that its "only honorarium is honor itself."[116] *Le
Journal*'s editors put the icing on the cake: "This is why our cries of victory
accompany you, you the vanquished who are victorious too. We have hope,
and with you we cry out: 'Vive la Plus Grande France!'" Fashoda was a momentary, perhaps necessary, setback en route to the ultimate triumph of the
greater imperial France.[117]

In terms of ideological commitment, if not realities on the ground, such
may have been the case. The republican embrace of the "hero of Fashoda"
doubtless reinforced pro-colonial sentiment on the moderate left. And com-

bined with the new militantly pro-colonial stance of the nationalist right, the heightened colonialism among republicans created a large constituency for empire in France. In the past, Radicals and right-wingers had argued strenuously against colonial expansion, worried as they were about diverting attention from the "bleeding wound" of Alsace and Lorraine.[118] But in the wake of Fashoda, pro-colonial sentiment would extend across the whole political spectrum, except for a tiny number of voices on the extreme left. Such near-unanimity would mean that French colonialism would weather an atrocities scandal in the Congo, though Brazza's investigation of French behavior there would give some people pause (see chapter 6). More important, when France became embroiled with Germany (1905) over conflicting claims to Morocco, the old idea of revanche against the Hun would assume a new and more dangerous import. Under those circumstances, Germany would do double duty as European threat and colonial threat, a Janus-faced menace against which war would seem the only way out.

It is difficult to find journalists or government officials who dissented from the portrait of Marchand as hero-martyr and agent of ultimate victory for France. One notable exception confirms just how deeply the idea of "glorious defeat" had taken root. Urbain Gohier, Clemenceau's colleague at *L'Aurore,* sputtered in frustration and rage over the victory-talk of his fellow journalists. When a people suffers a great loss, he wrote, they need to endure it in silence. But not the French. "We have no such decency. We triumph from our defeats and our humiliations as others triumph from their success." And because the French can never admit their defeats, Gohier added, they must compensate by taking their revenge on those too weak to resist: the Arabs, Annamites, and the blacks.[119] There was all too little of such commentary in the wake of Fashoda, as there would be too little in the aftermath of the world wars to come.

If nationalists and republicans ultimately allied over empire, in 1899, republicans reasserted control. On his triumphal return to Paris, Marchand left his right-wing admirers in the lurch, siding with the Republic and not with them. To cries of "*Vive Déroulède!* Down with the traitors!" Marchand dismissed the nationalist rebels who had pinned their hopes on him: "Let's all come together," he said. "*Vive la France!* That is all I have to say."[120] Nationalists had done everything they could to turn his visit to Paris, his "*journée Marchand,*" into an anti-republican coup d'état. Instead, they found themselves overwhelmed by a huge, vibrant, unifying "*fête populaire.*"[121] Nationalists found one perhaps insurmountable obstacle to their designs: never did the Third Republic's founding narratives depict France as divided in two and defeated by itself. Unlike the nationalist narratives, the Third Republic's heroic stories always located enemies outside France. In 1899, it was the republicans who breathed new life into those stories by presenting Marchand as symbol of a nation internally united against an often-hostile outside world.

The final act in the republican recuperation of Marchand took place on 14 July 1899, when Prime Minister René Waldeck-Rousseau made Marchand a main attraction of that year's "Fête Nationale." The commander and his officers led a group of handsomely uniformed *tirailleurs sénégalais* past an appreciative, good-humored crowd.[122] The acclaim Marchand received on this eminently republican and national day suggests that his heroic image had helped bring a measure of unity to a long-divided France.

SIX

Brazza and the Scandal
of the Congo

ON 15 FEBRUARY 1905, the *Petit parisien,* the daily paper boasting the largest circulation in the world (1.5 million), published a short front-page article entitled *"Arrestation Mysterieuse."* Details were sketchy, but the unsigned piece reported that a magistrate had charged one Georges Toquet with "assassination and violence against several natives" from the French Congo.[1] An interview with the colonial administrator's mother yielded no information beyond confirmation that her son had indeed been taken by the police.

The following day all the major Parisian papers and several provincial ones led with a much larger story of what the *Petit parisien* was already calling France's "Scandales Coloniaux." *Le Matin,* circulation 900,000, got the full, lurid scoop. In a front-page article entitled "The Black Man's Executioners," *Le Matin's* reporter narrated the details of this awful "colonial crime." The previous 14 July, Toqué (not Toquet) and two subordinates, Fernand-Léopold Gaud and Pierre Proche, decided to add a little drama to what was otherwise a dull celebration of France's national holiday. "After a copious meal, lubricated by frequent libations, the party-goers, inflamed all the more by the torrid climate, decided to treat themselves to a filthy drunken spectacle."[2] They laid their hands on a young black man, whom they bound tightly with rope. The drunkards then attached a stick of dynamite between the man's shoulder blades, but before lighting the fuse, one of the revelers had a better idea. Why not insert the dynamite into the African's anus and then blow him up? "The Negro screamed. An explosion rang out. Bloody debris, body parts, intestines were projected a great distance." Lest readers think that this "horrifying little pleasure, this bloodthirsty act of insanity" satisfied Toqué's macabre lust for violence, he and his friends thought it would be amusing to go one step further.[3] Their new idea was to ambush another black man and unceremoniously cut off his head. After disposing of the torso, Toqué dunked the head in a boiling caldron of water, the better to make a delectable soup. The French administrators then invited the decapitated man's friends and family to dinner, after which the sadists carried out the boiled head on a platter. "This new casserole," the journalist concluded, "produced the desired effect."[4]

The structure and style of this article closely resembles the typical fait divers, or miscellaneous (crime) story, of the Belle Epoque. Like the plethora of articles with titles such as *"Femme coupée en morceaux"* (Woman chopped in pieces), *Le Matin*'s "The Black Man's Executioners" focused on blood and guts, on the splattered body parts that made the full horror of crime palpable to readers avid for gory details.[5] As the audience of penny papers grew exponentially between the 1860s and the Great War, so did coverage of crime.[6] Interest in violence and the macabre was nothing new, but only since the 1860s had the technology and know-how existed for such tales to reach a huge newly literate public eager to be informed and entertained. Unlike the fictional literature that most people had read in the past, newspapers were devoted to reality, to actual events occurring in the world. Hence the widespread attention to crime, which satisfied both the public's interest in drama, violence, and gore and the journalists' professional obligation to narrate what was happening now.[7]

In reporting Toqué's *"crimes coloniales,"* the penny papers reproduced all the elements of a mainland crime story, only coverage of the Congo drama had potentially serious political consequences. The day after the Congo story broke, the *Petit parisien*'s reporter wrote, "The arrest of M. Emile-Eugène-Georges Toqué was just the prelude, it seems, to an enormous scandal in the colonial world."[8] What had begun as a fait divers now quickly earned promotion to the level of scandal, a much weightier category of journalistic interest. Sociologists define scandal as an event that implicates important people and often members of the government. It involves transgressions, or perceived transgressions, against widely accepted moral standards and as such can call the reputations of key individuals into question.[9] Scandals can change the relations of power in a society, as the Panama controversy of the early 1890s did, or reaffirm existing values and mores, as in the Caillaux Affair of 1914.[10] Although the Congo scandal would ultimately serve to reinforce prevailing ideas about the merits of colonialism in France, government officials could not, at the outset, be confident that such would be the case. When journalists from the mass-circulation press aired the word "scandal" in 1905, it necessarily worried French leaders, who knew full well that horrible, shameful things had occurred in the Congo on their watch.

If reporters were to represent Toqué's acts as typifying a widespread pattern of abuse, a pattern built into the structure of French colonial rule in Equatorial Africa, the legitimacy of France's colonial project, with its loudly proclaimed "civilizing mission," could be challenged. Such was especially true given the contemporaneous international scrutiny of King Leopold's Congo Free State and the reports of atrocities committed there on a very large scale.[11] If the French Congo resembled Leopold's Congo, how could a liberal republican government justify its colonial rule? How could government leaders and ordinary people continue to ground their support for imperial expansion in the moral and humanitarian comforts of the mission civilisatrice? For French leaders and the public at large, the greatness and superiority of French culture had made France uniquely responsible for nurturing, educating, and improving the lives of those privileged to live under colonial rule. The French took pride in their empire, not as an agent of conquest and economic exploitation but as a means of elevating and enlightening the "savage" masses of the South.[12] As we have seen, Brazza appeared to exemplify the humanitarian mission of French colonialism, and his charismatic persona helped attach a great many of his countrymen and women to this soothing set of beliefs. The Congo revelations threatened these widespread views, which is why a ferocious debate erupted in France over the meaning of what had occurred.

In response, the government launched a powerful campaign to play down the significance of the Congo reports, a campaign whose outcome remained in doubt for nearly a year. In the competitive market of the penny press, scoops as sensational as this took on a life of their own, often resisting efforts at the highest levels to frame the narrative or change the subject. Toqué's arrest had convinced a wide array of journalists that they had a big story on their hands—a story of "horrible crimes," of crimes so "fantastic and bizarre" that "they seemed to emerge from the pages of Edgar Allen Poe."[13] The resulting frenzy of attention from the press revealed examples of colonial violence that local administrators normally succeeded in covering up: the kidnapping and rape of Congolese women, the death of prisoners held under inhumane conditions, the harsh punishment of "rebels," and varieties of forced labor, often involving portage. Such revelations, the *Petit parisien* declared, "inspire a set of general reflections about our entire colonial oeuvre."[14] These were sentiments the Ministry of Colonies did not want to see on the front page of France's largest-selling paper.

For this reason, it is doubtful that government officials orchestrated this story, as certain prominent historians have maintained.[15] The evidence suggests, rather, that political leaders tried to keep it under wraps. Investigating these events, the *Petit parisien*'s journalists found the Ministry of Colonies "extremely unhappy about the publicity being given to this affair. So upset are they, that we wonder how the truth about the abominable deeds attributed to M. Toqué and his colleagues MM. Gaud et Proche could have leaked out, especially since the Minister had issued the strictest orders not to divulge anything of what had happened."[16] The answer, according to the paper's anonymous sources, was that several natives had confided in a colonial administrator known for his honesty, telling him what Toqué and his friends had done. That administrator, "justly indignant," reported the allegations to judicial authorities in Brazzaville, who immediately arrested Gaud. He, in turn, implicated his immediate superior, Toqué. At that point, the Congo's chief administrator, Commissaire General Emile Gentil, ordered Toqué to cut short his Parisian leave and return to the colony. Gentil hoped perhaps that by bringing the young administrator back, he could keep the story out of the press. If that was Gentil's strategy, it unraveled when Toqué refused to obey the governor's order. Under these circumstances, the only way to return him to Africa was to charge him with a crime and have him arrested in Paris. But that "*arrestation mysterieuse*" is what put reporters on the scent.

To bring the story under control, the colonial ministry and pro-government and pro-colonial newspapers claimed that such atrocities represented the isolated acts of "two crazy men . . . two lost sheep *(brébis galeuses)*," and not the "colonial crimes" of a system beset with structural flaws. They then proceeded to build a case against Toqué. The pro-government *Le Matin* sent its journalist to the administrator's hometown, Lorient, where former teachers described him as a sickly adolescent, almost deformed, his habits and bearing highly "irregular." The reporter asked one if he believed Toqué "capable of the atrocities he's accused of?" "I don't know and can't say," the instructor responded, "except that he wasn't honest, even if extremely intelligent. Perhaps he gave way in a moment of madness."[17]

If *Le Matin's* interviews put Toqué on trial, the more independent *Petit parisien* expressed a large measure of doubt over his guilt. It quoted Britain's "native-loving" *West African Mail,* a newspaper highly critical of France's Congolese regime, as calling Toqué "one of France's most humane colonial administrators." Sent to the accused's hometown, the *Petit parisien's* correspondent presented him in an even more sympathetic light. Toqué was warm and appealing, sympathized with the Congolese, and warned that French policies could "lead to the extermination of the tribes in question, half of whose population has already been lost." These sentiments, the correspondent concluded, "hardly seem compatible with those of a torturer."[18]

In response, *Le Matin* turned its front page over to the pro-colonial deputy René Le Hérissé, who concluded that men like Toqué and Gaud "constitute an exception, an extremely rare exception, among our colonial administrators," the vast majority of whom were "admirable for the zealousness of their devotion and their abnegation." If Toqué and Gaud's "methods resembled those practiced in certain foreign colonies," they were the exceptions that proved France's humanitarian rule. "In France," Le Hérissé declared, "we use a completely different method of colonization."

Writers for the *Petit parisien* seemed less certain of the difference between France's colonial practices and those all too common in the Congo Free State next door. To investigate the story behind the Toqué-Gaud atrocities, reporters for the paper interviewed several anonymous sources identified only as former colonial officials in Africa. Virtually all of these informants maintained that the crimes attributed to Toqué and Gaud represented the tip of the iceberg of a much deeper structural problem. "What took place in Krebedjé [Toqué's district]," one interviewee maintained, "happens essentially everywhere in the dark continent . . . where white torturers reign as sovereign masters over immense territories and populations."[19] Knowledge of atrocities, "which occur regularly," rarely seeped out. "My absolute belief," the interviewee said, "is that if Toqué had not returned to France, we would have known nothing of the accusations against him. These accusations would never have been made."

Although top officials in the colonial ministry presented French colonists in the Congo as "devoted and humane," they knew perfectly well that a great many were anything but. Since 1893, four successive government inspections of the French Congo had documented the negligence and incompetence of colonial officials posted there, the paucity of resources, and the abuses committed both by government agents and by individuals in the rubber trade.[20] Officials also knew of the atrocities attributed to

Toqué and Gaud, because the Congo's *commissaire general* had sent the former colonial minister, Gaston Doumerge, a detailed report about the affair the previous August.[21] The report had remained confidential until Toqué's arrest the following February.

The Entente Cordiale with Britain (1904) encouraged the French government all the more to keep the Toqué story under wraps and then to downplay its importance once it broke.[22] The British government was already unhappy over French policy in the Congo because the concessionary companies granted monopolies there prevented British traders from operating in the region. The Berlin Congress of 1885 had explicitly guaranteed free trade in much of what would become the Congo Free State and French Equatorial Africa, and British commercial interests reacted angrily to France and Belgium's flagrant violations of the Berlin accords. Since the 1860s, two British firms, Hatton-and-Cookson and John Holt, had between them owned about half of the major trading stations in the Congo. Most of these stations stood in regions granted to the different concessionary companies. When those companies attempted to prevent Holt from doing business and went so far as to confiscate his rubber in 1899, the British trader protested to his government.[23] The *Times* and other papers took up the matter, as did the skillful humanitarian advocate E. D. Morel, who often cooperated with British commercial interests in Liverpool.[24] Holt was not without his own humanitarian concerns: he saw how concessionary companies in both Congos deprived Africans of the right to harvest rubber on their own and trade directly with foreign merchants. The Congolese lived at the mercy of monopolistic firms.

Meanwhile, Britain's Aborigines Protection Society, largely indifferent to Holt's commercial concerns, joined him and Morel in publicly condemning the humanitarian consequences of France's "deplorable imitation" of the Congo Free State and the "manifest danger of further incalculable mischief ensuing."[25] Given the growing international outcry against Leopold's Congo, the last thing France's republican government wanted was to share in the opprobrium directed against Belgium. With an international commission due to issue a scathing report on the Free State, the French wanted to mark as much distance between them and Leopold as they could.[26] Otherwise, the developing scandal could bring down the French government.

On 26 February 1905, the new minister of colonies, Etienne Clémentel, announced the formation of a commission charged with investigating the Congo situation. By taking the initiative in creating such a commission, the French government hoped to avoid being required to make it an international body, as Leopold had been forced to do. Instead, the government would be free to stack the commission with reliable people who would produce a favorable, exculpatory report. But almost immediately, Clémentel met with an unanticipated problem. The docile bureaucrat Etienne Dubard, asked to head the commission, declined the assignment. While the colonial ministry looked for a replacement, the president of the Republic, who rarely intervened in day-to-day political affairs, publicly suggested Pierre Savorgnan de Brazza.

President Loubet had long been friendly with Brazza and his family, and he likely knew the celebrated explorer eagerly sought a role in this affair.[27] But Brazza was the last person to whom top colonial officials wanted to turn. Many of them had helped engineer Brazza's dismissal in 1898 as the Congo's commissaire general, and they rightly feared he would be disinclined to make them look good.[28] Worse, the explorer's public stature and the political authority granted this charismatic figure would give him a large measure of independence in pursuing his investigation and writing his report. With Brazza involved, the scandal would be hard to contain. But once the president had put forth his name, the Colonial Ministry had no choice but to accept it. Brazza was a national hero and founding father of France's new African empire; to reject him would raise suspicions that there was something to hide. As it happened, the commission of inquiry, hastily conceived and prematurely announced, nearly proved a disaster for the French imperial project in Central Africa. Brazza would develop serious doubts about the justice and morality of French colonialism in Central Africa, and perhaps elsewhere as well.

At the beginning of 1905, Brazza, now fifty-three, lived in retirement and semi-exile in Algiers. His wife's family was well-to-do, and Thérèse, née de Chambrun, ensured her husband and their young children a comfortable existence. In 1902 the French parliament had awarded the former explorer an annual pension of 10,000 francs in recognition of his extraordinary service to France.[29] This award made Brazza's life all the more comfortable, and after twenty-five arduous years in Central Africa he could enjoy the leisured, gentlemanly existence that others of his noble birth took for granted. His was a quiet life; unlike his old rival Stanley, Brazza did not much intervene in public affairs. Although he nursed a great many grievances against those who had unceremoniously dismissed him seven years earlier, he kept those grievances to himself. Still, his friends and family knew how devastated he had been.[30]

Anointed a national hero in the 1880s, the explorer found himself a decade later the victim of a harsh press campaign designed to remove him from office and destroy his reputation. By the late 1890s, official French policies and attitudes had become tougher and less idealistic than those of the budding republic in which Brazza had become famous. In that earlier time, it had been important to temper imperialism with the humanistic ideals that the "pacific conqueror" seemed to represent. Although the harsher attitudes of the 1890s would soften again in the new century, by the time of the Dreyfus Affair, France's leaders had come to emphasize national grandeur and the country's renewed status as a Great Power far more than the founding values of the Republic. Leaders had concluded a realpolitik alliance with czarist Russia, reconciled with the pope, cracked down on leftists and revolutionaries, chosen raison d'état over Dreyfus's individual rights, and fought, often brutally, a great many colonial wars. The rhetoric of revenge against Germany remained strong, and in addition, France took an increasingly aggressive stance against Great Britain, seen as an opponent, even an enemy, in the "scramble for Africa."[31] For both countries, the scramble had led not just to a great many wars against African states and rulers but had also raised the specter of military conflict between them.

In this bellicose 1890s context, military strength and manly virtues became dominant themes on both sides of the Channel. Britain eschewed the Christ-like martyrdom of Charles Gordon for the ruthless military prowess of Horatio Herbert Kitchener. In France, a tough, manly Jean-Baptiste Marchand prevailed over the gentle Savorgnan de Brazza, who now appeared too soft, too friendly toward the Africans, and ironically, given his once-exalted status as "pacific conqueror," too reluctant to fight. Increasingly, the journalistic verdict of the late 1890s was that France needed a fiercer, more classically military man who could whip the Congo into line economically and stand fast against Britain's desire to control Africa from "Cairo to the Cape." Newspapers that had routinely praised Brazza for giving France a huge new colony "without spilling a drop of blood" now compared him unfavorably to Stanley, once condemned for rampaging through Africa. *La Croix* went so far as to complain, "Brazza has not used against the Negroes the same cruelty as Stanley."[32] Marchand, who merited no such complaints, sarcastically denounced his rival's "negrophilic politics with all its prestigious purity." *Le Matin*, meanwhile, summed up the new verdict on Brazza: he "practiced philanthropy, not colonization."[33]

These complaints contained a large measure of truth. Brazza lacked the ruthlessness characteristic of many European colonists, and he was guilty as charged of "respecting [the natives'] mores and customs" rather than trying to develop "the material riches of the colonized country" at all costs.[34] Administration and governance, moreover, did not hold the interest of this restless explorer, more at home in the bush than behind a desk. Even so, most of the attacks against him were unfounded. Although Brazza had exaggerated the economic prospects of the Congo, he cannot be fairly accused of blocking its development. The same structural problems that stymied the Congo's economic progress in the 1890s—low investment, poor transportation, resistance to European methods, and sparse indigenous population—would continue to thwart French development of the colony for decades to come.[35]

Although economic malfeasance formed the official explanation for Brazza's recall, the more fundamental reason is that the hard-nosed French Republic of the 1890s no longer needed a "conquérant pacifique." At century's end, politicians, journalists, and the public in France temporarily preferred Marchand to Brazza. But this preference was not destined to last. The nationalists' loss in the Dreyfus Affair combined with Marchand's "glorious defeat" at Fashoda returned French domestic and foreign policy to a more moderate stance. France had to accommodate its new ally across the Channel, which meant that it could not afford to be seen as another Belgium, mercilessly exploiting its colonial subjects and violating Britain's economic interests in Central Africa. If the French government had banished Brazza in 1898, his recall from retirement in March 1905 suggested that he had been right all along. Thanks to the Congo scandal, he could exact a measure of revenge against his enemies in the colonial ministry and attempt to salvage a civilizing mission in which he wanted to believe.

The popular press lauded Brazza's 1905 appointment as head of the Congo Commission. In an editorial entitled "A Great Frenchman," the *Petit parisien* recalled the explorer's reputation as a "pacific conqueror," "an apostle of peace," and as the Frenchman who had "acquired among the natives the same moral authority as Livingstone."[36] Brazza was the good colonizer, the man who understood that the "basis of all truly lasting colonial activity was to improve the natives' lives, to conciliate their interests with ours." Thanks to his efforts, the Congolese had gained "such a high and pure idea of what the French flag represents that they wanted to take refuge within its folds." Neither this nor any other popular article on the Brazza Commission discussed what steps the explorer—or the government—might take to rectify the situation in the Congo, or even to understand how and why the abuses of the Congolese had been allowed to occur. It was as if Brazza's charismatic presence alone would "restore in our African colonies the principles of generosity that belong to the patrimony of France, of which Brazza, throughout his career, has been one of the most eminent representatives." Because Brazza's "name is synonymous with humanity and goodness," declared the *Petit parisien,* the commission needed no specific objectives. "It was enough to have charged Brazza with leading it," which is why the newspaper could "loudly proclaim our confidence in the mission's success." What exactly "success" would mean remained unsaid. The assumption was, as *La Nature* put it, that Brazza had remained such "a demigod among the Africans that one sign of friendship from him" would remind them of the goodness of French colonialism and make memories of its atrocities go away.[37]

Although top officials at the Ministry of Colonies publicly endorsed such sentiments—Brazza's mission constituted a "new apostolate," declared Clémentel—in private they expressed horror over his selection.[38] "The appointment of Brazza," wrote Gustave Binger, director of African affairs at the Ministry, "resulted from the idiotic press campaign in response to the Gaud and Toqué affairs. To put a stop to it and give public opinion a certain amount of satisfaction, the Minister, on my advice, decided to create a low-key commission of inspection." Ministry officials never intended that Brazza head the commission, but the former explorer "went to see several cabinet ministers, who . . . without thinking things though, reflexively agreed" to appoint him.[39]

Binger's comment provides further evidence that the government found itself responding to developments it did not control. Colonial officials had not only to contend with Brazza but also to allow him to approve commission members, a prerogative the explorer, with President Loubet's blessing, imposed as a condition for accepting the assignment. Particularly worrisome to the Colonial Ministry was the selection of Félicien Challaye, a young left-leaning philosopher and recent graduate of the elite Ecole normale supérieure. A talented writer, Challaye had agreed to cover the mission for *Le Temps.* His dispatches for this prestigious, quasi-official paper amounted to a serious indictment of France's entire Congolese regime.[40]

To make the best of a bad situation, Clémentel directed Congo commissaire general Gentil not to cooperate with the Brazza inquiry. The minister then limited its duration to six months, including travel to and from

Africa. He issued instructions designed to narrow the scope of the investigation and framed questions intended to evoke the kinds of answers the ministry wanted to hear. Brazza was asked, for example, to confirm that abuses were "extremely rare" and "limited to individual acts that cannot be seen as part of an organized system."[41] The minister also instructed Brazza not to include anything in his final report that would provoke "a sterile theoretical discussion of the advantages or dangers, in the French Congo, of the concessionary system." Above all, Clémentel made it clear, the commission of inquiry was to "show the difference between the rules that [France] applies to its possessions in the Congo and the methods used in the Free State." Brazza was to find, in other words, that the damning international criticism of Leopold's Congo did not apply to France.[42]

These kinds of instructions might have succeeded with a commission appointed by the ministry; with Brazza, they would have only minimal effect. Having spent twenty years in the Congo, Brazza knew what to look for, and he seemed convinced that his stature and prestige, both in France and in Africa, would permit him to root out the violence and injustice he found.[43] Never a writer, Brazza did not produce a narrative account of his mission, but Challaye's dispatches allow us to follow most of the inquiry, as do books written after the fact by another member of the commission, Jules Saintoyant, and by Georges Toqué himself.[44]

The dozen members of the commission, including Brazza's wife Thérèse, left Marseille on 4 April 1905.[45] They reached Libreville (present-day Gabon), a first destination of French ships heading for equatorial Africa, three weeks later. There, Brazza greeted the chiefs he knew from his days as commissaire general and acknowledged former slaves who owed their freedom to him. Despite poor health and lingering grief over the recent death of his five-year-old son, Brazza seemed in his element. "M. de Brazza," wrote Challaye, "put his hands on Chief Goya's shoulders. The old man placed his black hands on Brazza's white jacket. In this position, both bowed their heads three time, thrice repeating a mantra of greeting."[46]

From the Gabon coast, the commission sailed south to the former slave-trading port of Loango, where Challaye reported that the men "dress like us, without appearing too ridiculous." The philosopher marveled over the Africans' ability to speak and write French correctly, and he extolled the beauty of the countryside. "It's just like Normandy," he wrote.[47] Continuing on, they steamed into the mouth of the Congo River and then up the vast estuary to Matadi, the last town before the succession of cataracts that made the lower Congo impassable. From there, Brazza and company boarded the narrow-gauge Belgian train that chugged slowly overland to Leopoldville (now Kinshasa), capital of the Congo Free State. The four-hundred-kilometer journey took forty-eight hours, slow by European standards, but immeasurably faster than the slavers' caravan route that Marchand and others had had to take before Leopold completed his railroad in 1898. Once in Leopoldville, the French team took a ferry across the wide expanse of Stanley Pool, landing in Brazzaville on May 16. The commission had been *en voyage* for six weeks, and the inquiry had yet to begin.

During his brief stay in the town he founded, Brazza held tense meetings with Gentil and the longtime Catholic bishop of the region, Monseigneur Augouard. Neither tried to disguise their suspicion of the former commissaire general nor their hostility to his mission of inspection.[48] Both men had things to hide, and they worried about what Brazza might find. The mission stayed in the capital only two weeks; time was short and Brazza sought to visit as much of the colony as possible. He wanted especially to make it to Chad, where he understood some of the worst atrocities had taken place.

On 29 May the group boarded a steamer for the 750-kilometer trip up the Congo and then the Ubangi River to the town of Bangui, capital of the present-day Central African Republic. This was the same trajectory Marchand had followed in 1896, except that after Bangui the captain had headed east at the bend in the Ubangi River. The Brazza group continued north, abandoning its steamer for an oar-powered whaling boat that took the party up the Gribingui River to a pair of the most distant outposts in France's central African colony: Fort-Lamy and Fort-Crampel. This leg of the journey took five weeks. Saintoyant's narrative emphasizes just how arduous the trip was for the typical low-level colonial administrator assigned to one of these forts. Petty officials, who benefited from none of the special travel arrangements made for the Brazza commission, spent five months in transit from southern France to Fort-Crampel, a trip that left them ill, exhausted, and numbed by the sheer discomfort of the equatorial climate.

As for the outposts themselves, inexperienced colonial administrators served there with only one or two other European companions and no supervision by any higher authority. The nearest officers were weeks or months away and thus incapable of exercising any effective control, even had they wanted to. The forts were ill equipped and uncomfortable. Colonial agents had to procure much of their own food, since great distances and uncertain means of travel made it extremely difficult for authorities to supply the outposts with sufficient provisions. There were no books or even newspapers, and little else to relieve the monotony of this grim colonial life. For all these reasons, Saintoyant wrote, the Frenchmen stationed there "live in a state of nervous exhaustion that deprives them of the level-headedness required for good public administration." Not only did this situation "destroy the cadres' physical vigor, it extinguishes their ardor to create" a well-functioning colony, making lapses in judgment, even criminal behavior, inevitable.[49]

Saintoyant did not conclude from this sorry description that colonialism was a bad idea, but rather that building an empire required a huge commitment of resources and that politicians in Paris were remiss in refusing to provide them. Aggravating the problem was the refusal by French investors to sink capital into the region, whose economic potential they doubted. Large investment banks preferred to finance government loans and railroad building in "semicolonies" like Russia and Turkey. They shied away from the actual French Empire and, in particular, from unknown places like the Congo.[50] So did potential French settlers, repelled by the Congo's harsh climate and vast distance from France. And few French businesses showed interest in operating there, given the British dominance of African coastal trade. To lure firms to Equatorial Africa, the benefits would have to appear especially good.

For inspiration, French colonialists looked to the Belgian model. France's Congo could not be an exact replica of the Free State, since the latter had become the private property of the Belgian king. But the French were attracted to Leopold's method of dividing his colony into several large pieces and granting "concessionary" companies monopoly control over one or more of them. These monopolies had produced huge profits for a handful of Belgian firms and especially for the Belgian king. Perhaps they would do the same for France?

In 1899 the country's colonial minister established forty "concessions," each granting a single company the exclusive right to exploit the domain it received for thirty years.[51] The smallest concession covered 1,200 square kilometers, the largest 140,000. These sizes were approximate at best; no one knew the Congo's geography well enough to map the different concessions precisely. In fact, no one even knew exactly how big the Congo colony was. Large as these monopolies were, their advocates remained unsatisfied. Pro-colonial journalists argued that too much land had been reserved for the natives, who might therefore refuse to work for the companies, and that the French government's 15 percent share of the companies' profits was too high. Colonialists worried about the amount of rubber growing in the colony, the declining stocks of ivory, competition from firms in the Free State, and the cost of exploiting what proved to be there.[52]

In fact, business conditions in the French Congo were not very good. To operate profitably in this part of the world, a firm required more than a monopoly over a particular piece of land, even a very large one. Concessionary companies needed sizable state investment in means of transport and paramilitary police. Lacking other colonies to administer, King Leopold could focus all of his overseas resources on the Free State. He built a railway from Stanley Pool to the Atlantic and developed a thick apparatus of command and repression that worked in tandem with the different monopolistic firms.

The French government, by contrast, had created essentially no infrastructure, save for building a modest administrative center in Brazzaville and staffing the major towns and a few outposts with a skeleton crew of low-ranking officials. Paris proved unwilling to deploy French soldiers in the Congo, engaging instead a tiny force of African paramilitary policemen charged with overseeing more than a million square miles of land. If these problems alone likely doomed the colony to economic failure, two further obstacles ensured its financial ruin: a pitiful transport system and an inadequate supply of labor. The absence of an unbroken waterway from either the Congo or the Ubangi River to the Atlantic coast meant that human porters had to carry goods and supplies from the Congo to the Ogooué or the Alima River before they could be floated to an Atlantic port. To reach the northern part of the colony also required lengthy treks on foot over particularly arduous terrain. As Marchand had learned, indigenous people shunned the exhausting, unforgiving labor of portage, and neither the colonial administration nor the companies would—or could— pay the large sums needed to recruit porters from other regions of Africa. To solve the manpower problem, officials regularly forced men to work.

Reluctant as the Congolese were to serve as porters, they proved even less interested in harvesting rubber, especially for the minuscule wages Europeans tended to pay. Leopold solved the manpower problem by using his large paramilitary *force publique* to compel indigenous people, en masse, to work. As Adam Hochschild has shown, the *force* did so at a grotesque human cost.[53] French officials and agents of the concessionary companies imitated Leopold's methods of compulsion, but they lacked the means to employ them on such a large scale. As a result, economic extraction in the French Congo depended on the opportunistic, and often creative, use of violence—especially exemplary violence—to squeeze work out of the Congolese at the lowest possible price.

Banking on the prospect of doing just that, groups of investors eagerly bought shares of stock in France's new concessionary companies. Journalists extolled the supposed value of these companies, stirring a speculative interest in the stock. Shares of the Société de l'Ibenga that had sold for 500 francs each in late 1899 nearly doubled in value by April 1900. At that point, the original owners began to sell their holdings, reaping profits of 80 to 100 percent. By November 1900, the share price had dropped to 550 francs. After another two years of gyrating, values settled at extremely low levels, at which point some of the original investors returned to the market. Many of these financiers were Belgians heavily invested in the Congo Free State, and they proceeded to sweep up French equities at rock-bottom prices. Although the original decree establishing the concessions stipulated that most owners be French, the Belgian presence turned out to be very large. Several of the putatively French companies served as de facto subsidiaries of Belgian firms operating next door in Leopold's state.

Despite the heavy involvement of Belgians experienced in the rubber and ivory economies of Equatorial Africa, many of the French firms would fail. None would earn the high profits common in the Free State.[54] By 1904, five years after the French concessions were formed, 25 percent had already ceased to exist; the rest grouped themselves into nineteen operating companies. Thanks to cartographical confusion, one of those nineteen possessed no land at all, and another found itself on the wrong side of the border between the Congo and the German colony Cameroon. By the end of the concessions' thirty-year life, only six firms remained. As for the financial performance of the concessionary companies, in 1902, just a single firm earned enough to distribute dividends to shareholders. Seven reported dividends in 1906, the number falling back to two in 1908.[55] Overall, the companies lost nearly 10 million francs between 1899 and 1904.[56]

Such miserable performance added to the French government's troubles once news of the Congo scandal leaked out. Political leaders understood that violence and the threat of violence alone kept the concessionary system from collapsing altogether. But for obvious reasons, they could never admit as much. The government's best hope was to narrowly restrict the flow of information to the Brazza commission, limit the depth and duration of its inquiry, and keep its findings, certain to include some uncomfortable revelations, confidential. Unfortunately for the governing elite, enterprising journalists made extensive use of anonymous sources whose revelations kept the Congo story very much alive, even after the commission left for Africa in April 1905.

The colonial ministry had doubtless hoped the crush of dramatic domestic and international news of that extraordinary year—the law separating church and state, the Russo-Japanese War, the Russian revolution, the Franco-German crisis over Morocco—would make the Congo story go away. But former officials, businesspeople, and others familiar with the situation continued to leak damning information. A retired concessionary company manager told France's fourth-largest-selling paper, *Le Journal,* that his firm routinely forced Africans to deliver ivory and rubber to them by "tying them down and whipping them 50 times with a *chicotte*"—a cruelly ingenious lash made of raw, sun-dried hippopotamus hide, twisted to form hundreds of razor-sharp spokes. "After each blow, the victims screamed in pain, their blood spurting out." The next day, "they returned with ivory and rubber." *Le Journal*'s source also claimed to have frequently seen the companies' armed agents "enter into villages, where they forced terrorized blacks to give them their ivory." The Africans received not a sou in payment, a common practice, the former official said.[57] Worse, another popular paper not only confirmed the prevalence of such extortion and theft but also reported, "The administration [of the colony] tolerated such things; judicial officials left them unpunished; and successive [colonial] governors hid them from authorities in Paris."[58]

With reports such as these persistently leaking out, the colonial ministry must have been horrified when Challaye's detailed and compelling dispatches began to appear in *Le Temps.* The special correspondent, who doubled as Brazza's personal secretary for the mission, was a socialist openly hostile to the concessionary companies and suspicious from the outset of France's Congolese regime. It is unclear why *Le Temps* hired him, but impressive that it did. His remarkable series of articles, written between April and September 1905, added to the explorer's legend while covering the trial of Toqué and Gaud and, most important, confirming the extent of French abuses in the Congo. Challaye also made a notable contribution to French travel literature, painting perhaps the best portrait to date of equatorial Africa. Other members of the Brazza commission wrote about the Congolese mission, but without Challaye's journalistic flair and his front-page access to the mainstream press.[59]

In many ways, Challaye's narrative followed the pattern of the travel writing he knew very well. "Sitting in front of my tent," Challaye tells his readers early on, "I read Stanley's book, *Across the Dark Continent.*"[60] With the earlier literature in mind, Challaye reproduced many of the most familiar European images of Africa. For him, as for so many others, the voyage from Europe to the Dark Continent was an excursion into another world, a world so exotic as to seem unreal. In Challaye's first stop, the Moroccan city of Tangiers, "a blur of people fills the streets and the marketplace square: veiled Arab women, Moroccans, Jews, Negroes, priests, soldiers, beggars, a beautiful French woman on horseback, a few British tourists looking ridiculous and out of place. . . . A series of spectacles—the most colorful, animated, amusing spectacles I've ever seen—follow one another without any apparent link, just like in a dream."[61]

For Challaye, as for Joseph Conrad and so many others, Africa's shimmering exotic dream would gradually morph into a gruesome nightmare as he traveled into the savage midsection of the continent. Returning to Europe in 1898, Charles Castellani, Challaye's French predecessor in Equatorial Africa, felt as though he had just emerged from a "nightmare," from horrific visions that had taken him to the very "vestibule of death."[62] In Challaye's socialist-inflected telling, the nightmare had as much to do with the evils of French colonialism as with Africa itself. Even so, the young French philosopher escaped few of the era's standard images of the Dark Continent. His dispatches reproduced Conrad's portrait of Africa as a trip not just into uncharted recesses of space but into the distant mists of time.[63] "On the banks of the Congo," Challaye wrote, "we relive an age anterior even to prehistoric times."[64] Like most other European travelers, Challaye portrayed Africans as animalistic, the women parading naked and unashamed. He took voyeuristic delight in describing their unclothed bodies and in assumptions about their uninhibited sexuality. "Every afternoon," said Challaye, "the most elegant Banziri women smear their bodies, head to toe, with oil. They then coat themselves with a red powder. Naked (or almost) . . . they wait for I don't know what, love perhaps. From time to time, one of them performs a few steps of a brutal, erotic dance."[65]

Challaye endorsed the practice, common at the time, of taking these women as "temporary wives." By doing so, European men could avoid the rigors of sexual abstinence without incurring any ethical debts. Becoming mistress to a white man, he wrote, "poses no problem for the temporary wife, as native morals are anything but severe."[66] This idea was, of course, pure fantasy. African concubines often found themselves rejected by their own societies after their European lovers left them for home. Life proved even harder for the children of Euro-African unions, consigned as they were to a no-man's-land between the two worlds. Europeans feared that mixed-race children signaled racial decay, and Africans often rejected them as an alien breed.[67]

Beyond his stock images of African women, Challaye also found cannibalism everywhere he went. "One finds no gray hair, no senility and no blindness: children eat their parents at the first sign of decline." As for intelligence and maturity, Challaye found little of either. "The black man," he wrote, "can be compared to a young child and even to an animal, so narrow is his psychological life." They think only of the here and now, preoccupied as they are by the "satisfaction of physical needs" and especially "sexual pleasure." All this, Challaye hastened to add, is no reason to despise them or take advantage of their primitive brains. And it was wrong, he maintained, to impose hard, disciplined work on "races accustomed since time immemorial to do nothing."[68]

This conclusion prepared Challaye's readers for a detailed exposé of the atrocities committed or tolerated by French officials. It is interesting that he made no explicit references to these crimes until mid-August, three months into his trip. Why he waited so long is difficult to say; records of the Brazza commission make clear that it had found evidence of atrocities shortly after arriving in the Congo in May 1905.[69] It was as if Challaye understood that the readers of Le Temps, long a pro-colonial newspaper, had little interest in knowing what had really happened in France's equatorial possessions.

Still, there were hints early on of the revelations to come. In late May, Challaye described Brazza's meeting with a Protestant missionary who told him, "Here, the natives aren't treated too badly; there's no rubber." A few days later a Catholic missionary reported, "The neighboring villages, once populated, are now almost abandoned. . . . The demands of the whites caused many of the natives to flee." Arriving at Fort-Crampel (in present-day Chad), Challaye framed his dispatch around the image of "an enormous mass of black rock [that] gives the entire countryside an air of mourning, a sinister look."[70]

Challaye delayed his revelations, in part, to give the hero of his story, Brazza, full credit for discovering what had happened in this ominous place. During a bizarre "native dance" staged for the Europeans' benefit, Brazza saw in it "a symbolic representation of the Calvary the inhabitants of this region had had to suffer. . . . Overwhelmed with emotion," Brazza now understood the terrible significance of the human bones he had discovered en route to the village of Dékoa, where the dance had taken place. Duly impressed with his hero's intelligence, Challaye voiced a condescending respect for the locals as well: "The natives, primitive as they are, are not incapable of symbolism."[71]

Strangely, Challaye fails to mention an element of this scene reported by another member of the commission, an *inspecteur des colonies* named Saurin. According to him, Brazza also understood from the dance that a great many villagers had recently been taken captive. Questioning the local administrator, who had hoped to hide this crime, Brazza found evidence of a nearby "concentration camp" with 119 women and children held hostage under miserable conditions.[72] The women appeared to have been raped, and press accounts depicted them as suffering from venereal diseases contracted from their captors.

The dance scene, occurring on 30 June 1905, constitutes the turning point of Challaye's story.[73] Over the following six weeks, Brazza would uncover the full extent of the crimes and horrors that had turned his once peaceful colony into a grotesque hell on earth. The 119 hostages represented in the dance were at least still alive. Descending further toward Bangui, Brazza unearthed a history that had not ended so well. In the town of Mongoumba, just south of Bangui, the commissioners discovered "one of the most painful events in the recent history of the French Congo." In 1904 an administrator stationed in the regional capital of Bangui received an official circular from Gentil notifying him and his colleagues that all future promotions would depend on their ability to increase the amount of taxes collected from the indigenous population. The circular prompted the Bangui official to dispatch an assistant administrator, along with several members of the paramilitary regional guard, into areas where rubber grew wild. Settling in the town of Mongoumba, the assistant sent two guardsmen into each neighboring village to order the different chiefs to pay taxes in the form of rubber. In the process, guardsmen "brutalized the natives and took advantage of the women they desired."[74] Terrified, the villagers began to flee across the river into the Congo Free State.

Desperate to collect a quantity of rubber before everyone left, the assistant had his guards seize fifty-eight women and ten children from the different villages. He promised to release them only when their husbands and fathers paid their taxes in full. The chief of one village had his mother, two wives, and two children taken by the guardsmen, who locked them and sixty-three other hostages in a building in Mongoumba. The men then began to deliver the rubber required of them, which the assistant immediately handed over to an agent for the concessionary company. (Companies gave the colonial government cash in exchange for the rubber.) Weighing the product collected, the government agent judged the quantity too small; he decided not to release the hostages, taking them back to Bangui. There, he locked all sixty-eight in a windowless hut six meters long and four meters wide. During their first twelve days in captivity, twenty-five hostages died, their bodies dumped in the river. Several days later, a doctor, newly arrived in the town, heard cries and moans coming from the hut. He pushed open the door and to his horror found a small number of skeletally thin women and children barely alive amid the stench of dead bodies and human excrement. "The skin was peeling away," wrote Dr. Fulconis, "muscles atrophied, intelligence gone, movement and speech no longer possible."[75] Of the sixty-eight hostages originally squeezed into the makeshift prison, only twenty-one had survived. One of the women gave birth before passing away, and a woman survivor adopted her child. "In this horrible drama," Challaye wrote, "it was the women cannibals who gave the cruel white men a lesson in humanity."[76]

After freeing the survivors, the young doctor notified the colonial administration of the atrocities he had seen. The court in Brazzaville took up the case, only to dismiss it on grounds of insufficient evidence. The lone action taken was to transfer the administrator responsible for the hostage taking. He was, however, moved from the outback of Bangui to the capital city of Brazzaville, where everyone wanted to be. Having uncovered this atrocity, Brazza and his colleagues proceeded to accumulate evidence of one chilling abuse after the other. "The book one needs to reread here," Challaye remarked, "is Dante's *Inferno.*"

By shipping Toqué to Brazzaville for trial, the Colonial Ministry had hoped that the proceedings against him would occur offstage, outside the French press's range. Officials did not expect that Challaye, as special correspondent for *Le Temps,* would be on the spot. The young philosopher was in fact the only journalist to cover the trial, so his dispatches stood as the lone public account of the event.

The trial unfolded over six days in mid-August 1905. Brazzaville's makeshift courtroom possessed none of the majesty of a French *palais de justice.* The judge, M. de Kersaint-Gilly, had come down from Libreville, and his court included two other magistrates plus two jurors chosen by lot from a list of ten "notables" of the colony. There was a prosecutor, and a single defense attorney for the two defendants, Toqué and Gaud. In fact, their "attorney" did not belong to the bar; he was a colonial administrator who knew nothing of the law. Twenty spectators, all Europeans, filled out the room. Save for a handful of Africans called in as witnesses, the trial was a whites-only affair. French officials considered the Congolese too uncivilized even to watch a trial; according to Challaye, they should not have served as witnesses either. "It is universally recognized," he wrote, "that the black man, especially the primitive blacks of the Congo, have no understanding of truth. They take as reality the things they invent, and they lie with extreme ease."[77]

This statement sets up Challaye's sympathetic portrayal of Toqué, whom he saw as trapped between the falsehoods of the blacks and the self-interest of the commissaire general. The latter, Challaye said, intended that Toqué and Gaud shoulder all the blame for crimes that stemmed from the very structure of the colonial system. The journalist clearly preferred Toqué to Gaud, whom he described as "fat, hairy, and bearded, his face bestial and ugly." If Toqué was no matinee idol—"small, stooped, skinny, dark, and nervous"—he displayed a youthful energy, spoke well, and had an expressive face.

Both Toqué and Gaud faced charges of murdering or ordering the murders of several Congolese men and women. The two defendants denied all accusations leveled by Africans, admitting wrongdoing only when a European, including either Toqué or Gaud, had endorsed or brought a charge. Since Toqué had himself accused his colleague of blowing up an African named Pakpa, Gaud could not deny responsibility. He did, however, claim that Toqué had told him to execute the man. Asked why he had used dynamite, his only response was that he had a few sticks in his hut and thought they would work well as a method of execution. In the pretrial phase, Gaud had testified that death by dynamite would be an ideal form of exemplary violence. The natives would see Pakpa's demise as a magical, divine intervention, something that would instill fear in their hearts and prevent future rebellions. So he hung the dynamite around Pakpa's neck, lit the fuse, and the man exploded. "Gaud recounted his crime," Challaye wrote, "with a stupefying calm."[78]

On the witness stand, Toqué confirmed what he had said during the pretrial investigation. His superiors had told him that nothing was more important than recruiting porters and collecting taxes. Finding the natives unwilling to work or pay imposts voluntarily, Toqué sent his agents to round up porters by force and take their wives and children hostage.

Members of the regional guards routinely raped the women hostages, many of whom later died, along with their children, of hunger and disease. Toqué testified that he believed himself authorized to render justice and even execute Africans he judged guilty of rebellion or insubordination. When he told his superior that he had summarily shot a "rebel" named Pikamandji, Toqué claimed his boss had replied, "You have done the right thing; in the future keep such information to yourself."[79] Only later would the younger man be charged with murder.

Toqué's courtroom representative introduced evidence showing that his client's superiors had given him nothing but praise. One official had even wanted him rewarded with the cross of the Legion of Honor. The indigenous people who testified found him either "un peu bon," "bon," or "beaucoup bon." Their evaluations of Gaud showed less support. Some witnesses recognized his intelligence and his linguistic, ethnological, and technical knowledge. But others considered him a loser—megalomaniacal, bitter, authoritarian, violent, and cruel. The indigenes labeled him "mauvais."[80] A doctor called by the defense claimed that his violence and megalomania constituted signs of mental illness and that he shouldn't be held fully responsible for his actions.

After hearing all the testimony, the court took a full day to reach a verdict. It declared Toqué guilty as an accomplice to murder and Gaud guilty of murder without premeditation. In both cases, the court found "extenuating circumstances," sentencing the pair to five years in prison. Most white residents of Brazzaville found the penalty outrageously harsh. "Accustomed to treating blacks as machines or slaves," Challaye wrote, "to exploiting them and abusing them, they [the white population] were amazed that anyone could judge the lives of these 'dirty niggers' so valuable."[81] On leaving the courtroom, the journalist heard a young civil servant cry out: "It's as if we have been naturalized as niggers."[82]

The lone whites who endorsed the sentence—only five years, after all, for murder—were military officers from Chad who deplored the indiscipline they found rampant in the Congo. As for Challaye himself, he reported mixed feelings about the outcome of the trial, especially in the case of Toqué. "A hero," Challaye wrote, "would have refused to obey his superiors." But Toqué was a green recruit worried about his career and afraid to resist. Hence his complicity in an untenable colonial system he had done nothing to create.

Challaye noted that Toqué had failed to use all possible means of defense. He failed to highlight contradictory testimony, to call potential supporters as witnesses, and even to demand a real attorney to represent him. His counsel belonged to a colonial administration eager to deflect all blame from itself. Challaye claimed that an eminent Parisian lawyer was ready to represent Toqué.[83] Above all, Challaye was struck by Toqué's failure to implicate any member of the colony's high administration. The journalist suspected a deal had been made promising an acquittal for Toqué in exchange for his silence in court.[84] He had no idea why the apparent bargain had not held up. "A painful mystery weighs on the witnesses in this tragic trial, which seems like some drama by Maeterlinck— obscure, overwhelming, and beyond anyone's control."

Challaye's questions about the trial and his revelations of atrocities and colonial abuse turned him against the existing regime in the Congo. But he nonetheless retained his allegiance to the most fundamental ideological pillar of the French colonial system, the mission civilisatrice. For him, it was the hero Brazza who incarnated and legitimized that mission. Brazza's was "the only form of colonialism compatible with a democracy such as ours, a democracy that civilizes and liberates." His successors had allowed his achievements to collapse, leaving an angry and terrified population that no longer recognized the greatness of French civilization. Whether Challaye believed a new civilizing mission could have redeemed the Congo is unclear, but given the views of other socialists at the time, it's likely he did. Only in the 1930s did Challaye become an ardent opponent of colonialism in all its forms.[85]

Brazza was destined to die on the continent long dear to his heart. He became so sick on the last leg of the journey back to Brazzaville that he could barely stand up. He forced himself, Challaye writes, to hold one final meeting with Gentil, who appeared increasingly evasive, increasingly unwilling to let Brazza's commission do its work. In a letter written just before his return trip home, Brazza claimed that Gentil had attempted to block his efforts at every turn. In the Ubangi-Chari region, where Brazza had discovered "the destruction pure and simple of the population," local officials, doubtless acting on the governor's orders, "went to great lengths to prevent me from seeing what had happened in the past and especially what is going on now."[86] Brazza could understand why: he found evidence of serious abuses committed even after his commission had sailed for Africa. Worse, he had caught the commissaire general in an outright lie. Although Gentil had loudly announced the end of portage, the commission saw that it had continued even more ruinously than before. Brazza's conclusion was that

Gentil should be removed from office. "I return home," Brazza wrote, "with the belief that my mission was necessary. Without it, we would have had a scandal on our hands worse . . . than those of the Belgians."

After locking horns one last time with Gentil, Brazza headed back across Stanley Pool and down to the Atlantic coast via the Belgian railway. His illness became so severe on the steamship home that he was taken ashore at Dakar, where he died on 14 September 1905. The explorer, Challaye wrote, was so brokenhearted by what he had seen in the Congo, so upset over the ruin of the great humane colony he had built, that he could no longer soldier on. Having presciently refused early on to serve King Leopold, he had been horrified to discover in the French Congo the same evils that shamed its Belgian neighbor. Brazza's "heroic sorrow," Challaye wrote, "his sublime sadness, sapped his strength and hastened his death."[87] He died a martyr to the mission civilisatrice.

Brazza had long been portrayed as a martyr, working selflessly and at the cost of his health and well-being to create a great empire for France. His death allowed this figurative martyrdom to come true. The great man, this "laic missionary" and "apostle" of freedom, wrote the *Petit parisien*'s Lucien Vrily, had anticipated, even embraced, his sacrifice to a larger cause. Before leaving for the Congo, he had told the journalist, "I will happily surrender all my remaining strength" to prevent the moral ruin of the colony.[88] In announcing Brazza's death, the mass-circulation press and pictorial weeklies depicted the martyr in quasi-religious terms. They showed a saintlike, emaciated Brazza being helped toward his deathbed. Photographs pictured him lying there, his withered face looking old far beyond his fifty-three years, his blank eyes about to close for good. Brazza's biographer and brother-in-law, Jacques de Chambrun, later put these pictures to words: "Those who kneel before his emaciated body, stretched out on the whiteness of a small narrow bed, were struck by the expression on his features seemingly frozen in anguish. Suddenly, they perceived a new look to this face they all had known for so long. No longer was it the face of a hero; it was the face of a martyr."[89]

Brazza had hoped that the prestige of his name would add strength to his findings and move the Republic to make amends. Now his fame would have to exert a posthumous force. Clémentel, who had never wanted the truth of the Congo to come out, decided to play down Brazza's report, even while associating himself—and France as a whole—with the saintliness and martyrdom of the great man. With Brazza out of the picture, the colonial minister appears to have decided on a three-pronged strategy: ex-

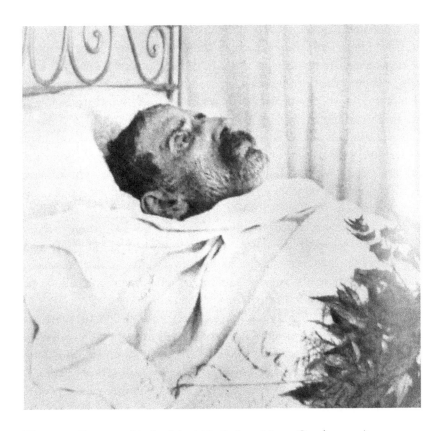

Figure 19. Brazza on his death bed (*Le Petit parisien,* 5 October 1905).

tol the martyr Brazza, silence the returning members of his commission, and bring Gentil to Paris to defend his colonial administration. In the short run, the strategy did not work very well. Although Brazza's second-in-command, Hoarau-Desruisseaux, a respected civil servant, agreed to keep quiet, another member gave copies of documents and other information to his brother Robert de Jouvenel, a prominent writer. Jouvenel then leaked this material, much of it written by Brazza himself, to the press.[90] The explorer's notes sharply criticized Gentil, whom he accused of heinous crimes. Brazza charged not only that Gentil had been complicit in the Congo's atrocities but that he had committed many himself.

The popular press jumped on the sensational new controversy, creating another episode in the ongoing Congo scandal. What could be juicier than a set of disturbing accusations coming "from beyond the grave," as one paper put it? According to "an individual well placed for being perfectly informed [Jouvenel]," Brazza had explicitly charged that Gentil's demands for ever increasing tax receipts and a huge force of porters had led to the hostage camps, the burning of villages, and the constant native rebellions, all repressed with excessively harsh tactics. Worse, Brazza's occult voice was now accusing Gentil of having personally "chicotted" a Gabonese man to death. Gentil had also ordered a woman flogged and then hung by her feet and several others whipped severely and placed in irons for theft and other petty crimes. He had meted out these punishments without so much as notifying the colony's judicial officers. Summarizing this damning information, the *Petit parisien*'s article gave what it said was a direct quote from Brazza: "Tortures and summary judgments proliferated. M. Gentil paraded through the streets with a personal bodyguard whose members whipped people who failed to salute the Governor."[91] Such quotations seemed all the more eerily real when Brazza's letter, mentioned above, surfaced in *Le Temps* the following day (27 September).

These accusations against Gentil escalated into an "affair" when the commissaire and his associates, having returned to France a few days earlier, adamantly rejected Brazza's charges, accusing commission members of spreading outright lies. The commissaire's men hesitated to criticize the charismatic Brazza directly, focusing their attack on other members of the commission, said to be "determined adversaries" prejudiced against Gentil from the start. The commissaire's associates implied that Brazza was too ill to conduct a genuine investigation of his own, so he took as gospel the falsehoods circulated by members of his group, and accepted suspect native testimony at face value. Since even a socialist like Challaye believed that blacks routinely made things up, the colonialists around Gentil knew they could cast doubt on Brazza's report by impugning his native sources.[92] If Gentil had at times been involved in violent conflict, said his chief of staff, M. Pelletier, it was only in the context of warfare against native rebels trying to overthrow French colonial authority.[93]

In a series of interviews with the press, Pelletier denied that many of the now notorious atrocities attributed to mid-level French colonial administrators and indirectly to Gentil had actually occurred. According to Pelletier, the case of the sixty-eight women and children found in a concentration camp, many of them dead, had nothing to do with Europeans; it was a wholly African affair. In Pelletier's account, members of an enemy tribe had kidnapped the victims in question after eating several others. Those kept alive were to be used as slaves.[94] In other, similar accounts, Gentil's surrogates attempted to explain away most of the cruelties attributed to the French. This tactic, combined with the widespread belief that African testimony could not be trusted, raised doubts not only about the information leaked from the Brazza documents but also about all prior reports of French abuses. Had Brazza still been alive, his fame and personal reputation might have enabled him to foil these efforts, but without him, Gentil and his allies in the colonial ministry could circulate a counternarrative designed to discredit the leaks coming from the commission of inquiry.

With two opposing explanations of the Congo situation, centering on a pair of antagonists, one deceased, the press polemic continued unabated. Most vocal were the conservative newspapers and the socialist *L'Humanité,* which proved as thorough as it was relentless. *L'Humanité*'s Gustave Rouanet, who represented the Seine Department in the Chamber of Deputies, did an extraordinary job of investigating the Congo affair. He obtained access to the Brazza commission's notes and found many sources willing to reveal what they knew. Beginning in late September 1905, Rouanet wrote no fewer than twenty-nine articles on *"La Barbarie Coloniale,"* almost one a day.[95] Taken together, his pieces constitute a masterpiece of advocacy journalism and the effective use of anonymous sources. The portrait he painted was devastating, not just for individuals like Toqué and Gentil but for the colonial system itself, Rouanet's real target. His articles would have been more influential had they appeared in a mainstream newspaper, and the intensity of his critique may have alarmed papers like *Le Temps* and the *Petit parisien,* whose journalists had already revealed much of what Rouanet would say, if in less detail. The editors of these two papers likely felt uncomfortable with the socialist writer now repeating, and reinforcing, what they had published. Shortly after Rouanet's series began, *Le Temps* and the *Petit parisien* backed off, leaving *L'Humanité* to face Gentil's counterattack largely alone. The socialists remained marginal enough in 1905 that opponents could dismiss their journalism on ideological grounds, without having to prove their information wrong.

Under these circumstances, Colonial Minister Clémentel decided to cool things down by announcing the formation of a new commission of inquiry. Its task would be to evaluate the respective claims of the two sides and recommend any reforms that might be needed. The new panel's membership was distinguished: Jean-Marie de Lanessan, the former governor-general of Indochina and minister of colonies, chaired the group, and his collaborators included a well-known academic and several high-level civil servants from Clémentel's ministry, all favorable to Gentil.[96] It is unclear exactly how Lanessan's panel did its work, but most members seemed eager to challenge Brazza's view that the origins of the Congo atrocities lay in the structure of France's colonial organization, especially as directed by Gentil. Lanessan's 120-page report followed to the letter Clémentel's original instructions to the Brazza commission: the abuses, deplorable as they were, resulted from the isolated acts of errant individuals. The colonial system itself was not to blame, nor was Gentil, whose career emerged from the second inquiry completely intact.

If the government found itself exculpated by the committee its leaders had named, the same was not true of the concessionary companies, whose operations, already compromised by market forces, Lanessan called into question. Even though his report explicitly—and repeatedly—pinned the blame on a few individuals, a close reading of the text suggests that the former minister had indeed found structural reasons for the Congo's problems. Those reasons were solely economic; the government bore no responsibility for the colony's ills, though it did hold the keys to their resolution. The concessionary companies, Lanessan wrote, had been a bad idea, and the government should allow no more. In the meantime, the National Assembly would have to fund the Congo more generously, and above all, the Republic would need to redouble its devotion to the mission civilisatrice. The colonial government, committed as always to the well-being and advancement of the native people, would have to protect the Congolese from exploitation. It must provide food, education, and medical care and ensure that natives living outside the concessionary zone could freely sell the products they raised.[97]

What the Lanessan report ignored was the close structural relationship between the colonial government and the concessionary economy. Both the local administration and the companies required indigenous people to provide labor and tax payments, neither of which the Congolese wanted to give. The only way to obtain the manpower needed for portage and harvesting rubber was to compel people to work. The assessment of taxes served as a crucial means of compulsion, but it was rarely enough. Authorities continued to recruit porters by force, and the Congolese continued to flee from recruiters into the brush, where they not infrequently starved to death. When colonial officials finally built roads and introduced automobiles during the Great War, the need for porters declined. But the humanitarian situation improved only briefly; throughout the 1920s, railway construction required massive, forcible conscription of labor. Local people fled from the recruiters or rebelled against them, reproducing the same kinds of abuses Brazza had found decades earlier.[98]

Despite its flaws, the Lanessan report, with its explicit, if muted, criticism of the concessionary companies, went further than the government wanted to go; officials at the Foreign Ministry forbade its publication. They feared it would give ammunition to France's colonial rivals and open the government to lawsuits from the companies. Despite the efforts of socialists and left-leaning Radicals like Joseph Caillaux, who wanted full disclosure of both the Lanessan text and the Brazza commission's notes, the chamber ultimately voted overwhelmingly to keep everything secret. Only ten copies of the Lanessan report saw print, and all ten were consigned to the archives, where they remain today.[99]

It is, of course, impossible to know what would have happened had Brazza been able to return home bearing his report. In the past, he had been an effective publicist, and the colonial ministry would have found it extremely difficult to dismiss him and his conclusions. As a national hero and charismatic personality, he would have caught the interest of the mass press, which would have given him a great deal of attention. The scandal would have remained alive, and the Congo might have enjoyed some genuine reforms. This is why the Colonial Ministry had been so upset by Brazza's appointment to head the commission of inquiry and why the minister and his associates had worked exceedingly hard to circumscribe the commission's activities. Brazza was considered so dangerous that his wife, Thérèse, who had traveled with him on the final African trip, believed to the end of her days that her husband had not died from dysentery. He had been poisoned, she maintained, to silence him and bury his findings.[100]

With Brazza dubbed a martyr and out of the picture, his opponents ignored his troublesome, divisive conclusions and diverted attention to the unifying, patriotic themes he and his friends had so carefully nurtured during his lifetime. "He was a conqueror," proclaimed *Le Matin,* "but one who conquered with kindness."[101] Essentially every newspaper and magazine rehearsed Brazza's now famous biography—the glorious rivalry with Stanley, the pacific conquest, the Makoko treaty, the self-sacrifice, the martyrdom for France. Brazza had always rallied a great many French men and women around his image as selfless patriot and intrepid explorer; political leaders now sought to use that image to overcome the divisions the Congo scandal had caused.

What better way to accomplish that goal than a great national communion around the fallen hero lying serenely in state? With fanfare and éclat, the French government organized an impressive public funeral for Brazza, a national event of the kind usually reserved for presidents, prime ministers, and luminaries like Victor Hugo.[102] On 3 October 1905, virtually the entire French elite thronged the Church of Sainte Clotilde, sumptuously decorated in black and white. Government ministers, business leaders, military figures—including Colonel Marchand—high civil servants, celebrities, and socialites representing the "tout Paris" all came to pay their respects.[103] People who rarely associated with one another rubbed shoulders as they strained to glimpse the ornate coffin of the great man and martyr to France. Such was the national unity expressed in the Church of Sainte Clotilde that clericals and secularists, putting aside their feud over the separation of church and state, pressed together to hear the Reverend Father Leroy extol the Catholic virtues of Savorgnan de Brazza.[104] For one day, at least, conflicts seemed forgotten as the country drew together around the hero's casketed body.

After representatives of the French army, resplendent in their full dress uniforms, gave an elaborate military salute, a long funeral procession set out for Père Lachaise, where Brazza would be lowered into his in-laws' tomb. En route, thousands of ordinary Parisians poured out of their homes and businesses to pay the hero their last respects. Brazza, like Marchand, enjoyed such immense popularity that he brought crowds into the street. "The entire nation is in mourning," declared *Le Journal*, "When a great man like M. de Brazza draws his final breath."[105]

At the gravesite, four eulogies contributed to the secular beatification of the French martyr; all emphasized national unity, the civilizing mission, and Brazza's benevolent "conquête pacifique." Brazza's work, intoned the colonialist deputy Paul Deschanel "is pure of human blood." His heroism, Deschanel added, had "widened [France's] borders" and made him "the brilliant artisan of justice and France's ideals."[106] Brazza, in short, had served as exemplar of the mission civilisatrice, the man whose explorations had enabled France to illuminate the Dark Continent with the radiance of its superior form of life. The unspoken subtext of this speech was that Brazza embodied the true nature of French colonialism. French men and women should think of *him* and not the dynamiters and the decapitators of colonized peoples when they seek to understand the meaning and value of French expansion.

More than anyone else, Colonial Minister Clémentel associated the French Republic and its empire with the prestige and reputation of the fallen hero. Clémentel asserted that far from harming the Congolese, France, like Brazza, had sacrificed to make them civilized and free. The explorer's recent mission to the Congo, he declared, had "consolidated our moral credit." No one more than Brazza, the minister continued, "incarnates the France of liberty and civilization" or prevented his compatriots from ever doubting "the eternal traditions of justice and humanity that are the glory of France."[107] Having buried the explorer's report, Clémentel deftly used Brazza's image as charismatic hero and martyr to obscure what the explorer had wanted to expose.[108]

With the ceremony concluded, the Congo scandal quickly faded away. Neither *L'Humanité*'s well-documented articles, nor an elaborate parliamentary debate could revive it. In the end, the scandal had served not to challenge deeply held French values, but to affirm them. It reinforced the widespread notion that France's colonial project was noble and good. The Congo scandal had proved to be one of those wrenching public phenomena that ultimately brings people together rather than pulling them apart. Such was the unifying power of Brazza's pubic image that political leaders could use it to create common perceptions diametrically at odds with what the explorer had ultimately wanted to say.

SEVEN

Hubert Lyautey and the French Seizure of Morocco

AFTER THE HUMILIATING DEFEAT OF 1870, French commentators of all ideological stripes turned, as we have seen, to the celebration of heroes past and present.[1] With the exception of Joan of Arc, a female warrior who dressed as a man, all these heroes were male. In a post-defeat atmosphere of fear at the prospect of national decline, and even extinction, French writers emphasized the heroes' exemplary courage and selflessness, their willingness to sacrifice themselves to save the nation. In response, a great many French men looked to fencing, dueling, and sport as the means to nurture a manly courage and prepare for an anti-German revenge.[2] But despite the surge of interest in these virile arts, until the Dreyfus Affair, most commentators continued to represent France's standing army as the deepest reservoir of valor the nation possessed. The great past heroes—Vercingetorix, Roland, Napoleon—had, after all, been soldiers. But the French army's failures in 1870–71 and the lack of Western European wars after that time made it difficult to identify new military heroes in mainland France. One alternative was to resurrect heroes of the past—the late century saw the revival of Napoleonic cults and the embrace of Joan of Arc; the other was to extol the colonies, where the near-constant warfare of the 1880s and '90s allowed a different kind of military heroism to emerge.

It was partly for this reason that then-colonel Hubert Lyautey, soon to become one of France's leading colonial actors and propagandists, began in the 1890s to seek the potential for national regeneration among those who served in colonies. But that service had to seem relatively peaceful, for the gruesome colonial battles of the late nineteenth century, many of which went poorly for the French and disturbed their republican sensibilities, made commentators squeamish about the prospect of continuing blood-shed in the colonies.[3] In this context, national salvation seemed to require military heroes at once virile and pacific, forceful and gentle, men who wielded an "iron fist in a velvet glove."[4] Lyautey, like Brazza, came to represent such a heroic ideal. As a "pacific conqueror" and advocate of benign colonial rule, Lyautey succeeded in attracting broad support among the French public, conservative and republican alike, both for himself as military hero and for his effort to make Morocco the jewel in France's imperial crown. Lyautey's eventual status as a colonial hero suggests, once again, that colonialism could command widespread interest in France, but on two conditions: that it appear to revolve around and be identified with a single charismatic individual and that it seem to take place in a peaceful, civilized way.

In the late 1890s, Lyautey developed a novel theory of colonization while serving under General Joseph Gallieni in Indochina and then Madagascar. The approach had originated with Gallieni, but it was Lyautey who articulated it for a nonmilitary public in an influential article of 1900, "The Colonial Role of the Army."[5] In that essay, Lyautey maintained that a successful process of colonization required a unified military and political leadership—a single man, "the right person in the right place," to direct the entire operation.[6] Algeria, Lyautey wrote, had demonstrated the irrationality of a military-civilian administrative divide, and he sought to bring together as a seamless whole the process of conquest, economic development, and pacification. Translated into our own contemporary language, Lyautey's method was to bring under unified military command the processes of military occupation, nation building, and the effort to win hearts and minds.[7]

Since none of this could take place without an army, the "right man" had to be a military officer, normally a general, who possessed both strategic acumen and administrative skills. The general should, that is, be the individual charged with running the new colony. He should possess a margin of independence from Paris in order to respond properly to local conditions, and he should control the resources, in terms of both money and manpower, to develop the country economically. Above all, the leader needed to understand his duties in political terms far more than military ones. Gallieni had long condemned a purely military approach to colonization in which a traditional column of forces conquers a territory and then moves on, leaving the subdued area to civilian administrators. The latter, he said, were unprepared to control lands that inevitably remained unpacified for a significant period of time.

The Gallieni-Lyautey alternative was to have colonial troops occupy a territory and remain in place. The officers and men would immediately begin the process of stabilization and economic development. Pacification, Lyautey wrote, came not through military measures but through the army's successful effort to improve the lives of indigenous people. Earlier, Lyautey had described this process as the *tache d'huile* or oil-stain approach to colonization.[8] The army would establish an initial presence and then, by bringing in markets, telegraph lines, roadways, medical care, and other services, show the locals the benefits of French civilization. As new resources poured in, people living on the fringes of the area would be convinced to join in, thus extending the reach and effectiveness of the original military occupation. In this way, French influence, and eventually French rule, would seep gradually, like an oil stain, into an ever expanding spread of territory. Colonization would be a largely "pacific" process, requiring only an initial military intervention. Once the army had established its beachhead, all the subsequent steps would, of necessity, be nonviolent. The army would thus "create life," as Lyautey put it, rather than sow destruction, as in the case of European wars or old-fashioned colonial campaigns. Lyautey's was an alternative version of Foreign Minister Delcassé's "pacific penetration" (exercising control by coaxing the Sultan into debt), one that recalled Brazza's "conquête pacifique."

The preference for protectorates over direct French rule became another key element of the method Lyautey attributed to Gallieni but which he had actually learned from Jean-Marie de Lanessan, France's governor-general in Indochina from 1891 to 1894.[9] As Lyautey wrote: "Instead of abolishing the traditional systems, make use of them: Rule with the mandarin and not against him. . . . Offend no tradition, change no custom, remind ourselves that in all human society there is a ruling class, born to rule, without which nothing can be done, and a class to be ruled: Enlist the ruling class in our service. Once the mandarins are our friends, certain of us and needing us, they have only to say the word and the country will be pacified."[10]

In hindsight, such a comment seems almost bizarrely naïve; to understand it properly requires two elements of context. The first is the earlier history of French colonization in Indochina, the place to which Lyautey's comments refer. There, French forces encountered such resistance in the 1880s that the government's political opponents called its entire colonial effort into question.[11] The second context is Lyautey's own royalist and aristocratic culture. For him, a republican government was a contradiction in terms; it violated a Burkean "natural order of things" by forgetting that one class was "born to rule" and everyone else "to be ruled."[12]

Colonialism, if managed properly, would maintain abroad the social hierarchy republicanism had overturned in France. Nothing did Indochina more harm than direct French rule, which extended the republic's unnatural administrative state to the colonial situation. The result was a chaos of violent rebellion, which required violent repression in return. This is why, according to Lyautey, French colonialism had encountered so much resistance. By reverting to mandarin leadership and the natural order of things, French colonial governors would allow themselves to profit from the traditional hierarchy of rulers and the ruled. The mandarins would say the word, and pacification would ensue. In practice, colonial administration never became so simple, although Lanessan and Gallieni's willingness in certain cases to return local authority to traditional elites helped make their Indochinese regime of the 1890s more successful than those of earlier years.[13]

After the turn of the century, France's colonial lobby embraced Lyautey's views and quickly adopted Lyautey himself, making him a key member.[14] Promoted to general in 1904, the officer corresponded with virtually all of France's leading colonialists.[15] Most important among them was Eugene Etienne, the moderate republican who represented Oran, Algeria, in the Chamber of Deputies and stood out as one of the Chamber's leading members.[16] So central was his colonial role that a fellow representative, Etienne Flandrin, declared, "The man who holds the portfolio as minister of colonies changes regularly, but the real minister of colonies never changes; it's always M. Eugene Etienne."[17] At Lyautey's request, his correspondents circulated his missives widely within pro-colonial circles. The letters recounted Lyautey's military experiences after being appointed commanding general in the South Oranais region of Algeria, which bordered on some of Morocco's rebellious tribal zones. They also elaborated Lyautey's understanding of how the sharifian empire should be colonized: not by making the sultan's government, or Makhzan, economically dependent on France, as Delcassé advocated with his doctrine of "peaceful penetration," but by gradually infiltrating Morocco from the south and spreading French influence through the *tache d'huile* strategy. Lyautey's own version of peaceful penetration appealed to colonialists impatient for measurable success in Morocco. It also reassured ordinary French men and women uncomfortable with the atrocities all too evident in the Congo and with the colonial violence characteristic of the 1890s.[18]

Although Lyautey remained largely unknown to the broad public in the early 1900s, he would soon become one of France's great colonial heroes, especially among people of conservative and moderate political views. Even among leftists, Lyautey would attract a measure of support thanks to his stance as a latter-day "conquérant pacifique." The ardently republican and anti-militarist paper *Gil Blas* distinguished Lyautey from the typical colonial soldier for whom "the end all and be all [of military life] is to drink, swear, punish, and knock people around." Lyautey, by contrast, represented "a breath of fresh air, a new spirit." He was one of the rare officers who "subordinates warfare to diplomacy," making him "one of the most likeable figures of our time."[19] Lyautey's ability to reach beyond conservative and nationalist circles would prove crucial in the years following the Dreyfus Affair, when a great many French men and women placed intellectuals and republicans in one camp and army officers and priests in the other. Lyautey's standing as a man of letters—literally, as he wrote thousands of letters during his lifetime, carefully conserving copies for later publication—placed him partly in the military sphere and partly in the realm of literary and intellectual life.

Lyautey's letters enabled him to orchestrate his own image, both contemporary and historical, extremely well. The handwritten texts, which a great many politicians, journalists, and literary personalities avidly read, established his standing within the French elite. Soon, members of this elite would help a broad public see him as a charismatic hero and popular icon. The published letters have shaped virtually all historical and biographical accounts of the marshal's colonial career, and much of what we know of his early years comes from an unpublished memoir he wrote in 1919 and deposited among his family papers for future historians to see.[20] Although it is impossible entirely to escape Lyautey's attempts to shape the historical record to his liking, several recent scholarly biographies give us good critical distance on his life.

Lyautey's unusual personal and political trajectory began in 1854, in Nancy, capital of the old French province of Lorraine. He descended from a long line of high-ranking military officers, bourgeois on his father's side, noble on his mother's. His maternal lineage harked back to the eleventh century and the quintessentially Norman vicomté de Falaise.[21] All his biographers agree that a crucial turning point came very early in his life, when at eighteen months he tumbled from a second-floor balcony. He likely would have died save for a first-floor awning that broke his fall. The baby ricocheted off the shoulder of a soldier parading with his brigade and landed headfirst on the street. Doctors initially believed Hubert had suffered a minor injury to his skull, from which they pronounced him cured within a matter of weeks. But a year later, he began to experience severe pain in his lower back, and the agony resumed periodically over the next two years. At age five he found it difficult to walk. The family doctor grew concerned, and a young colleague discovered that his spinal cord had been injured in the original fall, creating a huge abscess above his groin. Local doctors had no idea how to treat the boy's condition, and they consulted, by telegraph, the leading specialist in Paris, one Dr. Velpeau. Unable to come to Nancy, Velpeau sent written instructions to a local surgeon courageous enough to attempt the delicate operation. As Lyautey later described the procedure, "The surgeon cut four holes in my back and through them they butchered me for a half-hour straight. Doctors didn't yet use chloroform!"[22]

With the abscess removed, the surgeon wrapped Hubert in an "orthopedic corset" that kept him completely immobilized for two solid years. Day in and day out, he lay prone on a metal bed. His mother, aunt, and grandmother showered him with loving care, relieving his pain and boredom while cheering him up. In his memoir of 1919, Lyautey depicts the warmth and affection of his convalescence as if it had happened in the recent past. Historians have made a great deal of this constant attention from the women of his family, suggesting that it feminized a young boy who would otherwise would have been outside in the rough-and-tumble with his peers. His long immobilization could not but have a powerful psychological affect, but it hardly follows that it would determine his future sexual orientation. In any event, once Hubert regained the ability to walk at age eleven, he made a point of competing harder in sports than the other boys and of taking the lead in their playful "military attacks" on neighboring towns.[23]

If Lyautey's enforced bed rest moved him to prove his maleness later on, it also accustomed him to a breadth of literature greater than almost any child his age. Confined to bed around the clock, Hubert had nothing else to do but read. Family records list many of the books he devoured: history, especially military history; travel literature; explorers' narratives and missionaries' accounts; works of geography and natural science. When not reading, he spent hours staring at atlases and at the globe perched near his bed. Even after doctors allowed him to get up and move about, relapses confined him to bed at regular intervals; he thus never lost the inclination to read.[24]

Had he come from a less military and traditionalist family, he might have gone into law or another intellectually oriented field. But for monarchist aristocrats like his parents, there were but two genuinely respectable vocations: the army and the church. The latter Lyautey ruled out, for even as a young man he experienced sharp religious doubt. At age eighteen, he entered France's officer training academy at Saint-Cyr. He did very well there, graduating near the top of his class. Lyautey moved on to the high officers' school in 1876. While at Saint-Cyr, he became associated with Albert de Mun, the Catholic social reformer who wanted to improve society by teaching discipline, morals, and concern for others. De Mun convinced Lyautey that the army was key to such conservative social reform and thus that it should be more than a mere fighting force.

After graduating as a full lieutenant, Lyautey found himself assigned to the cavalry, a prestigious posting, and then to Algeria. His two years there, 1880–82, taught him something of Arabs and Islam and gave him a taste for the heat and sun of the Maghreb. His royalist traditionalism remained intact. On leave after returning to France, Hubert went to Austria for a personal visit with the count of Chambord, the Bourbon pretender to the vacant French throne. "I have just left Him," Lyautey wrote afterwards. "The emotion from this is such, the soaring feeling so strong, that I cannot regain consciousness of my own personality . . . lost in Him during those hours of grace. The King of France!—I have seen Him, touched Him, heard Him."[25]

Surrounded by doting women while an invalid boy, Lyautey as a young adult seemed perpetually in search of father figures in whom he hoped to find himself. The first surrogate father was Albert de Mun, who gave Lyautey "a reason for living," if only for a short period.[26] Chambord came next, though he perhaps proved too overwhelming, as Hubert risked losing himself altogether. Not until a decade later did Hubert meet the man, Joseph Gallieni, who would show him his way.

After ten listless years in one provincial garrison after the other, Lyautey received an order in August 1894 to ship out for Indochina, where he would serve under Colonel Gallieni, widely respected in military circles for his colonial command. The assignment served as a belated reprimand for Lyautey's article of 1891, "The Social Role of the Officer," published in the prestigious, if stodgy, Revue des deux mondes. The piece had implicitly criticized the High Command for failing to use the army as an agent of (conservative) social reform. Far from brooding over his punishment, Lyautey, now a major, jumped at the chance to escape metropolitan France's gloomy military routines. En route, he already felt "far from the mummification of our moribund, idle, routine-plagued army. It is a resurrection."[27]

In Hanoi, Lyautey served under two men who greatly impressed him, Governor-General de Lanessan and especially Gallieni, whom Lyautey called "this magnificent specimen of a complete man."[28] From Gallieni, Lyautey would discover a stable identity and his true vocation in life. He was to be a modern colonial officer, a man who ruled subject peoples more by persuasion, charm, and energy than by brute military force—a man galvanized by the rejuvenating energy that percolated in the exhilarating colonial sphere. To his boyhood friend Antonin de Margerie, Lyautey wrote that his time in Indochina had made him realize he was an "animal of action," an individual "now in a position to be another Cecil Rhodes . . . one of those in whom others believe and in whose eyes thousands of other eyes look for order." Growing up, Lyautey had nourished himself on the dream that his "voice and pen" would make "avenues reopen, countries repopulate and cities spring to life." He now understood that any failure to realize these dreams would constitute a "sharp set-back," a debilitating disappointment. "More than ever, I feel that, deprived of productive action, powerful and immediate, I eat away at myself, corrupt myself, and all my abilities corrode from disuse."[29]

The problem was that at this point, age forty-one in 1896, he had not yet outgrown his need for a mentor, a surrogate father to guide his way. When Lyautey heard that Gallieni was leaving Indochina to assume command in Madagascar, the younger man sank into such despair that he threatened to leave the army and return to France.[30] Fortunately, Gallieni requested his presence in Madagascar, and nothing could have made him happier: "Wherever you are," he wrote Gallieni, "Whatever you want to do with me, I will always and everywhere be at your service."[31] In Madagascar he earned promotion to lieutenant colonel and was poised to become a soldier-administrator, the main pillar of Gallieni's approach to colonization. This new assignment moved him from depression to exhilaration and enabled him to take a large step toward personal independence. "The essential thing," he wrote, "is to know what one wants and where one is going. Now, I know what that is."[32]

Until 1897, when he arrived in Madagascar, Lyautey had mostly thought of colonies in terms of their apparent political, economic, and moral benefits for France, of their ability to awaken military valor, and of the possibilities they opened for him as an officer. In Madagascar he also formulated a version of the civilizing mission, of colonization as agent of progress for backward realms of the globe. "Even if France were to gain nothing [from colonization,] wouldn't we at least have been the makers of a providential transformation on this planet? If we have brought life, culture, and people to regions in the grip of banditry and economic sterility; if we have remade their rivers into channels of communication . . . if we have unleashed the productivity of their forests, resurrected their fertile but uncultivated valleys, . . . our presence, even if temporary, will have left a useful trace."[33]

As with most colonialists, these ideals largely remained just that; the reality of empire proved far bloodier and less altruistic than such a statement implied.[34] In Madagascar, the practice of French colonialism left little room for human progress and economic advance. The Malagasy elite had made their disinterest in a French protectorate abundantly clear, having successfully resisted it for nearly a dozen years when Lyautey set foot on the island in 1897. Under these circumstances, Gallieni, now a brigadier general, received a mandate to quell the "native insurrection" by all necessary means. A bloody campaign ensued, complete with the assassination and exile of indigenous rulers and their expulsion from positions of economic power. Madagascar revealed the gaping hole in the Gallieni-Lyautey method of colonization: it worked only if the existing elite and most of those it ruled agreed to collaborate with the French. Where such agreement did not exist, as in Madagascar, Gallieni put his methods aside. His troops imposed direct French governance leavened only by a local puppet regime he saw fit to install.[35]

These developments might have made Lyautey alter his assessment of the Gallieni method; instead he became its chief spokesman. The cynical view of this apparent contradiction holds that for Lyautey, as for his mentor, the "pacific," native-oriented approach to colonization served mainly as a propaganda tool designed to win over a French public eager for colonies but squeamish about the idea of killing a great many people to obtain them.[36] There is perhaps an element of such calculation in Lyautey's views, but no evidence of it exists in his voluminous correspondence.[37] Lyautey likely believed in the method he would articulate so well; it's just that to work properly, it required that indigenous people act in what he understood to be their best interests. When they behaved otherwise, the French were morally obliged to prepare them for civilized life. After Madagascar, Lyautey would apply these ideas to Morocco, forcing people at gunpoint to accept the "benign protectorate" he would have preferred to impose in peace.

When Gallieni returned to Paris for consultations in June 1899, he brought Lyautey along to serve as his public face. At a meeting of the Union Coloniale Française, the younger man advertised his mentor's method of "peaceful conquest" to an appreciative audience. The pro-colonial press gave the speech favorable coverage, and the *Revue des deux mondes* published it as "Du role colonial de l'officier" a few weeks later. With this article, Lyautey made himself a key member of the pro-colonial elite and propagandist of note. Soon he would eclipse Gallieni, who possessed none of Lyautey's elegance and social ease.

Lyautey's influential friends, Albert de Mun and the novelist Eugene Melchior de Vogüé, both well-connected aristocrats, introduced him to Parisian high society. There, he sparkled as a conversationalist and impressed with his wit, intelligence, and broad knowledge of art and literature. His lieutenant and confidant Alfred de Tarde would later call him a "Swann with epaulettes."[38] In fact, there was no one like Lyautey—no one at once a high-ranking officer and elegant literary man, a mustachioed soldier as much at home in desert and jungle as in drawing rooms of the elite. Those who knew him endlessly commented on his svelte body and impeccable grooming, his nervous energy and hypomanic personality. His personal charm and seductiveness were legendary as were his polemical and negotiating skills.

To contemporaries, what we would now call his sexual orientation largely remained unmentioned, at least in public, though people in the know often attributed the following remark to Clemenceau: "[Lyautey] is an admirable, courageous man who has always had balls between his legs . . . even when they weren't his own." In another, perhaps apocryphal comment, Madame Lyautey remarked to her husband's circle of young officers: "Gentlemen, I have the pleasure of informing you that last night I cuckolded you all."[39] No one has ever produced definitive proof that Lyautey was a practicing homosexual, and until recently, historians have largely danced around the subject. André Maurois's foundational biography, written while his subject was still alive, does not mention Lyautey's sexuality.[40] Other writers who knew him, like later historians, spoke of his admiration for ancient Greek statuary, his "androphilia," feminine traits, and explosive emotionality, but never broached the term "homosexual."[41]

Only recently have historians been more explicit. Christian Gury argues that Lyautey inspired Proust's gay character the baron de Charlus, a man virile on the outside and effeminate underneath. To support this and other claims, Gury brings together a great deal of circumstantial evidence about the general's sexual orientation. Lyautey did not marry until age fifty-five and fathered no children. The only women in his life were his mother and sisters, to whom he remained very close, and a young woman named Louise Baignères, who wanted desperately to marry him. Partly to escape pressure from Louise and her parents, he eagerly fled to Indochina in 1894, citing his personal incompatibility with the institution of marriage.[42] Lyautey, Gury suggests, wrote admiringly about the unclothed male body and penned homoerotic prose about Africans, Arabs, Greeks, and Ceylonese. He loved to dress up in elaborate Arab garb, and he decorated his headquarters, and even his tents, with Persian carpets, expensive silks, and delicate porcelain. He sipped his tea in fine china and brought tasteful furnishings from his native Lorraine.

Lyautey did, it turns out, have one intense friendship with a woman, the brilliant social rebel Isabelle Eberhardt, who flaunted every imaginable convention of female identity. The illegitimate daughter of a French-speaking mother and a defrocked Russian Orthodox priest, Eberhardt grew up in Switzerland, where her father taught her Latin and Greek, as well as classical Arabic, French, German, Italian, and Russian. From early adolescence, she dressed as a boy and spent her time working and playing with young men. In 1897 she escaped Europe for Algeria, where she joined the Sufi brotherhood and eventually married a Muslim Arab named Slimène Ehnni, a spahi, or native soldier in France's Algerian army. Eberhardt kept a diary, wrote short stories, and managed to scrounge a few paid writing assignments. In February 1901 an unknown Arab man tried to kill her, claiming afterwards that a voice had told him to attack her because she was a rich European dressed as a man. In 1903 an Algerian newspaper sent her to the South Oranais to cover Lyautey's raids into Morocco. The general found her deep knowledge of Arabic culture useful for his military campaigns, and he admired her nonconformist behavior. She, in turn, felt attracted to his combination of military toughness and aristocratic elegance. They became fast friends, and she was known to spend entire nights in his tent—for long conversations, they both said. It is possible that they slept together, and if so, it would mean that the one woman he had sex with was a Muslim convert who traveled with the Foreign Legion and dressed as a man.[43]

If Lyautey did in fact have a sexual preference for men, he kept his private behavior carefully hidden, as did most homosexual men at that time. The army was, in fact, one of the best places for gay men to remain discreet;

there, a homosexual could spend his life in the company of uniformed young soldiers while exhibiting the virility and honor seemingly inherent in a military career.[44] Service in the colonies only enhanced one's apparent masculinity, since after 1870 these were the only places where French soldiers actually fought. Whatever the realities of Lyautey's sexual practice, the general public learned nothing of his proclivities. The private life of public figures remained off-limits to mainstream journalists throughout the Third Republic, and such was especially the case for military leaders. In formal correspondence, people addressed the army brass in a familial way—"Mon Général," "Mon Colonel." As national father figures, generals, like priests, appeared to possess little or no sexuality. The same was true of most political leaders, with the notable exception of Joseph Caillaux. When the former prime minister's political opponents made his extramarital affairs an issue in 1914, they crossed an indelible political line, revealing the depth of their antagonism toward him and highlighting the rarity of sexual allegation in the political culture of pre-1914 France.[45]

As Lyautey's reputation grew during the first years of the twentieth century, his approach to "peaceful" colonialism came into conflict with a French government committed to its own version of soft imperialism forged in the wake of the Entente Cordiale with Britain (1904). Delcassé and others from the Foreign Ministry favored what they termed "pacific penetration," an effort to seize eventual control of Morocco by loaning its government increasing sums of money.[46] The assumption was that the Makhzan would be unable to repay the loans and that its defaults would allow French officials to seize Moroccan resources in compensation and progressively bring Morocco's economy under Parisian control. This assumption proved correct: French officials began to confiscate the country's income from customs receipts, taxes, and other sources and to serve as "advisers" to the Makhzan. Before long, the sultan found himself at the financial mercy of the French, who now exercised an effective veto over Moroccan fiscal policy, such as it was, and over important elements of its foreign trade.[47]

These developments pleased French bankers but failed to give France the kind of political control colonialists wanted. During the first decade of the twentieth century, so much of Moroccan society stood in open and often violent rebellion against the sultan that the mounting French domination of his government and bureaucracy did not extend to the country as a whole. Worse, as French control increasingly exposed the weakness and impotence of the Makhzan, growing numbers of tribes joined the rebellion against it and thus against the French.[48]

The limits of French authority became crystal clear in the international sphere when the kaiser landed, with great fanfare, at Tangiers in March 1905, symbolically asserting the right to intervene in Moroccan affairs. This bold demonstration of German claims, with its implicit rejection of the Entente Cordiale, angered and frustrated French colonialists and proved to the most ardent among them the need for a different approach to Morocco. This second group turned to Lyautey, who promised to extend French control over Morocco, not by miring the Makhzan in debt, but by taming the rebellious tribes. Lyautey had already shown his willingness to stage incursions into Morocco in open defiance of Delcassé, who had ordered him not to cross the Algerian border. Etienne, surrounded by his Comité du Maroc, egged the general on.

For Etienne and Lyautey, Morocco stood as the last potentially important piece of unclaimed African land. It had retained its independence throughout the nineteenth century because each European power sought to prevent any other from seizing control. No continental government wanted Britain to colonize Morocco, as London's possession of Gibraltar and the Suez Canal already made the Mediterranean too much a British lake. And Britain, jealous of its Mediterranean hegemony, was disinclined to allow another power to occupy a part of Africa only a stone's throw from its own precious rock. Beyond these strategic European concerns stood the reality of Morocco itself, a country whose mountain ranges, tribalism, and powerful Islamic traditions made it extremely difficult to conquer—as the French would soon discover.[49]

Such realities rarely deterred ardent colonialists. When the Entente Cordiale removed British objections to French predominance in Morocco, Etienne and his allies stepped up their efforts to promote French expansion into this unclaimed portion of the Maghreb. But once Lyautey and his French colleagues set foot in Morocco, they found themselves overwhelmed by political, social, religious, and incipient nationalist conflicts they did not understand. After the turn of the century, Morocco was a society at war with itself and with outsiders who sought to bring it peace.

Morocco had entered the twentieth century unprepared to confront the political and economic challenges the new era would bring. The country's economy was weak, its government and army largely unreformed. The young sultan, 'Abd al-'Aziz, who succeeded to the throne in 1900, attempted to bring his bureaucracy and military closer to European standards, but doing so only saddled him with a mountain of debt. To pay off his loans and strengthen his regime, 'Aziz had to impose higher taxes on the country's multitude of tribes. A sultan who enjoyed widespread legitimacy might have been able to make the tribal leaders pay, but 'Aziz was too young and inexperienced to impose his will on a society divided by so many competing loyalties.[50] The central government had always ruled Morocco's fractious tribal society with great difficulty, and the country's history turns on the complex relationship among the Makhzan, cities, tribes, great families, and religious leaders (ulama).

What made Morocco so difficult for Europeans to understand, let alone master, was its tradition of shifting alliances within a system in which everyone in theory owed allegiance and obedience to the sultan, believed to be a direct descendent of the Prophet. Like most Europeans, Delcassé and Lyautey mistakenly viewed Morocco as a country divided into two, essentially permanent contending forces—the Makhzan versus the tribes. Delcassé maintained that the French could capture Morocco by dominating the Makhzan and then gradually extending its influence. Lyautey thought he could colonize the country by pacifying one tribal area at a time until he had absorbed the entire realm. What neither man grasped was the tendency for the Makhzan and tribes to come together in the face of foreign intervention. European pressure on the Makhzan could produce tribal rebellions on its side, and attacks on the tribes could force the sultan to intervene, military or diplomatically, on their behalf.

If foreign intervention could bring Makhzan and tribes together, it could also split them apart, though not in ways helpful to the French. After 1900, Morocco witnessed a series of uprisings against a sultan perceived as too close to the Europeans and prone to levy taxes at London or Paris's behest. Such perceptions trapped the sultan in an impossible situation. He needed French money and advisers to prevail over the tribal revolt, but to obtain these resources, he had to make arrangements that alienated growing numbers of people. Either way, he risked losing the support of key notables and high Makhzan officials, who might abandon him if the revolt grew too powerful, but who opposed giving the French mounting influence over Moroccan affairs.

By intervening in sharifian affairs, the German government sought to take advantage of these conflicts, not out of any particular sympathy for the sultan but to maintain the Reich's share of the Moroccan trade and satisfy Germany's own colonial lobby. To profit from European rivalries, the Makhzan called for an international conference over the status of Morocco. The meetings took place in Algeciras, Spain, next door to Gibraltar.[51] At Algeciras, French diplomats outmaneuvered their German counterparts, convincing most of the other European representatives to give them preponderance in Morocco. In practice, this outcome meant broad power for France over most aspects of Morocco's political and economic life.

The sultan had no choice but to ratify the Algeciras agreement, but by doing so, he turned much of his country against him. The French, meanwhile, used the treaty to resume their policy of peaceful penetration. They solidified their control of Moroccan customs and the port police, deepened their influence on the Makhzan's army, and established medical facilities in the major cities. French settlers streamed into Tangiers and Casablanca, where they appeared to thicken their country's control. Neither the Moroccan elites nor the majority of their countrymen had accepted the idea of an increased French presence, and both began to express their opposition through acts of violence against Europeans.

In May 1906 a young Frenchman was murdered in Tangiers; ten months later, a French tourist taking photographs in Fez suffered a severe beating and would have been killed without the chance intervention of two Makhzan soldiers passing by. The most politically significant incident came when an angry Marrakech crowd brutally murdered the French medical missionary Emile Mauchamp.[52] Smug and abrasive, the young doctor found himself accused of spying for French commercial interests when he helped a scientist set up geological equipment. The Arabs mistook the equipment for a wireless telegraph post, a misperception Mauchamp deliberately encouraged by pretending to erect an antenna on his roof. Shortly afterwards, a dozen men attacked him with sticks, rocks, and knives, crushing his skull and slashing his body. The assailants stripped the corpse naked, tied a noose around its neck, and dragged it to an empty lot. As crowd members debated whether to ignite Mauchamp's body with kerosene, soldiers loyal to the sultan's brother and pretender to the throne confiscated the corpse and carted it to Mauchamp's dispensary. French officials later found the body elaborately dressed in a Moroccan Muslim's white *qamis* and *jallaba*, a turban covering the smashed head.

It is difficult to know exactly why soldiers dressed the body this way, but Ellen Amster plausibly interprets it as a "mock funeral" designed to convey a political message. In draping Mauchamp's remains in Muslim garb, Amster writes, soldiers meant to symbolize the replacement of French authority with Moroccan sovereignty and thus to protest the growing encroachment of French administration, finance, technology, medicine, and culture. If available sources do not allow us precisely to establish the Moroccan soldiers' motives, numerous accounts make the dominant French interpretation of it clear. Journalists depicted the ritual of stripping and reclothing as yet another savage indignity, one that symbolically deprived Mauchamp of his superior European identity.[53]

The French press, especially the illustrated press, elaborately reported the incident, emphasizing the barbarism and savagery of the Muslim crowd. The front page of the *Petit journal*'s illustrated supplement shows a barely human horde of Arabs hurling paving stones at a young European man lying on the ground (fig. 20).[54] Mauchamp bleeds from the head and his shirt is stained in red. He tries to get up, but the crowd seems almost on top of him. A particularly evil-looking man has drawn a dagger, set to strike a fatal blow. By 1907, images such as this had become stock features of a colonialist iconography that permeated the popular press. The *Petit journal* woodcut recalls George William Joy's portrayal of Gordon's murder at Khartoum in 1885.[55] These pictures feature an innocent, unarmed European man, often in the foreground, mortally wounded by a huge crowd in Muslim garb. Hideous faces make these bloody assailants look like furies from hell. In Mauchamp's case, as in Gordon's, journalists depicted the European as a tragic hero martyred in service to the very natives to whom he had devoted his life. The lack of gratitude stood as a key theme in European representations of those they sought to colonize, a theme that served to justify further intervention and even wholesale conquest. Whether Arabs appreciated the effort or not, Europeans would ensure that they shed their primitive culture and beliefs.[56]

The murder of Mauchamp, dramatized and sensationalized in the French press, moved the government to intervene. The French cabinet ordered Lyautey, headquartered just across the border in Algeria, to occupy the Moroccan city of Oujda, in the country's northeastern corner. He would stay until the sultan paid France an indemnity for the doctor's murder, dismissed the pasha of Marrakech, and arrested the guilty parties.[57] The sultan had no choice but to comply. He was powerless to retake Oujda militarily, as his own army operated with French advisers. And since Algeciras, his government had become so dependent financially on France that he could not afford to alienate the decision makers in Paris. 'Abd al-'Aziz's unwillingness to confront the French seemed to confirm his apparent betrayal of Islam to the Christians and stripped him of what little legitimacy he had left. The result was a rebellion of such massive proportions that it ultimately led to 'Aziz's abdication and a large-scale French

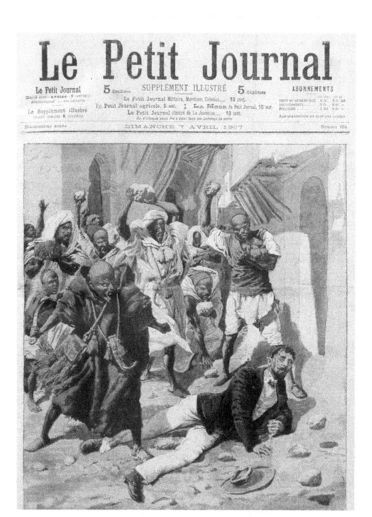

Le Petit Journal

SUPPLÉMENT ILLUSTRÉ

DIMANCHE 7 AVRIL 1907

Figure 20. The assassination of Doctor Mauchamp as depicted in
Le petit journal, 7 April 1907.

intervention. Between 1905 and 1914, French forces become a regular
presence in Morocco, fighting both with and against the Makhzan and
placing the Moroccan question at the center of both foreign policy and
public discussion.

Lyautey's occupation of Oujda earned him a large measure of praise in the
French press; although he had been mentioned frequently since the En-

tente Cordiale, he was now poised to become France's latest colonial hero, taking up Brazza's mantle as "conquérant pacifique." Already in July 1906, eight months before the killing of Mauchamp, the *Petit parisien* had described Lyautey as a military leader capable of "punishing brigands, restoring stolen goods, and bringing dissidents to order—and all this without firing any shots."[58] This description is reminiscent of Brazza's supposed ability to gain territory and native support "without spilling a drop of blood." Lyautey's method, wrote the *Petit parisien*'s Jean Frollo, was to marshal a large army for a "*mission pacifique*" designed to convince "*les indigènes*" that it would be futile to fight. "In making our power perpetually present," Frollo declared, "we have dispensed with the need to use it." Lyautey negotiates instead, "patiently but firmly," until the Moroccans agree to what the general has asked. This is "firmness without force," a "pacific strength" that enabled the French to gain the Moroccans' submission and respect, without causing any of the bitterness inherent in a traditional military campaign. The *Petit parisien*'s editors had doubtless read Lyautey articles and seen many of the letters sent to the general's colonialist friends; they endorsed without reservation the so-called Gallieni method of colonization. Under Lyautey, they wrote, we have turned our southern Algerian military posts into "centers of civilization and defense all at once."[59]

Le journal used almost exactly the same formulas to describe Lyautey, calling him "a tactician as skillful as he was prudent; he is completely pacific . . . displaying our power so as to use it as little as possible."[60] The reality, of course, was that war reigned far more often than peace during the decade before 1914 and that persuasion did not always work. When it didn't, or when tribal leaders promised to submit but kept fighting instead, Lyautey would bear down on them with deadly force.[61] In doing so, Lyautey saw himself not as a traditional military conqueror intent on crushing his opponent but as an agent of political and social change. In his mind, military efforts served merely to punctuate a larger peaceful conquest, the fighting and bloodshed viewed as regrettable, if necessary, efforts to make "today's adversary into the collaborator of tomorrow."[62] Moroccan "rebels" had been duped by a history they only dimly understood; Lyautey's task was not to punish them for their plight but to enable them to escape from it. For this reason, he considered himself not mainly a soldier, though he had to be ready always to fight, but rather an administrator, architect, engineer, agronomist, and judge.[63] Self-serving as such ideas appear, Lyautey seems to have believed them. He left no statements, either in his published or unpublished correspondence, that suggest deception, except perhaps self-deception, on his part.[64]

Although the *Petit parisien* and *Le Journal* articles quoted above appeared before Lyautey's occupation of Oujda, afterwards, he became an almost obsessive staple of journalistic concern. If the pictorial weekly *L'Illustration* consecrated heroes and celebrities with its cover drawings and photographs, Lyautey earned that distinction for the first time on 13 April 1907, shortly after his military intervention to avenge Mauchamp. The cover shows the general touring the streets of the Moroccan city he has subdued. *L'Illustration*'s caption emphasizes the "huge military apparatus" he commanded, but the magazine pictures him in wholly pacific pursuits. Another widely read pictorial weekly, *Le Monde illustré*, pushed the pacific imagery even further. Before Lyautey's arrival, Oujda's "streets were filthy"; now "they will be swept regularly and kept perfectly clean." It is as if Lyautey's army was a brigade of street sweepers rather than a well-equipped fighting force; the image of peaceful conqueror seems to have fully sunk in. But it was a peacefulness backed by the threat of force, an "iron fist," as *Le Figaro* put it, "sheathed in a velvet glove."[65]

Lyautey seemed so appealing, so different from the Third Republic's typical military leaders, that journalists returned again and again to his looks, bearing, and style. The incessant attention to Lyautey's body betrays an effort to understand manhood in new and reassuring ways, to feature men both powerful and unthreatening all at once. Unlike the thick, crude, bourgeois demeanor of the typical officer, wrote the editor of *Gil Blas*, Lyautey appeared "vigorous and refined." "He is tall and sharp, his svelte body proportioned harmoniously with his strong shoulders.... As a young man, he must have been very handsome. His allure is supple.... His head is round, unlike the squareness of typical military men ... and the roundness highlights, under the straight hair slightly tinted with silver, ... the glow of his thoughts."[66]

Here, *Gil Blas* expresses in literary language what would become the standard description of Lyautey: vigorous energy in a svelte body capped by an elegant, thoughtful-looking halo of silver-white hair. This portrait distinguished Lyautey from the thick, square-headed, and pot-bellied politicians and generals typical of the Third Republic. The dashing white-haired general exuded a form of masculinity partly aristocratic in character, a masculinity consistent with the culture of honor and the duel so prominent in France of the Belle Epoque.[67] That culture combined a bourgeois work ethic and belief in self-mastery with an aristocratic tradition of elegance

Figure 21. Lyautey and "the Occupation of Oujda" (*L'Illustration*, 13 April 1907).

Figure 22. Portrait of Lyautey (*L'Opinion,* July 1920).

and grace. Duelists practiced their craft assiduously, controlling their emotions in good bourgeois fashion. But they did so in a setting that harked back to the pre-industrial world, when the sword symbolized chivalric combat and fencing was the pastime of lords. Swordsmanship required superior skill, not superior strength; a combatant's goal was not to overwhelm his opponent, but calmly to demonstrate the ability to wound, even kill, while stopping short of such a violent denouement.[68] In fact, the most successful duelists were those whose reputed talents meant that they only rarely had to fight. The best fencers, in other words, were pacific conquerors—just like Brazza and Lyautey, aristocrats successful in a bourgeois, republican age. Lyautey's motto could have applied to them both: "Display your power so you don't have to use it."[69]

It was this semi-aristocratic ethic of the duel that Lyautey, in particular, seemed to represent. Lyautey's svelte form made him look like a fencer, and he carried his sword wherever he went. He intended not to obliterate his opponents but to convince them it was futile to fight. He would do so partly through skillful negotiation and partly through his reputation for power. Journalists focused on the general's aristocratic manliness because that cultural style seemed best suited for what was widely considered a dangerous and delicate point in time. Having made peace with Great Britain, France nonetheless faced the prospect of renewed conflict with Germany, and this at a time when Russia seemed unable to help. To prepare for the German threat, French men had to overcome the legacy of humiliation and emasculation they had suffered in 1870–71. But they had to do so without becoming so aggressive as to prompt a preemptive German strike.[70] The culture and practice of dueling seemed ideal for this purpose because it promoted a subtle form of masculine revival designed to enhance virility while keeping naked aggression in check. Such images could be reassuring to French men and women confronted with an assertive German neighbor, a once and potential enemy whose population, economy, and army greatly exceeded their French counterparts in strength. French commentators, and doubtless the general public as well, wanted to believe that their superior knowledge, skill, refinement, and self-discipline would compensate for what many feared was a deficit of masculinity and virile force.[71]

During the Belle Epoque, commentators widely agreed that virility, already wanting in 1871, had been further compromised by the feminizing effects of consumer society and of an economy in which machines dominated men and so many sat behind counters or desks. The novelist and ardent nationalist Maurice Barrès celebrated the mythic man who "strides through the high grass with his rifle in his hand . . . enveloped on all sides by danger," but worried about the omnipresence of bureaucratic "semimales." Barrès's ideological nemesis Emile Zola agreed, lamenting that "virility is fading away"; and the centrist Emile Faguet found it "revolting to see a [male] colossus performing the passive tasks of a petty functionary."[72] If "there were no longer any men," as the writer F. A. Vuillermet maintained, it was because they had been enervated and emasculated by a culture that paid too much attention to their minds and too little to their bodies.[73]

Dueling addressed this fin-de-siècle mind-body problem, echoing a time, as the sociologist Gabriel Tarde put it, "when courage was everything and said . . . to the softened and enervated man of our century: you must be brave."[74] But important as the duel seemed to be, for a military man like Hubert Lyautey it could not by itself produce the manly energy essential to revitalizing a decadent France weakened by luxury, republicanism, and decades of European peace. The main source of a heightened virility lay not in metropolitan France but in the colonies abroad.

Lyautey had doubtless been influenced by Barrès, who called for "professors of energy" to free his country from the egalitarian mediocrity and capitalist materialism of its republican regime.[75] But the general's innovation was to find those professors among the ordinary French men who served in the colonies. France's possessions in Indochina, Madagascar, the Sudan, and North Africa operated as "schools of virility," as Lyautey's confidant Alfred de Tarde would later put it, that trained the professors of energy who would eventually return home and, Lyautey wrote, "wrest this country from decomposition and ruin." Colonialists would do so, the general added, "not by changing [France's] constitutional forms, a mundane and fleeting remedy, but by acting powerfully on its mores, on its inertia and its passivity." Those returning from their lessons in virility abroad would "regenerate" the homeland by "awakening" its "physical fertility," which would in turn "awaken its economic activity, commerce, and the entrepreneurial spirit." If French men had become unsexed and infertile thanks to the "atrophied state [of their country] where everything melts into the soothing ease of a material semi-well-being," colonialists would help restore them to a more masculine life. Those who had served abroad would "fertilize the homeland with a virile seed."[76]

These passages from Lyautey's letters suggest an unintended irony. He had fled France partly to avoid marriage with a woman of childbearing age, a union that would have made him a father, still one of the essential characteristics of masculinity at that time.[77] His own complicated sexuality and male identity may have moved him to find in the colonies a fertility and virility that his sexual orientation denied him in his personal life. "The reason I became a dedicated colonial officer," he wrote, "was because, above all, our colonial expansion enlarges that wonderful nursery of will and energy" essential to making any nation great. Thanks to his experience abroad, he could "give fertility" to France.[78]

Among Lyautey's most faithful correspondents was Eugène Melchior de Vogüé, a diplomat, novelist, and Orientalist of noble lineage. In a letter to the vicomte, Lyautey responded to his friend's lamentation that the French were a "declining race" by telling him of the great potential their country-men could realize if only they would be "liberated from [metropolitan] France, like a sword from its sheathe." Here once again is the imagery of fencing and the duel, only it represents the manly energy released through colonial service abroad, rather than gentlemanly combat at home. If members of parliament could spend some time in Indochina, Lyautey wrote, they would see that France's colonies have begun to "educate a growing generation of strong young men, freed from routine and ready for bold and daring acts."[79]

Lyautey's letter may have inspired Vogüé's 1899 novel *Les Morts qui parlent,* in which a young parliamentary deputy named Jacques Andarran travels to Senegal to visit his brother Pierre, who serves as an officer there. If European writers of the fin-de-siècle typically portrayed Africa as a land riddled with disease and debilitating heat, Andarran characterized it as the source of vitality and good health. "Who calls it unhealthy and feverous, that Senegalese air? Jacques found it restorative." He had left behind in Paris the "pernicious fevers" of the Palais Bourbon, that cesspool of disgust where only "the dead speak," mouthing a "vain prattle," their "faces pinched, drab, hateful, and full of deceit." Africa may have been a nightmarish hell for Joseph Conrad and Félicien Challaye, but for Vogüé it was the place where the nightmare of parliaments and republican impotence vanished into air. There was nothing inherently wrong with members of the Chamber of Deputies; the institution held the blame. They would be cured if, like their countrymen in Senegal or Sudan, they could become "good students of virile work," laboring in the "school of action and responsibility" that the colonies represented.[80]

While in Africa, Jacques tells his brother and their comrades that, for his parliamentary colleagues, the goal of colonial expansion was the "*mis en valeur,*" or economic exploitation, of the territories in question. Pierre responds that he neither expects nor seeks any material benefits from his colonial efforts. His objective was the creation of new men, the formation of "the cadres of our national regeneration." Africa was the land, as Vogüé would put it in a later novel, from which France would "renew its spent energies."[81] When these forceful colonial men took charge of the metropolitan army, they would "make our European adversaries think twice" before trying to push the French around.[82]

Later in *Les Morts qui parlent,* Pierre, wounded, returns home. Marie, who loves him, urges him to remain with her but worries that Pierre has another love, the love of Africa, and that the continent's hold on him as "a man of action" is more powerful than hers. Marie is fiercely jealous of this Africa, her competitor in love. But despite her misery over the thought of losing Pierre again, "she instinctively loves in him this proof of male energy."[83] The colonies had made Pierre so viscerally male as to allow him to capture his beloved at an elemental, instinctive level, despite her fear that he would leave her behind. Vogüé's ideas, which echoed those of Lyautey, were consonant with the focus on heroes, heroism, and virility common in both fin-de-siècle France and late Victorian Britain.

Lyautey's reputation as a pacific conqueror, a lithe duelist on the colonial stage, received another boost in December 1908 when the general's forces defeated the Beni Snassen tribal army in its mountainous homeland in northeastern Morocco. The Berber tribe had risen in rebellion against the French forces based in Oujda, and after a month of inconclusive fighting, the Beni Snassen withdrew into their mountain redoubt. They planned to remain there until the French either left the region or let down their guard. Lyautey responded by turning their geographic position against them. Rather than invade their natural fortress, which would have placed French troops at a massive disadvantage, the general built a ring of military posts around the base of the mountains. This strategy cut the Beni Snassen's supply routes, preventing them from replenishing their dwindling stocks of food and ammunition. When these supplies ran out, tribal leaders sued for peace.[84]

Since Lyautey won this battle more through economic warfare than by taking a large number of Moroccan (or French) lives, journalists covering the campaign dubbed it yet another example of Lyautey's humane, pacific approach. "In just a few days with a small number of men," wrote a journalist for *Le Gaulois*, "General Lyautey won the complete submission of rebel tribes without causing [human] losses."[85] He earned loyalty from his soldiers and submission from Moroccans, added *Le Figaro*'s Jean Dautel, for one and the same reason: as Lyautey himself put it, "The art of command must be a labor of love."[86] Here was a manly man, whose best weapon was the art of love. Such an idea likely reassured French men and women of moderate and liberal temper who, since the Dreyfus Affair, had been wary of traditional military leaders. Ordinary citizens wanted to spread French civilization, and nothing could be more comforting than the notion of doing so in peace.

Still, if Lyautey subdued the Beni Snassen with a minimum of blood-shed, such would be the exception rather than the rule in Morocco between 1907 and 1914. Lyautey's fellow generals would prove extremely, even gra-tuitously, brutal in their campaigns against "rebel" Moroccan fighters, and Lyautey himself would soon find that violence alone succeeded in over-coming their resistance. But despite this bloody reality, Lyautey's reputa-tion as a peaceful conqueror would hold firm in France throughout the en-tire period and beyond. He established his peaceful bona fides early on, and that reputation would stick. An army, Lyautey wrote, was not just a fighting force but an "organization on the march," using diplomacy, intel-ligence, and economic incentives to minimize the amount of violence nec-essary to acquire territory abroad.[87] These ideas allowed Lyautey to ration-alize in his own mind the bloodshed of colonial conquest and to make an especially convincing case to French journalists, themselves eager to see colonialism as "a labor of love."

If most commentators transmitted the message Lyautey sought to im-part, contributing to the growing mythology surrounding him, there were nonetheless a few dissenters on the political extremes. For the left-wing *Les Hommes du jour,* the general was a master of public relations, a brilliant manipulator who "by his tact, his savoir-faire, and his subtlety . . . suc-ceeded in making the entire [mass-circulation 'bourgeois press'] dance to his tune." Unlike Gallieni, who wrote one weighty colonial tome after the other and influenced no one, Lyautey gave himself "a halo of generosity and humanitarianism" by placing a couple of short, cleverly-written ar-ticles in prestigious journals. Beyond this, he handled gullible journalists with impressive, if diabolical, skill.[88]

On the extreme right, Edouard Drumont agreed that Lyautey was a pa-cific conqueror but predicted—correctly as it turned out—that Morocco would become bloody. "All of our hesitations and our pacific proce-dures," Drumont's correspondent wrote, "will be interpreted as retreats by these tribes, against which force alone can succeed."[89] French pacifism would thus encourage the Arabs to fight harder, and before long the mur-ders and assassination of today would reach their "natural, logical, and fatal denouement: a mass uprising of the whole of Morocco, a Muslim crusade against the Roumis [Christians], a holy war by the sons of the Prophet." France would have no choice, Drumont added, but to inter-vene with force, leaving in Morocco "the bones of twenty or thirty thou-sand French soldiers."[90] Although the right-wing agitator overestimated the death toll, he proved generally accurate about the large-scale rebellion soon to erupt.

Lyautey's "peaceful" occupation of Oujda in April 1907, successful as it seemed at the time, became the last straw for tribal leaders and other Moroccan elites. France not only had seized control of Morocco's economy but had subjected the Makhzan to tight political oversight and now had brazenly occupied a Moroccan city. French troops would soon capture a second town, after nine Europeans, including three French citizens, were murdered in Casablanca on 30 July. Those who attacked the nine Europeans accused them of desecrating a Muslim cemetery. The French press, especially the mass-circulation dailies, splashed pictures and reports of the murders on the front pages. These killings, coming so soon after the highly publicized murder of Mauchamp, produced great outrage in France, whose government hastened to intervene. It did so with extraordinary clumsiness, triggering massive rioting and looting throughout Casablanca, especially in the Jewish quarter, where perhaps one hundred people were cut down and an equal number of girls abducted. In response, French gunboats bombarded the city, killing hundreds more, flattening buildings and making streets impassable. A corps of twelve hundred *tirailleurs sénégalais* and foreign legionnaires commanded by General Drude eventually came ashore and occupied the city.[91]

The huge French military presence triggered a powerful uprising among the tribes around Casablanca, which amassed some 10,000 men to face Drude's army. The French government, unprepared to endorse large-scale fighting in Morocco and fearing a hostile European reaction, forbade the general to move inland from the city. This reticence encouraged the Moroccan rebellion, which in turn moved the sultan to send his own army into the area. 'Aziz worried that the Casablanca rebellion would play into the hands of his half brother 'Abd al-Hafiz, who wanted to replace him as ruler of the country. Under these circumstances, the sitting sultan found himself with no good alternatives. If he did nothing, and rebellious tribes succeeded in ejecting the French from Casablanca, he would seem weak while allowing his brother, who supported the tribes, to look strong. But if the sultan's troops intervened in Casablanca, he would be accused of siding with the Roumi occupiers against his own people.

Even before the French landing in Casablanca, powerful local leaders such as Madani el Glaoui had begun to argue that 'Aziz had betrayed religion and country and should be deposed. Since the sultan was at once the country's political and spiritual leader, the position could not be abolished or left vacant. There had to be a new sultan, one who could claim a legitimate hold on the throne. Glaoui endorsed 'Abd al-Hafiz's claim to the throne, effectively giving the country a second ruler.[92] The mutual antagonism of the rival brothers would launch Morocco into a civil war, placing the French in an exceedingly awkward position. They were now fighting alongside a sultan who had lost much of his legitimacy and power. Any victories for French forces or for 'Aziz alienated Hafiz's followers all the more, making France's quest to rule Morocco indirectly through its sultan more elusive than ever.

Part jihad, part national rebellion, part anticolonial struggle, and part agrarian uprising, 'Abd al-Hafiz's "Hafiziya" movement radicalized much of Morocco and made it clear that broad sectors of the elite and population at large wanted nothing to do with France. The movement became so powerful that on 21 August 1908, 'Aziz abdicated and Hafiz became the new sultan.[93] This transfer of power did nothing, however, to lighten the load of Morocco's dependency on France. With the Makhzan heavily in debt, Hafiz could hardly shrug off French political and financial control. In submitting to it, he guaranteed that many of the social forces that had mobilized against his brother would soon rise against him. To confront this challenge, the French would have to abandon all pretense of a *penetration pacifique;* Lyautey would find himself charged with suppressing a holy war.

Lyautey retained his command on the border of Algeria and Morocco until the end of 1910, when he was named chief officer of the Tenth Army Corps at Rennes. Between the abdication of 'Aziz and his departure for France, Lyautey had established French control over the eastern third of Morocco and heightened the interest of French journalists who continued to portray him as a peaceful conqueror, despite his often-violent military campaigns. On 18 April 1908, *L'Illustration* pictured him on its cover for the second time, as he respectfully "received" the *qaid* (governor) of Mediouna. A year later, the magazine lauded Lyautey's putative success in organizing thriving markets in once rebellious provinces "without incident and without a single gunshot being fired." As a result, "the pacific penetration . . . of this vast region has [been] quickly assured," and local tribes now benefited from a "French peace . . . pursued and realized by General Lyautey."[94] The same was supposedly true of the Chaouia region, where, the *Petit parisien*'s correspondent observed, "respect for the natives has been scrupulous beyond anything we have seen before."[95] These overly rosy stories, with their happy, peaceful endings, glossed over a series of bloody battles between 10,000 tribal fighters and French troops during the two previous years.[96]

Thanks to such journalistic accounts, Lyautey assumed his command in Rennes surrounded by a halo of journalistic admiration equaled by no other military leader of the time. "His campaigns [in Morocco]," wrote his future collaborator Wladimir d'Ormesson, "have made him famous. He was considered one of the most brilliant commanders of the army, not only for his military talents, for the extraordinary authority that emanates from him, but also because of his reputation as a deeply cultured man, an artist and patron of the arts." Lyautey, added Ormesson, basked "in a kind of legend."[97] At this time, Lyautey began to think of himself as the general destined to lead France's looming war effort against Germany and as the man who would save his country from a new and devastating defeat.[98]

At it turned out, war between France and Germany nearly broke out in July 1911, when the kaiser sent his gunboat *Panther* to Agadir to protest an unprecedented French military penetration of Morocco's interior. In France, mainstream opinion viewed this latest German challenge as a grievous affront, while nationalists demanded blood—as did their counterparts across the Rhine. In the end, the two governments resolved their differences peacefully, postponing war for a few more years. The Germans acquiesced to a French protectorate over Morocco in exchange for a sliver of land from the Congo.[99] At long last, French colonialists had achieved their most cherished goal: Morocco now belonged to them. The sultan agreed to allow French forces to occupy any part of the country their leaders deemed necessary and to give France essentially complete control of his country's international relations and foreign trade. To enforce these provisions, a new treaty officially made Morocco a French protectorate and stipulated that France would be represented in Morocco by a "resident general" who would hold effective power there, serving at once as the sultan's prime minister and foreign minister.[100]

Once word of the protectorate treaty leaked out, Moroccan unrest erupted once again. It boiled over when French officials attempted to reshape the Makhzan's army along metropolitan lines. Prime Minister Raymond Poincaré's objective in doing so was to use Moroccan soldiers to complete the conquest of their country, thus sparing French manpower for the impending war against Germany. The military reorganization seemed humiliating to the Moroccans, who now had to take orders in French, follow what to them were alien military procedures, and worst of all, receive part of their pay in kind, which deprived them of cash needed to support their wives and children. The soldiers' protests quickly developed into a mutiny that targeted French military instructors, several of whom were killed. Soldiers then turned their rage against European residents of Fez, shooting people at random, looting stores, and burning houses. The mutineers, now with hundreds of townspeople behind them, turned on Fez's Jewish quarter, the *mallāh*, where Moroccan rioters usually ended up. The fighting lasted nearly three days (17–19 April); in the end, fifty-three French soldiers lay dead along with thirteen European civilians. The Jewish quarter was burnt to the ground, leaving ten thousand people homeless. Perhaps six hundred Moroccans lost their lives.[101]

The sultan proved powerless to stop the violence—he had, in fact, helped spark it by signing the protectorate agreement and giving his country to the infidel. Hafiz then fanned its flames by appearing to turn against the French and side with the rebels. In any event, the French, now in charge of Morocco, faced a full-scale insurrection. They needed an experienced military man to take charge, and Lyautey was waiting in the wings. Thanks in part to pressure from Etienne and the Comité du Maroc, Poincaré named Lyautey resident-general of Morocco—after he assured government leaders that he would subdue the rebellion as peacefully as possible.[102]

The French press lauded Lyautey's appointment, announced on 28 April 1912, with near unanimity. The only other times the country's commentators had responded to a French colonial personality with so little dissent had been when Brazza sought ratification of his Makoko treaty and when Marchand returned home from Fashoda. In Lyautey's case, we have evidence in his voluminous correspondence that broad swathes of the French public endorsed his selection as well.

Lyautey's most ardent journalistic support had long come from *Le Temps,* the austere, influential newspaper read by France's political elite. Dozens of Parisian and provincial papers reprinted or excerpted its articles nearly every day, especially those on foreign policy. For that reason, *Le Temps* enjoyed a degree of influence far beyond its relatively modest circulation (45,000 in 1912). The paper's leading writers and editors belonged to the colonial lobby, and, early on, Lyautey had convinced its main foreign affairs correspondent, André Tardieu, to endorse his method of colonial expansion.[103] Tardieu, a brilliant *normalien* (graduate of France's most selective school) who led a double life as journalist and high civil servant, had urged Poincaré to name Lyautey resident-general. When he did, *Le Temps* elaborately praised the decision, asserting, "The designation of General Lyautey as resident general has been received with a unanimous satisfaction. . . . He is the only man in France who has already done in Morocco exactly what he is now being asked to do," namely, to be "at once a soldier and an administrator."[104]

Virtually every major newspaper agreed, reminding readers of Lyautey's "self-assured command," his pacific conquest of the Beni Snassen, and his refusal to found "an empire through force alone."[105] Once again, commentators admired the general's distinctive looks and youthful, energetic allure, the "thin, well-proportioned body with tense military legs." A writer for the popular weekly *La Vie* claimed that even the Arabs worship him, too. When asked what he thought of Lyautey, a Moroccan soldier supposedly spread his arms and cried: "Allah! Mohammed! Lyautey!"[106]

Taken together, these articles and many more like them reached tens of millions of French readers. But how can we gauge their effect? We know from Lyautey's correspondence that long before his appointment as resident-general, his views had deeply influenced members of France's social and political elite, especially those of wealth and conservative values.[107] Lyautey corresponded with more than a thousand people, and because his epistolary partners circulated the letters among friends and acquaintances, it is likely that five thousand—perhaps even ten thousand individuals—had read one or more of his letters.[108] Since many of these people wrote back expressing admiration and support for his ideas and his work, we have good evidence that, within this large circle of correspondents at least, Lyautey's views about Morocco in particular and empire in general had sunk in. For these individuals, articles in the press likely confirmed ideas they already held, creating even stronger commitments to Lyautey and to the form of colonialism he represented.

The press proved especially influential among the general's correspondents because it reinforced a "private" relationship often too distant to stand on its own. Lyautey's long absences from France and the sheer impossibility of seeing so many people meant that in most cases he had little or no face-to-face relationship with the vast majority of those he wrote. And because the general could not communicate with each of his epistolary partners very often, most had to rely on the press for information about him. He was thus more a celebrity to them than a friend, more a distant public figure than an element of everyday life. But these correspondents possessed more than an ordinary fan's relationship with Lyautey. They formed, rather, a kind of elite fan club, all the more devoted to him and his ideas thanks to the letters they occasionally received.

Even some of Lyautey's family members related to him mainly in his role as a public persona. When Lyautey was named resident-general, a cousin wrote to say he had heard about it from the press, as did a great many who considered themselves his friends—including the rare individuals who addressed him with the familiar *tu*. As one wrote, "Je lis ta nomination dans la presse."[109] One particularly interesting set of reactions came from Max Lazard, the social reformer and scion of a top French banking family. Lazard enjoyed an epistolary relationship with Lyautey that extended over more than thirty years, though he saw him only rarely. In one early letter, Max writes: "If you have the time to respond, I hope you will talk to me about yourself for as long as I talk about myself. I hear about you only from the articles in newspapers, where you're cited very often." Lazard adds that he "would be happy to talk with you about the work of colonization that men like you can make so appealing and so attractive."[110] The combination of regular newspaper articles and the infrequent but intimate letters attached the young Max Lazard to Lyautey and made the then-colonel his hero. In an eight-page letter to Lyautey, Max's mother confirmed as much, telling him of her son's "complete admiration and affection for you." She confesses her own admiration as well, especially for Lyautey's colonial oeuvre. "Thanks to Mme Berenger, I was able to read a few of your *extremely vivid* letters [emphasis in original]. . . . I would have wanted all those interested in our colonies and in the grandeur of France to read them."[111] In Madame Lazard's letter we see the influence of Lyautey's missives beyond those to whom they were addressed.

For all that Lyautey curried favor with influential men, he did not neglect the obscure. He made a point of flattering and reinforcing unknown writers when they expressed ideas similar to his. Such individuals regularly joined the ranks of Lyautey's fans. Take Gaston Deschamps, a minor journalist who published articles here and there. After the general wrote Deschamps praising one of his pieces, the journalist responded in laudatory tones. He called Lyautey "the brilliant general who has served France so well," a man "well-known to each and every Frenchman."[112]

Although "serious" journalists like *Le Temps'* Tardieu wrote at length about foreign policy and colonial theory, the mass press did not limit itself to Lyautey's ideas and actions. As we have seen, popular journalists described—often elaborately—his looks, dress, mannerisms, idiosyncrasies, and the like. In doing so, the mass media of the era once again fostered an "intimacy at a distance," a familiarity gained without any direct interaction with the individual in question.[113]

The French National Archives contain vivid evidence of the role such "intimacy at a distance" played in making Lyautey a popular hero and celebrity and in attaching large numbers of French men and women to the colonial ideas and images he seemed to represent. Lyautey received hundreds, perhaps thousands, of letters congratulating him on his nomination as resident-general of Morocco in April 1912.[114] The majority of these letters came from people who knew him only distantly or not at all. This correspondence provides evidence not only of Lyautey's popularity but also of a widespread support for the Moroccan conquest he had come to represent. It also reveals the importance he had assumed in the mental worlds of a great many French women and men.

Several people wrote asking Lyautey to take them—or their sons—to Morocco with him, and others expressed regret that they could not join his efforts. As one writer put it, "The task to accomplish is so elevated, so important to our country, that all those unable to accompany you must suffer a broken heart." In any event, "the hearts of all Frenchmen accompany you [to Morocco] and God is on your side." The writer, who hadn't seen Lyautey in many years, expressed the disappointment that can result from intimacy at a distance: "I would have been very happy to talk with you about this for a few minutes."[115]

Echoing the mass press, a great many of Lyautey's correspondents claimed that "the whole of France" or "all Frenchmen" rejoiced in his nomination as resident-general and that in naming him to this post, the government was only responding to the popular will. As one put it, "for once, public opinion will be unanimous in ratifying your choice [as head of Morocco.]"[116] The word "patriotic" appears over and over again in these letters, as numerous writers identified the conquest and control of Morocco as one of France's most cherished interests, both in terms of its civilizing mission and as the bulwark against German expansion. "You will know how to make sure the flag of our Fatherland is respected and to show that a strong nation knows how to avenge the affronts it has suffered."[117]

Because Lyautey's appointment as proconsul of Morocco made him one of France's most important and visible people, many letter writers saw him as a celebrity and themselves as fans.[118] Several correspondents asked for his autograph, some enclosing a special card for that purpose. A great many others revealed an intense emotional connection to the celebrity Lyautey and a personal, if vicarious, involvement in his deeds: "When this morning's newspapers brought me, deep in my provincial backwater, the news of your great [new] dignity . . . I felt not just a joy but a profound sense of relief." For another correspondent, the emotional connection with Lyautey was such that "I will follow you, in my thoughts, along the path you have chosen. The path will be littered with obstacles, but it will take you into the realm of glory."[119]

For these writers, Lyautey was not just a celebrity but a hero as well. Like the other anointed heroes of the Belle Epoque, Lyautey seemed to reproduce the greatness of ancient myth, offering guidance, protection, and inspiration in this prewar era of uncertainty and unease. His Moroccan quest made him an "indispensable man," a "necessary man," an "indispensable leader," the "man of all men of energy and courage," the "only man capable of solving the grave Moroccan problem."[120] For one writer, Lyautey's heroism recalled "the aura of Bonaparte on the eve of his conquest of Egypt."[121] "Without a doubt," wrote another, "the prestige of your name alone, a name that means loyalty, courage, protection for the humble . . . will attract the [rebellious] natives to you and make them your servants."[122] They would, in other words, submit to Lyautey's conquête pacifique.

Many correspondents expressed dissatisfaction with the state of their country, but in Lyautey, they found hope for the future: "Your nomination is, in itself, the best proof of the restoration of our national sentiment, and nothing else could bring more joy and hope to our fighting men."[123] Such writers, and many others, believed the new resident-general would restore the national honor by bringing order and discipline to the colonies. "You and you alone have the strength to undo the chaos and to establish, step by step, a French peace."[124] In Lyautey, national and imperial sentiments came together, making him a French hero of overwhelming importance on the eve of 1914.

The ideas and emotions expressed in these letters to Lyautey announced what Daniel Rivet, the best historian of this period, has called a "Morocco Mania."[125] During a period of nationalist revival and looming fears of war, French men and women were comforted by the "heroic" victories over Moroccan "rebels" and especially by the emergence of a potential savior in Lyautey.[126] The elegant, aristocratic general—the manly, though pacific, conqueror—appealed to an unusually broad sector of the French population: nationalists who saw him as a Barrésian "professor of energy"; republicans who believed in the civilizing mission and the peaceful extension of French power; even socialists for whom Lyautey seemed the least of evils among generals who might be sent to Fez.[127]

Such generalized support underlay Lyautey's emergence as a colonial hero in the years before the First World War. It enabled him to embody in his person not just the French presence in Morocco but the essential qualities of Frenchness itself. When Lyautey was elected to the Academie Française in October 1912, journalists framed this honor as evidence of his ability to incarnate the nation as a whole. "At pivotal moments," wrote the editors of *La Liberté*, "certain names appear before us. All at once everyone finds himself drawn to these names, and we all come together in a kind of national fervor. Today, that name is Lyautey." Because the *academie* represented not just the country's intellectual life but its most essential spirit, "it wanted to acclaim as resoundingly as possible the man who, at this moment, best honors the fatherland.... What France loves above all in Lyautey is France itself."[128]

At a time of mounting tension with Germany, nothing proved more encouraging to the French public than newspaper tales of brave, triumphant fighters lead by a resident-general whose toughness and resolution were tempered by intelligence, *finesse,* and a zeal for French civilization. If Lyautey could defeat Moroccan barbarism with the promise of a humane, French peace, there was reason for confidence that other French generals—or perhaps Lyautey himself—would overcome German barbarism as well. "France has recognized Lyautey," wrote the *Petit journal,* "and Germany has noted it."[129] In 1899 the image of Jean-Baptiste Marchand had helped French men and women recover from the national disasters of Fashoda and the Dreyfus Affair; now the apparent heroism of Lyautey would steel them for the new trials to come.

Epilogue

STANLEY, BRAZZA, GORDON, MARCHAND, AND LYAUTEY—five men who became charismatic heroes and exemplars of empire—resonated in their countries after the end of their African careers, and in some cases even, or especially, after their deaths. For most of the five, charisma gave way to celebrity and fame, as they no longer exercised authority in a Weberian sense. In Stanley's case, for example, the excess violence associated with his expeditions deprived him of charismatic authority—his ability to inspire people to imitation and action—but not his celebrity status. And in the long run, his fame has endured. The word "fame" comes from the Greek and Latin "to speak" and applies to those "much talked about."[1] Stanley's fame has lasted not just because everyone knows the greeting "Dr. Livingstone, I presume?" but because an endless stream of biographies and other writings have kept his memory—and thus his fame—alive.

Although the five men played comparable roles, there were important differences among them. Gordon stood out as the sole religious hero of the group, though Brazza and Marchand joined him in appearing to martyr themselves to the imperial cause. Like Gordon, Brazza died in Africa in a brave but futile effort to achieve his goals. But the purposes and implications of the two final missions differed significantly. Gordon was sent to extricate British subjects and dependents trapped by an anticolonial rebellion. The long-term outcome of his intervention served to extend British control over Egypt and Sudan. Brazza's purpose was to investigate France's colonial transgressions, and he ultimately raised grave questions about his country's Congolese rule. His findings did not substantially change French policy, but they left him with a considerably better reputation in Africa than most Europeans enjoyed. As for Marchand, he returned from Africa alive but became a figurative martyr to political exigency, to France's need to avoid war with Britain and eventually ally with her.

Neither Lyautey nor Stanley achieved martyrdom, though both appeared to suffer on their countries' behalf—the French general less than the "intrepid" Welsh-American explorer. Of our five heroes, Lyautey alone actually conquered an African country and left a long-standing administrative imprint there, effectively ruling Morocco for more than a dozen years. Although he succeeded in making the country France's protectorate and in attracting a fair number of European colonists there, he failed to overcome the persistent resistance to France's colonial control. Morocco had long been the homeland of fiercely independent tribes, and to his credit, Lyautey proved unwilling to use the overwhelming force necessary to defeat their unceasing guerilla war.[2] Even so, Lyautey's actions caused far more deaths than Stanley's, since the latter did not engage in all-out war. And although the explorer played a key role in King Leopold's efforts to colonize the Congo, he bore no direct responsibility for the nightmare of death, suffering, and abuse endemic to the Free State. Still, Stanley never criticized Leopold in public and refused to blame his former employer for the atrocities committed there. Stanley did take reports of severed hands, whippings, and murders seriously and wrote cautiously about them.[3] But given his stature and fame, not to mention his position as member of Parliament, he more than anyone in the 1890s could have placed obstacles in Leopold's path.

Until recently, few observers have concerned themselves with Stanley's failings in this domain, and his historical reputation remained relatively unblemished for most of the twentieth century. He owed a good many of those positive memories to his wife, Dorothy Stanley, who worked tirelessly to tout her husband's accomplishments. She censored parts of his manuscript diary, prepared a Stanley "autobiography" that left a great deal unsaid, and carefully preserved his papers while keeping journalists and historians at arm's length. Tim Jeal argues that these efforts to protect his reputation, however successful for a time, backfired in the end. Her secrecy—and that of her adopted son—suppressed evidence of kindness, warmth, and generosity that came out only when scholars gained full access to Stanley's papers in 2002.[4]

The efforts of Brazza's wife, Thérèse, a descendent of Lafayette's, proved far more positive. She subscribed to a press clipping service that allowed her to preserve for posterity an extraordinary number of articles, most of them highly favorable, about her husband.[5] And after his death in 1905, she cultivated journalists and writers eager to amplify Brazza's legend and keep it alive. Thérèse helped ensure his lasting reputation as a peaceful conqueror by having Charles de Chavannes' epitaph engraved on his tomb: "His memory / Is pure of human blood." She protested vehemently in her husband's name when in 1911 the French government ceded a sliver of its Congolese territory to Germany in exchange for a free hand in Morocco. In the 1930s, Thérèse worked with prominent colonialists to revive Brazza's memory and give it a major role in France's huge International Colonial Exhibition of 1931. And at age eighty-three, she joined de Gaulle in Brazzaville (February 1944) when the Free French leader dedicated a monument in her husband's honor.[6]

Lyautey's wife played no similar role as guardian of the great man's memory, but throughout his life he corresponded regularly with his sisters and countless other women, who faithfully wrote him back. The marshal's nephew Pierre preserved his voluminous collection of letters, organizing it in ways that presented his uncle in a highly favorable light. This collection has done a great deal to shape Lyautey's historical reputation.[7] Gordon never married, but his sister Augusta loomed large throughout his life, strongly shaping his religious and spiritual views and giving him lifelong emotional companionship. W. T. Stead's interview in her Southampton home helped launch Gordon's final, fateful trip to the Sudan, and after his death, she worked assiduously to preserve his memory as a Christian philanthropist and surrogate father to troubled, abandoned boys.[8]

Of our five heroes, Marchand alone had no women prominently in his life. Does that absence help explain why he slipped most quickly from the press and public's radar screen? After Castellani's worshipful books about Marchand, biographers largely ignored him, though two of France's most prominent nationalist writers, Maurice Barrès and Léon Daudet, published laudatory essays extolling his extraordinary character and abilities. Recounting a dinner party for Marchand, Daudet wrote, "When Marchand came into the room . . . glory, honor, and courage entered with him."[9] But while Marchand relished his status as charismatic leader, he appeared uninterested in harnessing that authority to a political movement. The hero of Fashoda seemed especially reluctant to join the nationalists in seeking to overthrow a Republic that had, in the end, treated him well, promoting him quickly to lieutenant colonel, colonel, and eventually general.[10]

In 1900 he fought with French troops against the Boxer Rebellion in China and took a great interest in Lyautey's activity in Algeria and Morocco. The two began a correspondence in 1900 and saw each other regularly in Paris before the army assigned Lyautey to Algeria in 1903. Shortly after arriving there, Lyautey received a letter from Marchand in which the hero of Fashoda seemed to pass the mantle to the hero-to-be. "I salute your stars, and if they can rise at the same time as the sun of France, somewhat darkened today, . . . it would be thrilling beyond words to perceive their first rays of light."[11]

As a general, Marchand served brilliantly during the First World War, commanding the French army's Colonial Division on the western front. Journalists briefly took note when in 1915 Marchand's second-in-command at Fashoda, Albert Baratier, now a general, shook hands with his old nemesis Horatio Herbert Kitchener, Britain's secretary of state for war. Kitchener sent his regards to Marchand, prompting L'Illustration's correspondent to ask, "Who would have predicted such a turnabout at Fashoda seventeen years ago?"[12] Although Marchand disappeared from the news after 1918, Lyautey would not forget him. As head of France's International Colonial Exposition of 1931, a world's fair of colonialism, Lyautey placed a large monument commemorating Marchand near the fair's most prominent building. The monument still stands today, though the building, once the Colonial Museum, now houses France's new National Center for the History of Immigration.

If Marchand's memory lived on, by the post–World War I era, Gordon's had faded into a no longer relevant time. Lytton Strachey's *Eminent Victorians,* published in 1918, served as an epitaph to a Victorian era eclipsed, like France's Belle Epoque, by the shadow of war. As emblematic of that era, Gordon seemed to offer little to the jaded denizens of the brave new twentieth-century world. After the rigors of mechanized war, Gordon's belief in divine providence appeared naïve, his martyrdom trivial after the death of so many military men. By the Second World War, Gordon had become a historical curiosity at best. Madame Tussaud's dismantled its long-standing Gordon panorama in 1941, and his once prominent statue in Trafalgar Square lost its perch as city engineers stored it out of sight. Not until 1953 did it find a home in London's museum-like Victoria Embankment. The Victorian era had become quaint, its heroes now speaking to us only in the pages of biographies, where we can enjoy the romance of the past.

In Africa, too, Gordon's memory has all but vanished. The Gordon Memorial College, established in Khartoum in 1902 to commemorate the general's martyrdom and Kitchener's "reconquest" of the Sudan, lost its connection with Gordon and British imperialism when the country achieved its independence in 1956. That year, the former Gordon College became the University College of Khartoum.

The reputation of Hubert Lyautey has enjoyed a much longer life. Having "pacified" the coastal and lowland areas of Morocco, though not the mountains by 1914, Morocco's resident-general had reason to hope he might be chosen to lead the war effort against Germany. But the republican government, conservative as it had become, remained wary of the aristocratic, royalist general. Army leaders, meanwhile, worried that the intellectual, individualistic Lyautey would never be one of them. Save for a brief and unsuccessful stint as minister of war in the winter of 1916–17, the resident-general of Morocco remained outside mainland France. For that reason, no one could blame him for the stalemated slaughter of the war; his reputation grew as the luster of Joffre, Gallieni, Nivelle, and the other French commanders eventually wore off.[13]

In 1920, Lyautey traveled to Paris for his formal induction into the Academie Française, a ceremony postponed since his election eight years earlier amid Moroccan fighting so intense he could not leave. The French press elaborately covered the induction, during which he became known as "Lyautey L'Africain." Many of the journalistic themes were familiar. He had "given us Morocco and then preserved it for us almost without shedding any blood."[14] His oeuvre represented "the vast deserts penetrated, the inaccessible mountains crossed, the peoples made to submit, the roads opened to the Cross as well as the flag, the cities built, the land made fertile, French civilization under way."[15] Not "since Hercules," the journalist declared, have "the Atlas Mountains . . . seen so great a chief."[16] Perhaps most important for so many of France's postwar writers, Lyautey was at once a man of action and a man of letters. The resident-general, concluded Amadée Britisch, "has lived his novel before writing it."[17]

For all the hero worship of Lyautey, conservative writers appreciated the resident-general more than those on the left. Only the socialists condemned him outright, but republicans disliked the criticism Lyautey leveled against ancient Athens in his speech before the Academie. He held democracy responsible for the city-state's defeat, and to republican writers, this comment seemed a not-so-veiled criticism France's own form of government. Lyautey went on to laud Napoleon and the Bourbon kings, saying little about the French Revolution and the republics it spawned. Still, all but those on the far left made a distinction between Lyautey's anti-republican politics and his great service to France for making Morocco the "jewel in the French colonial crown." Republicanism and empire had long gone hand in hand, and governments of the Third Republic eagerly associated themselves with heroes of the empire, even those who shared their ideology as little as Lyautey and Marchand.

In 1921 the republic named Lyautey marshal of France, a distinction that only seven living generals enjoyed. The resident-general became the lone marshal not to have served in the Great War. His new status did not, however, prevent the government from removing him as proconsul of Morocco in 1925. During the Rif War of the mid-1920s, the French government judged him insufficiently tough, ordering Lyautey's fellow marshal, Philippe Pétain, to crush Berber insurgents. The deposed resident-general had reached age seventy, making him two years older than his rival. His long career seemed to have reached its end.

He returned to his native Lorraine, only to find himself recalled to Paris in 1928 to organize the massive colonial exhibition scheduled for 1931. This event would present France to itself and the world as a great colonial power, as the country whose civilizing mission had released huge swaths of Asia and Africa from their primitive state. Running from May to November 1931, the Exposition coloniale internationale de Paris received 4 million Parisian visitors, 3 million provincials, and 1 million foreigners, each of whom went four times on average.[18] This was, by any standard, a huge turnout. Afterwards, Lyautey wrote that the event had achieved its goal of "making the French conscious of their empire . . . and making them proud of being a citizen of 'la plus grande France.'"[19] The exhibition did in fact brilliantly advertise France's empire, with dozens of carefully designed buildings purporting to represent indigenous architecture and hundreds of displays of colonial peoples and production. But it was the expo's exotic, even wondrous, entertainment value that drew a great many of its visitors.

A short metro ride from anywhere in Paris, the gates of the colonial fair opened onto what organizers advertised as a "*Tour du Monde en Un Jour*" (A Tour of the World in a Single Day). Once inside, visitors could imagine themselves far from Europe as they moved from the Madagascar section, complete with a miniature village, to the Avenue des Colonies Françaises, where they could walk among the palm trees of Martinique and Guadeloupe before transporting themselves to the forests of Guyana, the palaces of French India, and the shaded dwellings of Tahiti and New Caledonia.

Strollers could visit a Tonkin village, take in the Muslim architecture of Sudan, inspect the straw huts of Equatorial Africa, and penetrate the "Casbah" of Morocco, Algeria, and Tunisia. Along the way, visitors observed native artisans fashioning their wares and watched Kanak dancers, whose exotic movements and rhythms had attracted French spectators even before the colonial exhibition began. Journalists later revealed that these dancers, so popular with the paying public, had been abused and exploited first by private entrepreneurs and then by exposition organizers themselves.

Beyond the dancing and the zoolike observation of real-life natives, the colonial fair offered even lower-brow forms of entertainment: an amusement park with the latest scary rides; two Islands of Delight in Lake Daumesnil, whose Thousand and One Nights area featured restaurants, dance halls, and concession stands; a camelback excursion through "West Africa"; and a water ride across the lake in vessels piloted by African or Indochinese boatmen. "Lake Daumesnil," enthused one journalist, had turned into the "soft waters of Asia and Africa combined, [offering] its embarcaderos to those who want to fish cod off Saint-Pierre and Miquelon [sic] or, in pirogues dug from the trunks of trees, lose themselves in the foliage of the Amazon."[20]

Appealing as these carnivalesque attractions were, most commentators agreed that the highlight of the *tour du monde* was the partial reconstruction of Cambodia's famed temple Angkor Wat. Lyautey had directed the exposition's architects to design "authentic" colonial buildings, and those who created the replica of Angkor Wat showed such concern for authenticity that they used plaster molds taken from the original. Despite this quest for exactitude, architects departed in significant ways from their model, refashioning the ancient temple according to contemporary French aesthetic norms and ideological preconceptions.[21]

If the exposition's success helped revive Lyautey's reputation, he never again became a figure around whom French men and women could unite. In the late 1920s and early 1930s, he flirted with ultra-right-wing paramilitary leagues, ensuring widespread hostility to him on the republican and socialist left. The majority of French men and women may have found themselves attracted to the marshal's simulacrum of "La Plus Grande France," but his role in the extraordinarily polarized French politics of the 1930s pushed a great many of them away.

His death in 1934 created no outpouring of public sentiment as Brazza's "martyrdom" had three decades earlier, and his desire to be buried in

Casablanca evoked the discrete but clear opposition of nascent nationalist forces in the French protectorate. Morocco's sultan only reluctantly agreed to the marshal's burial in a hillside mausoleum overlooking Rabat. Twenty-seven years later, after Morocco had achieved its independence (1956) and amid the bloody conclusion of the Algerian War, French president Charles de Gaulle had Lyautey's remains returned home. The president's advisers feared the Rabat mausoleum would be desecrated after French troops left neighboring Algeria.[22] In Paris, Lyautey's coffin earned pride of place in France's military pantheon, Les Invalides, and in celebrating his memory, de Gaulle subtly transformed the marshal from exemplar of empire to prophet of decolonization. The French president faced an extraordinarily delicate situation in the spring of 1961 when the reburial took place. He had to acknowledge the end of the Algerian War, whose outcome meant not only that France had fought for almost six years in vain but that the country's experience as a colonial power had come to an end. De Gaulle had to do so without denigrating France's colonial past, about which a great many French citizens retained positive, if now bitterly disappointed, feelings. De Gaulle used Lyautey's memory to serve these ends.

On the one hand, the president represented the marshal as a "good colonizer," a gentle, pacific conqueror who had seen to the "social, moral, and economic progress" of the Moroccans, while "respecting their [religious] customs and traditions." On the other, De Gaulle presented the deceased marshal as an avatar of decolonization, as agent of the maturation process through which all of France's colonies, including Algeria, would enter the modern world as sturdy independent powers grateful to France. To make this point, the president quoted Lyautey's words: "At some point, North Africa, highly evolved and living its own autonomous life, will detach itself from the metropole . . . and this should be the ultimate goal of our colonial policy." If so, "the separation will occur painlessly and Africans will continue to look for guidance to France."[23]

Such sentiments displayed wishful thinking when Lyautey wrote them in 1920; they bordered on fantasy in 1961 as Algeria ripped itself free of France. After Algeria's independence in 1962, most French men and women wanted to forget about a colonial empire whose cataclysmic conclusion had left an unthinkable number of Algerians and French soldiers dead. In this new, postcolonial situation, a willed amnesia buried Lyautey's words and deeds beneath layers of embarrassment, regret, and shame. Only rarely does anyone mention the white-haired marshal today. What remains of his public memory persists only in a sprinkling of street signs—

Figure 23. Rue Lyautey, Paris (photograph courtesy of
J. P. Daughton).

the one in figure 23 defaced with xenophobic propaganda—and a shrinking corps of conservative writers nostalgic for the supposed *grandeur* of
their country's colonial past.[24]

Strangely enough, Lyautey's legacy has survived in the United States,
though without the French marshal's name attached. The "oil stain" approach to counterinsurgency in Iraq, a method associated with General
David Petraeus's Team Phoenix, closely resembles the political-military
technique Lyautey articulated for Morocco. If Lyautey's oil stain strategy,
the effort to establish a small political and military stronghold and gradually extend it, generally failed to control Moroccan territory, the American
version, combined with the troop "surge" of early 2007, seems to have
enjoyed a measure of success.[25]

Turning now to Henry Morton Stanley, we see an individual whose
fame—and recent notoriety—have endured to our own time. As noted, the
greeting "Dr. Livingstone, I presume?" repeated almost obsessively in the
late nineteenth century, has enjoyed a long afterlife. Two biographies of
Stanley use the phrase as its title, as does a new book on the Livingstone-
Stanley duo. The New York Public Library's online catalog lists eighteen
books with "I Presume" in the title—*Africa, I Presume; America, I Presume;*

Murder, I Presume; and even "Dr. Frankenstein, I Presume—or, the Art of Vivisection."[26]

Beyond such bibliographical uses, the Stanley greeting has sunk deep into Anglo-American popular culture. It forms the centerpiece of *Stanley and Livingstone* (1939), a big-budget prewar adventure movie starring Spencer Tracy as Stanley. A national geographic version of the encounter appeared in 1997.[27] In the 1940s, a classic Jack Benny radio routine had a Stanley character practice saying, "Dr. Livingstone, I presume?" again and again. Artie Shaw made a recording entitled "Dr. Livingstone, I Presume?" And the Gene Kelly, Frank Sinatra musical *On the Town* referred to Alfred Kinsey's then-notorious book on male sexual behavior with the quip "Dr. Kinsey, I presume?" More recently, *Sesame Street* featured a Bert-and-Ernie sketch in which the two search for Dr. Livingstone in the jungle. When Ernie finds him, he forgets what he's supposed to say, blurting, "What's up, Doc?" instead.[28]

Biographies of Stanley abound and must sell; otherwise, publishers would cease bringing them out. More interesting than their frequency, which remains constant at three or four a decade in English, is the shifting tone and perspective on Stanley. In the 1950s and earlier, they remained respectful, even worshipful. But everything changed with decolonization, when Stanley biographies became much more critical of his character, deeds, and accomplishments. The same has applied to Livingstone, whose saintly myth persisted until the 1970s, when Tim Jeal's exhaustive biography knocked the pedestal from under his feet. It is significant that, having dethroned Livingstone in the early postcolonial period, Jeal endeavored to rehabilitate Stanley after the turn of the twenty-first century, when the British Empire made something of a comeback in popular culture.[29] Still, Jeal's friendlier treatment of Stanley doubtless has more to do with his contrarian biographical style—and the discovery of untouched sources—than with any nostalgia for empire. And he especially wanted to challenge the sharply negative views of Stanley that appeared in a pair of biographies by Frank McLynn and John Bierman, published almost simultaneously in 1989 and 1990.[30] McLynn, in particular, focused on Stanley's "homicidal impulses" and his supposed ability to exercise them with impunity in Africa. The two biographers, as Jeal writes, "destroy[ed] Stanley's reputation in the 1990s."[31] Influenced by them, Adam Hochschild's powerful exposé, *King Leopold's Ghost* (1998), gave Stanley a central role in the horrors of the Congo state.[32]

Whatever Stanley's responsibilities for the evils of the Free State, he played a major role in creating and disseminating racist stereotypes of the

"Dark Continent" and of the primitive, animalistic Africans that structured the West's view of Africa throughout much of the twentieth century. Joseph Conrad's *Heart of Darkness* owed much of its imagery to Stanley's *How I Found Livingstone,* as did other writers with less talent but perhaps more influence. The French journalists Félicien Challaye and Charles Castellani belong to this latter category.

The American writer Edgar Rice Burroughs, who created the celebrated Tarzan character, claimed to have written his first book with a dictionary in one hand and Stanley's *In Darkest Africa* in the other.[33] The Tarzan books and the forty films they spawned, including a recent Disney version, have kept Stanley's Africa alive—an Africa of primitive tribes and half-naked bodies, of childlike simplicity and simmering violence, whose people turn to the white man Tarzan as their savior. Watching the immensely popular Tarzan movies, a viewer would never know that Africa contained great cities and powerful indigenous empires, that its population was extraordinarily diverse, or that nationalist movements and trade unions rocked the continent politically until the European colonists withdrew.

After independence, African leaders did their best to efface all palpable traces of Stanley's memory. The Congolese colonial city of Stanleyville became Kisangani in the early 1960s, and nationalists rebaptized Stanley Pool, the huge lakelike expanse of the lower Congo River, Pool Malebo. In the mid-1970s, Congolese dictator Mobutu Sese Seko removed a colossal statue of the explorer from central Kinshasa (formerly Leopoldville) and had it dumped in a vacant lot, where it still lies crumbling and defaced. Guy Tillim's photograph in figure 24 shows a boy urinating on the rusting steamboat that Stanley's statue seems to embrace.[34] Recently, the town council of the explorer's native Welsh village, Denbigh, expressed interest in making a replica of the rotting bronze. Spurred by the biographer Jeal, the council hopes to displace the center of Stanley memory from Belgium to Wales.[35]

In King Leopold's country, Stanley's reputation has remained very much alive. As recently as 1991, Belgium's Royal Museum of Central Africa held a commemorative exhibition entitled *H. M. Stanley, Explorer in the King's Service.* It made barely a mention of the Congo atrocities of the 1890s and 1900s and presented Stanley in an almost entirely positive light. The museum itself is a cavernous time warp of a place, a musty, poorly lit palace that eerily transports visitors back to the time when, as the catalog grandly put it, "Belgium played an important economic and geopolitical role thanks to the possession overseas of a huge territory in Central Africa." That role was due, the text continues, "to the initiative of a single

Figure 24. Toppled statue of Henry M. Stanley in a vacant lot, Kinshasa (photograph courtesy of Guy Tillum).

man, King Leopold II" [and to] "the indispensable collaboration [of] the explorer H. M. Stanley.[36] Even in a post-Hochschild exhibition (2005) at the Royal Museum, the organizers relativized, rather than confronted head-on, the immense human and moral cost of Belgium's colonial regime.[37] Its crimes extend beyond the atrocities of a century ago to encompass the Congolese colonial experience as a whole, one that left the country woefully unprepared for independence in 1960 and all too open to dictatorship, civil war, and the genocidal conflicts of the 1990s.[38]

If Belgians have ignored, relativized, or explained away their country's massive colonial violence, French commentators have, until recently, largely screened it out. They have focused on Brazza's "peaceful conquests" rather than the brutality of Algeria, the Western Sudan, or their own Congolese regime. Throughout the country's long colonial reign, French writers and public figures liked to see their compatriots as gentle peace-loving people whose superior civilization—not military prowess—earned them the right to possess colonies. Never mind that Brazza's "peaceful conquests" were the exception that proved the rule of violent military assaults accompanied by substantial local resistance virtually everywhere else (and that even

Brazza resorted at times to force). By the 1890s, the French had been "pacifying" Algeria for more than sixty years, and they had had to struggle hard and with considerable loss of life to overcome opposition in Tunisia, Tonkin, Madagascar, Niger, Sudan, and several other places. Despite the reality of violent colonial conquest—or perhaps because of that reality— Brazza's methods were the ones that enjoyed public acclaim.

Later, his image as a peaceful conqueror would attract hordes of biographers eager to cast French colonialism in a positive light. To present the civilizing mission, with its implied sense of French superiority, as the primary motive of the country's colonial effort, commentators had to portray France's colonizers as civilized themselves. More than anyone else, Brazza appeared to fit this picture. I have not found a single negative treatment of Brazza's life, even among the volumes written since the 1990s.[39] Recent French historians have identified the Brazza legend rather than debunking it; no one has done to his saintly memory what a variety of historians have done to Livingstone's, taxing the Scottish hero as given to violent mood swings, hostile grudges, racist outbursts, and self-glorification.[40]

Why have Brazza biographies been so persistently favorable—even in our own anti-imperial age? For recent historians, it may have to do with the explorer's evident sympathy for the Congolese and his commendable efforts in 1905 to expose French atrocities. But before the late twentieth century, the positive treatment of Brazza belonged to the French rhetorical effort to bridge the yawning gap between the lofty language of the civilizing mission, always more emphatic than its counterpart in Great Britain, and the deficient realities of colonial life. One function of the Brazza narrative has always been to recast the often sordid, inhumane, and unsuccessful history of French imperialism into the heart-warming story of a gentle explorer who persuaded Africans to devote themselves and their lands to a generous France. Another reason for the persistence of Brazza hagiography has to do with France's trauma in the Second World War and the role of Equatorial Africa in the country's wartime redemption. Finally, the ordeal of decolonization, considerably more painful than what Britain endured, moved writers and readers to seek refuge in the comforting— and exculpating—ready-made narrative of Brazza's life.

The extent to which biographical treatments of Brazza cluster together at three crucial points provides evidence for these claims. After an early spate of books about Brazza's "heroic" expeditions, and the eulogies that accompanied his state funeral, biographical accounts centered on three twentieth-century events: the Colonial Exposition of 1931, showcase of France's mission civilisatrice; the Second World War and its aftermath; and the extended crisis of decolonization that culminated in the Algerian War.[41]

Although a few biographical accounts of Brazza appeared within a year of his death, French men and women heard little more about the explorer until the opening of the Colonial Exposition in 1931. In connection with this event, L'Illustration ran several new portraits of Brazza, reviving stories of the explorer's rivalry with a violent and mercenary Stanley and reminding readers that Brazza was "the friend of the black race and protector of the oppressed."[42] This reminder perhaps seemed important in the wake of mounting anti-French nationalism in the colonies, which included a wave of terrorism in Indochina and the massacre of a French garrison in the Haut-Tonkin. André Gide had recently denounced his country's colonial record in two prominent works, both concerned with parts of Africa that Brazza had "opened" to French civilization: Voyage au Congo (1927) and Le Retour du Tchad (1928).[43] And it was in part to prevent such criticism from damaging the growing pro-colonial consensus that political leaders spared neither expense nor effort to make the Colonial Exposition a success.

The first in a series of Brazza biographies, a thick volume by the general Chambrun (1930) appeared shortly before the exposition began.[44] After the event, a new Brazza book appeared almost every year: Henri-Paul Eydoux's biography of 1932, which boasted a preface by none other than Maréchal Lyautey; Pierre Mariel's fictionalized account (1933), complete with colorful illustrations and invented dialogue of the genre ("Equatorial Africa asks only to be conquered, provided that the French flag is planted there first"); and finally Charles de Chavannes's three-volume treatment (1934, 1937, 1937).[45] What is striking about these biographies is that they all recite almost exactly the same story, each successive volume rewriting the ones that had come before. Even the anecdotes are the same, all designed to show Brazza's horror of violence—always through stark contrast with Stanley—and his heroism, love of the natives, ardent French patriotism, and status as a diplomat extraordinaire who gave France an empire without shedding a drop of blood.

No other colonial figure, not even Lyautey himself, the greatest living hero of French colonial conquest, received so much biographical attention during the 1930s. At a time when French leaders sought to solidify public support for empire, confronted as they were with new challenges to its legitimacy, there appeared to be widespread agreement that Brazza, buried twenty-five years earlier, remained imperialism's best and most effective case. In a sense, his charisma persisted even after he had gone.

After a brief lull at the end of the 1930s, a new cluster of Brazza biographies, one of them a film, surfaced during and immediately following the Second World War. The film, *Brazza, l'épopée du Congo,* directed by Léon Poirier, premiered in January 1940; its 150-page screenplay, thickened by dozens of stills, saw print in book form a few weeks later.[46] The story is familiar, the view of Africa a string of stereotypes. The movie features a barebreasted African woman whose plaintive chants narrate the film's transitions from one scene to the next. Unlike the film, made before the fall of France, the wartime Brazza books seem connected to the crucial role the country's African colonies played in legitimizing Charles de Gaulle's Free French forces and in the eventual liberation of France. After the war and France's brush with national annihilation, the country's political leaders and opinion makers believed even more fervently than they had before 1940 that France's standing in the world, and perhaps even its continued existence, depended on remaining a colonial power. Then, as before, that power, in the view of French leaders, drew its legitimacy—even its nobility—from the mission civilisatrice.

Of the ten films (three fictional, seven documentary) finished and distributed between November 1939 and the fall of France, only three were considered of national importance and received official approval from the Commissariat Général de l'Information. One of those films was Poirier's *Brazza* (fig. 25).[47] Its published screenplay opens with a still frame clearly inspired by Nadar's famous photograph of Brazza, the engraving of which had appeared in *L'Illustration* a half-century earlier.[48] The film, like the earlier photograph, has Brazza looking like Moses in the desert—like a prophet, staff in hand, ready to lead his people to freedom. In this case, the people were presumably Africans whom Brazza was about to liberate from the chains of slavery, ignorance, and superstition. In one later scene, a staple of all the Brazza biographies, the explorer buys a slave and then shows him the French flag. "Touch it," he commands. The slave obeys and the Brazza character declares, "You are free!"[49]

In yet another staple of Brazza biography, the film portrays the explorer's simple but loyal Senegalese assistant Malamine preventing Stanley from entering Congolese territory Brazza had claimed for France. *"Ici, la France!"* declares the African soldier, barring Stanley's way.[50] Those words, inscribed in bold letters, bring Poirier's film to a close. In the spring of 1940, *Ici, la France!* had many possible meanings. Most evident was the notion, widely held in the 1930s, that the Congo colony Brazza had founded was part of a "Greater France" no less French than Brittany or Provence.[51]

ROBERT DARÈNE

BRAZZA

ou l'ÉPOPÉE DU CONGO
film de LÉON POIRIER

Figure 25. Brazza in Leon Poirier's film of 1939 (cover of DVD, Les documents cinématographiques, Paris).

In the aftermath of Munich, the German invasion of Poland, and the seizure of Denmark and Norway, French audiences must have found especially comforting the idea that their country extended beyond the beleaguered European Hexagon. French filmgoers could also have been taken *Ici, la France!* as a proud declaration that despite all the dangers surrounding their country, France was still here, still sovereign in the face of the Nazi menace. What is perhaps most striking about the words *Ici, la France!* is their prophetic character. Although the filmmaker could not have known it, the declaration that France *was* Equatorial Africa—"This is France," said Malamine, referring to the banks of the Congo River—would be almost literally true just a few months hence, at least for those who supported a France free of foreign rule.

After June 1940, the African colonies loomed especially large for De Gaulle, whose legitimacy as an alternative to Pétain required the ability to claim control of some portion of French territory and, eventually, to acquire a base of operations for an independent military force. With the Vichy regime firmly ensconced in North and West Africa, de Gaulle focused on the center of the continent. By the end of November, the Free French occupied most of Equatorial Africa, making that area the only fully independent part of France.[52] It is fitting that the first organization de Gaulle established outside of London, the Conseil de Défense de l'Empire, made Brazzaville its home (October 1940).[53] Before the Second World War, certain colonial theorists had claimed that Brazzaville and Libreville would soon be just as French as Paris and Marseille. Little did they realize that, for a time, these equatorial outposts would be all the France there was.

The unprecedented importance of Equatorial Africa, for Vichy as for De Gaulle, turned attention once again to the life of the region's explorer, Brazza. Five new biographies appeared in quick succession between 1943 and 1947.[54] The wartime works linked Brazza to the Free French forces and to France's "tradition of honor, liberty, and pride."[55] The two biographies published in 1945 reflected the changes in France's colonial relationships wrought by the war. A volume by G. Froment-Guieysse concluded with a wish that the empire continue "to give France its help, collaboration, and love." In doing so, the biographer wrote, citizens and subjects alike should look to Brazza's example of heroism, patriotism, and courage as France awakened to the "luminous morning of its resurrection."[56] These lines suggest that already in 1945, the French could no longer take the colonies' allegiance and subordination for granted; after a period in which the African empire alone kept the French Republic alive, this Brazza biographer acknowledged the extent to which the mother country now depended on its possessions. The hierarchy of colonizer and colonized had been turned upside down.

Although a few new Brazza biographies appeared in the early 1950s, the most significant postwar example came out in 1960, amid the Algerian nationalists' battle to the death against French colonialism, a battle that mocked the mission civilisatrice and France's humanitarian claims. Calling

Brazza "the liberator of slaves," the new volume resurrected the image of the conquérant pacifique, of the gentle colonizer who gives Africans the benefit of French culture without shedding a drop of blood. "Colonize, perhaps, but above all civilize, that is to say make fully and completely human," the biographer wrote. "This was Brazza's holy grail until his very last breath."[57] Never more than during the Algerian War did French imperialists need to invoke Brazza's memory, a memory that deflected or obscured the cruelty, racism, and exploitation all too prominent in the country's colonial rule.

If Brazza's memory has served certain political ends in France, it has worked to similar effect in the Republic of the Congo. Of our five colonial heroes, Brazza stands alone in having an African city still named after him—and a capital city, Brazzaville, at that. In a sense, the country itself is named for him, given its popular appellation as Congo-Brazzaville—in part to distinguish it from the neighboring Democratic Republic of the Congo, formerly Zaire.

Having served as capital of de Gaulle's Free French forces during the Second World War, the Congo gained autonomy within a French colonial commonwealth in 1958 and independence two years later. Like other postcolonial African states, the Republic of the Congo has suffered from fierce ethnic conflicts, often exacerbated by ideological divides. Whether Marxist-Leninist or noncommunist, most postindependence governments have resorted to undemocratic rule. And the exploitation of offshore oil and natural gas beginning in the 1970s has raised the stakes of existing ethnic and political divisions. As the different forces struggle to control the (diminishing) Congolese share of the wealth, the French petroleum company Total (formerly Elf Aquitaine) operates the oil rigs and extracts much of the profit.

As in other oil-rich countries, the Congo's black gold has benefited only a tiny percentage of its people. Thanks in large part to oil revenues, the Congo expanded its civil service from 3,300 employees in 1960 to 80,000 in the 1990s—this for a country of less than 4 million people. Meanwhile, rural development declined and agricultural production plummeted. The large cadre of salaried government workers, most in patronage jobs, now had to buy imported foods at high prices, reducing their real incomes to a fraction of what they had been. Those without civil service salaries found themselves unable to pay these inflated bills, resorting in many cases to hunting wild animals and growing manioc, long Central Africa's subsistence crop.[58]

While much of the Congolese population suffered, the country's leaders benefited from "syndication rights," or kickbacks, that lined their pockets—and Swiss bank accounts—with a portion of the oil receipts. A percentage of these payments returned to France in the form of "retro-commissions" that landed in the coffers of France's different political parties. A web of oil money thus connected Elf executives, Congolese (and other Central African) leaders, and French politicians, including those at the highest levels of government.[59]

As Congo officials grew rich on Elf's "syndication rights," their country sank into a quicksand of debt. Declining industrial and agricultural production reduced tax revenues so much that the government could no longer meet its enormous civil service payroll. Elf executives offered loans to cover the growing budget deficits, but they collected their (high) interest payments in the form of oil, whose value the executives set at 10 percent of the market rate.[60] It took vast quantities of petroleum to finance the interest due, and through this process the oil that in theory belonged to the Congolese government reverted to Elf. Congo leaders found it difficult enough to meet their interest payments let alone reduce the principal, which continued to grow as Elf executives added new loans to the Congolese portfolio. In 2004 the Congo's debt reached $6 billion, a deficit twice its GDP and the largest per capita in Africa.[61]

By the early 1990s, Congo-Brazzaville found itself trapped in a classic neocolonial bind. Government corruption, combined with European political and economic domination, resulted in widespread poverty, which in turn exacerbated political agitation and unrest. Conflicts became especially acute during the presidential and parliamentary elections of the 1990s, when violent confrontations resulted in some 15,000 deaths and the displacement of 800,000 people, or nearly a quarter of the country's population. In 1997 Congo sank into a gruesome civil war, as the three main ethnic groups, each with its own militia, fought for political control. The French government supported the longtime dictator Denis Sassou-Nguesso and encouraged Angolan forces to intervene on his side. After more than a year of fighting, Sassou-Nguesso emerged as Congo's president. Much of the country, including large sectors of Brazzaville, lay in ruins. Violence and political instability have continued into the new century, though a relative calm set in after 2003, despite persistent flare-ups of violence in the Pool region north of Brazzaville.[62]

Congolese corruption has remained what it was. French police investigated President Sassou-Nguesso for embezzling Congo oil revenues to buy property on the Riviera, and local and international human rights groups accused the president of fraudulent practices in the legislative elections of June 2007.[63] In this context, Sassou-Nguesso has sought to ingratiate himself with French president Nicolas Sarkozy, whose country needs Congolese oil and whose major oil company, Total, wants to keep British and American firms out of Central Africa. France's support gives the Congolese leader a measure of legitimacy at home. Recently, French and Congo-Brazzaville leaders have bonded over a Congolese memorial to Brazza as conquérant pacifique, a memorial built to commemorate the hundredth anniversary of his death in 2005. In France, it would have been impossible officially to observe this event. When President Jacques Chirac's government enacted a law in February 2005 requiring schoolteachers to acknowledge the "positive aspects" of French colonialism, more than one thousand prominent historians, writers, and intellectuals signed a petition demanding the law's repeal.[64] The government's directive defied historical reality, the critics wrote, and besides, the state had no business telling educators how to interpret the past. In this context, to echo the Congolese government in celebrating Brazza as humanitarian colonizer and "father to slaves" would have been to emphasize one of those supposedly positive aspects of French colonialism now widely rejected on principle. Partly for that reason, the Brazza centennial passed largely unremarked in France, save for a modest online exhibit and published catalogue by the National Archives' "Overseas Center" in Aix-en-Provence.[65]

The situation in the Republic of the Congo could not have differed more. In Brazzaville, a group of people close to Sassou-Nguesso established the Fondation Pierre Savorgnan de Brazza, dedicated to the "duty to remember . . . the greatest symbol [of Congolese history]," and to pay homage "to a man whose 'memory is pure of human blood,' who was more a humanistic and visionary explorer than a colonizer, and who . . . amazed the indigenous people with his ability to understand their culture and mediate between theirs and his. That man is Pierre Savorgnan de Brazza."[66]

The Brazza Foundation's leaders included a Frenchman named Jean Paul Pigasse, publisher of Les Dépêches de Brazzaville, a pro–Sassou-Nguesso newspaper, and Belinda Ayessa, the Congolese editor of Dépêches' magazine. The two journalists, in concert with top Congolese officials, hatched a project to transfer the remains of Brazza and his immediate family from Algiers to Brazzaville. To do so, they needed permission from a descendant of the explorer, and because he had no direct living heirs,

Ayessa turned to a pair of distant Italian relations, the elderly professor De-talmo Pirzio Biroli and his niece, the filmmaker and writer Idanna Pucci.[67] Ayessa suggested that Brazza should be buried in the village of Mbé, the tra-ditional seat of the Bateke kings and the place where Brazza and the Makoko Ilo signed their original agreement in 1880. The ancient, elective monarchy still exists, and in September 2003 Biroli—accompanied by Pucci's husband Terrance Ward—went to meet the Makoko in office at the time, Gaston Ngouayoulou. Pucci understood that her uncle had agreed to release Brazza's remains to Ngouayoulou but later learned that the Bateke king had died, suddenly and mysteriously, and that the Congolese government had taken charge of the affair. Sassou-Nguesso now planned to bury the explorer and his family in an imposing mausoleum in the heart of Brazza-ville. Suspicious about the king's death, Pucci resolved to block the trans-fer of Brazza's bones to a resting place she considered an affront both to her ancestor's memory and to the people of Brazzaville, a great many of whom lack the most basic necessities of life.

Although she ultimately won some symbolic concessions, Pucci's oppo-sition did nothing to prevent the foundation from breaking ground on a huge memorial to the French explorer. In February 2005 then–French president Jacques Chirac, Omar Bongo of Gabon, and Sassou-Nguesso came together in Brazzaville to lay, with great ceremony, the mausoleum's foundation stone. This event took place just a few weeks before Chirac proposed his new law on the "positive aspects" of French colonialism. The huge, imposing tomb, a cross between a Greek-style pantheon and a Ma-sonic temple, went up in little more than a year—record speed for the Congolese capital. Made of shiny white marble imported from Italy, the mausoleum cost nearly $10 million; it appears utterly alien to Brazzaville's cityscape, looming incongruously over the town's squat and often-makeshift buildings (fig. 26).

On 3 October 2006, Congolese officials, with the French foreign minis-ter looking on, solemnly interred the remains of Brazza, Thérèse de Chambrun, and their four children in the mausoleum's spacious crypt. The Brazzaville memorial features a sculpture garden in the back and an outsized twenty-foot statue of Brazza in front. The sculpture resembles Nadar's iconic photograph taken for L'Illustration in 1882. It faces away from the Pool Malebo and from Kinshasa, where the old broken-down statue of Stanley lies facedown in an abandoned lot.

The Brazza Foundation's website celebrates the explorer with such élan that any of the hagiographers mentioned above could have written its text.

Figure 26. The Brazza Mausoleum, Brazzaville (*New York Times*, 30 November 2006).

It details the explorer's effort to free African slaves and his ability to impress Ilo, the Bateke king, with his "goodness, pacifism, integrity, and noble intentions." The foundation's authors praise the hero's "genuine passion" for their country and call him an "intrepid model of determination and courage" whose "encounter with Africa gave him a destiny beyond that of ordinary human beings." So laudatory is this portrait that Brazza appears as an archetypal charismatic hero, "an exceptional personality . . . whose personal magnetism continues in our own time to radiate throughout Africa as a whole."[68]

It may be that Brazza's image as charismatic outsider appeals to a great many citizens of the Congo Republic, long ruled by corrupt, divisive, and unpopular men. Despite the understandable criticism of those who think "we should be putting the colonial days behind us" and who find it "ridiculous to use the people's money to build such an extravagant thing for a European explorer," others find the monument beautiful, "a way to remember our history" and open the long-turbulent Congo to a wider world.[69] The foundation's website quotes a letter from Professor Biroli maintaining that "this transfer [of Brazza's remains] will contribute to the preservation of peace in the Congo by enabling its people to celebrate each year the ceremony of the tree of peace, a rite inaugurated by Pierre Savorgnan de Brazza in 1881 so that peace would reign eternally among the Congolese."[70]

A peaceful, undisturbed status quo would, of course, appeal to the Congolese regime in place, especially since it has faced so much violent opposition in the past. But after so many years of deadly confrontations, ordinary people doubtless long for peace as well. In 1998, after a terrible year of violence, the Makoko Ngouayoulou perhaps spoke for many Congolese in wishing he—or someone—could magically create a reign of peace. "When I listen to the news about the warfare near the Pool, I feel as though someone has sunk a knife into my heart." To end the fighting, Ngouayoulou planned to eat a sacred rock whose powers promised to make the head of state govern in peace.[71]

Under these circumstances, the memory of Brazza, a powerful, charismatic outsider implicated in none of the Congo's ethnic and ideological conflicts, could perhaps become a symbol around which the country's divided people could unite. As the prominent Congolese Egyptologist Théophile Obenga put it, albeit from a critical anticolonial point of view, "Because the Congolese don't like the Congolese, because the Congolese possess a political hatred for one another, they prefer to celebrate a foreign political leader like Savorgnan De Brazza. It make sense: since not a single of our politicians enjoys the people's esteem, . . . it is understandable that, through a inferiority complex, they adore a foreigner. . . . In our hearts, we are the children of Brazzaville, of De Brazza himself. . . . We feel better off adoring him, making him a God."[72]

Whatever Brazza's symbolic role, the importance of which many Congolese intellectuals vociferously deny, those close to the government clearly hope that by constructing a *lieu de mémoire* devoted to his charismatic myth, they will create political and cultural bridges to a Euro-American world they eagerly want to join.[73] "Brazza knew how to unite the destiny of Europe and the destiny of Africa," foundation leaders say. The transfer of his remains "symbolizes a solidarity between the South and the North long obscured by the travails of colonization and decolonization."[74]

Such sentiments give rhetorical cover to the material interests of a narrow political and economic elite, but they also express the desire of ordinary Congolese to connect to a developed world governed by the rule of law, a world whose benefits they can see in the media but never enjoy themselves. Many blame their leaders for denying them a decent, productive life. Congolese officials may have created the Brazza monument for distinct political and economic reasons, but their compatriots will use it to serve their own highly varied—and perhaps even subversive—ends.

NOTES

INTRODUCTION

1. The literature is vast. For a sampling, see Bernard Porter, *The Absent-Minded Imperialists: Empire, Society, and Culture in Britain* (New York: Oxford University Press, 2004); Porter, *Critics of Empire: British Radicals and the Imperial Challenge* (New York: Palgrave, 2008); Richard Price, *An Imperial War and the British Working Class* (London: Routledge, 1972); H. Pelling, *Popular Politics and Society in Late Victorian Britain* (New York: St. Martins, 1968); Jonathan Rose, *The Intellectual Life of the British Working Class* (New Haven: Yale University Press, 2001), ch. 10; S. M. Persell, *The French Colonial Lobby, 1889–1938* (Stanford, CA: Hoover Institution, 1983); C. M. Andrew and A. S. Kanya-Forstner, "The French 'Colonial Party': Its Composition, Aims and Influence, 1885–1914," *Historical Journal* 14, no. 1 (1971): 99–128; L. Abrams and D. J. Miller, "Who Were the French Colonialists? A Reassessment of the *parti colonial*, 1890–1914," *Historical Journal* 19, no. 3 (1976): 685–725; Henri Brunschwig, *French Colonialism, 1871–1914: Myths and Realities* (New York: Praeger, 1966); Raoul Girardet, *L'Idée coloniale en France de 1871 à 1962* (Paris: La table ronde, 1972).

2. Ronald Edward Robinson and John Gallagher, with Alice Denny, *Africa and the Victorians: The Climax of Imperialism* (New York: Anchor Books, 1968). I owe a great many insights about heroism and empire to John M. MacKenzie, especially for his chapter, "Heroic Myths of Empire," in MacKenzie, ed., *Popular Imperialism and the Military, 1850–1950* (Manchester: Manchester University Press, 1992), 109–38. Further inspiration has come from Graham Dawson, *Soldier*

Heroes: British Adventure, Empire, and the Imaging of Masculinity (London: Routledge, 1994); Kathryn Tidrick, *Empire and the English Character* (London: I. B. Tauris, 1990); Geoffrey Cubitt and Allen Warren, eds., *Heroic Reputations and Exemplary Lives* (Manchester: Manchester University Press, 2000); Walter E. Houghton, *The Victorian Frame of Mind, 1830–1870* (New Haven: Yale University Press, 1957), esp. ch. 12, "Hero Worship"; Peter Gay, *The Naked Heart,* vol. 4, *The Bourgeois Experience* (New York: W. W. Norton, 1995), esp. chs. 2–3; Pierre Centlivres, Daniel Fabre, and Françoise Zonabend, *La Fabrique des héros* (Paris: Editions de la Maison des sciences de l'homme, 1998). More generally, my thinking about this subject has been shaped by the "cultural turn" in colonial history, a powerfully important historiographical shift in which MacKenzie and his students have played a major, perhaps *the* major, role. Like Edward Said (*Orientalism,* 1978), MacKenzie sought to understand imperialism as a cultural phenomenon, but for MacKenzie it was popular culture, not elite culture, that mattered. Support for imperialism came not from listening to politicians or reading pro-imperial treatises but from imbibing cultural materials: theater, songs, advertisements, popular art and literature, textbooks, newspapers, and the like. For a detailed discussion—and full bibliography—of MacKenzie's work, see Edward Berenson, "Making a Colonial Culture? Empire and the French Public, 1880–1940," *French Politics, Culture and Society* 22 no. 2 (summer 2004): 127–49.

3. Jean Stengers, L'Impérialisme colonial de la fin du xix siècle: Mythe ou réalité," *Journal of African History* 3, no. 3 (1962): 469–91; Stengers, "King Leopold and the Anglo-French Rivalry," in Prosser Gifford and Wm. Roger Louis, eds., *France and Britain in Africa: Imperial Rivalry and Colonial Rule* (New Haven: Yale University Press, 1971); Brunschwig, *French Colonialism*; Brunschwig, "Les origines du partage de l'Afrique occidentale," *Journal of African History* 5, no. 1 (1964): 121–25; Freda Harcourt, "Disraeli's Imperialism, 1866–1868: A Question of Timing," *Historical Journal,* vol. 23, no. 1 (March 1980): 87–109; G. N. Sanderson, "The Origins and Significance of the Anglo-France Confrontation at Fashoda, 1898," in Gifford and Louis, *France and Britain in Africa,* 285–332.

4. For excellent recent commentaries on Robinson and Gallagher, see John Darwin, "Imperialism and the Victorians: The Dynamics of Territorial Expansion," *English Historical Review* 112, no. 147 (June 1997): 614–42; Anthony Webster, *The Debate on the Rise of the British Empire* (Manchester: Manchester University Press, 2006), 68–86.

5. Thomas Ferenczi, *L'Invention du journalism en France* (Paris: Plon, 1993); Mark Hampton, *Visions of the Press in Britain, 1850–1950* (Urbana: University of Illinois Press, 2004); Michael B. Palmer, *Des petits journaux aux grandes agences: Naissance du journalisme moderne, 1863–1914* (Paris: Aubier, 1983), 307n159; Harcourt, "Disraeli's Imperialism."

6. P. J. Cain and A. G. Hopkins, *British Imperialism, 1688–2000* (London: Longman, 2001).

7. Darwin, "Imperialism and the Victorians."

8. Andrew and Kanya-Forstner, "The French 'Colonial Party'"; Andrew, "The French Colonialist Movement during the Third Republic: The Unofficial Mind of Imperialism," *The Royal Historical Society: Transactions*, 5th Series, vol. 26 (1976): 143–66; Girardet, *L'Idée coloniale en France*; Charles-Robert Ageron, *France coloniale ou parti colonial?* (Paris: Presses universitaires de France, 1978).

9. For an up-to-date treatment of these and other matters, see Edward Berenson, Vincent Duclert, and Christophe Prochasson, eds., *The French Republic: A Transatlantic History* (Ithaca, NY: Cornell University Press, 2011).

10. Currently the chief proponent of the traditional view is Porter, *Absent-Minded Imperialists*. Central to the new historiographical enterprise is the Manchester University Press series "Studies in Imperialism," now at sixty volumes and counting. About half of these books consider what series founding editor John M. MacKenzie calls "popular imperialism," or imperial culture or the effects of empire and imperialism on everyday life. See especially MacKenzie's *Propaganda and Empire: The Manipulation of British Public Opinion, 1880–1960* (Manchester: Manchester University Press, 1984) and *Imperialism and Popular Culture* (Manchester: Manchester University Press, 1985). More recent contributions include Antoinette Burton, "Making a Spectacle of Empire: Indian Travelers in Fin-de-Siècle London," *History Workshop Journal* 42 (1996): 127–46; Andrew Thompson, *The Empire Strikes Back? The Impact of Imperialism on Britain from the Mid-Nineteenth Century* (London: Longman, 2005); Catherine Hall and Sonya O. Rose, eds., *At Home with the Empire: Metropolitan Culture and the Imperial World* (Cambridge: Cambridge University Press, 2006); Alex Windscheffel, *Popular Conservatism in Imperial London, 1868–1906* (London: Royal Historical Society, 2007), ch. 7. For the French case, see Tony Chafer and Amanda Sackur, eds., *Promoting the Colonial Idea. Propaganda and Visions of Empire in France* (New York: Palgrave, 2002); William H. Schneider, *An Empire for the Masses: The French Popular Image of Africa* (Westport, CT: Greenwood Press, 1982); Pascal Blanchard, Sandrine Lemaire, and Nicolas Bancel, eds., *Culture coloniale en France: De la Révolution française à nos jours* (Paris: Editions autrement, 2008); Pascal Blanchard and Sandrine Lemaire, *Culture coloniale: La France conquise par son Empire, 1871–1931* (Paris: Editions autrement, 2008); Martin Evans, *Empire and Culture: The French Experience, 1830–1940* (New York: Palgrave Macmillan, 2004).

11. David Cannadine, ed., *Admiral Lord Nelson: Context and Legacy* (New York: Palgrave Macmillan, 2005); Steven Englund, *Napoleon: A Political Life* (New York: Scribner, 2004). For the best general history of fame, see Leo Braudy, *The Frenzy of Renown: Fame and Its History* (New York: Vintage, 1986).

12. Robert H. MacDonald, *The Language of Empire: Myths and Metaphors of Popular Imperialism, 1880–1918* (Manchester: Manchester University Press, 1994), 82–83.

13. Hampton, *Visions of the Press;* Claude Bellanger, *Histoire générale de la presse française,* vol. 3 (Paris: Presses universitaires de France, 1969).

14. Centilivres, Fabre, and Zonabend, *Fabrique des héros,* esp. 25–26.

15. Linda Colley, "Britishness and Otherness: An Argument," *Journal of British Studies* 31, no. 4 (October 1992): 309–29; Hall and Rose, "Introduction: Being at Home with Empire," in Hall and Rose, *At Home with the Empire,* 19–22.

16. Norman Vance, "Roman Heroism and the Problems of Nineteenth-Century Empire: Aeneas and Caractacus," in Cubitt and Warren, *Heroic Reputations,* 142–49; Wolfgang Schivelbusch, *The Culture of Defeat: On National Trauma, Mourning, and Recovery,* trans. Jefferson Chase (New York: Picador, 2003); MacDonald, *Language,* 89; MacKenzie, "Heroic Myths."

17. On the notion of a "heroic moment," see Philip Nord, *The Republican Moment: Struggles for Democracy in Nineteenth-Century France* (Cambridge, MA: Harvard University Press, 1995).

18. Quoted in Malcolm Pearce and Geoffrey Stewart, *British Political History, 1867–2001. Democracy and Decline* (London: Routledge, 2002).

19. Schivelbusch, *Culture of Defeat.*

20. Pierre Rosenvallon, in *Le peuple introuvable: Histoire de la représentation démocratique en France* (Paris: Gallimard, 1998), writes, "The celebration of ordinary men and of obscurity substituted for the principle of eminence in the choice of political leaders." On the nearly unanimous desire to create a weak presidency, see Philippe Niets and Parick Harismendy, "Sadi Carnot: Un Président voyageur," in Jean-William Dereymez, Olivier Ihl, and Gérard Sabatier, eds., *Un cérémonial politique: Les voyages officiels des chefs d'Etat* (Paris: L'Harmatan, 1998), 16–17. Carnot, president of the Republic from 1887 to 1894, succeeded briefly in raising the visibility of his office by traveling around the country in monarchical style. Partly as a result of that visibility, he succumbed to an assassin's bullet in 1894. For general works on the individuals and institutions of the early Third Republic, see Dominique Lejeune, *La France des débuts de la IIIe République: 1870–1896* (Paris: A. Colin, 1994); Maurice Agulhon, *The French Republic, 1879–1992* (Cambridge, MA: Basil Blackwell, 1993).

21. On the 1857 rebellion and worries about the fragility of the empire, see Antoinette Burton, "New Narratives of Imperial Politics in the Nineteenth Century," in Hall and Rose, *At Home with the Empire,* 215. On Morant Bay, see Bernard Semmel, *Democracy versus Empire: The Jamaica Riots of 1865 and the Governor Eyre Controversy* (New York: Doubleday, 1969).

22. Daniel Pick, *Faces of Degeneration: A European Disorder, c. 1848–c. 1918* (New York: Cambridge University Press, 1989); Harcourt, "Disraeli's Imperialism," 94–95; G. R. Searle, *A New England? Peace and War, 1886–1918* (New York: Oxford University Press, 2004), 243–52.

23. Quoted in Searle, *New England?* 244.

24. Ibid., 245.

25. David Cannadine, *The Decline and Fall of the British Aristocracy* (New York: Vintage Books, 1990), 26–27.

26. On the staying power of the landed elite's political influence, see Arno J. Mayer, *The Persistence of the Old Regime: Europe to the Great War* (New York: Pantheon, 1981).

27. Quoted in Cannadine, *Decline and Fall,* 31.

28. Leonore Davidoff and Catherine Hall, *Family Fortunes: Men and Women of the English Middle Class, 1780–1850* (Chicago: University of Chicago Press, 1987); Boyd Hilton, *The Age of Atonement: The Influence of Evangelicalism on Social and Economic Thought (1795–1865)* (New York: Oxford University Press, 1988); Peter Mandler, *The English National Character: The History of an Idea from Edmund Burke to Tony Blair* (New Haven: Yale University Press, 2006); Andrew Porter, "Religion and Empire: British Expansion in the Long Nineteenth Century, 1780–1914," *Journal of Imperial and Commonwealth History* 20, no. 3 (1993): 370–90.

29. On "muscular Christianity," see Mark Girouard, *The Return to Camelot: Chivalry and the English Gentleman* (New Haven: Yale University Press, 1981), esp. 130–42; Olive Anderson, "The Growth of Christian Militarism," *English Historical Review* 86 (1971): 46–72; Martin Green, *The Adventurous Male: Chapters in the History of the White Male Mind* (University Park: Pennsylvania State University Press, 1993); Allen J. Frantzen, *Bloody Good: Chivalry, Sacrifice, and the Great War* (Chicago: University of Chicago Press, 2004); Susan Thorne, "Religion and Empire at Home," in Hall and Rose, *At Home with the Empire,* 143–65. For the religious qualities attributed to Sir Henry Havelock, hero and martyr of the Indian "Mutiny," see Dawson, *Soldier Heroes,* chs. 4–5.

30. On the idea of a "transfer of sacrality" from the religious to the political realm, see Mona Ozouf, *Festivals and the French Revolution* (Cambridge, MA: Harvard University Press, 1988), ch. 10; Roger Chartier, *The Cultural Origins of the French Revolution* (Princeton: Princeton University Press, 1989), ch. 6.

31. Elaine Showalter, *Sexual Anarchy: Gender and Culture at the Fin de Siècle* (New York: Viking, 1990), 79ff; John Tosh, *Manliness and Masculinities in Nineteenth-Century Britain: Essays on Gender, Family and Empire* (London: Pearson Longman, 2005), 199–201.

32. The pioneering work on representations of Africa in the penny press is Schneider, *Empire for the Masses.* See also Sylvain Venayre, *La gloire de l'aventure* (Paris: Aubier, 2002).

33. Richard A. Van Orman, *The Explorers: Nineteenth Century Expeditions in Africa and the American West* (Albuquerque: University of New Mexico Press, 1984), 38–39.

34. Ibid., 28–43; William B. Cohen, *The French Encounter with Africa: White Response to Blacks, 1530–1880* (Bloomington: University of Indiana Press, 1980).

35. Anne Hugon, *The Exploration of Africa: From Cairo to the Cape* (New York: Harry N. Abrams, 1993), 17.

36. Quoted in Van Orman, *The Explorers,* 43.

37. Annelise Maugue, *L'identité masculine en crise au tournant du siècle, 1871–1914* (Paris: Editions Rivages, 1987); Showalter, *Sexual Anarchy;* Robert Nye, *Masculinity and Male Codes of Honor in Modern France* (New York: Oxford University Press, 1993); Edward Berenson, *The Trial of Madame Caillaux* (Berkeley: University of California Press, 1992); Judith Surkis, *Sexing the Citizen: Morality and Masculinity in Modern France* (Ithaca, NY: Cornell University Press, 2006); Christopher E. Forth, *The Dreyfus Affair and the Crisis of French Manhood* (Baltimore: Johns Hopkins University Press, 2004).

38. Anne-Emmanuelle Demartini and Dominique Kalifa, *Imaginaire et sensibilités au XIXe siècle: Études pour Alain Corbin* (Paris: Creaphis, 2005).

39. Thomas Carlyle, *Past and Present* (London: Chapman and Hall, 1843); Frantzen, *Bloody Good,* 138–39.

40. Quoted in Frantzen, *Bloody Good,* 143. On Hughes, see Peter Gay, "The Manliness of Christ," in R. W. Davis and R. J. Heimstadter, *Religion and Irreligion in Victorian Society* (London: Routledge, 1992): 102–16.

41. J. A. Mangan, *The Games Ethic and Imperialism* (London: Frank Cass, 1998); Tosh, *Manliness and Masculinities;* John Lowerson, *Sport and the English Middle Classes, 1870–1914* (Manchester: Manchester University Press, 1993); John Springhall, "Building Character in the British Boy: The Attempt to Extend Christian Manliness to Working-Class Adolescents," in J. A. Magnan and James Walvin, eds., *Manliness and Morality: Middle-Class Masculinity in Britain and America, 1800–1940* (New York: St. Martins Press, 1987), 52–74; Patricia Tilburg, *Colette's Republic: Work, Gender, and Popular Culture in France* (New York: Berghahn Books, 2009), ch. 2; Bertrand Joly, *Déroulède: Inventeur du nationalisme français* (Paris: Perrin, 1998); Nye, *Masculinity and Male Codes of Honor;* Berenson, *Trial of Madame Caillaux,* ch. 5.

42. On dueling and the danger of oversensitive, "feminized" men, see Berenson, *Trial of Madame Caillaux,* ch. 5.

43. Martin J. Wiener, "The Victorian Criminalization of Men," in Pieter Spierenburg, ed., *Men and Violence: Gender, Honor, and Rituals in Modern Europe and America* (Columbus: Ohio State University Press, 1998), 197–212; Charles Tilly, "How Protest Modernized in France, 1845 to 1855," in William Aydelotte, Allan Bogue, and Robert Fogel, eds., *The Dimensions of Quantitative Research in History* (Princeton: Princeton University Press, 1972); Alain Corbin, *The Village of Cannibals* (Cambridge, MA: Harvard University Press, 1992), ch. 4. Fenian protest in Ireland was quickly suppressed, and political moderates in France proved fairly successful in burying memories of the violent Paris Commune (1871). After that event, republican leaders sought to cleanse the republican tradition by downplaying its episodes of violence. See Maurice Agulhon, *Marianne au pouvoir: L'imagerie et la symbolique républicaines de 1880 à 1914* (Paris: Flammarion, 1989).

44. Norbert Elias, *The Civilizing Process*, 2 vols. (New York: Pantheon, 1982).

45. Schivelbusch, *Culture of Defeat*.

46. Franzen, *Bloody Good*, 2–3, 17–18.

47. Marc Michel, *La Mission Marchand* (Paris: Mouton, 1972), 109; Jean Autin, *Pierre Savorgnan de Brazza: Un prophète du tiers monde* (Paris: Perrin, 1985), 201–6.

48. Winston Churchill, *The River War. An Account of the Reconquest of the Sudan* (New York: Carroll and Graf, 2000 [1899]).

49. Dea Birkett, *Spinsters Abroad: Victorian Lady Explorers* (New York: Dorset Press, 1989); Birkett, *Mary Kingsley: Imperial Adventuress* (London: Macmillan, 1992); Annette Kobak, *Isabelle: The Life of Isabelle Eberhardt* (London: Chatto and Windus, 1988); Joëlle Désiré-Marchand, *Les itinéraires d'Alexandra David-Néel: L'espace géographique d'une recherche intérieure* (Paris: Arthaud, 1996).

50. Tim Jeal, *Livingstone* (New York: Putnam, 1973).

51. Robert Aldrich, *Colonialism and Homosexuality* (New York: Routledge, 2003), 36–47.

52. Van Orman, *The Explorers*.

53. Ann Laura Stoler, *Carnal Knowledge and Imperial Power: Race and the Intimate in Colonial Rule* (Berkeley: University of California Press, 2002); Phillippa Levine, "Sexuality and Empire," in Hall and Rose, *At Home with the Empire*, 122–42.

54. Stephen Turner, "Charisma and Obedience: A Risk Cognition Approach," *Leadership Quarterly* 4, nos. 3–4 (1993): 237–40; Turner, "Charisma Reconsidered," *Journal of Classical Sociology* 3, no. 1 (2003), 6. In the second article, Turner notes the use of "charisma" as the stage name of a movie star (Charisma Carpenter) and on the doorplates of a German modeling agency, a British record company, and a Florida hairdressing salon. See also Philip Reiff, *Charisma: The Gift of Grace and How It Has Been Taken Away from Us* (New York: Pantheon, 2007).

55. Max Weber, *Economy and Society: An Outline of Interpretive Sociology*, ed. Guenther Roth and Claus Wittich (Berkeley: University of California Press, 1978), 244.

56. Ibid., 241.

57. Ibid., 242. William H. Friedland, "For a Sociological Concept of Charisma," *Social Forces* 43, no. 1 (October 1964): 18–26.

58. Weber, *Economy and Society*, 242.

59. Turner, "Charisma and Obedience," 245. For a skeptical view of the term *charisma*, see K. J. Ratman, "Charisma and Political Leadership," *Political Studies* 12 (1964): 341–54.

60. Turner, "Charisma and Obedience," 246–47.

61. David S. Meyer and Joshua Gamson, in "The Challenge of Cultural Elites: Celebrities and Social Movements," *Sociological Inquiry* 65, no. 2 (May

1995): 181–206, show that in contemporary America, even those celebrities active in social movements possess little ability to advance the cause in question. Either they dilute its aims in an effort to avoid controversy and alienate fans, or they attract so much media attention to themselves that the ideas and issues in question get overlooked.

62. Weber, *Economy and Society,* 1117.

63. This and the following paragraphs summarize Panksepp, *Affective Neuroscience: The Foundations of Human and Animal Emotions* (New York: Oxford University Press, 2004), 51–55 and passim.

64. Ibid., 52.

65. Ibid., 53.

66. See Sylvain Venayre, "L'invention de l'invention: L'histoire des représentations en France depuis 1980," in Laurent Martin and Sylvain Venayre, eds., *L'histoire culturelle du contemporain* (Paris: Nouveau Monde, 2005), 31–54.

67. Eric Hobsbawm, *The Age of Extremes* (New York: Vintage, 1996); Weber, *Economy and Society,* 1120.

68. On the "recharismazation" of the German monarchy in the late nineteenth century, see Martin Kohlrauch, "The Workings of Royal Celebrity: Wilhelm II as Media Emperor," in Edward Berenson and Eva Giloi, eds., *Constructing Charisma: Celebrity, Fame, and Power in Nineteenth-Century Europe* (New York: Berghahn Books, 2010), 52–66.

69. James Gordon Bennett, the *New York Herald's* founding editor, is credited with conducting the first interview in the 1840s. The British journalist and editor of the *Pall Mall Gazette,* William T. Stead, popularized the interview in the 1880s, and Emile Zola, among others, complained of its effects. "Whenever the smallest event occurs," he said, "dozens of interviewers congregate at my door . . . and I can't get anything done." "Zola interviewé sur l'interview," *Le Figaro,* 12 January 1893.

70. Bellanger, *Histoire générale,* 3:95–98; Bonnie Brennen and Hanno Hardt, eds., *Picturing the Past: Media, History, and Photography* (Urbana: University of Illinois Press, 1999).

71. Daniel J. Boorstin, *The Image: A Guide to Pseudo-Events in America* (New York: Harper and Row, 1961), 57. Joshua Gamson, in *Claims to Fame: Celebrity in Contemporary America* (Berkeley: University of California Press, 1994), rightly argued that analysts of celebrity have generally made too much of this distinction.

72. Weber, *Economy and Society,* 1116, 1134.

73. On this crowd phenomenon, see Gregory Shaya, "The *Flâneur,* the *Badaud,* and the Making of a Mass Public in France, circa 1860–1910," *American Historical Review* 109, no. 1 (February 2004), 41–77.

74. Weber discusses the appropriation of charisma by traditional and bureaucratic leaders in a section of *Economy and Society* entitled "The Charismatic Legitimation of the Existing Order."

75. Marshall McLuhan, *Understanding Media: The Extensions of Man* (New York: McGraw Hill, 1964).

76. Edward Shils, "Charisma, Order, and Status," *American Sociological Review* 30, no. 2 (April 1965), 201 (emphasis in original).

I. HENRY MORTON STANLEY AND THE NEW JOURNALISM

1. Stanley's most recent biographer, Tim Jeal, maintains that the explorer did not actually say those famous words. In his otherwise favorable portrait, Jeal depicts Stanley as a chronic fabricator, an insecure man anxious to hide his real and imagined shortcomings under layers of obfuscation and outright lies. The Livingstone greeting must have been one of those inventions, Jeal claims, because it appears nowhere in Stanley's manuscript diary, his most accurate source. The pages where the explorer should have recorded this greeting have been removed. For our purposes, it doesn't matter whether Stanley actually uttered these words. What's important is that they are indelibly associated with him. Tim Jeal, *Stanley: The Impossible Life of Africa's Greatest Explorer* (New Haven: Yale University Press, 2007), 117–19. The date of the famous Stanley-Livingstone meeting has been the subject of considerable scholarly debate. See François Bontinck, "La date de la rencontre Stanley-Livingstone," *Africa: Rivista trimestrale di studi e documentazione dell'Istituto Italo-Africano* 24 (1979): 225–41. Jeal situates the meeting either in late October or the first part of November (504n10).

2. The literature on Stanley and Livingstone is large, and much of the best work has taken the form of biography. On Stanley, see Jeal, *Stanley;* John Bierman, *Dark Safari: The Life behind the Legend of Henry Morton Stanley* (New York: Knopf, 1990); Frank McLynn, *Stanley: The Making of an African Explorer* (London: Scarborough House, 1989); McLynn, *Stanley: Sorcerer's Apprentice* (London: Constable, 1991); Richard Hall, *Stanley: An Adventurer Explored* (Boston: Houghton Mifflin, 1975). Stanley was himself a prolific author; see, in particular, *How I Found Livingstone* (London: Sampson, Low, Marston and Searle, 1872) and *The Autobiography of Henry Morton Stanley,* ed. Dorothy Stanley (Boston: Houghton Mifflin, 1909). On Livingstone, see Tim Jeal, *Livingstone* (London: Heinemann, 1973); Joanna Skipwith, ed., *David Livingstone and the Victorian Encounter with Africa* (London: National Portrait Gallery, 1996); Dorothy O. Helly, *Livingstone's Legacy: Horace Waller and Victorian Mythmaking* (Athens: Ohio University Press, 1987); John M. MacKenzie, "David Livingstone: The Construction of the Myth," in Graham Walker and Tom Gallagher, eds., *Sermons and Battle Hymns: Protestant Popular Culture in Modern Scotland* (Edinburgh: Edinburgh University Press, 1990). For a comprehensive bibliography of works on Stanley and Livingstone, see James A. Casada, *Dr. David Livingstone and Sir Henry Morton Stanley: An Annotated Bibliography* (New York: Garland, 1976).

3. F. M. L. Thompson, *The Rise of Respectable Society: A Social History of Victorian Britain, 1830–1900* (Cambridge, MA: Harvard University Press, 1988).

4. On Livingstone, see Jeal, *Livingstone*. The recent biographies that look most closely at Stanley's personality are those by Bierman and McLynn.

5. Ian Anstruther, *Dr. Livingstone, I Presume?* (New York: Dutton, 1957), vii, 145–46.

6. Henry Morton Stanley, "Journal," 10 November 1871. A photocopy of Stanley's manuscript journal is housed in the British Library under Stanley Family Archives, RP 2435 (i) Box 3. The original, along with a mass of other Stanley papers, resides in Belgium's Musée Royal de l'Afrique Centrale, which purchased the archive for 30 million Belgian francs in 1962 and has only recently made it available to researchers.

7. *New York Herald*, 15 July 1872, dispatch dated 10 November 1871. Stanley omitted from his dispatch the admission that he wanted to do somersaults.

8. That, at least, was the assessment of Stanley's contemporary Richard Burton, who knew the region's culture extremely well. See McLynn, *Stanley: The Making of an African Explorer*, 358n7.

9. Quoted in Anstruther, *Dr. Livingstone*, 191. Again, if Jeal is right, even this apparently candid remark masks a truth we will never know.

10. Steven Ambrose, *Undaunted Courage: Meriwether Lewis, Thomas Jefferson, and the opening of the American West* (New York: Simon and Schuster, 1996).

11. As recently as 1840, news had taken more than a week to travel from Paris to Marseille. David H. Pinkney, *The Decisive Years in France, 1840–1847* (Princeton: Princeton University Press, 1986), 111; Eric Hobsbawm, *The Age of Capital* (New York: Scribner, 1975), 4, 53–55.

12. Ernst Jünger, *Das Abenteuerliche Herz* (1929), quoted in Sylvain Venayre, *La gloire de l'aventure: Genèse d'une mystique moderne, 1850–1940* (Paris: Aubier, 2002), 165.

13. Antoine de Sait-Exupéry, *Terre des hommes;* André Malraux, *La corde et les souris*, both quoted in Venayre, *La gloire de l'aventure*, 166–67.

14. On the "new journalism" and the mass press, see John B. Thompson, *The Media and Modernity: A Social Theory of the Media* (Stanford, CA: Stanford University Press, 1995); Hampton, *Visions of the Press*; Judith Walkowitz, *City of Dreadful Delight: Narratives of Sexual Danger in Late Victorian London* (Chicago: University of Chicago Press, 1992); George Boyce, James Curran, and Pauline Wingate, *Newspaper History: From the Seventeenth Century to the Present Day* (London: Constable, 1978); Joel H. Wiener, ed., *Papers for the Millions: The New Journalism in Britain, 1850s to 1914* (New York: Greenwood Press, 1988); Alan J. Lee, *The Origins of the Popular Press in England, 1855–1914* (London: Croom Helm, 1976); Lucy Brown, *Victorian News and Newspapers* (Oxford: Clarendon Press, 1985); Thomas Ferenczi, *L'invention du journalism en France* (Paris: Plon, 1993); Marc Martin, *Médias et journalistes de la République*

(Paris: Odile Jacob, 1997); Palmer, *Des petits journaux*; Michael Schudson, *Discovering the News: A Social History of American Newspapers* (New York: Basic Books, 1978); Dan Schiller, *Objectivity and the News: The Public and the Rise of Commercial Journalism* (Philadelphia: University of Pennsylvania Press, 1981).

15. Clare Pettitt, in *Dr. Livingstone, I Presume? Missionaries, Journalists, and Empire* (Cambridge, MA: Harvard University Press, 2007), writes interestingly about Stanley's greeting and the role journalism played in making it a notable, memorable event. See especially, 69–70 and ch. 2.

16. Michelle Perrot, "Fait divers et histoire au XIXe siècle," *Annales ESC* 38, no. 4 (July–August 1983): 914. See also Marie-Eve Thérenty, *La Littérature au quotidien: Poétiques journalistiques au XIXe siècle* (Paris: Seuil, 2007), 269–91.

17. Dominique Kalifa, *L'Encre et le sang: Récits de crimes et société à la Belle Epoque* (Paris: Fayard, 1995).

18. Anne-Claude Ambroise-Rendu, *Petits récits des désordres ordinaires: Les faits divers dans la presse française des débuts de la Troisième République à la Grande Guerre* (Paris: Seli Arslan, 2004), 53–54; Marc Martin, "Journalistes parisiens et notoriété (vers 1830–1870): Pour une histoire sociale du journalisme." *Revue historique* 266 (1981): 31–74.

19. Vanessa R. Schwartz, *Spectacular Realities: Early Mass Culture in Fin-de-Siècle Paris* (Berkeley: University of California Press, 1998); Timothy J. Clark, *The Painting of Modern Life: Paris in the Art of Monet and His Followers* (New York: Knopf, 1984). See also Peter Fritsche, *Reading Berlin 1900* (Cambridge, MA: Harvard University Press, 1996). Much of this work has been inspired by Walter Benjamin's now canonical studies of Paris in the nineteenth century: *The Writer of Modern Life: Essays on Charles Baudelaire*, ed. Michael Jennings (Cambridge, MA: Belknap Press of Harvard University Press, 2006).

20. Henry du Roure, *La presse d'aujourd'hui et la presse de demain* (Paris: au Sillon, 1908), 14–15.

21. Describing the *New York Herald*, the British writer Edward Delille declared, "It would pay any price for 'news': if true, so much the better." Quoted in Hampton, *Visions of the Press*, 93.

22. Hall, *Stanley*, 112–14.

23. Cadwalader Rowlands, *H.M. Stanley: The Story of His Life* (London: 1872), quoted in McLynn, *Stanley*, 1:85.

24. See Kay Redfield Jamison, *Touched with Fire: Manic-Depressive Illness and the Artistic Temperament* (New York: Free Press, 1993), for a description of the disease. Stanley shared many of the characteristics of personality and mood that distinguished the artists Jamison describes.

25. See for example, McLynn, *Stanley*, vol. 1.

26. Jeal, *Stanley*, 34–40.

27. Ibid., 37–38 and passim.

28. Paul Starr, *The Creation of the Media: Political Origins of Modern Communications* (New York: Basic Books, 2004), ch. 2. See also Joyce Appleby, "Radicalizing the War for Independence: American Responses to the French Revolution," *Amerikastudien/American Studies* 41, no. 1 (1996): 7–16.

29. Quoted in Starr, *Creation of the Media,* 48.

30. Ibid., 87.

31. Richard R. John, *Spreading the News: The American Postal System from Franklin to Morse* (Cambridge, MA: Harvard University Press, 1996).

32. There is a vast literature on the history of journalism. On the origins of the newspaper in England and France, see Bob Harris, *Politics and the Rise of the Press: Britain and France, 1620–1800* (New York: Routledge, 1996); C. John Sommerville, *The News Revolution in England* (New York: Oxford University Press, 1996); Claude Bellanger et al., *Histoire générale de la presse française,* 2 vols. (Paris: Presses universitaires de France, 1969). For the United States, see the works by Starr, Schudson, and Schiller, among many others. See also Lucy Maynard Salmon, *The Newspaper and the Historian* (New York: Oxford University Press, 1923).

33. Schudson, *Discovering the News,* ch. 1; Schiller, *Objectivity,* chs. 1–4; James Crouthamel, *Bennett's* New York Herald *and the Rise of the Popular Press* (Syracuse, NY: Syracuse University Press, 1989); Helen MacGill Hughes, *News and the Human Interest Story* (Chicago: University of Chicago Press, 1940); Don C. Seitz, *The James Gordon Bennetts* (Indianapolis: Bobbs-Merrill, 1928).

34. Patricia Cline Cohen, *The Murder of Helen Jewett* (New York: Knopf, 1998); Amy Gilman Srebnick, *The Mysterious Death of Mary Rogers: Sex and Culture in Nineteenth-Century New York* (New York: Oxford University Press, 1995).

35. Quoted in Schiller, *Objectivity,* 80.

36. Around the turn of the century, French papers, for example, staged bicycle and auto races and a variety of contests whose results became major stories they covered. See Berenson, *Trial of Madame Caillaux,* 233.

37. Stanley, *How I Found Livingstone,* xxxvii.

38. Bierman, *Dark Safari,* 65.

39. Stanley, *How I Found Livingstone,* xxxviii–xxxix.

40. McLynn, *Stanley,* 1:95.

41. Bierman, *Dark Safari,* 75–76.

42. Stanley to Bennett, 17 January 1871, Musée royal de l'Afrique centrale (hereinafter MRAC), Stanley Papers, 6926. The King Baudouin Foundation purchased this letter, among other Stanley documents, in a Christie's auction in 2001. Christie's had acquired the papers after the death of Richard M. Stanley, the stepson of Denzil Stanley, himself the adopted son of Henry Morton and Dorothy Stanley. The foundation then turned these materials over to Belgium's Royal Museum of Central Africa, which had established the Stanley Archives in 1987 in a pavilion adjacent to the huge Leopoldian museum building. Today, the entire col-

lection of Stanley materials—those acquired in an original sale by the Stanley family in 1982 and those auctioned by Christie's in 2001–3—reside in this Stanley Pavilion. To my knowledge, no Stanley biographer has noted the significance of this letter. See "Inventory of the Stanley Archives," www.africamuseum.be/ research/dept4/history/histocoll/research/dept4/history/Stanley.

43. All quotes in the preceding two paragraphs, in ibid.

44. Jeal, *Livingstone*, 337–38.

45. Nor did he possess the sickle-cell genetic mutation that makes many Africans and people of African descent resistant to malaria. Those with two copies of the gene get sickle-cell anemia, which is often fatal. Matt Ridley, *Genome: The Autobiography of a Species in 23 Chapters* (New York: Harper-Collins, 1999), 141; Van Orman, *The Explorers*, 37.

46. Frederick Cooper, *Plantation Slavery on the East Coast of Africa* (New York: Heinemann, 1997); Edward A. Alpers, *Ivory and Slaves: Changing Patterns of International Trade in East Central Africa to the Later Nineteenth Century* (Berkeley: University of California Press, 1975).

47. Hall, *Stanley*, 188.

48. Stanley's dispatches have been collected, with a useful introduction, in Norman R. Bennett, ed., *Stanley's Dispatches to the* New York Herald (Boston: Boston University Press, 1970).

49. Hall, *Stanley*, 177.

50. On Stanley as a travel writer, see Tim Youngs, *Travellers in Africa: British Travelogues, 1850–1900* (Manchester: Manchester University Press, 1994), esp. chs. 4–5. See also Mary Louise Pratt, *Imperial Eyes: Travel Writing and Trans-culturation* (London: Routledge, 1992).

51. For an illuminating description of the caravan trade, see Tippu Tipp, *L'autobiographie de Hamed ben Mohammed el-Murjebi Tippo Tipp*, ed. François Bontinck (Brussels: Koninklijke Academie voor Overzeese Wetenschappen, 1974). See also Stanley, *How I Found Livingstone*, ch. 1.

52. Stanley, *How I Found Livingstone*, 85.

53. See Bennett, *Stanley's Dispatches to the* New York Herald, 1–126. The best description of Stanley's first African voyage based on those dispatches is in McLynn, *Stanley*, vol. 1, chs. 6–7.

54. The dispatch dated 4 July 1871 was published in the *New York Herald* on 22 December 1871.

55. G. W. Hartwig and K. D. Paterson, *Disease in African History: An Introductory Survey and Case Studies* (Durham, NC: Duke University Press, 1978).

56. Stanley, *How I Found Livingstone*, quoted in McLynn, *Stanley*, 1:115–16.

57. Mirambo ultimately seized control of the greater part of what is now Tanzania.

58. So Stanley claimed the meeting went. See the *New York Herald*, 10, 15 August 1872.

59. Quoted in McLynn, *Stanley*, 1:164.

60. Quoted in Seitz, *James Gordon Bennetts*, 293.

61. McLynn, *Stanley*, vol. 1, ch. 8; Hall, *Stanley*, ch. 14; Bierman, *Dark Safari*, ch. 9; Jeal, *Livingstone*, ch. 22.

62. Jeal, *Livingstone*, ch. 22; Helly, *Livingstone's Legacy*, ch. 1.

63. *New York Herald*, 22 December 1871.

64. Hobsbawm, *Age of Capital*, 4, 53–55.

65. For the early rumors, see the *Times*, 2 May 1872. For the first full report, see the *New York Herald*, 2 July 1872.

66. Hosmer to Stanley, telegram, 6 July 1872, MRAC, Stanley Archives, 2664.

67. Bierman, *Dark Safari*, 121.

68. *New York Herald*, 23 December 1871.

69. *Frederick (Md.) Herald*, 30 December 1871; *Indianapolis News*, 23 December 1871.

70. *Memphis Appeal*, 29 December 1871.

71. *New York Herald*, 2 July 1872.

72. *London Daily Telegraph*, 3 July 1872.

73. Robert A. Stafford, "Scientific Exploration and Empire," in Andrew Porter, ed., *The Oxford History of the British Empire* (Oxford: Oxford University Press, 1999), 3:294–319; Agnes Murphy, *The Ideology of French Imperialism* (New York: Fertig, 1968); Girardet, *L'Idée coloniale en France*.

74. *London Daily Telegraph*, 3 July 1872.

75. *Manchester Guardian*, 13 August 1872.

76. Christophe Charle, *La crise des sociétés impériales: Allemagne, France, Grande-Bretagne, 1900–1940: Essai d'histoire sociale comparée* (Paris: Seuil, 2001).

77. *London Daily News*, 26 July 1872 (emphasis added).

78. For an excellent general discussion of Stanley's critics, see Felix Driver, "Henry Morton Stanley and His Critics: Geography, Exploration, and Empire," *Past & Present*, 133 (1991), revised and reprinted in Driver, *Geography Militant: Cultures of Exploration and Empire* (Oxford: Blackwell, 2001), ch. 6.

79. Quoted in McLynn, *Stanley*, 1:206.

80. Grant to H. W. Bates, 12 July 1872, quoted in ibid., 206n16.

81. *London Times*, 5 July 1872.

82. *Pall Mall Gazette*, 3 July 1872.

83. *Spectator*, 3 August 1872. Livingstone's letter thanking Bennett for the Stanley expedition appeared in the *New York Herald* on 26 July 1872. Within a week that letter and others by the British explorer were reprinted in papers in virtually every country reachable by telegraph.

84. *Le Temps*, 3 August 1872.

85. Stanley, "Journal," 1 August 1872. With government support, the RGS had sent an expedition to find Livingstone, whose leaders called off the search after learning in Zanzibar that Stanley had already found him.

86. *London Times,* 3 August 1872.

87. *Daily Telegraph,* 3 August 1872.

88. Hall, *Stanley,* 215–16.

89. McLynn, *Stanley,* vol. 1, ch. 11; Hall, *Stanley,* ch. 15.

90. Brown, *Victorian News and Newspapers,* 2.

91. *Daily Telegraph,* 2 August 1872.

92. Brown, *Victorian News and Newspapers,* 100–102.

93. On the *Petit journal,* see Ferenczi, *L'Invention;* Palmer, *Des petits journaux,* ch. 1; Berenson, *Trial of Madame Caillaux,* ch. 6.

94. Leonard R. N. Ashley, *George Alfred Henty and the Victorian Mind* (San Francisco: International Scholars Publications, 1999); Mawuena Kossi Logan, *Narrating Africa: George Henty and the Fiction of Empire* (New York: Garland, 1999).

95. The *Herald* reprinted press reactions to the Stanley story from around the world.

96. *London Daily News,* 4 July 1872.

97. See Venayre, *La gloire de l'aventure.*

98. Casada, *Dr. David Livingstone and Sir Henry Morton Stanley.* Jeal thinks Stanley deliberately exaggerated the amount and degree of violence he used in an attempt to appear masterful and tough. It seems more likely, however, that in recounting episodes of violence, Stanley obeyed the narrative conventions he had learned in covering the American Civil War, conflicts with American Indians, and colonial battles in West Africa. In these earlier reports, as in his dispatches from the Livingstone mission, Stanley saw no need to disguise his violent acts. On the contrary, he knew readers would be drawn to them.

99. Armand Sinval, *Les explorateurs contemporains (Livingstone, Stanley, Nordenskiold, Crevaux, Savorgnan de Brazza)* (Limoges, France: Barbou, 1888), 103.

100. Quoted in Hall, *Stanley,* 210.

101. Ibid.

102. *Pall Mall Gazette,* 2 August 1872. According to Donald Matheson, in "The Birth of News Discourse: Changes in News Language in British Newspapers, 1880–1930," *Media, Culture, and Society* 22, no. 5 (2000): 568, British newspapers did not abandon their "dignified," "gentlemanly" style until the 1880s and 1890s, or even later. American papers had done so several decades earlier.

2. PIERRE SAVORGNAN DE BRAZZA AND THE MAKING OF THE FRENCH THIRD REPUBLIC

1. The full typescript text of Stanley's speech, translated into French by the Havas news agency, is in the Archives nationale d'outre-mer, Aix-en-Provence (hereinafter ANOM), Fonds Brazza (hereinafter FB) PA 16 II/4. The English text was later published as a pamphlet entitled "Count Brazza and His Pretensions."

2. Ibid. Since I have not been able to find the pamphlet, I'm translating from the French version of Stanley's speech, delivered to the Stanley Club in English.

3. The king's actual name was Ilo, but Europeans preferred his dynastic title, Makoko; it seems least confusing to use the latter name here. For the text of this treaty, see Henri Brunschwig, ed., *Brazza explorateur: Les Traités Makoko, 1880–82* (Paris: Mouton, 1972).

4. Schivelbusch, *Culture of Defeat.*

5. The origins of this discourse lay not in the debacle of 1870–71, but in Napoleon's defeat at Waterloo. See Jean-Marc Largeaud, *Napoléon et Waterloo: La défaite glorieuse de 1815 à nos jours* (Paris: Boutique de l'histoire, 2006).

6. Alice Conklin, *A Mission to Civilize: The Republican Idea of Empire in France and West Africa, 1895–1930* (Stanford, CA: Stanford University Press, 1997).

7. William B. Cohen, "Gambettists and Colonial Expansion before 1881: The *République française,*" *French Colonial Studies/Etudes Coloniales Française* 1 (spring 1977): 55–56.

8. On republican education, see Mona Ozouf, *L'école, l'église, et la république 1871–1914* (Paris: A. Colin, 1963); Pierre Nora, "Lavisse, instituteur national: Le 'Petit Lavisse,' évangile de la République," in *Les lieux de mémoire,* vol. 1, ed. Pierre Nora (Paris: Gallimard, 1997), 239–76; James R. Lehning, *To Be a Citizen: The Political Culture of the Early Third Republic* (Ithaca, NY: Cornell University Press, 2001), esp. Ch. 3; Patricia Ann Tilburg, *Colette's Republic: Work, Gender, and Popular Culture in France, 1870–1914* (New York: Berghan Books, 2009). On republican goddesses, see Maurice Agulhon, *Marianne au combat* (Paris: Flammarion, 1979), and *Marianne au pouvoir* (Paris: Flammarion, 1989). See also Lynn Hunt, *Politics, Culture, and Class in the French Revolution* (Berkeley: University of California Press, 1984), chs. 1–3. On the 14th of July and republican festivals, see Olivier Ihl, *La fête républicaine* (Paris: Gallimard, 1996). Sudhir Hazareesingh locates the beginnings of local festivals of national unity not in the 1880s but in the early Second Empire. Sudhir Hazareesingh, *The Saint-Napoleon: Celebrations of Sovereignty in Nineteenth-Century France* (Cambridge, MA: Harvard University Press, 2004).

9. Joan B. Landes, *Women and the Public Sphere in the Age of the French Revolution* (Ithaca, NY: Cornell University Press, 1988); Landes, *Visualizing the Nation: Gender, Representation, and Revolution in Eighteenth-Century France* (Ithaca, NY: Cornell University Press, 2001).

10. Ihl, *Fête républicaine.*

11. Avner Ben-Amos, *Funerals, Politics, and Memory in Modern France 1789–1996* (New York: Oxford University Press, 2000). See also, Katherine Verdery, *The Political Lives of Dead Bodies: Reburial and Postsocialist Change* (New York: Columbia University Press, 1999).

12. Avner Ben-Amos, "Les funérailles de Victor Hugo," in Nora, *Lieux de mémoire,* 1:456.

13. Ernest Kantorowicz, *The Kings Two Bodies. A Study in Medieval Political Theology* (Princeton: Princeton University Press, 1966).

14. Gabriel Tarde, "Le Public et la foule," *La Revue de Paris* 4 (15 July 1898): 287–306, (1 August 1898): 615–35; Tarde, "L'Opinion et la conversation," *La Revue de Paris* 5 (15 August 1899): 689–719, (1 September 1899): 91–116. The two articles were republished in Tarde, *L'Opinion et la foule* (Paris: Presses Universitaires de France, 1989).

15. Tarde, *L'Opinion et la foule*, 36.

16. Ibid., 32.

17. Ibid., 47.

18. Ibid.

19. Tarde's "Opinion" resembles Habermas's "public opinion" in that it represents the consensus of members of a public constituted outside the confines of the state. But Tarde's public is quite different from Habermas's public. The latter, at least as an ideal type, enjoys considerable independence both from the state and from economic relations and for that reason possesses the ability to reflect rationally and disinterestedly on the issues of the day. Tarde's Opinion is, by contrast, not the product of mature reflection but the immediate result of a commercial mass medium's unprecedented ability to flood people with the same ideas at the same time. See Jürgen Habermas, *The Structural Transformation of the Public Sphere*, trans. Thomas Burger (Cambridge, MA: MIT Press, 1989); Craig Calhoun, ed., *Habermas and the Public Sphere* (Cambridge, MA: MIT Press, 1992). In the Calhoun volume, particularly valuable essays are those by Keith Michael Baker, "Defining the Public Sphere in Eighteenth-Century France," and Geoff Eley, "Nations, Publics, and Political Cultures: Placing Habermas in the Nineteenth Century."

20. Tarde, *L'Opinion et la foule*, 49. Writing at the same time as Tarde, the British observer Frank Taylor echoed the French sociologist's views in many ways, except that Taylor cast the press's ability to shape opinion in more negative terms. See Frank Taylor, *The Newspaper Press as a Power Both in the Expression and the Formation of Public Opinion* (Oxford: Blackwell, 1898). See also, Hampton, *Visions of the Press*, 99.

21. Benedict Anderson, *Imagined Communities: Reflections on the Origin and Spread of Nationalism* (London: Verso, 1983), 35

22. *République française*, 30 September 1882.

23. Joan of Arc is the exception that proves the rule.

24. Berenson, *Trial of Madame Caillaux*, chs. 3, 5.

25. Alexandre Dumas, *L'homme-femme, réponse à M. Henri d'Ideville* (Paris: Michel Lévy frères, 1872); Dumas, *Les femmes qui tuent et les femmes qui votent* (Paris: C. Lévy, 1880). William M. Reddy, *The Invisible Code: Honor and Sentiment in Postrevolutionary France, 1814–1848* (Berkeley: University of California Press, 1997); Nye, *Masculinity and Male Codes of Honor*.

26. For recent accounts of Brazza's life, see Idanna Pucci, *Brazza in Congo: A Life and a Legacy* (New York: Umbrage Editions, 2009); Jean Martin, *Savorgnan de Brazza (1852–1905): Une épopée aux rives du Congo* (Paris: Les indes savantes, 2005); and "Pierre Savorgnan de Brazza," online exhibit by the French National Archives, Centre des archives d'outre-mer, Aix-en-Provence, www.brazza.culture .fr/fr/index.html. These books and materials were timed to commemorate the hundredth anniversary of Brazza's death (1905–2005). Most Brazza biographies have relied on the hagiographic account by the explorer's brother-in-law, General [Jacques Aldebert de Pineton] de Chambrun, *Brazza* (Paris: Plon, 1930). See also René Maran, *Savorgnan de Brazza* (Paris: Editions du Dauphin, 1951); Charles de Chavannes, *Le Congo français* (Paris: Plon, 1937); Autin, *Brazza.* Much of the best information, biographical and otherwise, comes from four excellent volumes of analysis and primary materials relating to Brazza's work: Henri Brunschwig, *Brazza explorateur: L'Ogooué 1875–79* (Paris: Mouton, 1966); Brunschwig, *Brazza explorateur: Les traités Makoko, 1880–82* (Paris: Mouton, 1972); Catherine Coquery-Vidrovitch, *Brazza et la prise de possession du Congo français, 1883–85* (Paris: Mouton, 1969); Elisabeth Rabut, *Brazza, commissaire général: Le Congo français, 1886–1897* (Paris: Editions de l'Ecole des hautes études en sciences sociales, 1989).

27. Maria Petringa, *Brazza: A Life for Africa* (Bloomington, IN: Author House, 2006). On the Italian nobility of the nineteenth century, see Anthony Cardoza, *Aristocrats in Bourgeois Italy: The Piedmontese Nobility, 1861–1930* (New York: Cambridge University Press, 1997).

28. On Stanley as explorer, see chapters 1 and 4.

29. See, for example, Charles de Chavannes, *Avec Brazza* (Paris: Plon, 1935).

30. *Exposition universelle internationale de 1878, à Paris,* Tome V, *Catalogue des produits des colonies françaises* (Paris: Challamel aîné, 1878).

31. Bennett, *Stanley's Dispatches to the* New York Herald.

32. Roland Barthes, "L'Effet de reél," *Communications* 11 (1968): 84–89.

33. Alfred Ferro, *La Société de Géographie, 1821–1946* (Geneva: Droz, 1983); Dominmique Lejeune, *Les sociétés de géographie en France et l'expansion coloniale au XIXème siècle* (Paris: Albin Michel, 1993); Emmanuelle Sibeud, *Une science impériale pour l'Afrique? La construction des savoirs africanistes en France, 1878– 1930* (Paris: EHESS, 2002).

34. C. M. Andrew and A. S. Kanya-Forstner, "Centre and Periphery in the Making of the Second French Colonial Empire, 1815–1920," *Journal of Imperial and Commonwealth History* 16 (1988): 9–34; Michael J. Heffernan, "The Science of Empire: The French Geographical Movement and the Forms of French Imperialism, 1870–1920," in Anne Godlewska and Neil Smith, eds., *Geography and Empire* (Oxford: Blackwell, 1994), 95–97. The classic works on French imperialism are Henri Brunschwig, *French Colonialism, 1871–1914* (New York: Praeger, 1966); Girardet, *L'Idée coloniale en France*; Charles-Robert Ageron, *France*

coloniale ou parti colonial? (Paris: PUF, 1978). For more recent treatments, see Denise Bouche, *Histoire de la colonisation française,* vol. 1 (Paris: Fayard, 1991); Jean Meyer et al., *Histoire de la France coloniale* (Paris: Armand Colin, 1991).

35. Andrew and Kanya-Forstner, "The French 'Colonial Party.'"

36. Anatole Prévost-Paradol, *La France nouvelle* (Paris: Michel Lévy frères, 1868). The Bibliothèque nationale de France's online catalog lists many of the different editions.

37. Prévost-Paradol, *France nouvelle,* quoted in Heffernan, "Science of Empire," 2.

38. Quoted in Rosaline Eredapa Nwoye, "The Public Image of Pierre Savorgnan de Brazza and the Establishment of French Imperialism in the Congo" (M.A. thesis, Aberdeen University African Studies Group, 1981), 7. I am particularly indebted to this work, which has to be one of the best M.A. theses ever written.

39. Quoted in Heffernan, "Science of Empire," 103.

40. Quoted in ibid., 106.

41. The best overall contemporary summary of these views is Paul Leroy-Beaulieu, *De la colonisation chez les peuples modernes* (Paris: Guillaumin, 1874). The second edition, published in 1882, was particularly influential.

42. Ageron, *France coloniale,* 72–73; Ageron, "Jules Ferry et la colonisation," in François Furet, ed., *Jules Ferry, fondateur de la République* (Paris: Editions de l'Ecole des hautes études en sciences sociales, 1985), 194–95.

43. The most thorough work on Ferry the imperialist remains Thomas F. Power, *Jules Ferry and the Renaissance of French Imperialism* (New York: Octagon Books, 1966).

44. Richard West, *Brazza of the Congo: European Exploration and Exploitation in French Equatorial Africa* (Newton Abbot, UK: Victorian Book Club, 1973), pt. 11, ch. 2.

45. www.bateke.com/bateke/organisation_du_royaume.htm.

46. Descriptions of these events are in all the biographies of Brazza. See also Brunschwig, *Brazza explorateur: Les traités Makoko.*

47. Autin, *Brazza,* 110–11.

48. Brazza to Marius Fontane, secretary general of the French section of the Association Intérnationale Africaine, April 1881, reprinted in Brunschwig, *Brazza explorateur: Les traités Makoko,* 188.

49. Ibid.

50. Proceedings of the PGS, 19 February 1881, quoted in Nwoye, "Public Image," 91.

51. For such a *transfert de sacralité,* see Mona Ozouf, *La fête révolutionnaire* (Paris: Gallimard, 1976).

52. *Le petit parisien,* 25 june 1882.

53. *Le Temps,* 11 June 1882.

54. Maunoir to Brazza, 19 June 1882, ANOM, FB PA 16 III/2.

55. Lejeune, *Les sociétés de géographie.*

56. Jean-Pierre Albert, "Du martyr à la star: Les métamorphoses des héros nationaux," in Centlivres, Fabre, and Zonabend, *La Fabrique des héros,* 18. A theme prominent in nineteenth-century writing on heroism held that "the more the hero is 'small' at the beginning, the more his later acts appear heroic."

57. *L'Illustration,* 8 July 1882, 25, 28. On images of Africa drawn or inspired by nineteenth-century explorers, see Guy Gauthier, "Photographies et gravures sur les explorations africaines des années 1880," in Pascal Blanchard et al., eds., *L'autre et nous, scènes et types* (Paris: Association connaissance de l'histoire de l'Afrique contemporaine, 1995). See also Anne-Claude Ambroise-Rendu, "Du dessin de presse à la photographie (1878–1914): Histoire d'une mutation technique et culturelle," *Revue d'histoire moderne et contemporaine* 39, no. 1 (January–March 1992).

58. Jeal, *Stanley,* 108, 255.

59. Jean Suret-Canale, "Brazza ou la dernière idole," *Recherches africaines* 2 (January–March 1960): 12–16; Brunschwig, *Brazza explorateur: Les traités Makoko,* 190.

60. *Le Temps,* 4 October 1882.

61. *République française,* 2 October 1882.

62. *L'Illustration,* 7 October 1882.

63. Stengers, "L'Impérialisme colonial," 475.

64. All newspaper reports of this event—and there were a great many—agreed on the essentials of what took place. See *Le Temps,* 21 October 1882; *Petit parisien,* 22 October 1882; *Le Figaro,* 20–21 October 1882; *Times,* 21 October 1882.

65. English text in ANOM, FB PA 16 II/4.

66. McLynn, *Stanley: Sorcerer's Apprentice,* 56. Brazza also knew that the Havas agency would be there to transmit news of the proceedings to newspapers in every city and town in France.

67. West, *Brazza of the Congo,* 122.

68. Henri Malo, *A l'enseigne de la petite vache: Souvenirs, gestes et figures d'explorateurs* (Paris: Editions de la nouvelle France, 1946).

69. Andrew and Kanya-Forstner, "Centre and Periphery."

70. *Le Constitutionnel,* 7 October 1882, quoted in Stengers, "L'Impérialisme colonial," 475.

71. "Savorgnan de Brazza et Stanley," *Revue des deux mondes,* 1 November 1882, 206.

72. See, for example, *Le Siècle,* 23, 29 September 1882; *Le Temps,* 30 September and 4, 6, 31 October 1882; *La République française,* 30 September, 2, 23 October 1882; *Journal des débats,* 22 September and 21, 23 October 1882; *L'Intran-*

sigeant, 7, 20 October 1882; *Le Voltaire,* 1–10 October 1882; *Le Constitutionnel,* 4, 7, 10, 12 October 1882.

73. *Le Petit journal,* 30 November 1882.

74. *Le Parlement,* 3 October 1882, quoted in Stengers, "L'Impérialisme colonial," 474.

75. Autin, *Brazza,* 78.

76. D. Neuville and Charles Bréard, *Les Voyages de Savorgnan de Brazza* (Paris: Berger-Levrault, 1884), xii.

77. ANOM, FB PA 16 III/2.

78. Quoted in *Le Petit journal,* 30 November 1882.

79. Henri Brunschwig, *Le Partage de l'Afrique noir* (Paris: Flammarion, 1971), 48; Autin, *Brazza,* 78. Four hundred forty-one deputies voted yea, along with a unanimous Senate.

80. Quoted in Andrew and Kanya-Forstner, "Centre and Periphery," 19n54.

81. *Le Temps,* 30 November 1882.

82. *London Times,* 30 November 1882, quoted in Stengers, "L'Impérialisme colonial," 475.

83. On Nadar, see Jean Prinet and Antoinette Dilaser, *Nadar* (Paris: Armand Colin, 1966).

84. The image, reproduced in virtually every biography of Brazza, first appeared in *L'Illustration* at a time when the journal's circulation was relatively large, 30,000 to 40,000. See Bellanger, *Histoire de la presse française,* 3:387.

85. Autin, *Brazza,* photo following 184. This quote is from Autin's caption to the photograph, written as if the image had not been staged.

86. Roland Barthes's comments on this photograph in *La Chambre claire* (New York: Hill and Wang, 1981), 51–53. What Barthes says about the picture is not particularly relevant to the analysis here.

87. *L'Univers,* 23 January 1886.

88. On the *ralliement,* see Debora Silverman, *Art Nouveau in Fin-de-Siècle France* (Berkeley: University of California Press, 1989), 48–49.

89. Image in *Journal des voyages* 11, no. 263 (23 July 1882): 48. On the colonial army, see A. S. Kanya-Forstner, *The Conquest of the Western Sudan: A Study in French Military Imperialism* (Cambridge: Cambridge University Press, 1969); Douglas Porch, "Bugeaud, Gallieni, Lyautey: The Development of French Colonial Warfare," in Felix Gilbert, Gordon A. Craig, and Peter Paret, eds., *Makers of Modern Strategy: From Machiavelli to the Nuclear Age* (Princeton: Princeton University Press, 1986).

90. Front cover of *Les Hommes d'aujourd'hui* 289 (1886), ANOM, FB PA 16/VIII, carton 16.

91. G. Froment-Guieysse, *Brazza* (Paris: Editions de l'Encyclopédie coloniale et maritime, 1945), 90.

92. Schwartz, *Spectacular Realities,* 133–34.

93. Ibid., ch. 3.

94. West, *Brazza of the Congo,* 124.

95. Ibid.

96. Chavannes, *Avec Brazza,* 14–15.

97. A. Berthet, ANOM, FB 16/VII, carton 12. Brazza scrupulously saved his correspondence, which the family kept until the 1960s in a private archive.

98. Thompson, *The Media and Modernity.*

99. A. Berthet, ANOM, FB 16/VII, carton 12.

100. ANOM, FB 16/VII, carton 12. Both poems published in Saint-Paul-Trois-Chateaux, Drôme, 4–5 June 1884.

101. The two copies are dated 5, 6 October 1882.

102. ANOM, FB 16/VII, carton 12. The poem is dated 24 September 1885; the author's last name is illegible, the first name Alexis.

103. Ferry to G. de Courcel, 1 December 1884, quoted in Andrew and Kanya-Forstner, "Centre and Periphery," 20.

3. CHARLES GORDON, IMPERIAL SAINT

1. On Gordon's death and its perceived meanings, see John Wolffe, *Great Deaths: Grieving, Religion, and Nationhood in Victorian and Edwardian Britain* (New York: Oxford University Press, 2000), ch. 5.

2. Lytton Strachey, *Eminent Victorians,* illustrated ed. (London: Bloomsbury, 1988), 160–61.

3. John Laband, *The Transvaal Rebellion: The First Boer War, 1880–1881* (New York: Pearson Longman, 2005).

4. In May 1857, tens of thousands of Indian troops rebelled against their British officers in and around Delhi, the capital of Britain's informal empire on the subcontinent. The British East India Company imposed order there with only a small contingent of British troops and a thin layer of British officers. The overwhelming majority of soldiers hailed from India itself. To properly load their new Lee-Enfield rifles, fighters had to "bite the bullet," chomping on the end of each greased cartridge as they inserted it in the firing chamber. Soldiers believed the grease had come from pigs and cows; the apparent disrespect to the two Indian religions—Muslims considered pigs unclean, Hindus venerated cows—triggered a violent and powerful rebellion. Before long, forty-five of the Bengal army's seventy-four infantry regiments stood in open revolt. Much of the civilian population joined in.

5. Edward M. Spiers, *The Army and Society, 1815–1914* (London: Longman, 1980), 219.

6. Freda Harcourt, "Disraeli's Imperialism, 1866–1868: A Question of Tim-

ing," *Historical Journal* 23, no. 1 (March 1980): 87–109. Harcourt argues that Disraeli reinvigorated imperialist sentiment when as Conservative leader in Parliament he organized a successful military expedition to Abyssinia to punish King Theodore for holding British captives.

7. Pearce and Stewart, *British Political History*, 146–56.

8. John Ruskin, inaugural lecture as Slade Professor (8 February 1870), reprinted in Elleke Boehmer, ed., *Empire Writing: An Anthology of Colonial Literature, 1870–1918* (New York: Oxford University Press, 1998), 18–19.

9. Spiers, *Army and Society*, 129.

10. Pearce and Stewart, *British Political History*, 157.

11. Webster, *Debate on the Rise of the British Empire*, 33–38.

12. *Pall Mall Gazette*, 4 February 1885.

13. Jeffrey A. Auerbach, *The Great Exhibition of 1851: A Nation on Display* (New Haven: Yale University Press, 1999); Louise Purbrick, ed., *The Great Exhibition of 1851: New Interdisciplinary Essays* (New York: Palgrave, 2001). Kate Colquhoun, *The Busiest Man in England: A Life of Joseph Paxton, Gardener, Architect, and Victorian Visionary* (London: Godine, 2006).

14. *Pall Mall Gazette*, 4 February 1885. On the European challenge, see Bernard Porter, *The Lion's Share: A Short History of British Imperialism*, 4th ed. (London: Pearson, 2004), ch. 3.

15. Pearce and Stewart, *British Political History*, ch. 5; Duncan Bell, *The Idea of Greater Britain: Empire and the Future of World Order* (Princeton: Princeton University Press, 2007).

16. Stewart J. Brown, *Providence and Empire: Religion, Politics, and Society in Britain and Ireland, 1815–1914* (London: Longman, 2008), 302.

17. Porter, *Lion's Share*, 116–19.

18. Pearce and Stewart, *British Political History*, 156–59.

19. MacDonald, *Language of Empire*, 83–86.

20. Quoted in John Pollock, *Gordon: The Man behind the Legend* (London: Constable, 1993), 142.

21. Violet Barnes, quoted in ibid., 178.

22. Quoted in ibid., 296, 259.

23. Ibid., 253.

24. On Havelock and Gordon, see Dawson, *Soldier Heroes*, 79–154.

25. Porter, *Lion's Share*, ch. 4.

26. The title of Strachey's magnificent biographical portrait in *Eminent Victorians* is "The End of General Gordon." See also, Wolffe, *Great Deaths*, ch. 5.

27. Lee, *Origins of the Popular Press*, 59–61; Dawson, *Soldier Heroes*, 85.

28. Biographies of Gordon are legion, though more of them saw print in the nineteenth century than in the twentieth. Recent efforts include Pollock, *Gordon*; Charles Chenevix Trench, *The Road to Khartoum: A Life of General Charles Gordon* (New York: Norton, 1978); Anthony Nutting, *Gordon of Khartoum:*

Martyr and Misfit (London: Constable, 1966); Lord Elton, *General Gordon* (London: Collins, 1954).

29. Quoted in Pollock, *Gordon,* 31. This description appeared in Wolseley's memoir, *A Soldier's Life,* published long after Gordon's death.

30. Gordon to Augusta, 11 November 1880, quoted in Pollock, *Gordon,* 32.

31. On the Taiping Rebellion, see Jonathan D. Spence, *God's Chinese Son: The Taiping Heavenly Kingdom of Hong Xiuquan* (New York: W. W. Norton, 1996).

32. Nutting takes pains to disassociate his own biography from this pattern (*Gordon of Khartoum,* 73–75).

33. Ibid., 75–76; Pollock, *Gordon,* 96.

34. On the "hero industry," see Dawson, *Soldier Heroes,* 145–47; MacKenzie, "Heroic Myths of Empire"; Showalter, *Sexual Anarchy,* ch. 1; Jeffrey Richards, ed., *Imperialism and Juvenile Literature* (New York: St. Martins Press, 1989).

35. Quoted in Pollock, *Gordon,* 100.

36. Quoted in Strachey, *Eminent Victorians,* 145.

37. Charles George Gordon, *Letters of General C. G. Gordon to His Sister* (London: MacMillan, 1888), 117 (3 January 1876).

38. See Braudy, *Frenzy of Renown,* part V.

39. Quoted in Pollock, *Gordon,* 131.

40. On the Egyptian colonization of the Sudan, see Eve M. Troutt Powell, *A Different Shade of Colonialism: Egypt, Great Britain, and the Mastery of the Sudan* (Berkeley: University of California Press, 2003); Alice Moore-Harell, *Gordon and the Sudan: Prologue to the Mahdiyya, 1877–1880* (London: Frank Cass, 2001); John O. Udal, *The Nile in Darkness,* 2 vols. (Norwich, UK: Michael Russell, 1998 and 2005).

41. Malcolm Holt, *The Mahdist State in the Sudan, 1881–1898* (Oxford: Clarendon Press, 1958), pp. 9–16, ch. 1.

42. Dominic Green, *Three Empires on the Nile* (New York: Free Press, 2009), 28–29.

43. This volume has long been a staple source for Gordon biographers, especially those focused on his religious views.

44. On Gordon's religious views, see Strachey, *Eminent Victorians,* 143–44.

45. Stewart, *Providence and Empire,* 303; Pollock, *Gordon,* 256–57.

46. Gordon, *Letters to His Sister,* 104 (27 June 1875) (italics added).

47. Troutt Powell, *Different Shade of Colonialism,* 2; Moore-Harell, *Gordon and the Sudan,* 23–23; Udal, *Nile in Darkness,* 2:335–52.

48. Udall, *Nile in Darkness,* 2:338.

49. Quoted in ibid. (17 September 1877) (emphasis in original).

50. Moore-Harell, *Gordon and the Sudan,* 23–25.

51. Troutt-Powell, *Different Shade of Colonialism.*

52. Green, *Three Empires,* ch. 5.

53. Andrew and Kanya-Forstner, "Centre and Periphery," 19.

54. The best general discussion of this resistance is David Levering Lewis, *Race to Fashoda: Colonialism and African Resistance* (New York: Henry Holt, 1995).

55. Jean Stengers, "Aux Origines de Fachoda: L'Expédition Monteil." *Revue belge de Philologie et d'Histoire* 36 (1958): 436–50; 38 (1960): 366–404, 1040–65; G. N. Sanderson, "Contributions from African Sources to the History of European Competition in the Upper Valley of the Nile," *Journal of African History* 3 (1962): 69–90; Sanderson, *England, Europe, and the Upper Nile, 1882–1899: A Study in the Partition of Africa* (Edinburgh: Edinburgh University Press, 1965).

56. Sanderson, in *England, Europe and the Upper Nile*, tells the diplomatic story in impressive detail.

57. Holt, *Mahdist State*, 17–31.

58. Stewart, *Providence and Empire*, 302.

59. Moore-Harell, *Gordon and the Sudan*, 239–45; Udal, *Nile in Darkness*, vol. 2, chs. 12–13; Fergus Nicoll, *The Sword of the Prophet: The Mahdi of the Sudan and the Death of General Gordon* (Stroud, UK: Sutton, 2004); Holt, *Mahdist State;* Alan Buchan Theobald, *The Mahdiya: A History of the Anglo-Egyptian Sudan, 1881–1899* (London: Longman, 1951).

60. Quoted in Roland Anthony Oliver, J. D. Fage, and G. N. Sanderson, *The Cambridge History of Africa*, vol. 6, *1870–1905* (Cambridge: Cambridge University Press, 1985), 609.

61. Holt, *Mahdist State*, ch. 3.

62. Gladstone quoted in Trench, *Road to Khartoum*, 252; Earl of Cromer, *Modern Egypt* (London: MacMillan, 1908), 1:388n.

63. On the government and the public sphere, see Porter, *Lion's Share*, 116–22.

64. Pollock, *Gordon*, 173.

65. Ibid., 215.

66. *Vanity Fair*, 19 February 1881.

67. Beginning with its inaugural issue of 7 November 1868.

68. Pollock, *Gordon*, 219.

69. Quoted in ibid., 217.

70. Strachey, *Eminent Victorians*, 144.

71. Quoted in Pollock, *Gordon*, 268. Gordon, like Stanley, managed to write several thousand words a day, even after long, arduous travels or military campaigns.

72. Ibid., 267. On the Gordon family and Southampton, see Miles Taylor, "Gordon of Khartoum: Reluctant Son of Southampton," in Taylor, ed., *Southampton: Gateway to the British Empire* (London: I. B. Tauris, 2007).

73. *Pall Mall Gazette*, 9 January 1884.

74. On the widely disseminated nineteenth-century images of Turkish pashas, see Katherine E. Fleming, *The Muslim Bonaparte: Diplomacy and Orientalism in Ali Pasha's Greece* (Princeton: Princeton University Press, 1999), ch. 9.

75. Anderson, *Imagined Communities*; Holt, *Mahdist State*; Haim Shaked, *The Life of the Sudanese Mahdi: A Historical Study of* Kitab sa'adat al-mustahdi bi-sirat al-Imam al-Mahdi *(The book of the bliss of him who seeks guidance by the life of the Imam the Mahdi)* (New Brunswick, NJ: Transaction Books, 1978).

76. *Pall Mall Gazette*, 9 January 1884. The paper kept up its drumbeat of pressure with frequent editorials and articles pressing the idea of having Gordon rescue the Sudan. See especially, 1 January, 2 February, 13 March, 22 May 1884.

77. W. T. Stead, "Chinese Gordon," *The Century: A Popular Quarterly* 28, no. 4 (August 1884): 556–61.

78. *Times*, 11 January 1884.

79. Strachey, *Eminent Victorians*, 160.

80. Ibid., 161.

81. *Illustrated London News*, 26 January 1884.

82. *Birmingham Post*, 28 January 1884.

83. *Illustrated London News*, 26 January 1884.

84. *Manchester Examiner*, 21 January 1884.

85. *London Spectator*, 25 January 1884.

86. *Tablet*, 25 January 1884.

87. Trench, *Road to Khartoum*, 201. Gordon consistently underestimated the Mahdi's power and influence. As late as 5 March 1884, a month after reaching the Sudan, he wrote his sister, "I believe the Mahdi is in a greater fix than I am, for he fears his *own* people, which I do not." *Letters to His Sister*, 5 March 1884.

88. Quoted in Trench, *Road to Khartoum*, 198.

89. Ibid., 199–200.

90. Ibid., 203.

91. Ibid., 200.

92. Baker later wrote, "As soon as I heard Gordon was to go to the Sudan, I knew there would be a fight." Quoted in ibid., 240.

93. Ibid., 213.

94. *London Times*, 31 January 1884.

95. Holt, *Mahdist State*, 92–99.

96. Quoted in ibid., 93.

97. Quoted in Stewart, *Providence and Empire*, 304.

98. Trench, *Road to Khartoum*, 231.

99. Previous two quotes in Douglas H. Johnson, "The Death of Gordon: A Victorian Myth," *Journal of Imperial and Commonwealth History* 10 (1982): 300.

100. Trench, *Road to Khartoum*, 235–36.

101. Ibid., 245.

102. *Pall Mall Gazette*, 14 February 1884.

103. Holt, *Mahdist State*, 97.

104. Trench, *Road to Khartoum*, 244.

105. Ibid., 249–50.

106. *London Times,* 8 May 1884, letter from Baroness Burdett-Coutts.

107. *London Times,* 3 May 1884. See all issues of *Lloyd's* for February 1885.

108. Holt, *Mahdist State,* 99–103.

109. Rudyard Kipling, *The Light That Failed* (New York: United States Book Company, 1890).

110. Green, *Three Empires,* 193.

111. James Morris, *Heaven's Command: An Imperial Progress* (New York: Harcourt Brace, 1973), 512–13. Morris refers here to Rudolf Slatin, *Fire and Sword in the Sudan: A Personal Narrative of Fighting and Serving the Dervishes, 1879–95* (London: Arnold, 1896).

112. Holt, *Mahdist State,* 104.

113. *London Daily Telegraph,* 6 February 1885.

114. *Daily News,* 5 February 1885; *Morning Advertiser,* 5 February 1885.

115. *London Times,* 5 February 1885.

116. *London Daily Chronicle,* 6 February 1885.

117. *London Daily Telegraph,* 9 February 1885; second quote, *Birmingham Gazette,* 6 February 1885.

118. *London Daily Telegraph,* 11 February 1885.

119. *Pall Mall Gazette,* 20 February 1885.

120. *London Morning Advertiser,* 11 February 1885.

121. *London Daily Telegraph,* 11 February 1885.

122. *Pall Mall Gazette,* 20 February 1885.

123. *London Daily News,* 10 February 1885.

124. *London Times,* 11 February 1885.

125. Pick, *Faces of Degeneration.*

126. *London Daily Telegraph,* 11 February 1885.

127. *Liverpool Courier,* 6 February 1885.

128. *Pall Mall Gazette,* 5 February 1885.

129. Green, *Three Empires,* 200.

130. Quoted in ibid., 198–99.

131. Quoted in Strachey, *Eminent Victorians,* 190.

132. *Standard,* 9 February 1885.

133. Quoted in *Pall Mall Gazette,* 16 February 1885.

134. Quoted in ibid.

135. *Manchester Examiner,* 8 February 1885.

136. *Edinburgh Scotsman,* 11 February 1885.

137. *London Daily Telegraph,* 11 February 1885.

138. Field-Marshall Viscount Garnett Wolseley, *In Relief of Gordon: Lord Wolseley's Campaign Journal of the Khartoum Relief Expedition, 1884–85,* ed. A. Preston (London: Hutchinson, 1967), 139–59.

139. Stewart, *Providence and Empire,* 305.

140. *Pall Mall Gazette,* 6 March 1885.

141. MacDonald, *Language of Empire,* 86.

142. Stewart, *Providence and Empire,* 305.

143. Quoted in MacDonald, *Language of Empire,* 85.

144. William MacDonald Sinclair, *Gordon and England* (London: Hatchards, 1885) (sermon preached on 22 February 1885).

145. Weber, *Economy and Society,* 399–401.

146. Sinclair, *Gordon and England.*

147. William Boyd Carpenter, *In Commemoration of the Death of General Gordon* (London: Sheffington and Son, 1899), 1.

148. The letters are conserved in the British Library's Gordon Papers (BLGP), ADD 52404. The dossier consists of a giant folio with hundreds of poems dedicated to Gordon, most handwritten and many anonymous or with signatures like "A working-man." Some of the verses are prefaced with a brief note. All quotations up to the end of this section come from this source.

149. Doreen M. Rosman, *The Evangelicals and Culture* (London: Croon Helm, 1984).

150. Dawson, *Soldier Heroes,* 82–83.

151. Morris, *Farewell the Trumpets,* 28. See also MacKenzie, "Heroic Myths," 125–30. For an earlier example of popular mythmaking, see Helly, *Livingstone's Legacy.*

152. MacKenzie, "Heroic Myths," 129.

153. MacDonald, *Language of Empire,* 94–98. Gordon's family showed little enthusiasm for such public displays. Rather than monuments and statues, Augusta preferred to commemorate her brother by establishing schools for indigent and wayward boys. She wanted Gordon remembered as a Christian philanthropist and mentor to troubled youth. See Taylor, "Gordon of Khartoum."

154. Johnson, "Death of Gordon," 299. The evidence suggests that Gordon was shot while resisting the Mahdist troops who invaded his palace. See also Strachey, *Eminent Victorians,* 188–90.

155. Wingate rewrote and oversaw the publication of two accounts of Gordon's death ostensibly by a pair of Austrian captives of the Mahdi. The two books are Joseph Orhwalder, *Ten Years' Captivity in the Mahdi's Camp* (1892), and Rudolf Slatin Pasha, *Fire and Sword in the Sudan* (1895).

156. Winston S. Churchill, *The River War* (New York: Caroll and Graff, 2000 [1898]), 66.

157. Johnson, "Death of Gordon," 303–4.

158. Ibid.

159. Robinson and Gallagher, *Africa and the Victorians*; Porter, *Lion's Share,* ch. 4.

160. Cromer, quoted in Sanderson, *England, Europe, and the Upper Nile,* 1.

161. *London Times,* 15 October 1889, quoted in Stengers, "L'impérialisme colonial," 488.

162. Michel, *La Mission Marchand*, 20.

163. Holt, *Mahdist State*, chs. 7–12.

4. THE "STANLEY CRAZE"

1. The best book on the EPRE remains Iain R. Smith, *The Emin Pasha Relief Expedition, 1886–1890* (Oxford: Clarendon Press, 1972).

2. The satirical newspaper *Moonshine* may have coined the term "Stanley craze" in its issue of 25 May 1890. The term also appears in Sidney Webb's anti-Stanley pamphlet, *The Stanley Craze: Or, the True Story of the Quest and Rescue of Emin Pasha* (London, 1890).

3. Bierman, *Dark Safari*; McLynn, *Stanley: The Making of an African Explorer*; McLynn, *Stanley: Sorcerer's Apprentice*; Jeal, *Stanley*.

4. W. G. Barttelot, ed., *The Life of Edmund Musgrave Barttelot, from his Letters and Diary* (London: Richard Bentley and Son, 1890); James S. Jameson, *The Story of the Rear Column* (London: John W. Lovell, 1890); John Rose Troup, *With Stanley's Rear Column* (London: Chapman and Hall, 1890).

5. McLynn, *Stanley: Sorcerer's Apprentice*, 350–54.

6. Weber, *Economy and Society*, 458, 1143.

7. Showalter, *Sexual Anarchy*; Leo Braudy, *From Chivalry to Terrorism: War and the Changing Nature of Masculinity* (New York: Knopf, 2003); George L. Mosse, *The Image of Man: The Creation of Modern Masculinity* (New York: Oxford University Press, 1996), 78–82; Tosh, *Manliness and Masculinities*.

8. Venayre, *La gloire de l'aventure*; Showalter, *Sexual Anarchy*, 79ff; Tosh, *Manliness and Masculinities*, 199–201.

9. MacKenzie, "Heroic Myths of Empire"; Frantzen, *Bloody Good*.

10. Davidoff and Hall, *Family Fortunes*; John Tosh, *A Man's Place: Masculinity and the Middle-Class Home in Victorian England* (New Haven: Yale University Press, 1999).

11. Christopher Lasch, *Haven in a Heartless World* (New York: Basic Books, 1977).

12. Mangan, *Games Ethic*, 18.

13. Bierman, *Dark Safari*, 204–10.

14. Felix Driver, "Henry Morton Stanley and His Critics: Geography, Exploration and Empire," *Past & Present* 133 (November 1991): 138.

15. Tosh, *Manliness and Masculinities*, 112–13.

16. On degeneration, see Pick, *Faces of Degeneration*. On masculine decline, see Showalter, *Sexual Anarchy*; Tosh, *Manliness and Masculinities*.

17. Quoted in Smith, *Emin Pasha Relief Expedition*, 13.

18. On the phenomenon in an earlier period of crossing over, see Linda Colley, "Going Native, Telling Tales: Captivity, Collaborations, and Empire," *Past*

and Present 168 (August 2000): 170–93. On sexuality and "going native," see Stoler, *Carnal Knowledge.*

19. Smith, *Emin Pasha Relief Expedition,* 3.

20. Richard Gray, *A History of the Southern Sudan, 1839–1889* (London: Oxford University Press, 1961), 140–44.

21. Smith, *Emin Pasha Relief Expedition,* ch. 3.

22. Quoted in ibid., 45.

23. Green, *Three Empires,* 200.

24. On Mackinnon, see John S. Galbraith, *Mackinnon and East Africa* (Cambridge: Cambridge University Press, 1976).

25. Roger T. Anstey, *Britain and the Congo in the 19th Century* (Oxford: Oxford University Press, 1962).

26. Smith, *Emin Pasha Relief Expedition,* 55.

27. *England, Europe, and the Upper Nile,* 33; Smith, *Emin Pasha Relief Expedition,* 59.

28. Smith, *Emin Pasha Relief Expedition,* 64.

29. Ibid., 87. In Africa, Stanley added Herbert Ward to his officer corps.

30. Tipp, *L'Autobiographie.*

31. François Renault, *Tippo Tip: Un potentat arabe en Afrique central au XIXe siècle* (Paris: Société française d'histoire d'outre-mer, 1987), 8–14. See also R. P. P. Ceulemans, *La question arabe et le Congo, 1883–1892* (Brussels: Académie royale des sciences d'outre-mer, 1959).

32. Smith, *Emin Pasha Relief Expedition,* 99–101. Renault's title calls Tippu Tip a "*potentat arabe.*"

33. Henry M. Stanley, *Through the Dark Continent,* 2 vols. (New York: Dover, 1988 [1878]), 2:74.

34. McLynn, *Stanley,* 2:146; Bierman, *Dark Safari,* 265.

35. Driver, "Stanley and His Critics"; Bierman, *Dark Safari,* 269; McLynn, *Stanley,* 2:149.

36. Smith, *Emin Pasha Relief Expedition,* 111–13; Barttelot, *Letters and Diary,* 90–91; Jameson, *Story of the Rear Column,* 24–26.

37. Jameson, *Story of the Rear Column,* 58–59.

38. Quoted in Smith, *Emin Pasha Relief Expedition,* 115.

39. Barttelot, *Letters and Diary,* 79, 121.

40. Adam Hochschild, *King Leopold's Ghost. A Story of Greed, Terror, and Heroism in Colonial Africa* (Boston: Houghton Mifflin, 1998).

41. The letter is included as appendix 2 of Jameson's *Story of the Rear Column,* 378–81.

42. Smith, *Emin Pasha Relief Expedition,* 122.

43. Jameson, *Story of the Relief Column,* 75.

44. Quoted in Bierman, *Dark Safari,* 275.

45. Smith, *Emin Pasha Relief Expedition,* 179.

46. Ibid., 126.

47. A. J. Mounteney-Jephson, manuscript diary, quoted in ibid., 128.

48. Quoted in William Stairs, *African Exploits: The Diaries of William Stairs, 1887–1892,* ed. Roy Maclaren (Montreal: McGill-Queen's University Press, 1998), 109.

49. Thomas Heazle Parke, *My Personal Experiences in Equatorial Africa* (New York: Scribners, 1891), 345.

50. Quoted in McLynn, *Stanley,* 2:203.

51. Quoted in ibid., 2:154.

52. Smith, *Emin Pasha Relief Expedition,* 168–69, 261–65.

53. Henry M. Stanley, *In Darkest Africa,* 2 vols. (Santa Barbara: Narrative Press, 2001 [1890]), 1:444.

54. Ibid., 1:445. On Ward, see note 29.

55. Parke, *Personal Experiences,* 335.

56. Smith, *Emin Pasha Relief Expedition,* ch. 9; McLynn, *Stanley: Sorcerer's Apprentice,* 261.

57. Smith, *Emin Pasha Relief Expedition,* 266.

58. McLynn, *Stanley: Sorcerer's Apprentice,* 317.

59. Quoted in Driver, "Stanley and His Critics," 158.

60. Quoted in Hall, *Stanley,* 49.

61. *London Spectator,* 28 September 1888.

62. *Truth,* 11 April 1889.

63. *Morning Post,* 28 April 1890.

64. *Daily Chronicle,* 26 November 1889.

65. *Leeds Mercury,* 15 April 1990.

66. Ibid.

67. *London Times,* 28 April 1890.

68. *Saturday Review,* 30 November 1889; *Leeds Mercury,* 15 April 1889; *Morning Post,* 28 April 1890.

69. *London Daily Telegraph,* 28 April 1890.

70. *Morning Post,* 28 April 1890.

71. Gregory Shaya, "The Flaneur, the Badaud, and the Making of a Mass Public in France, circa 1860–1910," *American Historical Review* 109, no. 1 (February 2004): 41–77.

72. *Morning Post,* 28 April 1890.

73. *London Daily Chronicle,* 28 April 1890.

74. *Morning Post,* 28 April 1890.

75. *London Times,* 28 April 1890.

76. See the thousands of letters collected in MRAC, Stanley Archives, especially files 3393–3750.

77. As the *Times* (28 April 1890) wrote, "For once . . . the season will have a real hero for its lion."

78. *Illustrated London News,* 10 May 1890.

79. Press book, 3 May 1890, MRAC, Stanley Archives, file 5362.

80. *London Times,* 3 May 1890.

81. *Illustrated London News,* 10 May 1890; *Daily Telegraph,* 3 May 1890.

82. Ibid.

83. MRAC, Stanley Archives, files 3393–3750.

84. These talks did not bear fruit until 1898, because, at the time, Stanley was still an American citizen and thus ineligible for the honor the queen had in mind. See Bierman, *Dark Safari,* 335.

85. *London Daily Telegraph,* 14 May 1890.

86. Montagu Butler, Trinity College, Cambridge, to Stanley, 26 April 1890, MRAC, Stanley Archives, file 3493.

87. *London Daily Telegraph,* 14 May 1890.

88. *Self Help* (London: Murray, 1858).

89. Reported in *Gentlewoman,* 12 July 1890.

90. *Pall Mall Gazette,* 9 June 1890.

91. This menu is included in the volume of press clippings in MRAC, Stanley Archives, file 5362.

92. *Illustrated London News,* 7 December 1889 and 8 February 1890.

93. *Pall Mall Budget,* 20 February 1890.

94. *Graphic,* 30 April 1890.

95. *Graphic,* 7 May 1890.

96. De Winton to Stanley, 12 March 1890, MRAC, Stanley Archives, file 3438.

97. De Winton to Stanley, 13 February 1890, ibid., file 3418.

98. Moberly Bell to Stanley, 26 March 1890, ibid., file 3446.

99. London: Sampson, Low, Marston, Searle and Rivington, 1890.

100. Marston, *How Stanley Wrote "In Darkest Africa,"* 13.

101. Ibid., 51.

102. Ibid., 73.

103. Ibid., 63.

104. *World,* 16 July 1890; E. H. Hunt, "Industrialism and Regional Inequality: Wages in Britain, 1760–1914," *Journal of Economic History* 46, no. 4 (December 1986): 964.

105. For sales figures, see the journal *Oracle,* 12 July 1890; McLynn, *Stanley,* 2:327.

106. See, for example, the huge article in *Le Monde illustré,* 14 July 1890. See also Marston, *How Stanley Wrote "In Darkest Africa,"* 71.

107. "The New-found World and Its Hero," *Blackwood's Magazine* 233 (August 1890): 35.

108. Ibid., 246.

109. Ibid., 250.

110. *London Times,* June 28, 1890.

111. *Westminster Review* 134, no.2 (August 1890): 119. On muscular Christianity, see Mosse, *Image of Man,* 49–50.

112. *Queen, the Lady's Newspaper,* 8 February 1890.

113. Stanley's journal, 6 March 1889, quoted in McLynn, *Stanley: Sorcerer's Apprentice,* 271.

114. *London Times,* 28 June 1890.

115. See, for example, Bierman, *Dark Safari,* 248–49; McLynn, *Stanley,* 2:118–20. For a thorough examination of Stanley's (homo)sexuality, see Aldrich, *Colonialism and Homosexuality,* esp. 36–47.

116. See the narrative of their courtship, such as it was, in McLynn, *Stanley,* 2:328–32.

117. *Pall Mall Gazette,* 17 May 1890.

118. *Scotsman,* 14 July 1890.

119. *Westminster Review* 134, no. 2 (August 1890): 118. On Rider Haggard and Stanley, see also *Spectator,* 10 May 1890.

120. *Globe,* 26 June 1890.

121. MRAC, Stanley Archives, files 2264–2452.

122. McLynn, *Stanley,* 2:332.

123. *Lady's Pictorial,* 5 June 1890.

124. Ibid., 2 July 1890.

125. *Society,* 19 July 1890; *Lloyd's,* 13 July 1890; *Dundee Advertiser,* 14 July 1890; *Scottish Leader,* 14 July 1890.

126. *Aberdeen Free Press,* 14 July 1890.

127. *Country Gentlemen,* 19 July 1890.

128. *Scotsman,* 14 July 1890.

129. *Pall Mall Gazette,* 12 July 1890.

130. *Evening Sun,* 13 July 1890. On the idea of "intimacy at a distance," see Thompson, *The Media and Modernity.*

131. *Scotsman,* 14 July 1890.

132. Mont to Stanley, 25 March 1890, MRAC, Stanley Archives, file 3445.

133. T. Burt to Dorothy Tennant, 28 May 1890, ibid., 2290.

134. Burcombe to Stanley, 3 July 1890, ibid., 2306.

135. General Garnet Wolseley to Stanley, 10 July 1890; Frederick Ellis to Stanley, 27 May 1890, ibid., 3712, 2289.

136. Emma Cecilia Thursley to Stanley, 16 January 1890, ibid., 3399.

137. B. Threlfall Vickers to Stanley, 26 April 1890, ibid., 3504.

138. Roland H. Blades to Stanley, 27 March 1890, ibid., 3447.

139. Amy Skirm to Stanley, 27 April 1890, ibid., 3511.

140. Quoted in Marston, *How Stanley Wrote "In Darkest Africa,"* 53.

141. Hans and Carry Luthy to Stanley, 26 May 1890, MRAC, Stanley Archives, file 2288.

142. Viles to Stanley, 28 April 1890, ibid., 3521.

143. Quoted in Marston, *How Stanley Wrote "In Darkest Africa,"* 53.

144. Nellie Lumley to Stanley, 20 May 1890, MRAC, Stanley Archives, file 2279.

145. *London Daily Telegraph,* 13 June 1890.

146. Stanley, "Personal Journal of the Emin Pasha Relief Expedition," December 1886–9 April 1890, MRAC, Stanley Archives, file 64. Stanley made these comments in mid-January 1890.

147. Peter Loewenberg, *Decoding the Past* (New York: Knopf, 1982), 54.

148. Stanley, "Personal Journal."

149. Quoted in Hall, *Stanley,* 18.

150. Stanley, "Personal Journal."

151. Ibid.

152. All quotations in this paragraph in ibid.

153. Leo Braudy, in *The Frenzy of Renown*, pays considerable attention to this phenomenon.

154. John B. Thompson, in *The Media and Modernity,* downplays to some extent the disappointments inherent in "intimacy at a distance" (207–8, 219–25).

155. Stanley, "Personal Journal."

156. MRAC, Stanley Archives, files, 5357–5366.

157. *Pall Mall Gazette,* 12 July 1890.

158. Braudy took the title of his book from Matthew G. Lewis, whose novel *The Monk* (1796) referred to a new post-Revolutionary "frenzy of renown." Braudy, *Frenzy of Renown,* 14.

159. *Pall Mall Gazette,* 3 May 1890.

160. *Moonshine,* 25 May 1890; *Truth,* 17 July 1890.

161. *Punch,* 12 June 1890.

162. "The Stanley Scandal" was a headline published in the *Scotsman,* 17 November 1890.

163. Jeal, Stanley's most recent biographer, is a notable exception. His portrait of the explorer is largely favorable.

164. John Rose Troup, in *With Stanley's Rear Column,* vii–ix, discusses this contract and the special agreement he had negotiated with Stanley about his own book.

165. On scandals as media and political phenomena, see Damien de Blic and Cyril Lemieux, "Le scandale comme épreuve," *Politix* 71 (September 2005): 9–38; John B. Thompson, *Political Scandal: Power and Visibility in the Media Age* (Cambridge, UK: Polity Press, 2000); and Eric de Dampierre, "Thèmes pour l'étude du scandal," *Annales ESC* 9 (1954): 328–36.

166. *Times, Daily Telegraph, Daily News, Pall Mall Gazette, Morning Post, Daily Chronicle,* 7 November 1890; *Times, Daily Graphic, Scotsman,* 10 November 1890.

167. Stanley, "Personal Journal," entry for 23 October 1890.

168. The *London Times* and other papers, 8 and 10 November 1890.

169. *Times,* 14 November 1890.

170. *Globe,* 15 November 1890.

171. *Speaker,* 22 November 1890.

172. Stanley, "Personal Journal," entries for 1, 12, 18, and 25 May 1891.

173. Bierman, *Dark Safari,* 341.

174. Stanley, "Personal Journal," 17 March 1891.

175. On Stanley's election and his brief and relatively undistinguished role in conservative politics, see Windscheffel, *Popular Conservatism.*

176. On this point and the question of "sub-imperialism" in general, see Darwin, "Imperialism and the Victorians," 638. See also Galbraith, *Mackinnon.*

5. JEAN-BAPTISTE MARCHAND, FASHODA, AND THE DREYFUS AFFAIR

1. *L'Aurore,* 29 May 1899, called the week of 29 May 1899 *la semaine sanglante.* This is, of course, the same label given to the final, murderous week of the Paris Commune.

2. Ruth Harris, *Dreyfus: Politics, Emotion, and the Scandal of the Century* (New York: Henry Holt, 2010).

3. *L'Intransigeant,* 2 June 1899.

4. Quoted in Jean-Denis Bredin, *The Affair: The Case of Alfred Dreyfus,* trans. Jeffrey Mehlman (New York: George Braziller, 1986), 383.

5. Ibid., 385–86.

6. Archives Nationales, Pantheon, Mi 25350, dossier Marchand 1899–1915, Renseignements généraux, 27 May 1899; Archives de la Prefecture de Police, Serie B/A, dossier Marchand.

7. This is not, of course, to say that Marchand's image single-handedly saved the regime. The new prime minister, René Waldeck-Rousseau, who took office in late June 1899, proved resolute in dismissing the generals overly complicit in the campaign against Dreyfus; in prosecuting right-wing extremists who agitated against the regime; and in bringing certain politicized religious orders to heel. Even so, when Alfred Dreyfus came before a newly constituted military court in August and September 1899, he was convicted anew, albeit with "extenuating circumstances." The conviction might have rent the country once again; instead, most French men and women seemed to put the affair behind them with unexpected dispatch. See Bredin, *The Affair,* 390–451.

8. For narratives of Marchand's expedition, see Michel, *La Mission Marchand;* Lewis, *Race to Fashoda;* A. Baratier, *Souvenirs de la Mission Marchand,* 3 vols. (Paris: Fayard and Grasset, 1914–41).

9. Charles Castellani, "De Courbevoie à Bangui avec la Mission Marchand," *L'Illustration,* 22, 29 January; 12, 19, 26 February; 5, 19 March; 2 April 1898.

10. Charles Castellani, *Marchand L'Africain* (Paris: Flammarion, 1902), 332.

11. *La Patrie,* 18 October 1898.

12. Malcolm Carroll, *French Public Opinion and Foreign Affairs, 1870–1914* (New York: Century, 1931), 174.

13. *L'Aurore,* 25 October 1898.

14. *Petit parisien,* 23 September 1898.

15. Schivelbusch, *Culture of Defeat.* Schivelbusch argues that the culture of defeat enabled the French to "work through" the trauma of their military defeat. But in Freudian terms, the process of "working through" represents a healthy effort to come to terms with the trauma, to accept it, learn from it, and heal its wounds. My argument here is that many French commentators erected emotional defenses against the trauma of defeat rather working through it in ways that might have enabled them to give their country better guidance in the future. See George E. Vaillant, *Ego Mechanisms of Defense: A Guide for Clinicians and Researchers* (New York: American Psychoanalytical Association, 1992).

16. In the early 1890s, a huge political scandal rocked the Republic when journalists, mostly on the nationalist Right, revealed that dozens of republican politicians had taken bribes from shady financiers trying to raise money for the Panama Canal. Shortly afterwards, anarchists began a series of bombings and other attacks that culminated in the assassination of President Sadi Carnot in 1894.

17. Christian Amalvi, *De l'art et la manière d'accommoder les héros de l'histoire de France: Essais de mythologie nationale* (Paris: Albin Michel, 1988); Amalvi, *Les héros de l'histoire de France: Recherche iconographique sur le panthéon scolaire de la Troisième République* (Paris: Éditions Phot'œil, 1979); Schwartz, *Spectacular Realities*; Venita Datta, "'L'appel au soldat': Visions of the Napoleonic Legend in Popular Culture of the Belle Epoque," *French Historical Studies* 28, no. 1 (Winter 2005): 1–30.

18. Gerd Krumeich, *Jeanne d'Arc in der Geschichte: Historiographie, Politik, Kultur,* quoted in Schivelbusch, *Culture of Defeat,* 340n78.

19. Schivelbusch, *Culture of Defeat,* 141. The bipartisan interest of the early Third Republic would not last. As memories of the war receded in the 1880s and '90s, the Left largely abandoned her, while the Right embraced her. The image of Napoleon also gravitated to the right during these years. See Agulhon, *Marianne au combat*; Datta, "L'appel au soldat," 15. Nationalist writer Maurice Barrès, in particular, glorified Napoleon, the "virile hero" as antidote to a "dissociated," "decerebrated," and "feminized" France.

20. Few French leaders actually believed it would be politically or militarily possible to win a new war against Germany in the near future. Revanche was, above all, a tool of domestic politics. See Steven Englund, *Nation-Talk: The Political Significance of the "Nation" in French History,* unpublished manuscript in author's possession, ch. 2; Schivelbusch, *Culture of Defeat,* 147ff.

21. Quoted in Schivelbusch, *Culture of Defeat,* 142–43.

22. On Vercingetorix, see André Simon, *Vercingétorix, héros républicain* (Paris: Ramsay, 1996).

23. Keith Baker, *Inventing the French Revolution* (New York: Cambridge University Press, 1990), ch. 2.

24. As many historians have shown, the leaders of the Third Republic took this lesson to heart. They set out to imitate aspects of German culture and institutions believed to have contributed to their (momentary) military superiority. See Allan Mitchell, *The German Influence in France after 1870: The Formation of the French Republic* (Chapel Hill: University of North Carolina Press, 1979); Claude Digeon, *La Crise allemande de la pensée française, 1870–1914* (Paris, Presses universitaires de France, 1959).

25. ANOM, M42, M43, M44; ANOM Série Afrique III, 32–35; Bibliothèque de l'Institut, Fonds Terrier, IA CXXXIII (5891–6023); Marc Michel, "Deux lettres de Marchand à Liotard," *Revue française d'histoire d'outre-mer* 52 (1965): 41–91; M. A. Menier, "Une lettre inédite de Marchand à Gentil: La marche française vers le Nil et le Tchad en avril 1897," *Revue d'histoire des colonies* 40 (1953): 431–42.

26. There is no scholarly account of Marchand's life. The best portrait of him is buried in the middle of Michel, *Mission Marchand*, 66–70. See Jacques Delebecque, *Vie du général Marchand* (Paris: Hachette, 1937). Other biographies include Pierre Croidys, *Marchand, le héros de Fachoda* (Paris: Editions des Loisirs, 1942); Castellani, *Marchand l'Africain*.

27. Venayre, *La gloire de l'aventure,* chs. 1–2.

28. Delebecque, *Vie du général Marchand,* 11; Croidys, *Marchand,* 11.

29. Raoul Girardet, *La Société militaire de 1815 à nos jours* (Paris: Perrin, 1998), ch. 8; Hubert Lyautey, "Du rôle social de l'officier," *Revue des deux mondes* 140 (15 March 1891): 443–59.

30. See ch. 3, this volume. Kanya-Forstner, *Conquest of the Western Sudan.*

31. Lewis, *Race to Fashoda,* 79.

32. Quoted in ibid.

33. Jacques Thobie and Gilbert Meynier, *Histoire de la France coloniale*, vol. 2, *L'apogée* (Paris: A. Colin, 1991), 152.

34. Michel, *Mission Marchand,* 67.

35. Quoted in Lewis, *Race to Fashoda,* 83.

36. Venita Datta, *Birth of a National Icon: The Literary Avant-Garde and the Origins of the Intellectual in France* (Albany: State University of New York Press, 1999), 149.

37. Gil Mihealy, "Virility and Authority: Army and Masculinity in France from the Restoration to the Third Republic," paper presented at Society for French Historical Studies annual meeting, Stanford, CA, March 18, 2005. Mihealy argues that during the Restoration, military men began to sport moustaches as a sign of virility. By the Third Republic the moustache had became such a powerful symbol of masculinity that virtually all men wanted to wear

them, even those in "servile" professions such as waiters, who had been forbidden to grow them.

38. Léon Daudet, *Salons et journaux: Souvenirs 1880–1908* (Paris: Nouvelle librairie nationale, 1917), 182–83.

39. Ibid., 188–89, 196–98.

40. Quoted in Lewis, *Race to Fashoda*, 159.

41. On Barrès, see Datta, *Birth*, 159. See also Maugue, *L'Identité masculine en crise*.

42. Datta, *Birth*, 159–64; Berenson, *Trial of Madame Caillaux*, ch. 5; Nye, *Masculinity and Male Codes of Honor*.

43. Castellani, *Marchand*, 323. Boulanger was a French general and minister of war who briefly placed himself at the head of a militant right-wing movement in the late 1880s. He contemplated a coup d'état in early 1889, but his failure to act decisively led to an indictment for treason and exile from the country. Two years later, he committed suicide on his mistress's grave. See Bertrand Joly, *Nationalistes et conservateurs en France* (Paris: Les Indes savants, 2008), 13–116; Joly, *Déroulède*, ch. 6; William D. Irvine, *The Boulanger Affair Reconsidered: Royalism, Boulangism, and the Origins of the Radical Right in France* (New York: Oxford University Press, 1989).

44. Roger Glenn Brown, *Fashoda Reconsidered: The Impact of Domestic Politics on French Policy in Africa, 1893–1898* (Baltimore: Johns Hopkins University Press, 1969), 38.

45. Michel, "Deux lettres," 51.

46. The two most thorough treatments of the political and diplomatic history surrounding Fashoda disagree over the role of Gabriel Hanotaux. G. N. Sanderson, in *England, Europe and the Upper Nile*, 273, finds him generally opposed to Marchand's expedition to the Nile but outmaneuvered by the captain's friends and supporters in the government. Michel, in *Mission Marchand*, ch. 3, considers Hanotaux much more favorable to Marchand's project and willing to allow him to undertake it. Michel's evidence seems more thorough and more convincing.

47. Quoted in Sanderson, *England, Europe and the Upper Nile*, 214.

48. Quoted in ibid., 217.

49. Ibid., 214–24.

50. Van Orman, *The Explorers*.

51. Sanderson, "Contributions from African Sources."

52. Sanderson, *England, Europe and the Upper Nile*, 1; Michel, *Mission Marchand*, 57.

53. Michel, *Mission Marchand*, 59.

54. The *Petit parisien* was particularly Anglophobic in the 1890s, running regular editorials condemning the "barbarism" of British colonialism. See, for example, the issues of 29 July 1892, and 6 May 1893. See also Brown, *Fashoda*

Reconsidered, 121; Michel, *Mission Marchand*, 21–25; and Alan Pitt, "A Changing Anglo-Saxon Myth: Its Development and Function in French Political Thought, 1860–1914," *French History* 14, no. 2 (2000): 150–73.

55. *L'Autorité*, 10 December 1898, quoted in Carroll, *French Public Opinion*, 178.

56. Schivelbusch, *Culture of Defeat*, 185–86.

57. *Le Petit parisien*, 18 November 1897.

58. Quoted in Michel, *Mission Marchand*, 58. Englund, *Napoleon*.

59. Michel, *Mission Marchand*, 58.

60. On this point, Sanderson writes: "Behind this policy there was little rational calculation. It rested rather on a quite irrational conviction that a successful expedition to the Upper Nile *must* [italics in original] somehow lead to a favorable solution of the Egypt question." *England, Europe and the Upper Nile*, 391.

61. Maurice Barrès, *Scenes et doctrines du nationalisme* (Paris: Emile Paul, 1902), 369.

62. Michel, *Mission Marchand*, 102–16; Lewis, *Race to Fashoda*, ch. 7. Lewis reveals the resistance and suffering of the Bateke people, which Castellani and most contemporary newspaper accounts ignored. Brazza objected to Marchand's brutal tactics; shortly afterward, he was dismissed as colonial governor of the Congo.

63. Michel, *Mission Marchand*; Baratier, *A travers l'Afrique* (Paris: Fayard, 1900); J. M. Emily, *Mission Marchand: Journal de route* (Paris: Hachette, 1912).

64. Lewis, *Race to Fashoda*, 171–2; Joseph Conrad, *The Heart of Darkness* (New York: Barnes and Noble, 1994).

65. T. W. Riker, "A Survey of British Policy in the Fashoda Crisis," *Political Science Quarterly* 44, no. 1 (March 1929): 59.

66. Churchill, *The River War*, 273; George W. Steevens, *With Kitchener to Khartum* (New York: Dodd, Mead, 1899), 263–64.

67. *London Daily Mail*, 10 September 1898.

68. Brown, *Fashoda Reconsidered*, ch. 7.

69. Ibid., 8.

70. Eric Cahm, *The Dreyfus Affair in French Society and Politics* (New York: Longman, 1966), 125–29.

71. Michel, *Mission Marchand*, 222; Bertrand Joly, *Dictionnaire biographique et géographique du nationalisme français (1880–1900)* (Paris: Honoré Champion, 1998), 225–26.

72. Michel, *Mission Marchand*, 215; Sanderson, *England, Europe and the Upper Nile*, ch. 15.

73. Brown, *Fashoda Reconsidered*, 99–100.

74. Ibid., 113; Robinson and Gallagher, *Africa and the Victorians*, 373.

75. Quoted in *La politique coloniale*, 14 October 1898.

76. Quoted in ibid., 110.

77. Sanderson, "Origins and Significance," 304–5, 323.

78. Michael B. Palmer, "The British Press and International News, 1851–99: Of Agencies and Newspapers," in Boyce, Curran, and Wingate, *Newspaper History*, 218.

79. *Le Petit parisien*, 7 November 1898.

80. Palmer, *Des petits journaux*, 307n152.

81. Ambassador Geoffray, quoted in ibid., 197.

82. Ibid., 198.

83. Kennedy Jones, *Fleet Street and Downing Street*, quoted in ibid., 201.

84. Ibid., 307n159.

85. *London Daily Mail*, 6 October 1898.

86. Ibid., 10 October 1898.

87. Rachel Arié, "L'Opinion publique en France et l'Affaire de Fachoda," *Revue d'histoire des colonies* 41 (1954): 348–49.

88. *London Evening News*, 13 September 1898.

89. *Spectator*, 1 October 1898.

90. *Le Temps*, 6 October 1898.

91. *Depêche de Toulouse*, 24 October 1898.

92. Arié, "L'Opinion publique," 350.

93. *L'Intransigeant*, 22 October 1898; *La Patrie*, 22 October 1898.

94. *Revue du monde catholique*, October 1898; Carroll, *French Public Opinion*, 174.

95. Datta, *Birth*, 152–64.

96. Sanderson, *England, Europe and the Upper Nile*, 349.

97. MacKenzie, "Heroic Myths of Empire," 109.

98. On common sense, see Sophia Rosenfeld, "Before Democracy: The Production and Uses of Common Sense," *Journal of Modern History* 80, no. 1 (March 2008): 1–54.

99. Sanderson, "Origins and Significance," 292.

100. Archives Nationales, Pantheon, Mi 25350, dossier Marchand 1899–1915, 16 May 1899.

101. Joly, *Déroulède*, 304. The quotation is from the nationalist poet François Coppée.

102. Archives Nationales, Pantheon, Mi 25350, dossier Marchand, renseignements généraux, 27 May 1899. This file contains all the secret police reports on Marchand, especially numerous during the summer and fall of 1899.

103. Commissaire spécial de Marseille to Minister of the Interior, 30 May 1898, ibid.

104. Commissaire spécial, Toulon, to Minister of the Interior, 19 May 1899, ibid.

105. Commissaire spécial to Prefect of the Vosges, 31 May 1898, ibid.

106. Datta, *Birth;* Forth, *Dreyfus Affair and the Crisis of French Manhood.*

107. Besides that in *La Libre parole,* many other versions of this narrative appeared in the French press of this time. See, for example, *Le Monde illustré,* 30 May 1899; *Le Gaulois,* 2 June 1899.

108. See, for example, *L'Intransigeant,* 1 June 1899, and *Le Petit journal,* 2 June 1899.

109. *Le Matin,* 2 June 1899.

110. Ibid.

111. My thanks to Willa Silverman for providing this reference: Henri Vever Papers, archives of the Freer and Sackler Gallery, Washington, DC.

112. Michel, *Mission Marchand,* 240.

113. *Le Matin,* 2 June 1899.

114. Ibid.

115. *Le Figaro,* 28 May 1899.

116. *Le Journal,* 1 June 1899.

117. Ibid., 2 June 1899.

118. Girardet, *L'Idée coloniale,* 77–107.

119. *L'Aurore,* 29 May 1899.

120. Quoted in Michel, *Mission Marchand,* 240.

121. Ibid., 241.

122. Ibid.

6. BRAZZA AND THE SCANDAL OF THE CONGO

1. *Petit parisien* (hereinafter *PP*), 15 February 1905.

2. *Le Matin,* 16 February 1905.

3. Ibid.

4. *Le Matin,* 16 February 1905. Like most faits divers, the Toqué story, as reported, differed significantly from what had actually happened, although a more accurate account does little to exculpate the French colonial agents. The man blown up with dynamite was an individual accused of murder—probably falsely—and already in custody. The stick of dynamite was attached to his back, not placed in his anus. As for the individual whose head was boiled into a "soup," he was already dead. The events in question took place in 1903, not 1904. They belonged to no July 14th celebration, and no Europeans other than Toqué and Gaud were involved. It was the latter who did the dirty deed. Toqué, in bed with malarial fever, told Gaud "to do what he wanted" with Pakpa; he did not order Gaud to blow the man up. See *L'Humanité,* 17 February 1905; Félicien Challaye, *Le Congo français* (Paris: Felix Alcan, 1909), 108–44; Georges Toqué, *Les massacres du Congo* (Paris: L'Harmattan, 1996 [1907]), 109–10; Rémi Fabre, "Gustave Rouanet et les obscures espérances: Les socialistes et l'affaire du Congo 1905–1906," in Vincent Duclert, Rémi Fabre, and Patrick Fridenson,

eds., *Avenirs et avant-gardes en France, XIXe-XXe siècle: Hommage à Madeleine Rebérioux* (Paris: La Découverte, 1999).

5. On the fait divers, see Ambroise-Rendu, *Petits récits des désordres ordinaries*; Thérenty, *La littérature au quotidien*, 269–92; Georges Auchair, *Le mana quotidian: Structures et functions de la chronique des faits divers* (Paris: Editions anthropos, 1982); Perrot, "Fait divers et histoire au XIXe siècle"; Roland Barthes, "Structure du fait divers," in *Essais critiques* (Paris: Seuil, 1964).

6. Kalifa, *L'encre et le sang*.

7. Thérenty, *Littérature*, 90–152.

8. *PP*, 16 February 1905.

9. On scandals as media and political phenomena, see Blic and Lemieux, "Le scandale comme épreuve"; Thompson, *Political Scandal*; Dampierre, "Thèmes pour l'étude du scandal"; and James Lull and Stephen Hinerman, *Media Scandals: Morality and Desire in the Popular Culture Marketplace* (New York: Columbia University Press, 1997).

10. The press's revelations that more than one hundred French politicians had taken bribes to disguise the impending bankruptcy of the Panama Canal Company produced a scandal whose consequences changed the balance of power in France. It boosted anti-Semitism, weakened the republic, and leant credibility to extremists of the nationalist right, as large numbers of elected officials found themselves accused of violating the public trust. Panama opened the way to the Dreyfus Affair, a scandal that threatened to rock the very foundations of the French Republic. In this case, a scandal became an "affair" once a number of prominent people and widely read newspapers began to dispute the accusations against the French army captain accused of treason. In the Caillaux Affair, a scandal that began with a former prime minister's adultery and ended with accusations of murder against his wife, existing conceptions of masculinity and femininity were reaffirmed. So were prevailing ideas about sexual transgression and the relationship between politics and personal life. Damien de Blic, "Moraliser l'argent: Ce que Panama a changé dans la société française (1889–1897)," *Politix* 71 (September 2005): 61–82; De Blic and Lemieux, "Le scandale," 14–16; Berenson, *Trial of Madame Caillaux*.

11. E. D. Morel, *King Leopold's Rule in Africa* (London: Heinemann, 1904); Morel, *The British Case in the French Congo* (London: Heinemann, 1903); Pierre Mille, *Le Congo léopoldien* (Paris: Cahiers de la quinzaine, 1905); Hochschild, *King Leopold's Ghost*.

12. Conklin, *Mission to Civilize*; Girardet, *L'Idée coloniale*.

13. *PP*, 17 February 1905.

14. *PP*, 19 February 1905. In Central Africa all goods had to be carried by human porters because pack animals could not survive the diseases born by insects common to the region. There were no roads as yet for automobiles.

15. Given this campaign and the extraordinary difficulty of containing such a sensational story, it is extremely unlikely that Henri Brunschwig is correct in arguing that the French government either orchestrated the press campaign or was happy to see it unfold. The government's objective, Brunschwig maintained, was to persuade a parliament always stingy when it came to colonial credits to approve a sizable loan for its financially strapped Congo territory. Politicians would do so, Brunschwig claimed, only under pressure from a press campaign that revealed problems and called for reform. It is difficult, however, to believe that politicians who had been exposed to the mass press since the 1870s and had lived through the media storms over the Panama bribery scandal and the Dreyfus Affair could have thought they could control a story as juicy as the one surrounding Congo atrocities. See Henri Brunschwig, "Brazza et le scandale du Congo français (1904–1906)," *Bulletin des séances de l'académie Royale des sciences d'outre-mer* 23 (1977): 112–29. See also Jürgen Markstahler, *Die franzosiche Kongo-Affare 1905/1906: Ein Mittel in der imperialistischen Konkurrenz der Kolonialmachte* (Stuttgart: Franz Steiner, 1986).

16. *PP,* 17 February 1905.

17. *Le Matin,* 21 February 1905.

18. *PP,* 17 February 1905.

19. *PP,* 20 February 1905.

20. Brunschwig, "Brazza et le scandale," 115–16.

21. Ibid., 116.

22. Among other things, the Entente Cordiale resolved most outstanding Franco-British colonial conflicts. The French agreed to recognize British hegemony over Egypt, and Britain acknowledged France's paramount role in most of Morocco, leaving the rest of the country to Spain.

23. S. J. S. Cookey, "The Concession Policy in the French Congo and the British Reaction, 1898–1906," *Journal of African History* 7, no. 2 (1966): 263–64.

24. On Morel, see William Roger Louis and Jean Stengers, eds., *E. D. Morel's History of the Congo Reform Movement* (Oxford: Clarendon Press, 1968).

25. Quoted in Cookey, "Concession Policy," 266.

26. Brunschwig, "Brazza et le scandale," 117ff.

27. Martin, *Savorgnan de Brazza,* 193.

28. Autin, *Brazza,* 210–17.

29. Ibid., 218.

30. Ibid., 217.

31. On "revanche," see Bertrand Joly, "La France et la Revanche (1871–1914)," *Revue d'histoire moderne et contemporaine* 46 (April–June, 1999): 325–47.

32. *La Croix,* 17 April 1897.

33. Michel, *Mission Marchand,* 109; Autin, *Brazza,* 201–6.

34. *Le XIXe siècle,* 5 October 1897.

35. Catherine Coquery-Vidrovitch, "Les idées économiques de Brazza et les premières tentatives de compagnies de colonisation au Congo français, 1885–1898," *Cahiers d'études Africaines* 5, no. 1 (1965): 57–82; Coquery-Vidrovitch, *Le Congo au temps des grandes compagnies concessionnaires* (Paris: Mouton, 1972).

36. *PP*, 13 March 1905. For similar comments, see *PP, supplement illustré*, 19 March 1905; *Les Hommes du jour*, 1 April 1905.

37. *PP*, 23 September 1905.

38. Interview with Emile Clémentel, minister of colonies, *PP*, 2 March 1905.

39. All quotations in the paragraph are from Brunschwig, "Brazza et le scandale," 119–20. These are excerpts of letters written to Gentil and collected in the commissaire-général's papers, ANOM, PA 25, Papiers Gentil.

40. Challaye collected these newspaper articles, plus other material, in a book, *Le Congo français: La question internationale* (Paris: Alcan, 1909).

41. Brunschwig, "Brazza et le scandale," 121–22.

42. Ibid.

43. West, *Brazza of the Congo*, 177.

44. Jules Saintoyant, *L'Affaire du Congo 1905* (Paris: Editions Epi, 1960); Toqué, *Les massacres du Congo*.

45. Coquery-Vidrovitch, in *Compagnies concessionaires*, lists the ten members plus Brazza and his wife (172n2).

46. Challaye, *Congo français*, 13.

47. Ibid., 18.

48. Augouard's diaries were edited by Jehan de Witte and published as *Un explorateur et un apôtre du Congo français: Monseigneur Augouard, archevêque titulaire de Cassiopée, vicaire apostolique du Congo français* (Paris: Emile-Paul frères, 1924). On Gentil's reaction to Brazza, see Autin, *Brazza*, 245–46. On Augouard more generally, see Maurice Mahieu, *Monseigneur Augouard: Un poitevin roi du Congo* (La Crèche: Geste éditions, 2006).

49. Saintoyant, *L'Affaire du Congo 1905*, 60.

50. Coquery-Vidrovitch, *Compagnies concessionaries*, 62.

51. Renée Jaugeon, "Les Sociétés d'exploitation au Congo et l'opinion française de 1890–1906," *Revue d'histoire de l'Outre-mer* 48 (1961): 366. See also Coquery-Vidrovitch, *Compagnies concessionnaires*, ch. 2.

52. Jaugeon, "Sociétés d'exploitation," 365–71.

53. Hochschild, *King Leopold's Ghost*, 165.

54. Ibid., 62–65; Jaugeon, "Sociétés d'exploitation," 375–84.

55. Coquery-Vidrovitch, *Compagnies concessionnaires*, 65–67.

56. Jaugeon, "Sociétés d'exploitation," 411.

57. *Le Journal*, 28 April 1905.

58. *Le Soir*, 15 October 1905.

59. See Saintoyant, *L'Affaire du Congo 1905*.

60. Challaye, *Congo français*, 78.

61. Challaye, in *Le Temps*, 27 May 1905.

62. Castellani, in *L'Illustration*, 2 April 1898.

63. Pratt, *Imperial Eyes*; Cohen, *French Encounter with Africans*; Youngs, *Travellers in Africa*.

64. Challaye, *Congo français*, 59.

65. Ibid., 74–75.

66. Ibid., 41.

67. On mixed-race children, or métis, see Owen White, *Children of the French Empire: Miscegenation and Colonial Society in French West Africa, 1895–1960* (Cambridge: Cambridge University Press, 1999); Stoler, *Carnal Knowledge*; Emmanuelle Saada, *Les enfants de la colonie: Les métis de l'empire français entre sujétion et citoyenneté* (Paris: Découverte, 2007).

68. Challaye, *Congo français*, 156, 160–61.

69. ANOM, Afrique Equatoriale française, Serie D (Politique et administration générale), 3 D 1 à 43. Missions d'inspection des colonies. 1905–1939. ****1. Brazza. 1905.

70. Challaye, *Congo français*, 54, 57, 93.

71. Ibid., 91.

72. *L'Humanité*, 27 September 1905; Coquery-Vidrovitch, *Compagnies concessionnaires*, 176.

73. There is a discrepancy between Challaye's report and the ones cited by Coquery-Vidrovitch, *Le Congo*, 176n3. Challaye has the native dance taking place on 30 June and mentions nothing about the concentration camp. Coquery-Vidrovitch dates the dance to 15 July.

74. Challaye, *Congo français*, 102.

75. Fabre, "Gustave Rouanet et les obscures espérances," 265.

76. Challaye, *Congo français*, 104.

77. Ibid., 109.

78. Ibid., 121.

79. Ibid., 115.

80. Ibid., 124.

81. Ibid., 139.

82. Ibid.

83. Ibid., 143.

84. This is what Toqué would later claim. See Toqué, *Les massacres du Congo*, 166.

85. Challaye, *Congo français*, 150. On Challaye's opposition late in life to colonialism, see William Irvine, *Between Politics and Justice: La Ligue des Droits de l'Homme, 1898–1945* (Stanford, CA: Stanford University Press, 2007), 144.

86. Brazza's fellow commissioner Hoarau Desruisseaux had earlier written him that Gentil "has assiduously blocked our investigation. He has created one

obstacle after the other and refuses to give us the documents we have requested." Saintoyant, *L'Affaire du Congo 1905,* 175.

87. Challaye, *Congo français,* 147.

88. *PP,* 16 September 1905.

89. Chambrun, *Brazza,* 252.

90. *Le Matin* and *Le Journal,* 27–28 September 1905.

91. *PP,* 26 September 1905.

92. See the polemic on the truthfulness of Africans in *L'Humanité,* 30 September–1 October 1905.

93. *Le Temps,* 27 September 1905.

94. *La Liberté,* 2 October 1905.

95. Fabre, "Gustave Rouanet et les obscures espérances," 256.

96. Brunschwig, "Brazza et le scandale," 123–24.

97. Ibid., 126–27.

98. Coquery-Vidrovitch, *Compagnies concessionnaires,* 176–95; André Gide, *Voyage au Congo* (Paris: Gallimard, 1927), and *Le Retour du Tchad* (Paris: Gallimard, 1928).

99. Autun, *Brazza,* 262–64.

100. Ibid., 256. Idanna Pucci, in *Brazza in Congo* (New York: Umbrage, 2009), 188, writes, "To this day, the question of Brazza's death has remained unresolved."

101. *Le Matin,* 16 September 1905.

102. Ben-Amos, *Funerals, Politics, and Memory in Modern France.*

103. Martin, *Savorgnan de Brazza,* 210.

104. Jean Bauberot, *Laïcité 1905–2005: Entre passion et raison* (Paris: Seuil, 2004).

105. *Le Journal,* 4 October 1905.

106. Ibid.

107. Ben-Amos, "Les Funérailles de Victor Hugo," 459; *Le Journal,* 4 October 1905.

108. Although the government suppressed Brazza's draft report, it is clear from the writings of those who accompanied him to the French Congo in 1905 that his findings condemned the very structure of the colonial regime. See Saintoyant, *L'affaire du Congo;* Amédée Britsch, "Pour le Congo francais: Histoire de la dernière mission Brazza," *Le Correspondant,* 10 January 1906.

7. HUBERT LYAUTEY AND THE FRENCH SEIZURE OF MOROCCO

1. Edward Berenson, "Fashoda, Dreyfus, and the Myth of Jean-Baptiste Marchand," in "Myth and Modernity," special issue, *Yale French Studies* 111 (May 2007): 129–42. See also Schivelbusch, *Culture of Defeat*; Paul Gerbod,

"L'éthique héroique en France (1870–1914)," *Revue historique* 268, no. 2 (1982): 409–29; Jean-François Chanet, "La Fabrique des Héros: Pédagogie républicaine et culte des grands hommes de Sedan à Vichy," *Vingtième Siècle* 65 (January–March, 2000): 13–34; Amalvi, *De l'art et la manière d'accommoder les héros*; Datta, "'L'appel au soldat.'"

2. On fencing and sport, see Nye, *Masculinity and Male Codes of Honor,* chs. 8–10.

3. Porch, "Bugeaud, Gallieni, Lyautey," 394.

4. *Le Figaro,* 18 December 1907.

5. "Du rôle colonial de l'armée," *La revue des deux mondes,* 15 January 1900.

6. "The right person in the right place" appeared in English in the article, doubtless to refer to Britain's putative superiority over the French as colonizers.

7. Or in terms of current American counterinsurgency theory, the key elements are to "clear, hold, and build." See Bob Woodward, *State of Denial* (New York: Simon and Schuster, 2006), 418.

8. Lyautey to Margerie, 7 March 1895, in Lyautey, *Lettres du Tonkin et de Madagascar,* 2 vols. (Paris: A. Colin, 1920): 2:159–60.

9. Pascal Venier, "Lyautey et l'idée de protectorat de 1894 à 1902: Genèse d'une doctrine coloniale," *Revue française d'histoire d'outre-mer* 78 (1991): 499–517.

10. Lyautey to his sister, 16 November 1894, quoted in William A. Hoisington, Jr., *Lyautey and the French Conquest of Morocco* (New York: St. Martin's Press), 6.

11. Power, *Jules Ferry.*

12. Daniel Rivet, *Le Maroc de Lyautey à Mohammed V: Le double visage du protectorat* (Paris: Denoel, 1999), 35–41.

13. On Gallieni and pacification, see Marc Michel, *Gallieni* (Paris: Fayard, 1989), chs. 10–11. See also Bouche, *Histoire de la colonisation française,* 2:138–42.

14. Pascal Venier, *Lyautey avant Lyautey* (Paris: Editions L'Harmattan, 1997), 144–46.

15. Françoise Hildesheimer, *Papiers Lyautey* 475 AP (Paris: Archives nationales, 1990).

16. Andrew and Kanya-Forstner, "The French 'Colonial Party'"; Andrew, "The French Colonialist Movement"; Abrams and Miller, "Who Were the French Colonialists?"; Persell, *The French Colonial Lobby.*

17. Quoted in Venier, *Lyautey avant Lyautey,* 144.

18. See ch. 6, this volume; Porch, "Bugeaud, Gallieni, Lyautey"; Kanya-Forstner, *Conquest of the Western Sudan.*

19. *Gil Blas,* 19 May 1904.

20. Fonds Lyautey, Archives Nationales (hereinafter FL), 475 AP 243. The following are the major published collections of Lyautey's letters: *Lettres du Tonkin et de Madagascar* (Paris: A. Colin, 1920); *Paroles d'action: Madagascar, Sud-Oranais, Oran, Maroc (1900–1926)* (Paris: A. Colin, 1927); *Vers le Maroc, lettres du*

Sud-Oranais, 1903–1906 (Paris: A. Colin, 1937); *Choix de lettres, 1882–1919* (Paris: A. Colin, 1947); *Lettres d'aventures (1883–1913)* (Paris: Julliard, 1948); *Lyautey l'Africain (1912–1925),* 4 vols. (Paris: Plon, 1953–1957); *Les plus belles lettres de Lyautey* (Paris: Calmann-Lévy, 1962).

21. Among the countless biographies of Lyautey, the best and most recent are Venier, *Lyautey avant Lyautey*; André Le Révérend, *Lyautey* (Paris: Fayard, 1983); Arnaud Teyssier, *Lyautey* (Paris: Perrin, 2002).

22. Quoted in Venier, *Lyautey avant Lyautey,* 28.

23. Ibid., 37.

24. Ibid., 30–36.

25. Quoted in Alan Schram, *Lyautey in Morocco* (Berkeley: University of California Press, 1970), 5.

26. Ibid., 4.

27. Ibid., 7; Teyssier, *Lyautey,* 121.

28. Quoted in Hoisington, *Lyautey and the French Conquest of Morocco,* 8.

29. Lyautey to Margerie, 15 August 1896, in Lyautey, *Choix de lettres,* 112–14.

30. André Maurois, *Lyautey* (Paris: Club des éditeurs, 1959 [1931]), 47.

31. Quoted in ibid., 49.

32. Quoted in ibid., 50.

33. Quoted in Le Révérend, *Lyautey,* 236–37.

34. On the civilizing mission, see Conklin, *Mission to Civilize.*

35. Stephen D. K. Ellis, *The Rising of the Red Shawls: A Revolt in Madagascar, 1895–1899* (Cambridge: Cambridge University Press, 1985).

36. This is the view of Douglas Porch in *The Conquest of Morocco* (New York: Knopf, 1983) and "Bugeaud, Gallieni, Lyautey."

37. Which doesn't necessarily mean he never expressed such views, just that he didn't leave any traces of them for posterity.

38. Quoted in Daniel Rivet, *Lyautey et l'institution du protectorat français au Maroc (1912–1925),* 2 vols. (Paris: L'Harmattan, 1988), 1:148.

39. Both quotations in Robert Aldrich, "Homosexuality in the French Colonies," *Journal of Homosexuality* 41, nos. 3–4 (2001): 209.

40. Maurois, *Lyautey.*

41. Teyssier, *Lyautey,* 226–33.

42. Ibid., 98–100.

43. Annette Kobak, *Isabelle: The Life of Isabelle Eberhardt* (New York: Knopf, 1989); Laura Rice, "'Nomad Thought': Isabelle Eberhardt and the Colonial Project," *Cultural Critique* 17 (Winter 1990–91): 151–76; Porch, *Conquest of Morocco,* 131–33.

44. Nye, *Masculinity and Male Codes of Honor*; Nye, "Review Essay: Western Masculinities in War and Peace," *American Historical Review* 112, no. 2 (April 2007): 417–38.

45. Berenson, *Trial of Madame Caillaux,* esp. ch. 2.

46. Rivet, *Lyautey et l'institution du protectorat français au Maroc,* vol. 1, ch. 2; Kim Munholland, "Rival Approaches to Morocco: Delcassé, Lyautey, and the Algerian-Moroccan Border, 1903–1905," *French Historical Studies* 5, no. 3 (Spring 1968): 328–43.

47. Edmund Burke III, *Prelude to Protectorate in Morocco: Precolonial Conquest and Resistance, 1860–1912* (Chicago: University of Chicago Press, 1976), ch. 3.

48. Ibid., chs. 3–5; Hoisington, *Lyautey and the French Conquest of Morocco,* ch. 2; Porch, *Conquest of Morocco.*

49. On precolonial Morocco, see Rivet, *Lyautey et l'institution du protectorat français,* vol. 1, part 1; Burke, *Prelude to Protectorate,* chs. 1–3; Hoisington, *Lyautey and the French Conquest of Morocco,* chs. 1–2; Porch, *Conquest of Morocco.*

50. Burke, *Prelude to Protectorate,* chs. 3–4.

51. Ibid., 86–87.

52. Jonathan G. Katz, *Murder in Marrakesh: Emile Mauchamp and the French Colonial Adventure* (Bloomington: Indiana University Press, 2006).

53. Ellen Amster, "The Many Deaths of Dr. Emile Mauchamp: Medicine, Technology, and Popular Politics in Pre-Protectorate Morocco, 1877–1912," *International Journal of Middle Eastern Studies* 36 (2004): 409–28; Jonathan G. Katz, "The 1907 Mauchamp Affair and the French Civilizing Mission in Morocco," *Journal of North African Studies* (June 2001): 159.

54. *Le Petit journal,* 7 April 1907.

55. See ch. 3, this volume.

56. Rivet, "Lyautey, L'Africain," *L'Histoire* 29 (December 1980): 19; Alain Ruscio, *Le credo de l'homme blanc: Regards coloniaux français XIXe-XXe siècles* (Paris: Editions complexe, 1995).

57. Burke, *Prelude to Protectorate,* 92.

58. *PP,* 22 July 1906.

59. *PP,* 6 October 1906.

60. *Le Journal,* 6 October 1906.

61. Porch, "Bugeaud, Gallieni, Lyautey."

62. A favorite saying of Lyautey's ("L'adversaire d'aujourd'hui est le collaborateur du lendemain"), quoted in Rivet, *Lyautey et l'institution du protectorat français,* 1:205.

63. Ibid.

64. So concludes Daniel Rivet, the best and most subtle student of Lyautey. See Rivet, *Le Maroc de Lyautey à Mohammed V,* 23–34. For a different view, see Porch, "Bugeaud, Gallieni, Lyautey," which argues that Lyautey's rhetoric about the pacific conquest stemmed from a perception that this was what the folks back home wanted to hear. It is a plausible argument, except that Porch provides no evidence of a cynical awareness on Lyautey's part of saying one thing and doing another.

65. *Le Monde illustré,* 18 December 1907.

66. *Gil Blas,* 19 May 1904.

67. Nye, *Masculinity and Male Codes;* Berenson, *Trial of Madame Caillaux,* ch. 5.

68. Nye, *Masculinity and Male Codes,* 164–65.

69. In French: "Montrer sa force pour ne pas avoir à s'en servir." Rivet, *Lyautey et l'institution du protectorat français,* 1:203.

70. Joly, "La France et la Revanche (1871–1914)"; Schivelbusch, *Culture of Defeat,* 147ff.

71. Berenson, *Trial of Madame Caillaux,* ch. 5.

72. Barrès, Zola, and Faguet quoted in Maugue, *L'identité masculine en crise,* 73.

73. F. A. Vuillermet, *Soyez des hommes: À la conquête de la virilité* (Paris: P. Lethielleux, 1909), 12.

74. Tarde, *Etudes pénales et sociales* (Paris: A. Maloine, 1892), 61, 69.

75. Maurice Barrès, *Le culte du moi* (Paris: Emile Paul, 1910–12).

76. Alfred de Tarde, *Le Maroc, école d'énerie* (Paris: Plon, 1923); Lyautey to his sister, 20 February 1897, in *Choix de lettres,* 143–44. Alfred de Tarde was co-author, with Henri Massis, of the famous nationalist manifesto *Les jeunes gens d'aujourd'hui,* published on the eve of World War I.

77. See Nye, *Masculinity and Male Codes,* ch. 5. On the aborted marriage, see Teyssier, *Lyautey,* 101.

78. Lyautey to Antonin de Margerie, 15 October 1896, in *Choix de lettres,* 139.

79. Lyautey to Vogüé, 26 February 1897, in *Lettres de Tonkin et de Madagascar (1894–1899)* (Paris: A. Colin, 1921).

80. Eugène Melchior de Vogüé, *Les Morts qui parlent* (Paris: Nelson, 1910 [1899]), 263–64. See Girardet, *l'dée coloniale en France,* 154–56.

81. From Vogüé's novel *Le maître de la mer,* quoted in Teyssier, *Lyautey,* 84.

82. Vogüé, *Les Morts,* 261.

83. Ibid., 272. Pierre and Marie marry at the novel's end.

84. Burke, *Prelude to Protectorate,* 113; Porch, *Conquest of Morocco,* 191.

85. *La Gaulois,* undated clipping (probably December 1908), in FL, 475 AP 75.

86. *Le Figaro,* 18 December 1907.

87. Porch, "Bugeaud, Gallieni, Lyautey," 389–92.

88. P. Vigne d'Octon, "Le général Lyautey, pacificateur du Maroc," *Les Hommes du jour,* 18 May 1912.

89. *La Libre parole,* 2 August 1907.

90. Ibid., 5 August 1907.

91. For the most recent account of these events, see Katz, *Murder in Marrakech,* 228–32.

92. Hoisington, *Lyautey and the French Conquest of Morocco,* 31.

93. Ibid., 121.

94. *L'Illustration,* 10 September 1910.

95. *PP,* 13 February 1909.

96. Hoisington, *Lyautey and the French Conquest of Morocco,* 36–37.

97. Teyssier, *Lyautey*, 234.

98. Ibid., 259–60.

99. Joseph Caillaux, *Agadir: Ma politique extérieure* (Paris: A. Michel, 1919), 135ff. For an exhaustive study of the Agadir crisis, see Jean-Claude Allain, *Agadir 1911* (Paris: Publications de la Sorbonne, 1976).

100. Hoisington, *Lyautey and the French Conquest of Morocco*, 37–38; Burke, *Prelude to Protectorate*, 181–82.

101. Burke, *Prelude to Protectorate*, 183–87.

102. Ibid., 187.

103. On Tardieu and *Le Temps*, see Bellanger, Godechot, Guiral, and Terrou, *Histoire générale* 3:354–55.

104. *Le Temps*, 29 April 1912. A *normalien* is a graduate of the Ecole normale supérieure, the extraordinarily selective academy that during the Third Republic trained France's political and intellectual elite.

105. *PP*, 28 April 1912; *Le Journal*, 12 May 1912.

106. *La Vie*, 4 May 1912.

107. Lyautey's correspondence, the staple source of the many biographies devoted to him, is housed in the National Archives in Paris (FL, 475 AP 259–314). Most biographers and historians have focused on the letters Lyautey wrote, largely ignoring those written to him. For my purposes, the latter constitute the more interesting source.

108. See Hildesheimer, *Papiers Lyautey*.

109. Roger de Salvery to Lyautey, 28 April 1912, FL, 475 AP 110. "I read about your nomination in the press."

110. Max Lazard to Lyautey, n.d. (probably 1900), FL, 475 AP 289.

111. Mme. Lazard to Lyautey, 10 August 1900, ibid.

112. Gaston Deschamps to Lyautey, 18 June 1906, FL, 475 AP 274.

113. Thompson, *The Media and Modernity*, 219.

114. FL, 475 AP 110. This box contains five hundred letters, each numbered by Lyautey's secretary, and they may represent only a fraction of what he received. Lyautey lost a great many of his papers when German troops set fire to his family home early in the Great War.

115. G. Vallières to Lyautey, 29 April 1912, ibid., letter 438.

116. [Illegible] to Lyautey, 28 April 1914, ibid., letter 84.

117. P. Michel to Lyautey, 30 April 1912, ibid., letter 23.

118. See, for example, letters 13 and 167, ibid.

119. Roger Lusanne to Lyautey, 28 April 1912, ibid., letter 63.

120. Ibid., letters 62, 63, and an unnumbered letter of 28 April 1912, whose signature is illegible. Also G. Vallieres to Lyautey, 29 April 1912, letter 438.

121. Roger de Salvery to Lyautey, 28 April 1912, ibid. (unnumbered).

122. P. Michel to Lyautey, 30 April 1912.

123. Bellay to Lyautey, 3 May 1912, letter 326.

124. Lusanne to Lyautey, 28 April 1912.

125. Rivet, *Lyautey et l'institution du protectorat français*, 1:59 (English in original).

126. Eugen Weber, *The Nationalist Revival in France* (Berkeley: University of California Press, 1959).

127. Georges Oved, *La Gauche française et le nationalisme marocain, 1905–1955*, 2 vols. (Paris: L'Harmattan, 1984).

128. *La Liberté*, 18 October 1912.

129. *Le Petit journal*, 21 July 1912.

EPILOGUE

1. On fame, see Braudy, *Frenzy of Renown*; Stephen Minta, "Byron, Death, and the Afterlife," in Berenson and Giloi, *Constructing Charisma*, 119–33.

2. Rivet, *Le Maroc de Lyautey à Mohammed*.

3. Jeal, *Stanley*, 445–51; Bierman, *Dark Safari*, 352.

4. Jeal, *Stanley*, 465–68.

5. Thérèse de Brazza played a major role in collecting the papers that eventually became the Fonds Brazza at the Archives nationales d'outre-mer in Aix-en-Provence.

6. Autin, *Brazza*, appendix; Martin, *Savorgnan de Brazza*, 213, 229. *L'Illustration*, 13 December 1930; *Académie des sciences coloniales: Réception de Mme. de Brazza et de M. de Chavannes* (Paris: Société d'éditions géographique, maritimes et coloniales, 1932).

7. Hildesheimer, *Papiers Lyautey*.

8. Taylor, "Gordon of Khartoum."

9. Daudet, *Salons et journaux*, 182.

10. Joly, *Dictionnaire biographique et géographique*, 255–56.

11. Pierre Lyautey, "Lettres de Marchand à Lyautey," *Revue française d'études politiques africaines* 34 (1974): 699.

12. *L'Illustration*, 28 August 1915.

13. Teyssier, *Lyautey*, ch. 11.

14. *L'Éclair*, 9 July 1920; *L'Opinion*, July 1920.

15. *L'Echo de Paris*, 15 July 1920.

16. Raymond de Vogüé in *Le Tour du Monde*, 17 July 1920. See also *L'Echo de Paris*, 5 July 1920; and reception speech by Mgr. Duchesne, 8 July 1920, *L'Action française*, 9 July 1920.

17. *L'Opinion*, July 1920.

18. Charles-Robert Ageron, "L'Exposition coloniale de 1931: Mythe républicain ou mythe impérial?" in *Les Lieux de mémoire*, vol. 1, ed., Pierre Nora (Paris: Gallimard, 1997), 505.

19. Raoul Girardet, "L'Apothéose de la 'plus grande France': L'Idée coloniale devant l'opinion française (1930–1935)," *Revue française de science politique* 18 (1968): 1093.

20. Patricia A. Morton, *Hybrid Modernities: Architecture and Representation at the 1931 Colonial Exposition, Paris* (Cambridge, MA: MIT Press, 2000), 66.

21. Herman Lebovics, *True France: The Wars over Cultural Identity, 1900–1945* (Ithaca, NY: Cornell University Press, 1992), ch. 2; Morton, *Hybrid Modernities.*

22. Robert Aldrich, "Marshal Lyautey's Funerals: The Afterlife of a French Colonial Hero and the Death of an Empire," in Vesna Drapac and André Lambelet, eds., *French History and Civilization: Papers from the George Rudé Seminar* (Brisbane: George Rudé Seminar, 2009), 2:144.

23. All quotations in this paragraph from ibid., 147–48.

24. Teyssier, *Lyautey,* 426.

25. Michael R. Gordon, "The Last Battle," *New York Times Magazine,* 3 August 2008.

26. Anstruther, *Dr. Livingstone, I Presume?*; Alan Gallop, *Mr Stanley, I Presume? The Life and Explorations of Henry Morton Stanley* (London: Sutton, 2004); Pettitt, *Dr. Livingstone, I Presume?*; Alan Reeve, *Africa, I Presume?* (New York: Macmillan, 1949); Lewis Wyndham, *America, I Presume* (New York: Howell, Soskin and Co., 1940); Gillian Linscott, *Murder, I Presume* (New York: St. Martin's Press, 1990); Marcus Alessi Bittencourt, "Doctor Frankenstein, I Presume— or, The Art of Vivisection," Ph.D. dissertation, Columbia University, 2003.

27. *Forbidden Territory: Stanley's Search for Livingstone.* Also available on DVD is an A&E Biography entitled *Stanley and Livingstone.*

28. Pettitt, *Dr. Livingstone, I Presume?* 16–17.

29. Jeal, *Livingstone*; Jeal, *Stanley.* To wit, the British television series *Empire,* based on Niall Ferguson's book of the same title, a sympathetic, even nostalgic treatment of the British imperial past. See Ferguson, *Empire: The Rise and Demise of the British World Order and the Lessons for Global Power* (New York: Basic Books, 2003).

30. McLynn, *Stanley: The Making of an African Explorer*; McLynn, *Stanley: Sorcerer's Apprentice*; Bierman, *Dark Safari.*

31. Jeal, *Stanley,* 7.

32. Hochschild, *King Leopold's Ghost.*

33. Pettitt, *Dr. Livingstone, I Presume?* 208.

34. Ibid., 205; *The Guardian,* 30 August 2005.

35. BBC News, 5 July 2007.

36. Musée royal de L'Afrique Centrale, *H. M. Stanley, Explorateur au service du Roi* (Tervuren, Belgium, 1991) (introduction by D. Thys van den Audenaerde).

37. Musée royal de l'Afrique centrale, *La mémoire du Congo: Le temps colonial* (Ghent: Editions Snoeck, 2005). On this exhibit and Belgium's troubled relationship with its colonial past, see Adam Hochschild, "In the Heart of Darkness,"

New York Review of Books, 6 October 2005; Debora Silverman, "The Congo, I Presume? Tepid Revisionism in the Royal Museum of Central Africa, Tervuren, 1910–2005," paper presented at the American Historical Association meeting, January 2009.

38. Michela Wrong, *In the Footsteps of Mr. Kurtz: Living on the Brink of Disaster in Mobutu's Congo* (New York: Harpers, 2002); Thomas Turner, *The Congo Wars: Conflict, Myth, and Reality* (London: Zed Books, 2007); Georges Nzongola-Ntalaja, *The Congo, from Leopold to Kabila: A People's History* (London: Zed Books, 2002).

39. Marc Sich, *Pierre Savorgnan de Brazza* (Paris: Editions Jean-Claude Lattès, 1992); Henri Servien, *La Fabuleuse épopée de l'Afrique française* (Paris: Elor, 1991); Martin, *Savorgnan de Brazza*; Isabelle Dion, *Pierre Savorgnan de Brazza: Au cœur du Congo* (Paris: Images en Manoeuvres Editions; Marseille: Archives nationales d'outre-mer, 2007).

40. The most balanced recent biography is Jeal, *Livingstone.* Judith Listowel, in *The Other Livingstone* (New York: Scribner, 1974), is considerably more negative. See also Helly, *Livingstone's Legacy,* for a fascinating study of the making of the Livingstone myth. Very important as well is MacKenzie, "David Livingstone: The Construction of the Myth."

41. For early works, see A.-S. Doncourt, *Monsieur Savorgnan de Brazza et l'Afrique occidentale et centrale à notre époque* (Lille: J. Lefort, 1884); E. Genin, *Les Explorations de Brazza* (Paris: Librairie générale de vulgarisation), 1885; *Les Hommes d'aujourd'hui,* no. 289 (1886); D. Neuville and Charles Bréard, *Les Voyages de Savorgnan de Brazza* (Paris: Berger-Levrault et Cie., 1884); A. Sinval, *Savorgnan de Brazza* (Limoges: Barbou et Cie., 1884); Charles Vernes, *La France au Congo et Savorgnan de Brazza* (Paris: Fischbacher, 1887).

42. *L'Illustration,* 13 December 1930.

43. André Gide, *Travels in the Congo,* trans. Dorothy Bussy (Berkeley: University of California Press, 1962); Gide, *Le Retour du Tchad* (Paris: Gallimard, 1928).

44. Chambrun, *Brazza.*

45. Henri-Paul Eydoux, *Savorgnan de Brazza* (Paris: Labose, 1932); Pierre Mariel, *Savorgnan de Brazza au Congo* (Paris: Tallandier, 1933); Charles de Chavannes, *Avec Brazza: Souvenirs de la Mission de l'Ouest Africain (Mars 1883–Jan 1886)* (Paris: Plon, 1934), *Ma Collaboration avec Brazza, 1886–1894* (Paris: Plon, 1937), and *Nos relations jusqu'à sa mort, 1905* (Paris: Plon, 1937).

46. Léon Poirier, *Brazza: Le Livre film* (Tours: Maison Mame, 1940). The film now exists on DVD (Paris: Les documents cinématographiques, 2000).

47. Rémy Pithon, "French Film Propaganda, July 1939–June 1940," in *Film and Radio Propaganda in World War II,* ed. K. R. M. Short (Knoxville: University of Tennessee Press, 1983). All film production and distribution was halted during the first two months of the Phony War (September 1939–May 1940).

48. *L'Illustration,* 25 November 1882.

49. Poirier, *Brazza,* 38.

50. Ibid., 137.

51. Girardet, *L'Idée coloniale en France,* ch. 6, 9; Ageron, *France coloniale ou parti colonial?* 239–67.

52. Gerhard L. Weinberg, *A World at Arms: A Global History of World War II* (New York: Cambridge University Press, 1994), 159–61.

53. Ageron, *France coloniale ou parti colonial?* 274.

54. Médecin Général Guirriec, *Brazza, ses premières explorations* (Paris: Les lettres françaises, 1943); G. Froment-Guieysse, *Brazza* (Paris: Editions de l'Encyclopédie coloniale et maritime, 1945); Marie-Germaine Soeur, *La Pupille de Brazza* (Toulouse: Les Editions du Clocher, 1945); Maria de Crisenoy, *"Le Héros du Congo": Pierre Savorgnan de Brazza* (Paris: Editions Spes, 1946); Pierre Croidys, *Brazza, conquérant du Congo* (Paris: Les éditions des loisirs, 1947).

55. Guirriec, *Brazza,* 2.

56. Froment-Guieysse, *Brazza,* 147.

57. G. Cerbelaud-Salagnac, *Savorgnan de Brazza: Le Père des esclaves* (Paris: Letouzey et ané, 1960), 1.

58. Cassie Knight, *Brazzaville Charms: Magic and Rebellion in the Republic of Congo* (London: Frances Lincoln, 2007).

59. "Judges Clear Dumas in Elf Payoff Scandal," *International Herald Tribune,* 30 January 2003.

60. Knight, *Brazzaville Charms,* 140.

61. Ibid., 146; *The Globalist,* 19 April 2008.

62. Soni Benga, "La guerre du Congo-Brazzaville (du 5 juin au 15 octobre 1997): Les vérités non dites," in Boniface Mongo Mbousse and Ivan Vangu-Ngimbi, eds., *Crise des deux Congo* (Paris: L'Harmattan, 2001), 65–78; Edouard Etsio, ed., *Autopsie de la violence au Congo-Brazzaville* (Paris: L'Harmattan, 2007).

63. *Africa Confidential,* 20 July 2007.

64. For the historians' petition, see www.aidh.org/hist-mem/petition01.htm #1. See also *The Guardian,* 15 April 2005.

65. www.brazza.culture.fr/fr/index.html.

66. www.fondation-brazza.org.

67. Pucci narrates the following in *Brazza in Congo,* 23–63.

68. Ibid.

69. *New York Times,* 30 November 2006.

70. www.fondation-brazza.org; Dion, *Pierre Savorgnan de Brazza.*

71. www.fondation-brazza.org.

72. See the excerpts from Obenga's talk and its hour-long video at www .mwinda.org/article/obenga.html.

73. For a harsh condemnation of Brazza, whose "methods and barbarism" resembled nothing so much as those of Stanley, see Raphaël Okoundji, "De Brazza au Congo ou le scotome d'une vérité historique," in *Crise des deux Congo,* 95–100. See also the critiques collected by MwindaPress at www.mwinda.org.

74. www.fondation-brazza.org.

INDEX

Italicized page numbers refer to illustrations.

280; Paris gold medal given to, 71–72; patriotism of, 56–57, 64, 225, 276, 279; pension for, 203; poems about, 79–81; reburial of, 282–86, *284;* reputation of, 64, 204–5, 223, 226, 263–65, 274–80, *278,* 282–86, *284;* Sorbonne speech of, 65–68; Stanley Club intervention of, 68–71, 306nn64,66; Stanley compared to/contrasted with, 58–60, 64–67, 203–4, 207, 221, 276; writings of, 222, 332n108

Brazza, Thérèse de. *See* Chambrun, Thérèse de

Brazzaville, 63, 178, 200, 208, 210, 216, 218–19, 265, 279–86, *284*

Britisch, Amadée, 267

British East India Company, 308n4

British heroes. *See* Gordon, Charles George "Chinese"; Stanley, Henry Morton

British Museum, 43

British Reform Bills (1867, 1884), 5

Brunschwig, Henri, 329n15

Burcombe, H. S., 156

Burdett-Coutts, Baroness, 108–9

Burroughs, Edgar Rice, 273

Burton, Richard, Sir, 33, 35, 37, 57, 296n8

Caillaux, Joseph, 225, 239

Caillaux Affair (1914), 199, 239, 328n10

Cain, P. J., 3–4

cannibalism, 136, 163, 214

Canterbury, archbishop of, 114

Caractacus, 6

Carlyle, Thomas, 11

Carnot, Sadi, 322n16

Carpenter, William Boyd, 115

Casablanca, 242, 254, 269–70

Cassagnac, Paul de, 177

Castellani, Charles, 168, 175, 178, 213, 265, 273, 325n62

Catholicism, 9, 11, 52–53, 204; and Brazza, 56, 70, 73–75, 208, 214, 226; and Gordon, 103, 112; and Lyautey, 234

Caumel Decazés, Roseline, 80–81

celebrities, 17, 19, 226, 293–94n61. *See also* fame; Brazza as, 50–51, 65, 69, 79;

Lyautey as, 246, 258, 260–61; Stanley as, 122–24, 132, 140, 145, 148, 152, 155, 160–62, 164, 263

Chad, 61, 208, 214, 218

Challaye, Félicien, 206–7, 212–20, 251, 273, 331n73

Chamberlain, Joseph, 181–82

Chamber of Deputies, French, 177, 192, 231, 251. *See also names of members*

Chambord, 234

Chambrun, Jacques de, 220, 276

Chambrun, Thérèse de, 203, 207, 225, 265, 283, 338n5

charismatic individuals, 2, 5, 7, 9, 15–21; Brazza as, 50–51, 55, 63–64, 70, 72, 75, 77, 80–81, 102, 199, 203, 206, 214, 225, 227, 276, 284–86; Gordon as, 82, 102, 105–6, 108, 113, 115, 127; Kitchener as, 185; Lyautey as, 229, 232; the Mahdi as, 95; Marchand as, 167, 176, 178, 185, 194, 265; Panksepp on, 16–18; Stanley as, 24, 26, 28, 46, 102, 122–25, 263; state funerals for in France, 53–54; Turner on, 16–17, 293n54; Weber on, 15–17, 19–20, 124, 263

Charmes, Gabriel de, 72

Chavannes, Charles de, 79, 265, 276

Chevreau de Christiani, Fernand, 167

chicotte, 212

Chirac, Jacques, 282–83

chivalric men, 11, 13, 248; Gordon as, 112, 116–18; Stanley as, 125, 141, 146, 154

Christianity, 8–9, 11, 13. *See also* Catholicism; and Charlemagne, 170; Christ as charismatic individual, 15–16; and Gordon, 86–88, 92, 100, 109, 112, 114–16, 118, 120, 265; and literacy in U.S., 30; in Morocco, 243, 253–54; muscular Christianity, 9, 11, 116, 152; and Stanley, 41, 152, 156

Churchill, Seton, 118

Churchill, Winston, 13, 118, 120, 180

Church of Sainte Clotilde, 226

civilizing mission, 10, 12–13, 18. *See also* pacific conquest; and atrocities scandals in Congo, 199, 219–20, 224; and Brazza, 52, 62–63, 65, 69, 73, 199,

National Archives, French, 260, 282
National Center for the History of Immigration, French, 266
nationalism, British, 6–8, 12, 18, 21; and Gordon, 85–86, 103, 111, 113–15, 120; and Kitchener, 182–83, 186; and Stanley, 41, 44, 124, 126, 140–41, 143–46, 148
nationalism, French, 6–7, 12, 18, 21; and annexation of Congo, 51, 68, 70–72, 94; and Boulanger, 175, 324n43; and Brazza, 51–57, 60–64, 68, 70, 72–75, 81–82, 204–5, 226; and Dreyfus Affair, 167–68, 180, 185, 328n10; and Hugo, 53–54; and Lyautey, 228–29, 232, 256, 261–62; and Marchand, 167–69, 175, 177, 180–81, 183–92, *189, 190,* 195–96, 205, 265, 322n16
nation building, 229, 271, 333nn6,7
La Nature, 206
Nelson, Admiral Lord, 5, 112
Nelson, Robert, 129
neocolonialism, 281
neuroscience, affective, 17–18
new journalism: and Brazza, 51, 56; and Stanley, 25–31, 34, 40–41, 45, 47–48
newspapers. *See* press coverage; readers of newspapers; *names of newspapers*
New Woman, 14, 175
New York Herald, 22–23, 29–36, 38–43, 45–47, 49, 59, 69, 154, 160, 163, 294n69, 297n21, 300n83, 301n95
New York Sun, 30
Ngouayoulou, Gaston, 283, 286
Nightingale, Florence, 158
Nile River: and Baker, 33, 91–92; and Emin Pasha, 127, 137; and Gordon, 92–94, 96, 103, 105–6, 109; and Marchand, 1, 120, 173, 176–81, 184–85, 191, 325n60; source of in Ruwenzoris, 138; and Stanley, 121, 138; and Wolseley, 110
No, Lake, 178
Noaille, countess de, 130
Northbrook, Lord, 104
Nubar Pasha, 92

Obenga, Théophile, 286
objective journalism, 29–32, 45
Ogooué River, 58, 64–65, 210
oil revenues, 280–82
oil-stain strategy, 229–31, 271
Oliphant, Laurence, 87
Omdurman, 109–10; battle of (1898), 13, 180
On the Town (musical), 272
Opinion, 55, 70–71, 303nn19,20
Ormesson, Wladimir d,' 256
Ottoman Empire, 83, 85, 91, 94, 99, 106, 127
Oujda, 243–46, *247,* 252, 254

pacific conquest, 12–13, 15, 18, 292n43. *See also* civilizing mission; and Brazza, 13, 50, 55–60, 63–70, 72–73, 75, 78–79, 81, 97, 103, 199, 204–5, 225–27, 230, 245, 248, 265, 274–75, 280; and Gordon, 103, 118, 120; and Lyautey, 229–32, 236–37, 239, 241, 245–46, 248–49, 252–58, 261, 267, 270, 335n64; and Marchand, 178–80
pacific penetration, 230–32, 239, 242, 255
pagnes (waist cloths), 66
Pakpa, 217, 327n4
Pall Mall Gazette: on "dethronement of England," 86; and Gordon, 84, 86, 96, 99–102, 106, 108, 113, 312n76; and Stanley, 43, 47, 153, 160–61
Panama Canal, 322n16
Panama controversy (early 1890s), 199, 328n10, 329n15
Panksepp, Jaak, 16–18
Panther (German gunboat), 256
Paris Commune (1870–71), 7, 292n43
Paris Geographical Society (PGS), 59–60, 64–65, 68–69
Parke, Thomas H., 130, 138–39
Pasteur, Louis, 53
La Patrie, 185
peaceful conquerors. *See* pacific conquest
peaceful penetration. *See* pacific penetration
Pellegrini, Carlo. *See* Ape (caricaturist)
Pemjean, Lucien, 188, 191–92

public opinion *(continued)*
scandals in Congo, 199, 206; and
Brazza, 55, 63–65, 71–79, 199, 203,
205–6, 225–26; and Gordon, 96, 102,
104, 108–9, 111, 113–14, 128; and
Lyautey, 229, 232, 236, 256–62; and
Marchand, 178, 181–82, 184–86; and
popular culture of imperialism, 4–5,
287–88n2, 289n10; *public français,* 54–
55; and Stanley, 128, 139, 141, 144–45,
145, 146, 148, 153–57, 162, 164
publishing technologies, 9, 19, 26, 31, 54
Pucci, Idanna, 283
Punch, 162
pygmies, 136

Quarterly Review, 8
Queen, the Lady's Newspaper, 152
Quiller-Couch, Arthur, 115

racist stereotypes, 2, 35, 272–73, 277
railroads, 25, 31, 54, 103, 208–10, 220, 224
rape, 200, 215–16, 218
Rawlinson, Henry, Sir, 42–43, 47, 97
readers of newspapers, 3, 10–11, 17–21. *See
also* public opinion; Anderson's views
on, 55; and atrocities scandals in
Congo, 213–14; and Brazza, 55, 64,
79–80, 213–14; and Gordon, 87, 100,
102–3, 111; and Lyautey, 258; and Marchand, 174, 179, 183–85; and Stanley,
24, 27–28, 30, 35, 41–43, 45–46, 59,
126, 144, 154, 301n98; Tarde's views
on, 54–55, 303nn19,20
Rear Column scandal, 134–35, 138–39, 141,
150, 160, 162–64
Rede Lecture (Cambridge), 148
Red Sea, 99, 103, 109, 114
religious faith, 8–9, 12–13. *See also* Catholicism; Christianity; Islam; feminized,
11, 98, 103; and Gordon, 9, 86–87, 89–
93, 98–99, 103, 106, 112, 114–17, 263,
265–66; and images of Brazza, 73–75;
and Lyautey, 234; and Mahdist revolt,
95, 99–100, 106; and Stanley, 152,
156–57
Remiremont, 187

Rencesvals, 170
republicanism, French. *See* Third Repub-
lic, French
République française, 56, 68
Le Retour du Tchad (Gide), 276
revanche, 171, 186, 191–92, 195, 322n20
Revue des deux mondes, 234–35, 237
Rif War (mid-1920s), 268
River War, The (Churchill), 118, 120
Rivet, Daniel, 261, 335n64
Robespierre, 53
Robinson, Ronald, 3
Rochefort, Henri, 185, 192
Roland, 170–71, 228
Rosebery, Lord, 182, 186
Rouanet, Gustave, 223
Roure, Henry du, 27
Rowlands, John. *See* Stanley, Henry Morton
Royal Albert Hall, 122, 146, *147,* 149
Royal Engineers, 89–90
Royal Geographical Society (RGS), 42–44,
47, 90, 97, 122, 127, 146, *147,* 149, 159,
300n85
Royal Military Academy, Woolwich, 89
Royal Museum of Central Africa (Bel-
gium), 273–74
rubber trade, 201–2, 209–12, 214–16, 224
Ruskin, John, 85–86
Russia, 204, 209, 249; Russian Revolution,
212
Russo-Japanese War, 212
Ruwenzori Mountains, 138
Ryner, Maggie Cecil, 117

Saint-Exupéry, Antoine de, 25
Saintoyant, Jules, 207–9
saints: Brazza as, 73–75, 220, 275, 283–84;
Gordon as, 15, 97, 111–12, 115–16, 120;
Marchand as, 169; republican saints,
53; secular saints, 9, 64, 73
Sale, E. J., 117
Salisbury, Lord, 7–8, 186; and Fashoda cri-
sis (1898), 1, 3, 177, 181–86; and Gor-
don, 113; and Stanley, 123, 128, 164
Samori Turé, 173–74
Sand, George, 73
Sanga, 163

Stanley, Henry Morton *(continued)*
Emin Pasha Relief Expedition
(EPRE, 1886–90), 9, 88, 121–41, *130,
142,* 146, 149–50, 153, 158, 160, 162–
64; exhibitions of, 273–74; false
claims of being adopted, 28–29, 39;
films of, 272, 277–79; "find Livingstone" story of, 31–33, 42, 47, 158–59;
first journey into African interior
(1870–71), 34–42, 46, 299n45; "freedom of the city" honors for, 122, 146;
and French decolonization, 272; Gordon compared to/contrasted with, 84,
90, 96, 99, 102–3, 158; honorary doctorates of, 148; in illustrated press,
142, 143, 145, 147, 149, *155;* image in
wax museum, 122; knighthood of,
124, 146, 164, 318n84; lecture tours of,
126, 145–46, *147,* 162–64; Marchand
compared to, 168; marriage of, 152–
56, *155;* meeting with Livingstone, 22–
26, 38–40, 42–45, 137, 271–72, 295n1;
native town of Denbigh (Wales), 273;
personality problems of, 28, 37, 67,
132–33, 151–52, 158–59, 297n24; poems
about, 154, 157, 161–62; publicity campaign for, 148–49; and Rear Column
scandal, 134–35, 138–39, 141, 150, 160,
162–64; receptions for, 122, 140, 146,
148–49, 152–53, 158; reflections on perils of fame, 157–60, 163–64; as reporter for *Herald,* 29–36, 38–47, 160–
61; reputation of, 123–24, 139, 150,
164, 263–64, 271–74, *274;* ridicule/dis-
belief by British readers, 23–24, 28,
42–48, 137, 159, 297n21, 301n102;
Stanley Club speech of, 49–51, 68–70,
306nn64,66; and "Stanley craze," 123,
156, 160–62, 164, 315n2; statues of,
157, 273, *274,* 283; violent acts of, 12–
13, 27–28, 37–38, 59, 63–67, 70, 123,
132–33, 136–37, 140–41, 150–51, 160,
163–64, 263, 272–74, 276, 301n98;
women stalkers of, 159–60; writings
of, 20, 25–28, 31, 35–37, 39–47, 59, 90,
122–23, 126, 131, 138, 144, 149–52, 157–
59, 162, 164, 168, 213, 264, 273

Stanley and Livingstone (film, 1939), 272
Stanley Club, 49–51, 68–71, 306nn64,66
Stanley Pool, 63, 132–34, 208, 210, 220, 273
Stanleyville, 273. *See also* Kisangani
state funerals, French, 53, 225–27, 275
Stead, William T. (W. T.), 99–102, 105,
160–61, 265, 294n69
Steevens, George, 180
Stengers, Jean, 68
stereotypes, racial, 2, 35, 272–73, 277
Stevenson, Robert Louis, 125, 154
St. James Hall, 146
Strachey, Lytton, 2, 88, 98–99, 101–2, 104,
266, 309n26
strikes, 180–81
Suakin, 109, 114
Sudan/Sudanese: and Emin Pasha, 121, 123,
127, 137; Equatoria as province of, 91–
93, 110, 123, 127–28; and Gordon, 12,
83–84, 86, 88, 91–97, 99–115, 118, 120,
264–65, 267, 312nn76,87,92; independence (1956), 267; and International
Colonial Exhibition (France, 1931),
269; and Kitchener, 179–83, 267; and
Lyautey, 250–51; and Marchand, 173–
74, 176–86; and Stanley, 32, 137, 139
Suez Canal, 39, 85, 94, 109, 240
Swahili Arabs, 23–24, 35, 37–38, 45–46,
130–31, 296n8

Tablet, 103
Tabora, 37–38, 131, 139
tache d'huile, 229–31, 271
Taiping Rebellion (1860s), 84, 89–90, 92,
97, 100–101, 103, 105
Tanganyika, Lake, 22, 33–35, 38–40, 131
Tangiers, 213, 240, 242
Tarde, Alfred de, 237, 250, 336n76
Tarde, Gabriel, 54–55, 249–50, 303nn19,20
Tardieu, André, 257, 259
Tarzan books/films, 273
Tawfiq, 93–96
Taylor, Frank, 303n20
telegraph, 25–26, 54; and Gordon, 88, 108;
and Lyautey, 230, 233; and Mauchamp,
Emile, 242; and Stanley, 40, 43, 45,
132, 139, 300n83

Waldeck-Rousseau, René, 196, 321n7
Wales, 123, 148, 164, 273
Wales, prince of, 122, 146, 149
Walsin-Esterhazy, Ferdinand, 180
Walter, A. F., 149
war correspondents, 24, 46; Churchill as,
    180; Stanley as, 32
Ward, Herbert, 139
Ward, Terrance, 283
Warhol, Andy, 162
War of the Worlds, The (Wells), 8
Waterloo, 302n5
wax museums, 79, *80,* 118, 122, 170, 266
Webb, Francis, 34
Webb, Sidney, 315n2
Weber, Max, 15–17, 19–20, 124, 263
Wells, H. G., 8
West African Mail, 201
Westminster Abbey, 154–56, *155*
White Nile, 178
Whittier, John Greenleaf, 118
Wilhelm II, Kaiser, 140, 158, 240, 256
Wilson, Charles, Sir, 118
Wingate, F. R., 118, 120
Winton, Francis de, 149
Wolseley, Garnett, 84, 89, 91, 94, 101–2,
    104–5, 109–10, 113–14

women, indigenous: and Brazza, 66, *67,* 277;
    Challaye's description of, 213–14; kid-
    napping/rape of in Congo, 200, 215–
    18; as "temporary wives," 14, 213–14
women, white: as "angels of the home,"
    125; and Boulanger, 175, 324n43;
    emancipation of, 10–11, 124; excluded
    from citizenship in France, 52; as ex-
    plorers, 14; as image of Africa, 148;
    and Lyautey, 14, 233–34, 237–38, 250,
    265; and Marchand, 175, 265; mar-
    riage of to heroes of empire, 14–15,
    152–56, *155,* 237–38, 250, 264–65; and
    Stanley, 14, 146, 152–56, *155,* 159–60;
    as threat to French manliness, 57
World War I. *See* First World War
World War II. *See* Second World War

Yambuya, 133–36, 138, 162

Zanzibar/Zanzibaris: and Gordon, 113; and
    Mackinnon, 128; and Stanley, 32–35,
    129, 131–32, 137, 139, 300n85; and
    Tippu Tip, 130–31
Zola, Emile, 180, 249, 294n69
Zubayr Pasha, 93, 107–8
Zulus, 85

Text: 11.25/13.5 Adobe Garamond
Display: Adobe Garamond
Compositor: Westchester Book Group
Cartographer: Bill Nelson
Indexer: Sharon Sweeney